VACATION & SECOND HOMES

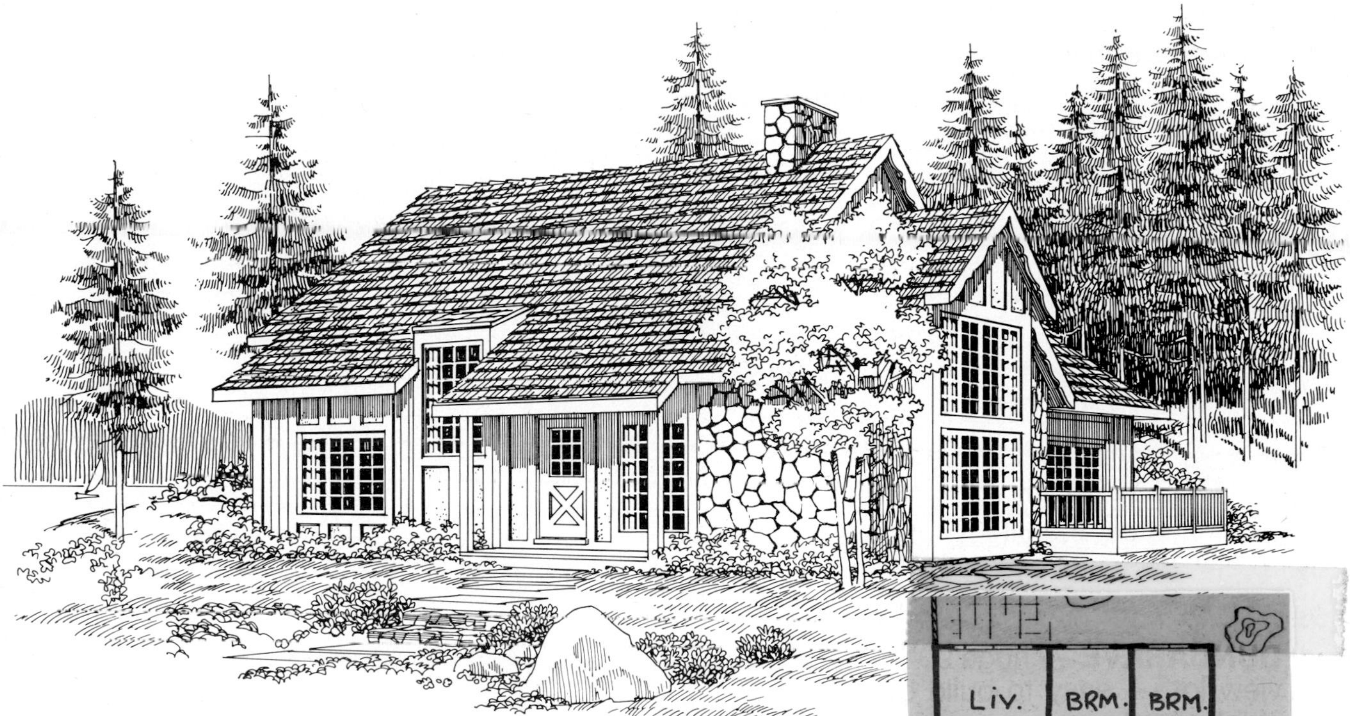

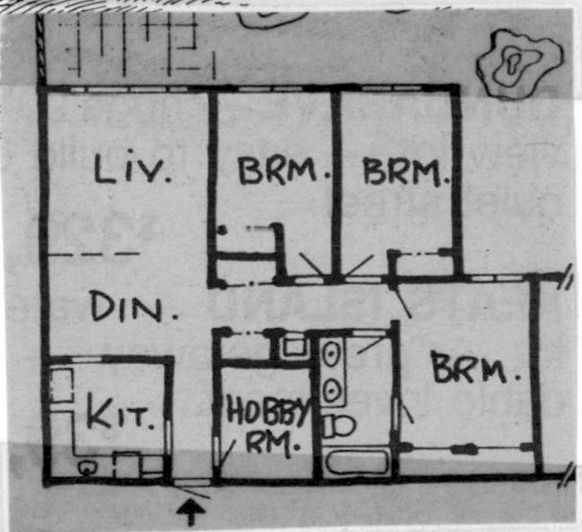

258 Designs For Recreation, Retirement and Leisure Living

440 to 4,400 square feet

Contents

Note: Many of the homes featured in this book have a matching or corresponding Landscape or Deck plan available from Home Planners, Inc. Some have both. These plans have an L or a D following their design number and square-footage notations. For information on how to order plans for landscapes and decks, see pages 238-245.

Published by Home Planners, Inc.
Editorial and Corporate Office:
3275 West Ina Road, Suite 110
Tucson, Arizona 85741
Distribution Center:
29333 Lorie Lane
Wixom, MI 48393

Chairman: Charles W. Talcott
President and Publisher: Rickard D. Bailey
Publications Manager: Cindy J. Coatsworth
Editor: Paulette Mulvin
Front Cover Graphic Design: Paul Fitzgerald

10 9 8 7 6 5 4 3

Library of Congress Number: 90-084447
ISBN: 0-918894-88-3

ON THE COVER: Plans for this charming Two-Story Vacation home, Design V42488, can be found on page 33.
Frankel/Rondo Residence, Oakland, Michigan
Photographer: Laszlo Regos

How To Read Floor Plans and Blueprints

Selecting the most suitable house plan for your family is a matter of matching your needs, tastes, and lifestyle against the many designs we offer. When you study the floor plans in this book, and the blueprints that you may subsequently order, remember that they are a two-dimensional representation of what will be a three-dimensional reality.

Floor plans are easy to read. Rooms are clearly labeled, with dimensions given in feet and inches. Most symbols are logical and self-explanatory. The location of bathroom fixtures, fireplaces, planters, tile floors, cabinets and counters, sinks, appliances, closets, and sloped or beamed ceilings will be obvious.

A blueprint, although much more detailed, is also easy to read; all it demands is concentration. The blueprints that we offer come in many large sheets, each one of which contains a different kind of information. One sheet contains foundation and excavation drawings, another has a precise plot plan. An elevations sheet deals with the exterior walls of the house; section drawings show precise dimensions, fittings, doors, windows, and roof structures. This provides all the construction information needed by your contractor. Also available is a helpful materials list with size and quantities of all necessary components. Using this list, your contractor and suppliers can make a start at calculating costs for you.

When you first study a floor plan or blueprint, imagine that you are walking through the house. By mentally visualizing each room in three dimensions, you can transform the technical data and symbols into something more real. Interior space should be organized in a logical way, based on the intended use of such space. Usually the space is divided into rooms which fall into one of three categories. The sleeping area includes bedrooms and bathrooms; the work area includes the kitchen, laundry, utility room, garage and other functional rooms; the living area includes the living and dining rooms, family room, and other gathering areas as well as entrance ways.

To begin a mental tour of the home, start at the front door. It's preferable to have a foyer or entrance hall in which to receive guests. A closet here is desirable; a powder room is a plus.

Look for good traffic circulation as you study the floor plan. You should not have to pass all the way through one main room to reach another. From the entrance area you should have direct access to the three principal areas of a house—the living, work, and sleeping zones. For example, a foyer might provide separate entrances to the living room, kitchen, patio, and a hallway or staircase leading to the bedrooms.

Study the layout of each zone. Most people expect the living room to be protected from cross traffic. The kitchen, on the other hand, should connect with the dining room—and perhaps also the utility room, basement, garage, patio or deck, or a secondary entrance. A homemaker whose workday centers in the kitchen may have special requirements: a window that faces the backyard; a clear view of the family room where children play; a garage or driveway entrance that allows for a short trip with groceries; laundry facilities close at hand. Check for efficient placement of kitchen cabinets, counter, and appliances. Is there enough room in the kitchen for additional appliances, for eating in? Is there a dining nook?

Perhaps this part of the house contains a family room or a den/bedroom/office. It's advantageous to have a bathroom or powder room in this section.

As you study the plan, you may encounter a staircase, indicated by a group of parallel lines, the number of lines equaling the number of steps. Arrows labeled "up" mean that the staircase leads to a higher level, and those pointing down mean it leads to a lower one. Staircases in a split-level will have both up and down arrows on one staircase because two levels are depicted in one drawing and an extra level in another.

Notice the location of the stairways. Is too much floor space lost to them? Will you find yourself making too many trips?

Study the sleeping quarters. Are the bedrooms situated as you like? You may want the master bedroom near the kids, or you may want it as far away as possible. Is there at least one closet per person in each bedroom or a double one for a couple? Bathrooms should be convenient to each bedroom—if not adjoining, then with hallway access and on the same floor.

Once you are familiar with the relative positions of the rooms, look for such structural details as:

- Sufficient uninterrupted wall space for furniture arrangement.
- Adequate room dimensions.
- Potential heating or cooling problems—i.e., a room over a garage or next to the laundry.
- Window and door placement for good ventilation and natural light.
- Location of doorways—avoid having a basement staircase or a bathroom in view of the dining room.
- Adequate auxiliary space—closets, storage, bathrooms, countertops.
- Separation of activity areas (will noise from the recreation room disturb sleeping children or a parent at work?).

As you complete your mental walk through the house, bear in mind your family's long-range needs. A good house plan will allow for some adjustments now and additions in the future.

Take time to notice special amenities: fireplaces and raised hearths, work islands in the kitchen, pass-through countertops between kitchen and breakfast nook, whirlpool baths. Note the placement of decks and balconies. Your family may find the listing of favorite features a most helpful exercise. Why not try it?

How To Shop For Mortgage Money

Most people who are in the market for a new home spend months searching for the right house plan and building site. Ironically, these same people often invest very little time shopping for the money to finance their new home, though the majority will have to live with the terms of their mortgage for as long as they live in the home.

The fact is that not all lending institutions are alike, nor are the loans that they offer.

- Lending practices vary from one city and state to another. If you are a first-time builder or are new to an area, it is wise to hire a real estate (not divorce or general practice) attorney to help you unravel the maze of your area's laws and customs.
- Before talking with a lender, write down all your questions and take notes so you can make accurate comparisons.
- Do not be intimidated by financial officers. Do not hesitate to reveal what other institutions are offering; they may be challenged to meet or better the terms.

A GUIDE TO LENDERS

Where can you turn for home financing? Here is a list of sources for you to contact:

Savings and Loan Associations
Savings Banks/Mutual Savings Banks
Commercial Banks
Mortgage Banking Companies
Some Credit Unions

Each of the above institutions generally offers a variety of loan types, interest rates, and fees. It is recommended that you survey each type of institution in your area to determine exactly what type of financing is available so that you can make an intelligent and informed decision.

A GUIDE TO LOAN TYPES

Conventional Loans

These types of loans usually require a minimum down payment of 10% of the lower of the purchase price or appraised value of the property. However, in many cases, this down payment requirement has been increased to 15% to 20% depending on the type of loan and the requirements of the lending institution. Often, the minimum down payment requirement is applied to owner-occupied residences and is usually increased if the property is purchased as a vacation home or investment.

The most common type of conventional loan is the **fixed-rate loan** which has a fixed interest rate and fixed monthly payments. The term of the loan may vary, but such loans generally are available in fifteen- and thirty-year terms. The obvious advantage of a fifteen-year term is an earlier loan payoff as well as reduced interest charges.

Other types of conventional loans are called **adjustable rate mortgages (ARM's)**. This type of loan usually has a lower initial interest rate than the fixed-rate loan, but the interest rate of payment may change depending on the loan terms and economic conditions. The frequency of these interest/payment adjustments depends on the individual loan, but they usually occur every twelve months.

Some key terms to understanding ARM loans are listed below:

Adjustment Period - The period between one rate change and the next. Therefore, a loan with an adjustment period of one year is known as a One Year ARM.

Index - The interest rate change is tied to an index rate. These indexes usually go up and down with the general movement of interest rates. If the index rate moves up, so does your monthly payment. If the index rate goes down, your monthly payment may also go down. There are a variety of indexes. Among the most common is the weekly average yield on U.S. Treasury securities adjusted to a constant maturity of one, three, or five years.

Margin - To determine the interest rate on an ARM, lenders add a few percentage points to the index rate. These percentage points are called the margin. The amount of the margin can differ from one lender to the next, but is usually constant through the life of the loan.

Caps - Most ARM loans limit the amount that the interest rate can increase. There are periodic caps which limit the increase from one adjustment period to the next and overall caps which limit the interest rate increase over the life of the loan.

Negative Amortization - Several ARM loans contain negative amortization which means that your mortgage balance can increase even though you are making regular monthly payments. This happens when the interest rate of the loan increases while your monthly payment remains the same.

Convertibility or Conversion Option - This is a clause in your agreement that allows you to convert the ARM to a fixed-rate mortgage at designated times. Not all ARM loans contain this option.

There are other types of less-common conventional loans which are offered by many institutions: Graduated Payment Mortgages, Reverse Annuity Mortgages, and Bi-Weekly Mortgages. Consult with a financial officer of a lending institution for details on these other loan types.

Government Loans

FHA loans are government insured and have substantially lower down payments than conventional loans; however, there are maximum allowable loan amounts for these loans depending on the location of the property.

Another type of government loan is through the Veteran's Administration (VA). Like the FHA, the VA guarantees loans for eligible veterans and the spouses of those veterans who died while in the service. Down payment requirements are also extremely low on these types of loans.

There are a variety of loan types available under these government programs including fixed rate, ARM's and graduated payment mortgages. The financial officer of the lending institution will be able to explain these various loan types and the qualification standards.

The Cost of a Mortgage

Monthly principal and interest per $1,000 of mortgage

Mortgage rate	15-year loan	20-year loan	25-year loan	30-year loan
9.00%	10.15	9.00	8.40	8.05
9.10%	10.21	9.07	8.47	8.12
9.20%	10.27	9.13	8.53	8.20
9.30%	10.33	9.20	8.60	8.27
9.40%	10.39	9.26	8.67	8.34
9.50%	10.45	9.33	8.74	8.41
9.60%	10.51	9.39	8.81	8.49
9.70%	10.57	9.46	8.88	8.56
9.80%	10.63	9.52	8.95	8.63
9.90%	10.69	9.59	9.02	8.71
10.00%	10.75	9.66	9.09	8.78
10.10%	10.81	9.72	9.16	8.85
10.20%	10.87	9.79	9.23	8.93
10.30%	10.94	9.85	9.30	9.00
10.40%	11.00	9.92	9.38	9.08
10.50%	11.06	9.99	9.45	9.15
10.60%	11.12	10.06	9.52	9.23
10.70%	11.18	10.12	9.59	9.30
10.80%	11.25	10.19	9.66	9.38
10.90%	11.31	10.26	9.73	9.45
11.00%	11.37	10.33	9.81	9.53
11.10%	11.43	10.40	9.88	9.60
11.20%	11.50	10.46	9.95	9.68
11.30%	11.56	10.53	10.02	9.76
11.40%	11.62	10.60	10.10	9.83
11.50%	11.69	10.67	10.17	9.91
11.60%	11.75	10.74	10.24	9.98
11.70%	11.81	10.81	10.32	10.06
11.80%	11.88	10.88	10.39	10.14
11.90%	11.94	10.95	10.46	10.21

Note: Multiply the cost per $1,000 by the size of the mortgage (in thousands). The result is the monthly payment, including principal and interest. For example, for an $80,000 mortgage for 30 years at 10 percent, multiply 80 x 8.78 = $702.40.

How To Choose A Contractor

Contractors are part craftsmen, part businessmen, and part magicians. Transforming your dreams and drawings into a finished house, they are responsible for the final cost of the structure, for the quality of the workmanship, and for the solving of all problems that occur quite naturally in the course of construction.

There are two types of residential contractors: the construction company and the carpenter-builder, often called a general contractor. Each of these has its advantages and disadvantages.

Carpenter-builders work directly on the job as field foremen. Because their background is that of a craftsman, their workmanship is probably good—but their paperwork may be slow or sloppy. Their overhead—which you pay for—is less than that of a large construction company. However, if the job drags on for any reason, their interest may flag because your project is overlapping their next job and eroding profits.

Construction companies that handle several projects concurrently have an office staff to keep the paperwork moving and an army of reliable subcontractors. Though you can be confident that they will meet deadlines, they may sacrifice workmanship in order to do so. Emphasizing efficiency, they are less personal to work with than a general contractor and many will not work with an individual unless there is representation by an architect.

To find a reliable contractor, start by asking friends who have built homes for recommendations. Check with local lumberyards and building supply outlets for names of possible candidates and call departments of consumer affairs. Keep in mind that these watchdog organizations can give only the number of complaints filed; they cannot tell you what percent of those claims were valid. Remember, too, that a large-volume operation is logically going to have more registered complaints against it than will an independent contractor.

Interview each of the potential candidates. Find out about specialties—custom houses, development houses, remodeling, or office buildings. Ask each to take you into—not just to the site of—current projects. Ask to see projects that are complete as well as work in progress, emphasizing that you are interested in projects comparable to yours. A $300,000 dentist's office will give you little insight into a contractor's craftsmanship.

Ask each contractor for bank references from both a commercial bank and any other appropriate lender. If in good financial standing, the contractor should have no qualms about giving you this information. Also ask about warranties. Most will give you a one-year warranty on the structure; some offer as much as a ten-year warranty.

Ask for references, even though no contractor will give you the name of a dissatisfied customer. Ask about follow-through. Was the building site cleaned up or did the owner have to dispose of the refuse? Ask about the organization of business. Did the paperwork go smoothly, or was there a delay in hooking up the sewer because of a failure to apply for a permit?

Talk to each of the candidates about fees. Most work on a "cost plus" basis; that is, the basic cost of the project—materials, subcontractors' services, wages of those working directly on the project, but not office help—plus a fee. Some have a fixed fee; others work on a percentage of the basic cost. A fixed fee is usually better for you if you can get one. If a contractor works on a percentage, ask for a cost breakdown of the best estimate and keep very careful track as the work progresses. A crafty contractor can always use a cost overrun to good advantage when working on a percentage.

Do not be overly suspicious of a contractor who won't work on a fixed fee. One who is very good and in great demand may not be willing to do so and may also be reluctant to submit a competitive bid.

Give the top two or three candidates each copies of the plans and your specifications for materials. If they are not each working from the same guidelines, the competitive bids will be of little value. Give each the same deadline for turning in a bid; two or three weeks is a reasonable period of time. Make an appointment with each of them and open the envelopes at this time.

If one bid is remarkably low, the contractor may have made an honest error in the estimate. Don't insist that the contractor hold to a bid if it is in error. Forcing a building price that is too low could be disastrous for both of you. You may want to review the bids with your architect, if you have one, or with your lender to discuss which to accept. They may not recommend the lowest. A low bid does not necessarily mean that you will get the best quality with economy.

If the bids are relatively close, the most important consideration may not be money at all. A bid from a contractor who is easy to talk to and inspires confidence may be the best choice. Any sign of a personality conflict between you and a contractor should be weighed when making a decision.

Once you have financing, you can sign a contract with the builder. Most have their own contract forms, but it is advisable to have a lawyer draw one up or, at the very least, review the standard contract. This usually costs a small flat fee.

A good contract should include:

- Plans and sketches of the work to be done, subject to your approval.
- A list of materials, including quantity, brand names, style or serial numbers. (Do not permit any "or equal" clause that will allow the contractor to make substitutions.)
- The terms—who (you or the lender) pays whom and when.
- A production schedule.
- The contractor's certification of insurance for workmen's compensation, damage, and liability.
- A rider stating that all changes, whether or not they increase the cost, must be submitted and approved in writing.

Of course, this list represents the least a contract should include. Once you have signed it, your plans are on the way to becoming a home.

A Checklist For Plan Selection

Developing an architectural plan from the various wants and needs of an individual or family that fits into lifestyle demands and design elegance is the most efficient way to assure a livable plan. It is not only possible but highly desirable to design a plan around such requirements as separate bedrooms for each member of the family, guest suites, a quiet study area, an oversized entertainment area, a two-car garage, a completely private master suite, and a living room fireplace. Incorporated into this can be such wants as Tudor styling, 1½-stories, a large entry hall, decks and balconies, and a basement.

While it is obviously best to begin with wants and needs and then design a home to fit these criteria, this is not always practical or even possible. A very effective way around this problem is to select a professionally prepared home plan which meets all needs and incorporates as many wants as possible. With careful selection, it will be possible to modify sizes and make other design adjustments to make the home as close to custom as can be. It is important to remember that some wants may have to be compromised in the interest of meeting budgetary limitations. The trick is to build the best possible home for the available money while satisfying all absolute needs.

Following are some cost-controlling ideas that can make a big difference in the overall price of a home:

1. Square or rectangular homes are less expensive to build than irregularly shaped homes.
2. It is less expensive to build on a flat lot than on a sloping or hillside lot.
3. The use of locally manufactured or produced materials cuts costs greatly.
4. Using stock materials and stock sizes of components takes advantage of mass production cost reductions.
5. The use of materials that can be quickly installed cuts labor costs. Prefabricating large sections or panels eliminates much time on the site.
6. The use of prefinished materials saves significantly on labor costs.
7. Investigating existing building codes before beginning construction eliminates unnecessary changes as construction proceeds.
8. Refraining from changing the design or any aspect of the plan after construction begins will help to hold down cost escalation.
9. Minimizing special jobs or custom-built items keeps costs from increasing.
10. Designing the house for short plumbing lines saves on piping and other materials.
11. Proper insulation saves heating and cooling costs.
12. Utilizing passive solar features, such as correct orientation, reduces future maintenance costs.

To help you consider all the important factors in evaluating a plan, the following checklist should be reviewed carefully. By comparing its various points to any plan and a wants-and-needs list, it will be possible to easily recognize the deficiencies of a plan or determine its appropriateness. Be sure to include family members in the decision-making process. Their ideas and desires will help in finding exactly the right plan.

CHECKLIST

The Neighborhood

1. _____ Reasonable weather conditions
2. No excess
   _____ *a.* wind
   _____ *b.* smog or fog
   _____ *c.* odors
   _____ *d.* soot or dust
3. _____ The area is residential
4. There are no
   _____ *a.* factories
   _____ *b.* dumps
   _____ *c.* highways
   _____ *d.* railroads
   _____ *e.* airports
   _____ *f.* apartments
   _____ *g.* commercial buildings
5. _____ City-maintained streets
6. No hazards in the area
   _____ *a.* quarries
   _____ *b.* storage tanks
   _____ *c.* power stations
   _____ *d.* unprotected swimming pools
7. Reasonably close to
   _____ *a.* work
   _____ *b.* schools
   _____ *c.* churches
   _____ *d.* hospital
   _____ *e.* shopping
   _____ *f.* recreation
   _____ *g.* public transportation
   _____ *h.* library
   _____ *i.* police protection
   _____ *j.* fire protection
   _____ *k.* parks
   _____ *l.* cultural activities
8. _____ Streets are curved
9. _____ Traffic is slow
10. _____ Intersections are at right angles
11. _____ Street lighting
12. _____ Light traffic
13. _____ Visitor parking
14. _____ Good design in street
15. _____ Paved streets and curbs
16. _____ Area is not deteriorating
17. _____ Desirable expansion
18. _____ Has some open spaces

19. _____ Numerous and healthy trees
20. _____ Pleasant-looking homes
21. _____ Space between homes
22. _____ Water drains off
23. _____ Near sewerage line
24. _____ Storm sewers nearby
25. _____ Mail delivery
26. _____ Garbage pickup
27. _____ Trash pickup
28. _____ No city assessments

The Lot

1. _____ Title is clear
2. _____ No judgments against the seller
3. _____ No restrictions as to the use of the land or the deed
4. _____ No unpaid taxes or assessments
5. _____ Minimum of 70 feet of frontage
6. _____ House does not crowd the lot
7. _____ Possible to build on
8. _____ Few future assessments (sewers, lights, and so forth)
9. _____ Good top soil and soil percolation
10. _____ Good view
11. _____ No low spots to hold water
12. _____ Water drains off land away from the house
13. _____ No fill
14. _____ No water runoff from high ground
15. _____ If cut or graded there is substantial retaining wall
16. _____ Permanent boundary markers
17. _____ Utilities available at property line
18. _____ Utility hookup is reasonable
19. _____ Utility rates are reasonable
20. _____ Taxes are reasonable
21. _____ Water supply is adequate
22. _____ Regular, simply shaped lot
23. _____ Trees
24. _____ Do not have to cut trees
25. _____ Privacy for outside activities
26. _____ Attractive front yard
27. _____ Front and rear yards are adequate
28. _____ Front yard is not divided up by walks and driveway
29. _____ Outdoor walks have stairs grouped

The Floor Plan

1. _____ Designed by licensed architect
2. _____ Purchased from a reputable stock plan company
3. _____ Supervised by skilled contractor

4. Orientation
   _____ *a.* sun
   _____ *b.* view
   _____ *c.* noise
   _____ *d.* breeze
   _____ *e.* contour of land

5. _____ Entry
6. _____ Planned for exterior expansion

7. Planned for interior expansion
   _____ *a.* attic
   _____ *b.* garage
   _____ *c.* basement

8. _____ Simple but functional plan
9. _____ Indoor recreation area
10. _____ Wall space for furniture in each room

11. Well-designed hall
   _____ *a.* leads to all areas
   _____ *b.* no congestions
   _____ *c.* no wasted space
   _____ *d.* 3' minimum widths

12. _____ Easy to clean
13. _____ Easy to keep orderly
14. _____ Plan meets family's needs
15. _____ All rooms have direct emergency escape

16. Doorways functional
   _____ *a.* no unnecessary doors
   _____ *b.* wide enough for moving furniture through
   _____ *c.* can see visitors through locked front door
   _____ *d.* do not swing out into halls
   _____ *e.* swing open against a blank wall
   _____ *f.* do not bump other subjects
   _____ *g.* exterior doors are solid

17. Windows are functional
   _____ *a.* not too small
   _____ *b.* enough but not too many
   _____ *c.* glare-free
   _____ *d.* roof overhang protection where needed
   _____ *e.* large ones have the best view
   _____ *f.* easy to clean
   _____ *g.* no interference with furniture placement
   _____ *h.* over kitchen sink
   _____ *i.* open easily

18. _____ No fancy gadgets
19. _____ Room sizes are adequate
20. _____ Well-designed stairs
   _____ *a.* treads are 9" minimum
   _____ *b.* risers are 8" maximum
   _____ *c.* 36" minimum width
   _____ *d.* 3' minimum landings
   _____ *e.* attractive
   _____ *f.* easily reached

21. _____ Overall plan "fits" family requirements
22. _____ Good traffic patterns
23. _____ Noisy areas separated from quiet areas
24. _____ Rooms have adequate wall space for furniture
25. _____ Halls are 3'6" minimum

The Living Area

1. _____ Minimum space 12' x 16'
2. _____ Front door traffic does not enter
3. _____ Not in a traffic pattern
4. _____ Windows on two sides
5. _____ Has a view
6. _____ Storage for books and music materials
7. _____ Decorative lighting
8. _____ Whole family plus guests can be seated
9. _____ Desk area
10. _____ Fireplace
11. _____ Wood storage
12. _____ No street noises
13. _____ Privacy from street
14. _____ Acoustical ceiling
15. _____ Cannot see or hear bathroom
16. _____ Powder room
17. _____ Comfortable for conversation

18. Dining room
   _____ *a.* used enough to justify
   _____ *b.* minimum of 3' clearance around table
   _____ *c.* can be opened or closed to kitchen and patio
   _____ *d.* can be opened or closed to living room
   _____ *e.* electrical outlets for table appliances

19. Family room
- _____ *a.* minimum space 10' x 12'
- _____ *b.* room for family activities
- _____ *c.* room for noisy activities
- _____ *d.* room for messy activities
- _____ *e.* activities will not disturb sleeping area
- _____ *f.* finish materials are easy to clean and durable
- _____ *g.* room for expansion
- _____ *h.* separate from living room
- _____ *i.* near kitchen
- _____ *j.* fireplace
- _____ *k.* adequate storage

20. _____ Dead-end circulation
21. _____ Adequate furniture arrangements

The Entry

1. _____ The entry is a focal point
2. _____ The outside is inviting
3. _____ The landing has a minimum depth of 5'
4. _____ Protected from the weather
5. _____ Has an approach walk
6. _____ Well planted
7. _____ Coat closet
8. _____ Leads to living, sleeping, and service areas
9. _____ Floor material attractive and easy to clean
10. _____ Decorative lighting
11. _____ Space for table
12. _____ Space to hang mirror
13. _____ Does not have direct view into any room

The Bedrooms

1. _____ Adequate number of bedrooms
2. _____ Adequate size—10' x 12' minimum
3. _____ Open into a hall
4. _____ Living space
5. _____ Children's bedroom has study and play area
6. _____ Oriented to north side
7. In quiet area
   - _____ *a.* soundproofing
   - _____ *b.* acoustical ceiling
   - _____ *c.* insulation in walls
   - _____ *d.* thermal glass
   - _____ *e.* double doors
   - _____ *f.* closet walls
8. _____ Privacy
9. _____ 4' minimum wardrobe rod space per person
10. Master bedroom
   - _____ *a.* bath
   - _____ *b.* dressing area
   - _____ *c.* full-length mirror
   - _____ *d.* 12' x 12' minimum
11. Adequate windows
   - _____ *a.* natural light
   - _____ *b.* cross-ventilation
   - _____ *c.* windows on two walls
12. _____ Room for overnight guests
13. _____ Bathroom nearby
14. _____ Wall space for bed, nightstands, and dresser
15. _____ Quiet reading area

The Bathroom

1. _____ Well designed
2. _____ Plumbing lines are grouped
3. _____ Fixtures have space around them for proper use
4. _____ Doors do not interfere with fixtures
5. _____ Noises are insulated from other rooms
6. _____ Convenient to bedrooms
7. _____ Convenient to guests
8. _____ Ventilation
9. _____ Heating
10. _____ Attractive fixtures
11. _____ No windows over tub or shower
12. _____ Wall area around tub and shower
13. _____ Light fixtures are water tight
14. _____ Large medicine cabinet
15. _____ Children cannot open medicine cabinet
16. _____ No bathroom tie-ups
17. _____ Good lighting
18. _____ Accessible electrical outlets
19. _____ No electric appliance or switch near water supply
20. _____ Towel and linen storage
21. _____ Dirty clothes hamper
22. _____ Steamproof mirrors
23. _____ Wall and floor materials are waterproof
24. _____ All finishes are easy to maintain
25. _____ Curtain and towel rods securely fastened
26. _____ Grab bar by tub
27. _____ Mixing faucets
28. _____ Bath in service area
29. _____ No public view into open bathroom door
30. _____ Clean-up area for outdoor jobs and children's play

The Kitchen

1. _____ Centrally located
2. _____ The family can eat informally in the kitchen
3. _____ At least 20' of cabinet space
   - _____ *a.* counter space on each side of major appliances
   - _____ *b.* minimum of 8' counter work area
   - _____ *c.* round storage in corners
   - _____ *d.* no shelf is higher than 72"
   - _____ *e.* floor cabinets 24" deep and 36" high
   - *f.* wall cabinets 15" deep
   - _____ *g.* 15" clearance between wall and floor cabinets
4. _____ Work triangle is formed between appliances
   - _____ *a.* between 12' and 20'
   - _____ *b.* no traffic through the work triangle
   - _____ *c.* refrigerator opens into the work triangle
   - _____ *d.* at least six electric outlets in work triangle
   - _____ *e.* no door between appliances
5. _____ No space between appliances and counters
6. _____ Window over sink
7. _____ No wasted space in kitchen
8. _____ Can close off kitchen from dining area
9. _____ Snack bar in kitchen
10. _____ Kitchen drawers are divided
11. _____ Built-in chopping block
12. _____ Writing and telephone desk
13. _____ Indoor play area visible from kitchen
14. _____ Outdoor play area visible from kitchen
15. _____ Exhaust fan
16. _____ Natural light
17. _____ Good lighting for each work area
18. _____ Convenient access to service area and garage
19. _____ Durable surfaces
20. _____ Dishwasher
21. _____ Disposal
22. _____ Built-in appliances
23. _____ Bathroom nearby

24. _____ Room for freezer
25. _____ Pantry storage

The Utility Room

1. _____ Adequate laundry area
2. _____ Well-lighted work areas
3. _____ 240-volt outlet
4. _____ Gas outlet
5. _____ Sorting area
6. _____ Ironing area
7. _____ Drip-drying area
8. _____ Sewing and mending area
9. _____ On least desirable side of lot
10. _____ Exit to outdoor service area
11. _____ Exit near garage
12. _____ Sufficient cabinet space
13. _____ Bathroom in area
14. _____ Accessible from kitchen
15. _____ Adequate space for washer and dryer
16. _____ Laundry tray
17. _____ Outdoor exit is protected from the weather
18. _____ Window

Working Areas

1. _____ Home repair area
2. _____ Work area for hobbies
3. _____ Storage for paints and tools
4. _____ Garage storage
5. _____ Incinerator area
6. _____ Refuse area
7. _____ Delivery area
8. _____ Near parking
9. _____ 240-volt outlet for power tools

Storage

1. _____ General storage space for each person
2. _____ 4' of rod space for each person
3. _____ Closet doors are sealed to keep out dust
4. _____ Minimum wardrobe closet size is 40" x 22"
5. _____ Cedar closet storage for seasonal clothing
6. _____ Bulk storage area for seasonal paraphernalia
7. _____ Closets are lighted
8. _____ Walk-in closets have adequate turnaround area
9. Storage for:
   _____ *a.* linen and towels
   _____ *b.* cleaning materials
   _____ *c.* foods
   _____ *d.* bedding
   _____ *e.* outdoor furniture
   _____ *f.* sports equipment
   _____ *g.* toys—indoor
   _____ *h.* toys—outdoor
   _____ *i.* bicycles
   _____ *j.* luggage
   _____ *k.* out-of-season clothes
   _____ *l.* storm windows and doors
   _____ *m.* garden tools
   _____ *n.* tools and paints
   _____ *o.* hats
   _____ *p.* shoes
   _____ *q.* belts
   _____ *r.* ties
   _____ *s.* bridge tables and chairs
   _____ *t.* camping equipment
   _____ *u.* china
   _____ *v.* silver
   _____ *w.* minor appliances
   _____ *x.* books
10. _____ Closets are ventilated
11. _____ Closets do not project into room
12. _____ Toothbrush holders in bathrooms
13. _____ Soap holders in bathrooms
14. _____ Adequate built-in storage
15. _____ Drawers cannot pull out of cabinet
16. _____ Drawers slide easily
17. _____ Drawers have divided partitions
18. _____ Adult storage areas easy to reach
19. _____ Children storage areas easy to reach
20. _____ Guest storage near entry
21. _____ Heavy storage areas have reinforced floors
22. _____ Sides of closets easy to reach
23. _____ Tops of closets easy to reach
24. _____ No wasted spaces around stored articles
25. _____ Sloping roof or stairs do not render closet useless
26. _____ Entry closet

The Exterior

1. _____ The design looks "right" for the lot
2. _____ Design varies from other homes nearby
3. _____ Design fits with unity on its site
4. _____ Definite style architecture—not mixed
5. _____ Simple, honest design
6. _____ Garage design goes with the house
7. _____ Attractive on all four sides
8. _____ Colors in good taste
9. _____ Finish materials in good taste
10. _____ Has charm and warmth
11. _____ Materials are consistent on all sides
12. _____ No false building effects
13. _____ Well-designed roof lines—not chopped up
14. _____ Window tops line up
15. _____ Bathroom windows are not obvious
16. _____ Does not look like a box
17. _____ Easy maintenance of finish materials
18. _____ Windows are protected from pedestrian view
19. _____ Attractive roof covering
20. _____ Gutters on roof
21. _____ Downspouts that drain into storm sewer
22. _____ Glass area protected with overhang or trees
23. _____ Dry around the house
24. _____ Several waterproof electric outlets
25. _____ Hose bib on each side
26. _____ Style will look good in the future

Outdoor Service Area

1. _____ Clothes hanging area
2. _____ Garbage storage
3. _____ Can storage
4. _____ On least desirable side of site
5. _____ Next to indoor service area
6. _____ Near garage
7. _____ Delivery area for trucks
8. _____ Fenced off from rest of site

Outdoor Living Area

1. _____ Area for dining
2. _____ Area for games
3. _____ Area for lounging
4. _____ Area for gardening
5. _____ Fenced for privacy
6. _____ Partly shaded
7. _____ Concrete deck at convenient places
8. _____ Garden walks

9. _____ Easy access to house
10. _____ Paved area for bikes and wagons
11. _____ Easy maintenance

Landscaping

1. _____ Planting at foundation ties
2. _____ Garden area
3. _____ Well-located trees
4. _____ Healthy trees
5. _____ Plants of slow-growing variety
6. _____ Landscaping professionally advised
7. _____ Garden walks
8. _____ Easy maintenance
9. _____ Extras as trellis or gazebo

Construction

1. _____ Sound construction
2. _____ All work complies to code
3. _____ Efficient contractor and supervision
4. _____ Honest builders
5. _____ Skilled builders
6. _____ Constructed to plans
7. Floors are well constructed
   _____ *a.* resilient
   _____ *b.* subfloor diagonal to joints
   _____ *c.* flat and even
   _____ *d.* slab is not cold
   _____ *e.* floor joists rest on 2" of sill—minimum
   _____ *f.* girder lengths are joined under points of support
8. Foundation is well constructed
   _____ *a.* level
   _____ *b.* sill protected from termites
   _____ *c.* vapor barrier
   _____ *d.* no cracks
   _____ *e.* no water seepage
   _____ *f.* no dryrot in sills
   _____ *g.* garage slab drains
   _____ *h.* waterproofed
   _____ *i.* walls are 8" thick
   _____ *j.* basement height 7'6" minimum
   _____ *k.* sills bolted to foundation
   _____ *l.* adequate vents
9. Walls are well constructed
   _____ *a.* plumb
   _____ *b.* no waves
   _____ *c.* insulation
   _____ *d.* flashing at all exterior joints
   _____ *e.* solid sheathing
   _____ *f.* siding is neat and tight
   _____ *g.* drywall joints are invisible
10. Windows are properly installed
   _____ *a.* move freely
   _____ *b.* weatherstripped
   _____ *c.* caulked and sealed
   _____ *d.* good-quality glass
11. Doors properly hung
   _____ *a.* move freely
   _____ *b.* exterior doors weatherstripped
   _____ *c.* exterior doors are solid-core
   _____ *d.* interior doors are hollow-core
12. Roof is well constructed
   _____ *a.* rafters are straight
   _____ *b.* all corners are flashed
   _____ *c.* adequate vents in attic
   _____ *d.* no leaks
   _____ *e.* building paper under shingles
13. _____ Tile work is tight
14. _____ Hot water lines are insulated
15. _____ Mortar joints are neat
16. _____ Mortar joints do not form shelf to hold water
17. _____ Ceiling is 8'0" minimum
18. _____ No exposed pipes
19. _____ No exposed wires
20. _____ Tight joints at cabinets and appliances
21. _____ Stairs have railings
22. _____ Neat trim application
23. _____ Builder responsible for new home flaws

The Fireplace

1. _____ There is a fireplace
2. _____ Wood storage near the fireplace
3. _____ Draws smoke
4. _____ Hearth in front (minimum 10" on sides; 20" in front)
5. _____ Does not project out into the room
6. _____ Has a clean-out
7. _____ Chimney top 2' higher than roof ridge
8. _____ No leaks around chimney in roof
9. _____ No wood touches the chimney
10. _____ 2" minimum air space between framing members and masonry
11. _____ No loose mortar
12. _____ Has a damper
13. _____ Space for furniture opposite fireplace
14. _____ Doors minimum of 6' from fireplace
15. _____ Windows minimum of 3' from fireplace
16. _____ On a long wall
17. _____ Install "heatilator"
18. _____ Install glass doors to minimize heat loss

Equipment

1. _____ All equipment listed in specifications and plans
2. _____ All new equipment has warranty
3. _____ All equipment is up to code standards
4. _____ All equipment is functional and not a fad
5. _____ Owner's choice of equipment meets builder's allowance
6. _____ Public system for utilities
7. _____ Private well is deep; adequate and healthy water
8. Electrical equipment is adequate
   _____ *a.* inspected and guaranteed
   _____ *b.* 240 voltage
   _____ *c.* 120 voltage
   _____ *d.* sufficient electric outlets
   _____ *e.* sufficient electric circuits—minimum of six
   _____ *f.* circuit breakers
   _____ *g.* television aerial outlet
   _____ *h.* telephone outlets
   _____ *i.* outlets in convenient places
9. Adequate lighting
   _____ *a.* all rooms have general lighting
   _____ *b.* all rooms have specific lighting for specific tasks
   _____ *c.* silent switches
   _____ *d.* some decorative lighting
   _____ *e.* light at front door
   _____ *f.* outdoor lighting
10. _____ Plumbing equipment is adequate
   _____ *a.* inspected and guaranteed
   _____ *b.* adequate water pressure
   _____ *c.* hot water heater—50-gallon minimum
   _____ *d.* shut-off valves at fixtures

_____ *e.* satisfactory city sewer or septic tank
_____ *f.* septic tank disposal field is adequate
_____ *g.* septic tank is large enough for house (1000 gallons for three-bedroom house, plus 250 gallons for each additional bedroom)
_____ *h.* water softener for hard water
_____ *i.* siphon vertex or siphon reverse-trap water closet
_____ *j.* clean-out plugs at all corners of waste lines
_____ *k.* water lines will not rust
_____ *l.* water pipes do not hammer
_____ *m.* waste lines drain freely
_____ *n.* cast iron with vitreous enamel bathtub

11. _____ Good ventilation through house and attic
12. Heating and cooling systems are adequate
_____ *a.* insulation in roof, ceiling, walls
_____ *b.* air conditioning system
_____ *c.* heating and cooling outlets under windows
_____ *d.* air purifier
_____ *e.* thermostatic control
_____ *f.* walls are clean over heat outlets
_____ *g.* comfortable in hot or cold weather
_____ *h.* automatic humidifier
_____ *i.* furnace blower is belt-driven
_____ *j.* quiet-heating plant
_____ *k.* ducts are tight
13. _____ Windows are of good quality
_____ *a.* storm windows
_____ *b.* secure locks
_____ *c.* screened
_____ *d.* double glazed in extreme weather (thermal)
_____ *e.* glass is ripple-free
_____ *f.* safety or safe thickness of glass
_____ *g.* moisture-free
_____ *h.* frost-free
14. Doors are of good quality
_____ *a.* secure locks on exterior doors
_____ *b.* attractive hardware
_____ *c.* hardware is solid brass or bronze
15. All meters easily accessible to meter readers
16. _____ Fire extinguisher in house and garage
17. _____ Acoustical ceiling
18. _____ Facilities to lock mail box
19. _____ Facilities to receive large packages
20. _____ Gas or electric incinerator
21. Adequate small hardware
_____ *a.* soap dishes
_____ *b.* toilet-paper holders
_____ *c.* toothbrush holders
_____ *d.* towel holders
_____ *e.* bathtub grab bars
_____ *f.* door and drawer pulls

The Garage

1. _____ Same style as the house
2. _____ Fits with house
3. _____ Single garage 12' x 22' minimum
4. _____ Double garage 22' x 22' minimum
5. _____ Larger than minimum size if used for storage or workshop
6. _____ Protected passage to house
7. _____ Doors are safe
8. _____ Access to overhead storage

Financial Checklist

1. _____ Do you understand conveyancing fees (closing costs)?
2. _____ Is the house a good investment?
3. _____ Is the total cost approximately three times your annual income?
4. _____ Have you shopped for the best loan?
5. _____ Do you have a constant payment plan (sliding principal and interest)?
6. _____ Is there a prepayment penalty?
7. _____ Will a week's salary cover the total housing expense for one month?
8. _____ Are all the costs itemized in the contract?
9. Do you understand the following closing costs?
_____ *a.* title search
_____ *b.* lawyer
_____ *c.* plot survey
_____ *d.* insurance, fire, and public liability
_____ *e.* mortgage tax
_____ *f.* recording mortgage
_____ *g.* recording deed
_____ *h.* bank's commitment fee
_____ *i.* state and county taxes
_____ *j.* state and government revenue stamps
_____ *k.* title insurance (protects lender)
_____ *l.* homeowner's policy (protects owner)
_____ *m.* transferring ownership
_____ *n.* mortgage service charge
_____ *o.* appraisal
_____ *p.* notarizing documents
_____ *q.* attendant fee (paying off previous mortgage)
_____ *r.* personal credit check
10. _____ Do you have extra cash to cover unforeseen expenses?
11. Can you afford to pay the following?
_____ *a.* closing costs
_____ *b.* old assessments or bonds
_____ *c.* new assessments or bonds
_____ *d.* downpayment
_____ *e.* immediate repairs
_____ *f.* immediate purchases (furniture, appliances, landscape, tools, fences, carpets, drapes, patio)
_____ *g.* adequate insurance
_____ *h.* mortgage payments
_____ *i.* general maintenance
_____ *j.* utilities (water, heat, electricity, phone, gas, trash pickup)
_____ *k.* special design features wanted
_____ *l.* extras not covered in plans and contract
_____ *m.* prepayment of interest and taxes for first month of transition
_____ *n.* moving
_____ *o.* gardener
_____ *p.* travel to work
_____ *q.* interest on construction loan
_____ *r.* advances to contractors
12. _____ Who will pay for the following?
_____ *a.* supervision costs of architect or contractor
_____ *b.* inspection fees
_____ *c.* increased costs during building
_____ *d.* building permits
_____ *e.* difficulties in excavation
_____ *f.* dry wells
_____ *g.* extra features the building inspector insists upon

The above Checklist is used with permission. It is taken from Home Planners' Guide to Residential Design *by Charles Talcott, Don Hepler, and Paul Wallach; 1986; McGraw-Hill, Inc.*

LIFESTYLE RECREATION HOMES . . .

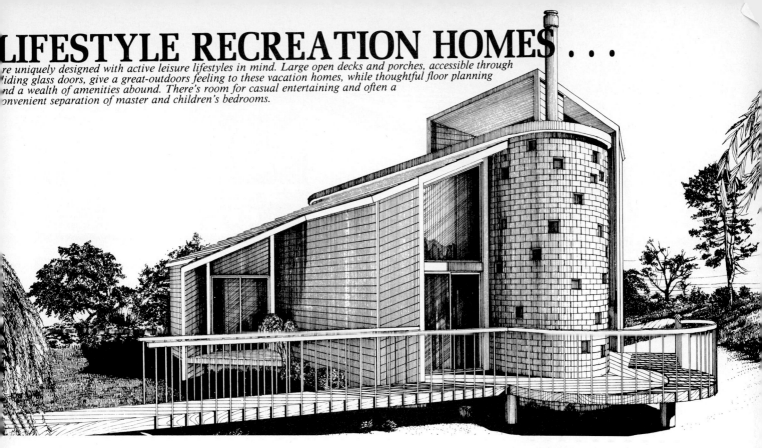

re uniquely designed with active leisure lifestyles in mind. Large open decks and porches, accessible through 'iding glass doors, give a great-outdoors feeling to these vacation homes, while thoughtful floor planning nd a wealth of amenities abound. There's room for casual entertaining and often a onvenient separation of master and children's bedrooms.

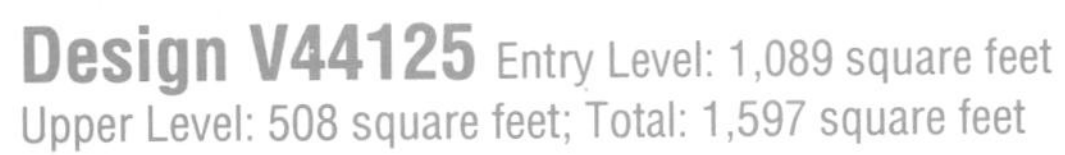

Design V44125 Entry Level: 1,089 square feet
Upper Level: 508 square feet; Total: 1,597 square feet

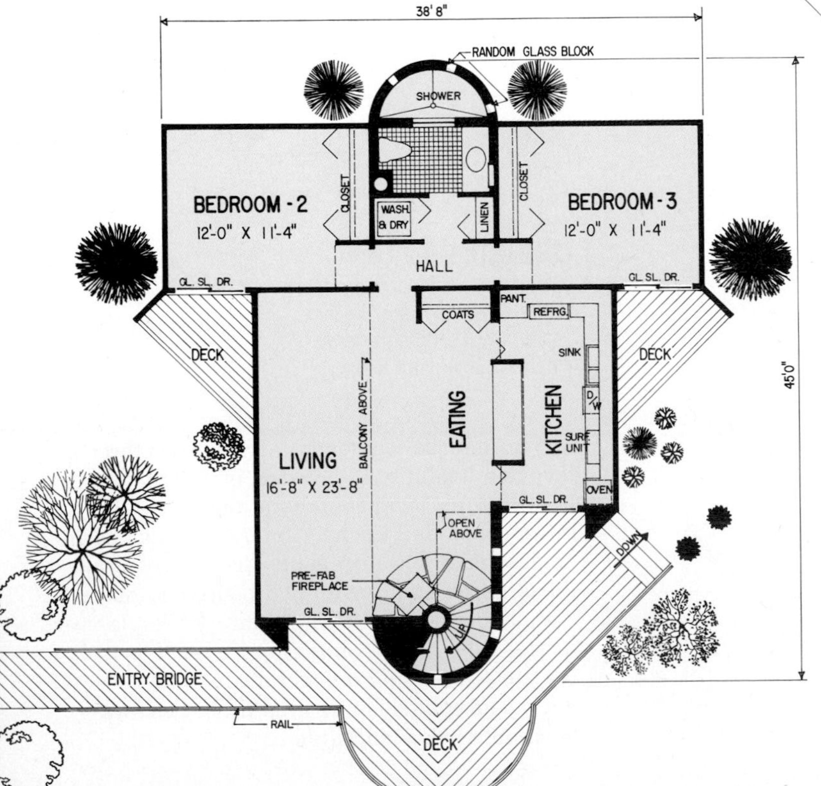

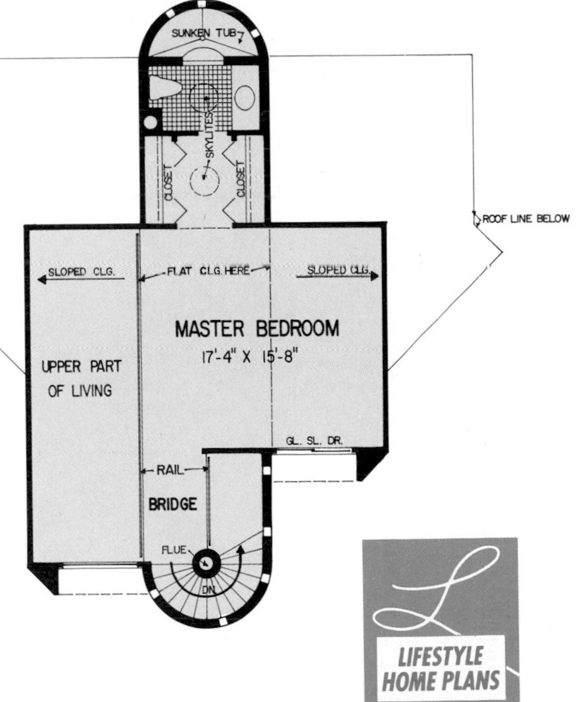

LIFESTYLE HOME PLANS

● Geometrical design elements are used to striking effect in this appealing contemporary. Several entrances lead into the open living and eating area. A pass-through to the kitchen saves steps in serving and cleaning up. Two rear bedrooms each have a private deck. A large circular tower encloses a spiral staircase leading up to the balcony master suite. Notice the semicircular sunken tub in the bath.

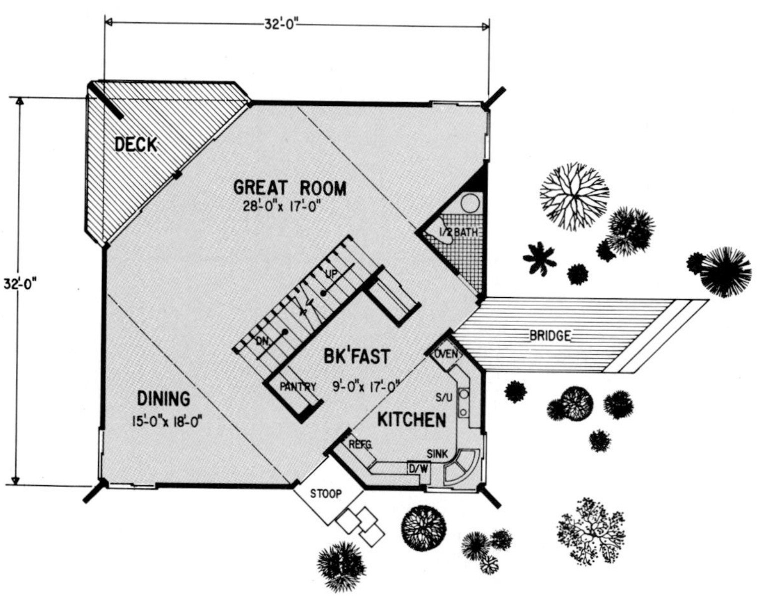

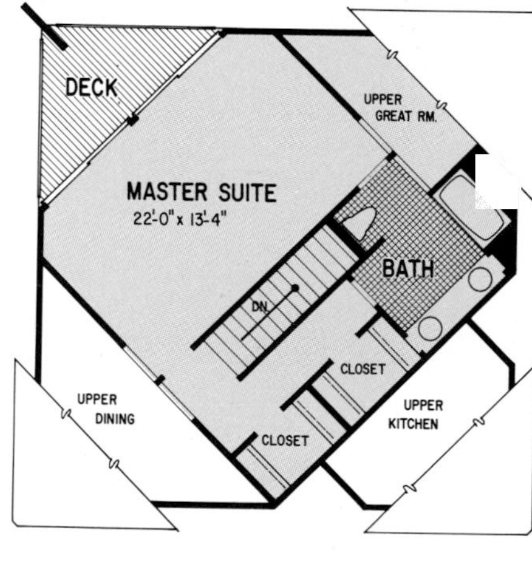

Design V44134

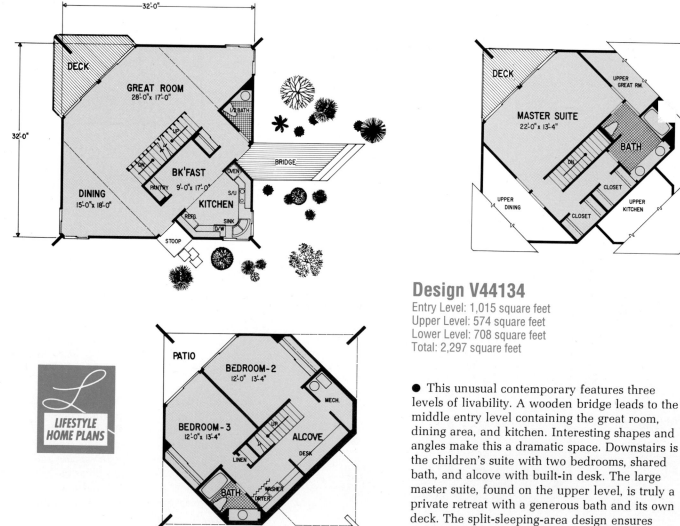

Entry Level: 1,015 square feet
Upper Level: 574 square feet
Lower Level: 708 square feet
Total: 2,297 square feet

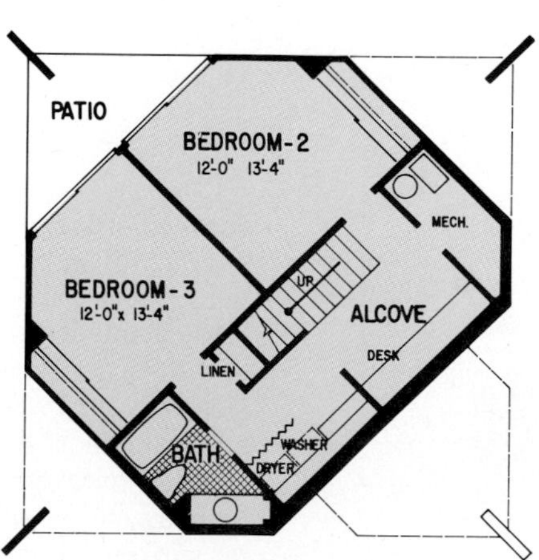

● This unusual contemporary features three levels of livability. A wooden bridge leads to the middle entry level containing the great room, dining area, and kitchen. Interesting shapes and angles make this a dramatic space. Downstairs is the children's suite with two bedrooms, shared bath, and alcove with built-in desk. The large master suite, found on the upper level, is truly a private retreat with a generous bath and its own deck. The split-sleeping-area design ensures maximum peace and quiet.

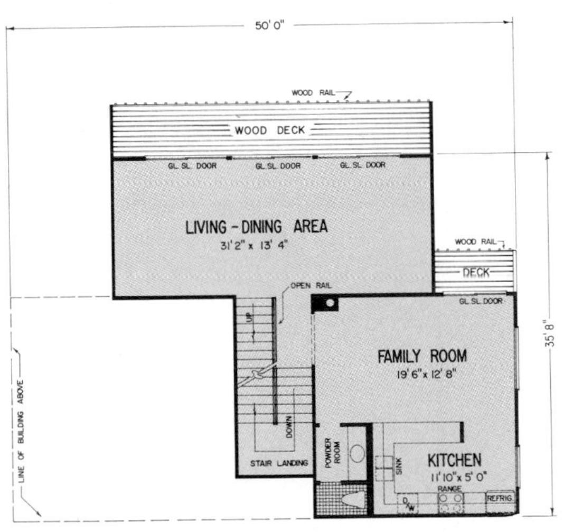

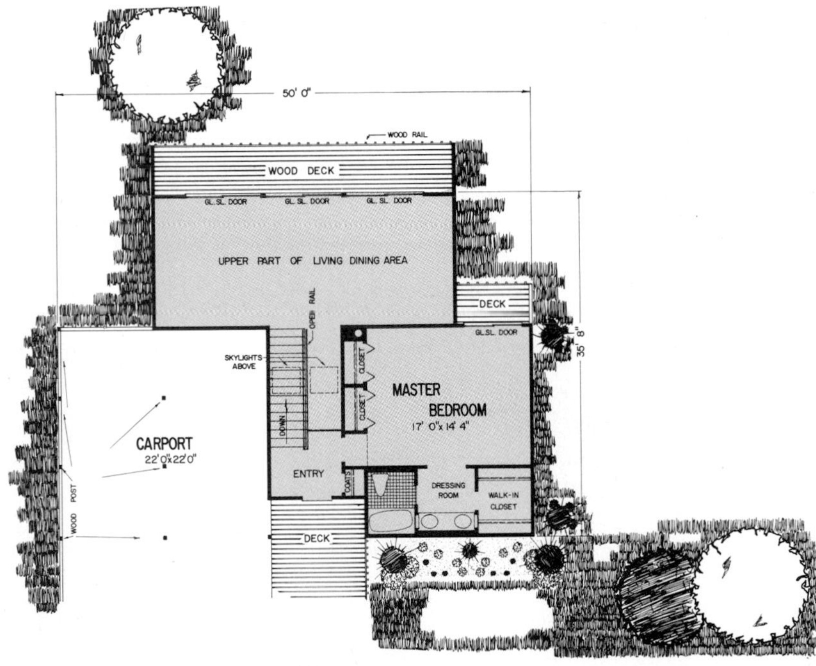

Design V44113

Main Level: 884 square feet
Upper Level: 576 square feet
Lower Level: 543 square feet
Total: 2,003 square feet

● With its glass doors and multiple decks, this striking multi-level was designed with a spectacular view in mind. The upper level houses the large master bedroom. Down the open stair is the spacious living and dining area. Just steps away is the open kitchen and family room, a communal spot for cooking and relaxing together. The lower level contains two more bedrooms, a full bath, and a shared deck. Both parents and children will appreciate the privacy of the split sleeping area.

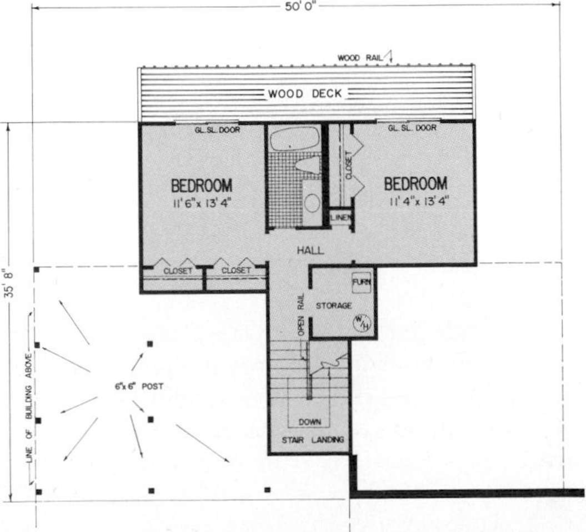

Design V44316

Entry Level: 873 square feet
Middle Level: 540 square feet
Upper Level: 600 square feet
Total: 2,013 square feet

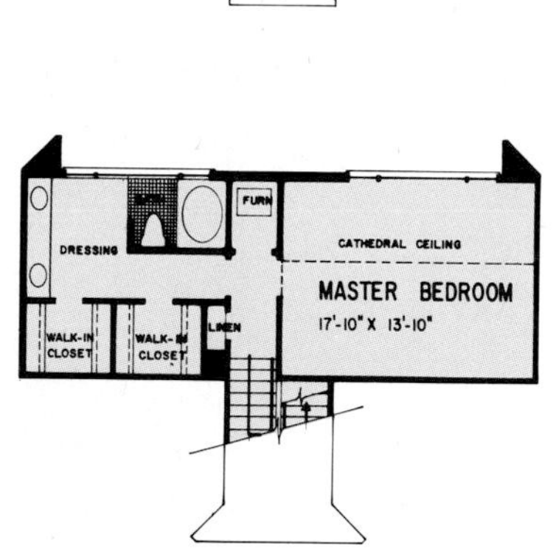

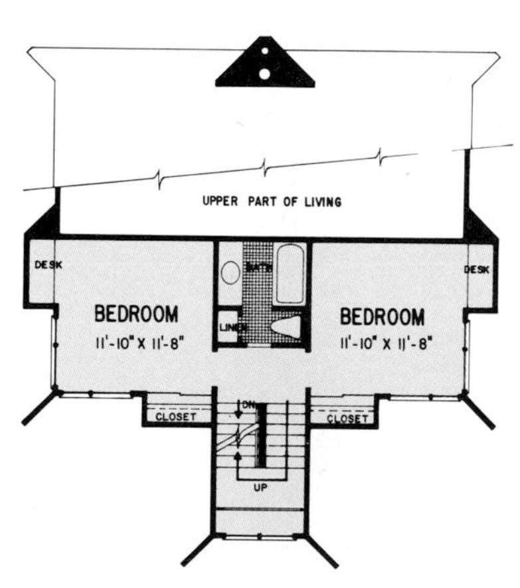

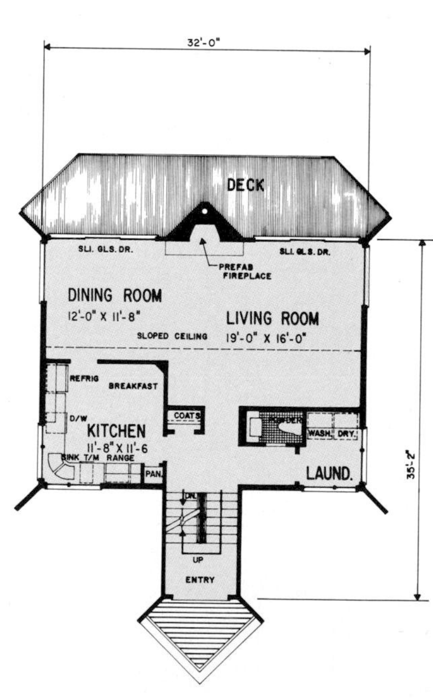

● Designs which cater to relaxed living patterns are much sought after in vacation homes. Informality is the rule in this plan which features an open living and dining area. Just a few steps away, a large deck extends the living area to the outdoors. Two bedrooms on the middle level share a bath. Contained on the upper level is a large master bedroom with cathedral ceiling and dressing area. Notice the matching walk-in closets — vacation doesn't have to mean roughing it!

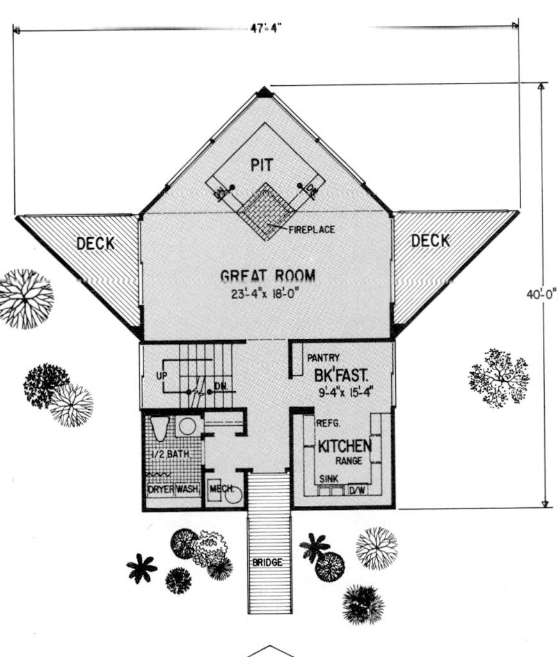

Design V44129

Entry Level: 802 square feet
Upper Level: 576 square feet
Lower Level: 577 square feet
Total: 1,955 square feet

● This design with its stacked levels of livability is ideal for a sloping site. The entry level contains the kitchen and the multi-purpose great room with its flanking decks. A large triangular projection contains a sunken conversation pit with fireplace — a cozy spot for chatting or curling up with a book. The two-bedroom lower level includes a deck; both parents and children will appreciate this extra space for playing or relaxing. The master suite is found on the upper level. Notice the large closet and oversized tub.

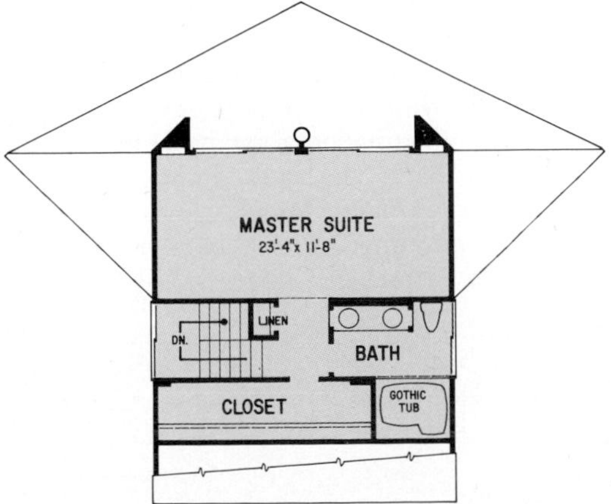

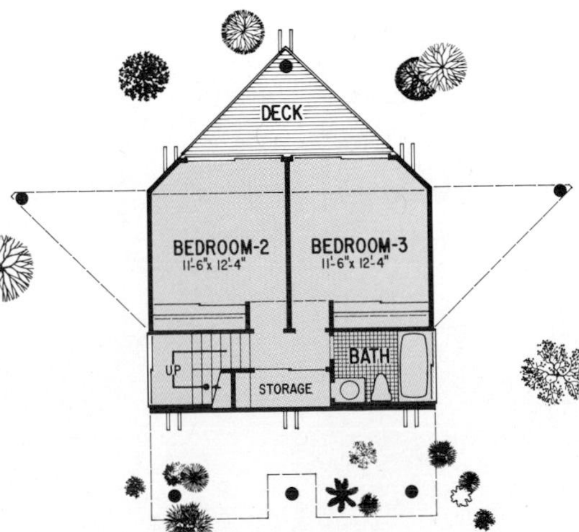

Blueprints show details for brick veneer and cavity wall construction.

Design V44187

Entry Level: 596 square feet
Upper Level: 680 square feet
Total: 1,276 square feet

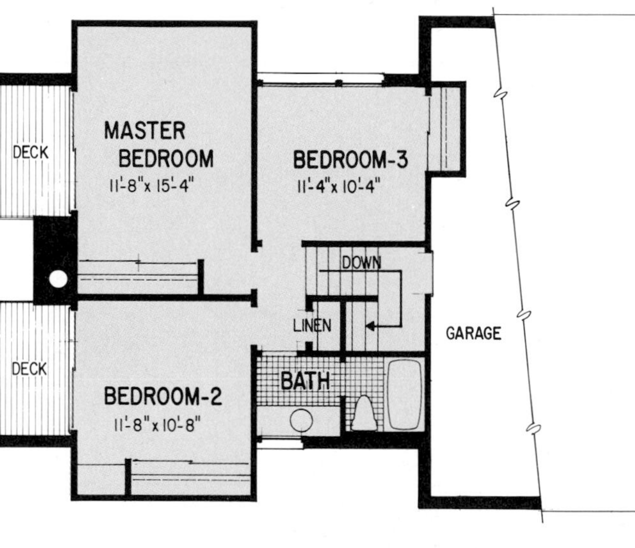

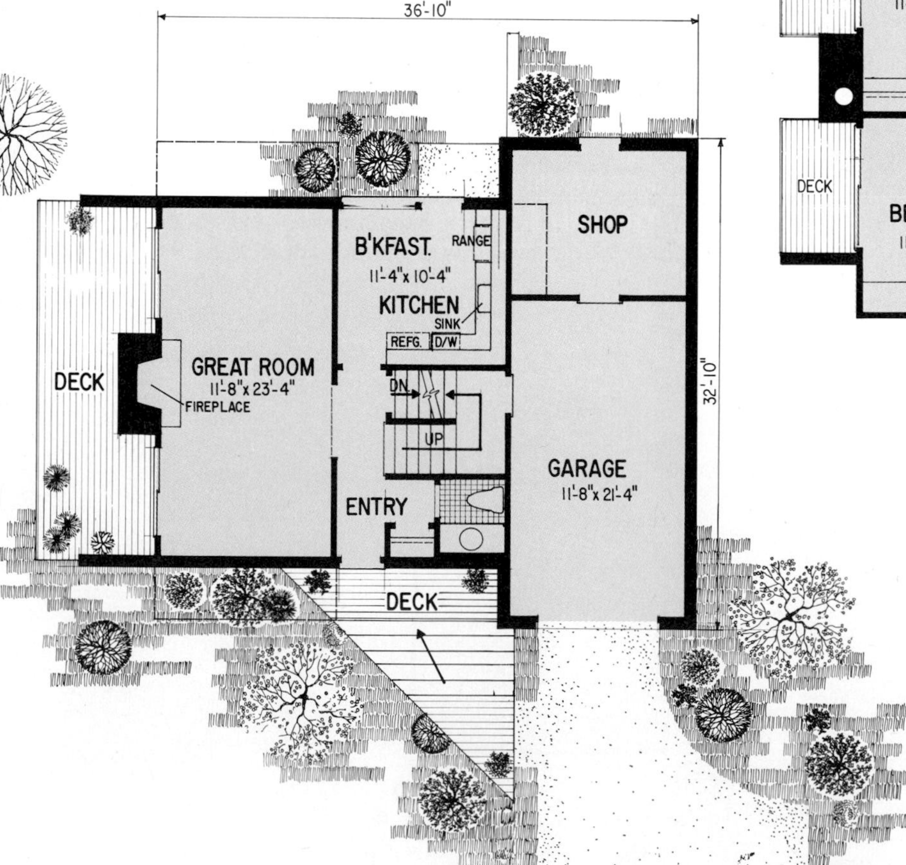

● Sloping rooflines and geometrical projections create a striking exterior for this home. The interior features all the relaxed informality of a vacation home. The enormous great room has enough space to accommodate a dining area, if desired, or several seating areas. An adjacent deck provides additional living space. The well-equipped kitchen includes a breakfast nook. Upstairs are three bedrooms and a shared bath. Two of the bedrooms feature private decks.

Design V44132

First Floor: 1,233 square feet
Second Floor: 915 square feet
Total: 2,148 square feet

● This home is designed to take full advantage of a spectacular view. Each room enjoys views and access to a deck through a sliding glass door. There's plenty of living space on the entry level with both a family room and living room. Notice the corner fireplace in the living room. The three-bedroom second level includes a large deck and an alcove which could accommodate a small sitting area.

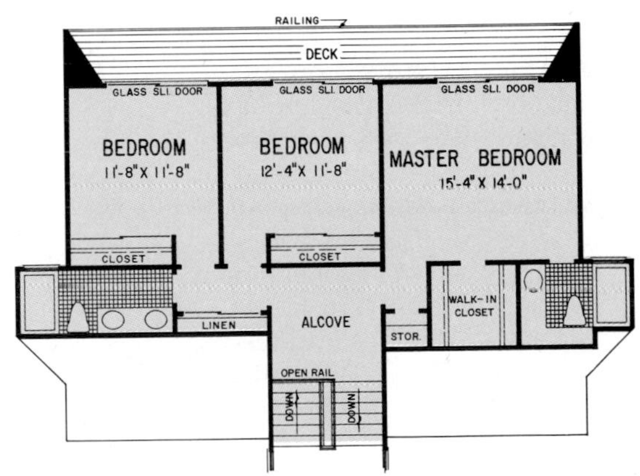

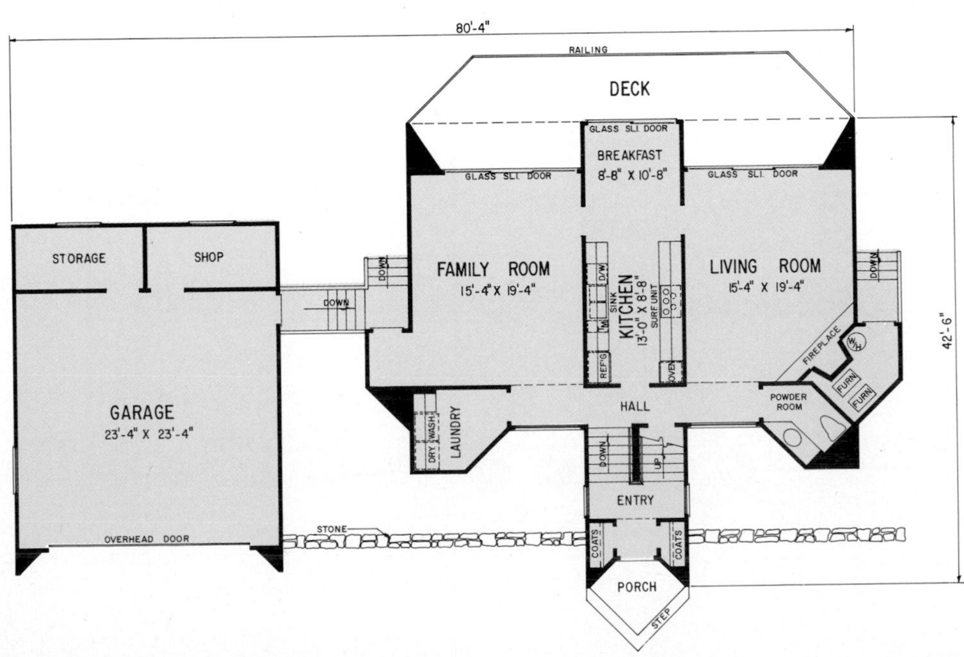

Design V44124

Square Footage: 1,772

● What an unusual entrance this home has! A wooden foot-bridge leads across a sunken garden for a dramatically different approach. The spacious great room will be a favorite gathering spot. The dining room is open to the great room, yet contained within its own distinct space. Three sliding glass doors provide access to the L-shaped deck and allow nice views of the back yard. Three good-sized bedrooms comprise a private sleeping wing away from the living and working areas.

Design V44114

Main Level: 852 square feet
Upper Level: 146 square feet
Total: 998 square feet

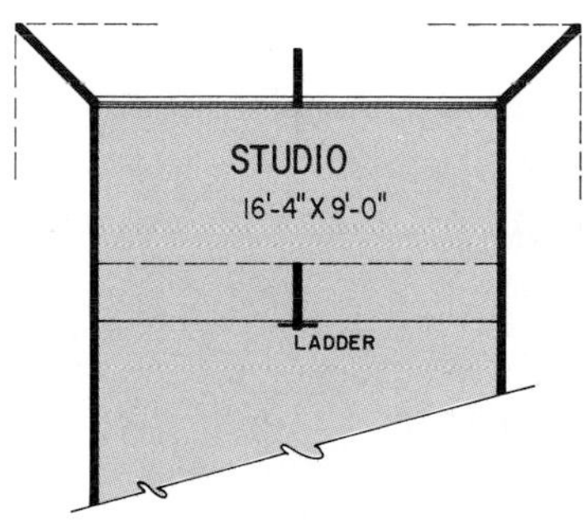

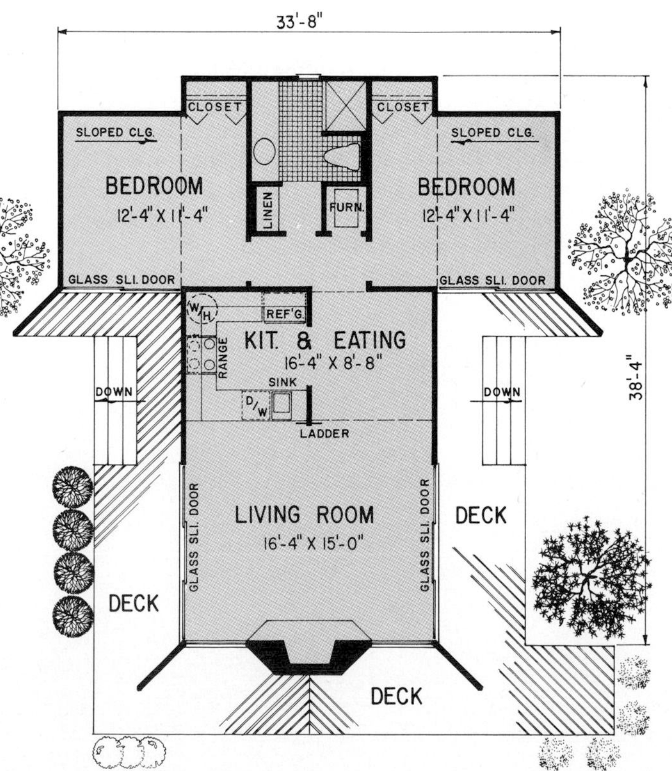

● This home was designed with the outdoors in mind. A large, wraparound deck provides ample space for sunning and relaxing. Huge windows and sliding glass doors open up the interior with lots of sunlight and great views — a must in a vacation home. Open planning makes for relaxed living patterns; the kitchen, living, and eating area flow together into one large working and living space. An upstairs loft provides added space for a lounge or an extra sleeping area.

Design V44539 Square Footage: 2,755 D

● This beach or resort house was planned with the main living area on an upper floor so that occupants can have a view of the water. The exterior walls of the lower floor are concrete block with concrete floors; the upper level is finished with boards and battens left to weather to a silver-gray driftwood color. The U-shaped kitchen, which looks out on the view, has a pass-through to the service hall for arriving groceries and a pass-through eating bar opening to the living room. The circular stair is the main entry and is reached through the lower-level game room, which has a fireplace and a bath with shower for swimmers. It is intended that the upper-level porch be screened.

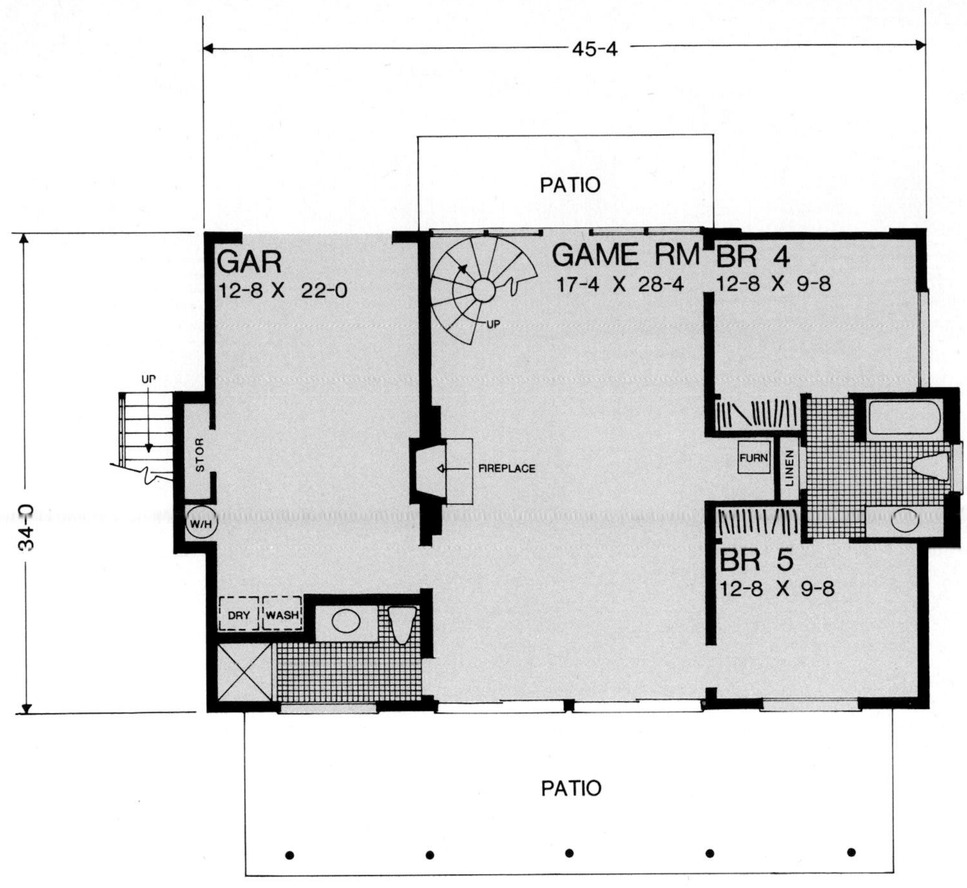
45-4
PATIO
GAR
12-8 X 22-0
GAME RM
17-4 X 28-4
BR 4
12-8 X 9-8
UP
STOR
FIREPLACE
FURN
LINEN
W/H
34-0
BR 5
12-8 X 9-8
DRY
WASH
PATIO

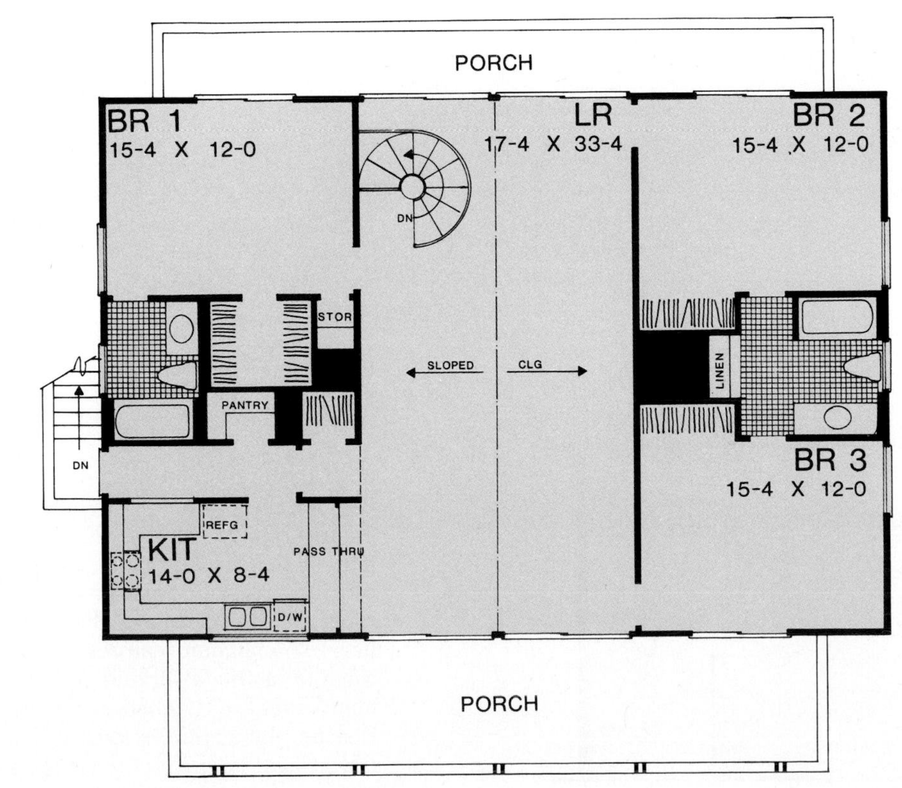
PORCH
BR 1
15-4 X 12-0
LR
17-4 X 33-4
BR 2
15-4 X 12-0
DN
STOR
SLOPED
CLG
LINEN
PANTRY
BR 3
15-4 X 12-0
DN
REFG
KIT
14-0 X 8-4
PASS THRU
D/W
PORCH

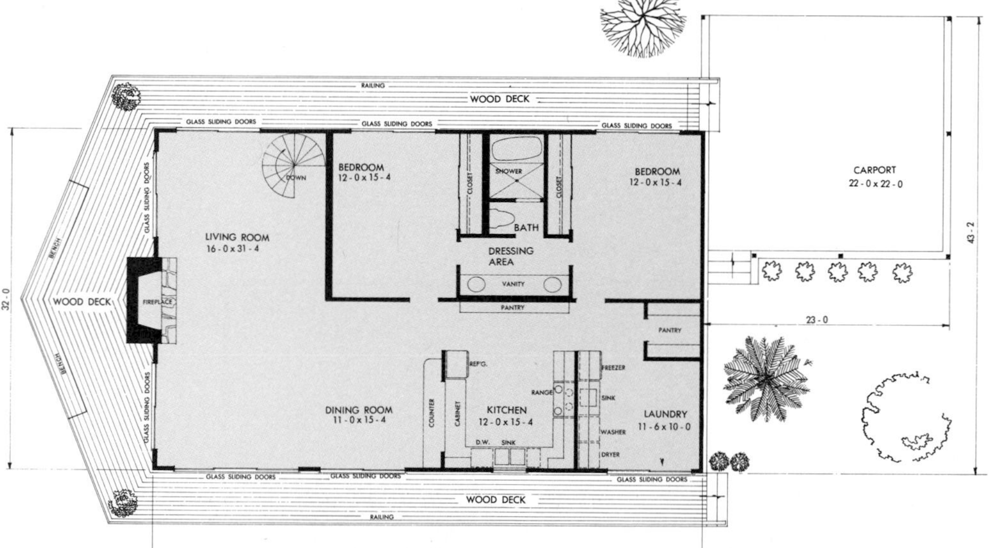

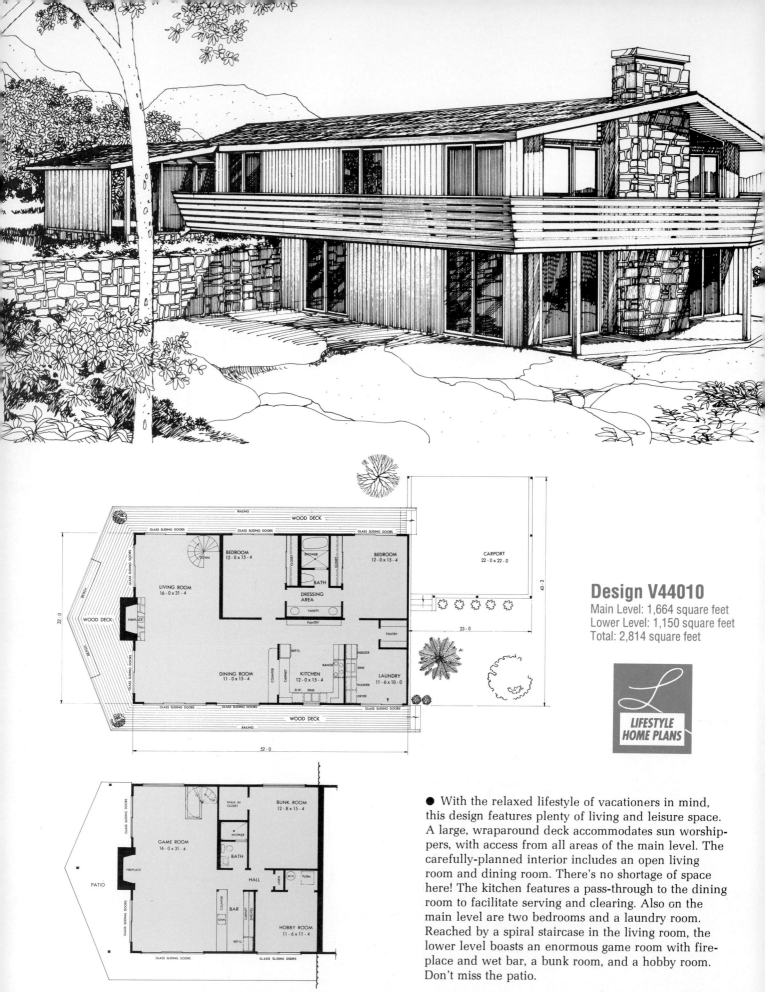

Design V44010

Main Level: 1,664 square feet
Lower Level: 1,150 square feet
Total: 2,814 square feet

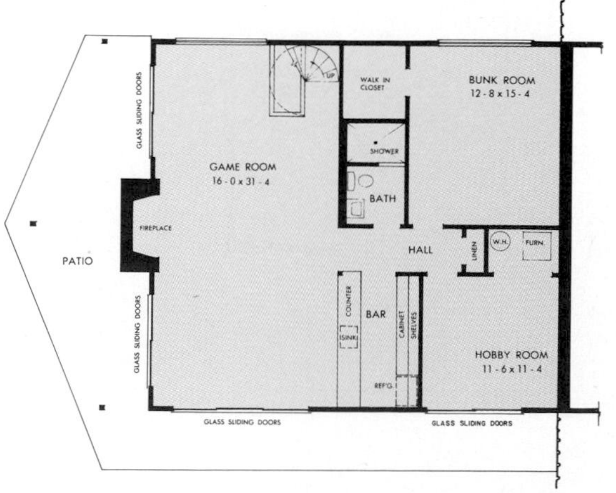

● With the relaxed lifestyle of vacationers in mind, this design features plenty of living and leisure space. A large, wraparound deck accommodates sun worshippers, with access from all areas of the main level. The carefully-planned interior includes an open living room and dining room. There's no shortage of space here! The kitchen features a pass-through to the dining room to facilitate serving and clearing. Also on the main level are two bedrooms and a laundry room. Reached by a spiral staircase in the living room, the lower level boasts an enormous game room with fireplace and wet bar, a bunk room, and a hobby room. Don't miss the patio.

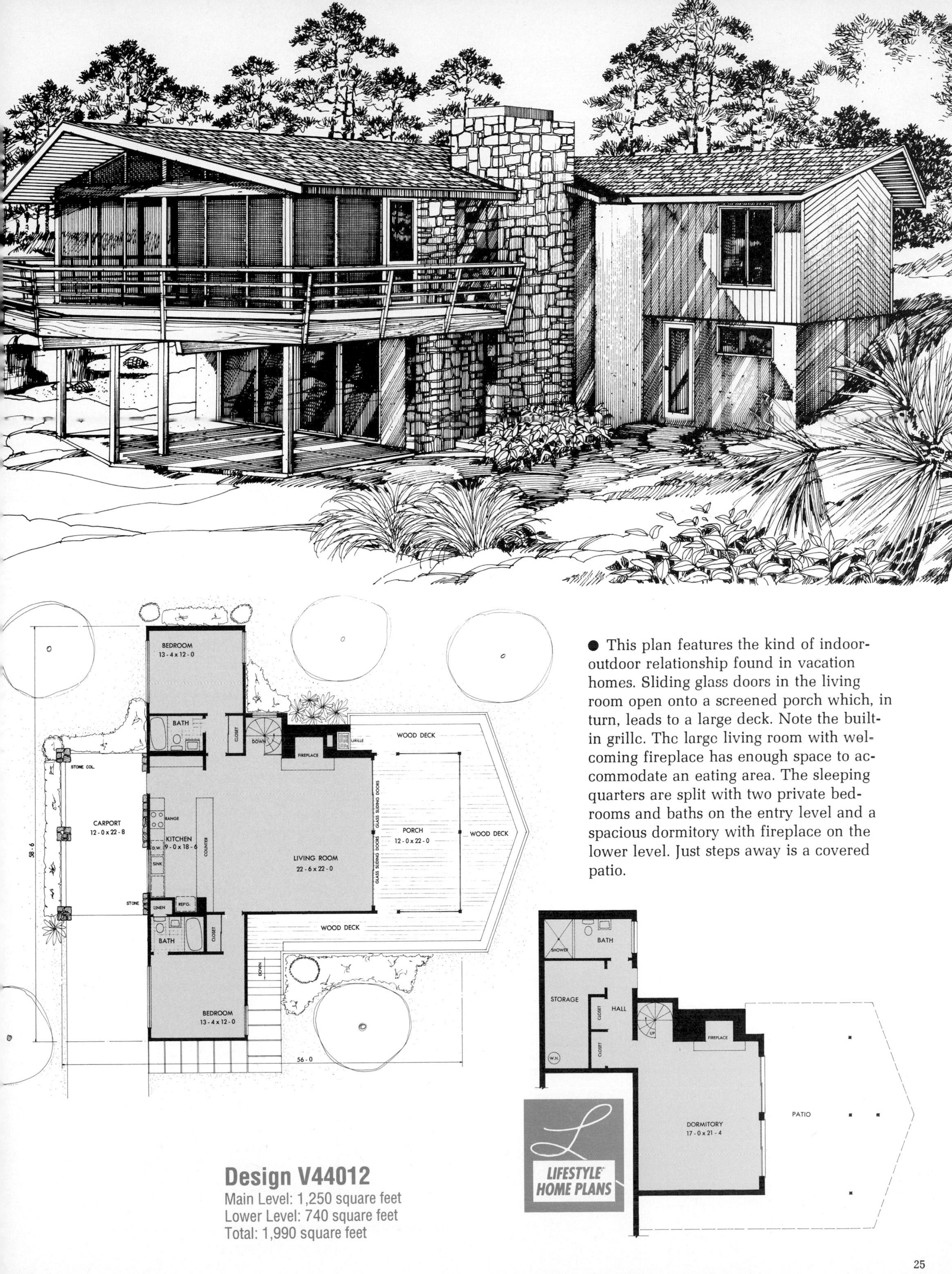

● This plan features the kind of indoor-outdoor relationship found in vacation homes. Sliding glass doors in the living room open onto a screened porch which, in turn, leads to a large deck. Note the built-in grillc. Thc largc living room with welcoming fireplace has enough space to accommodate an eating area. The sleeping quarters are split with two private bedrooms and baths on the entry level and a spacious dormitory with fireplace on the lower level. Just steps away is a covered patio.

Design V44012

Main Level: 1,250 square feet
Lower Level: 740 square feet
Total: 1,990 square feet

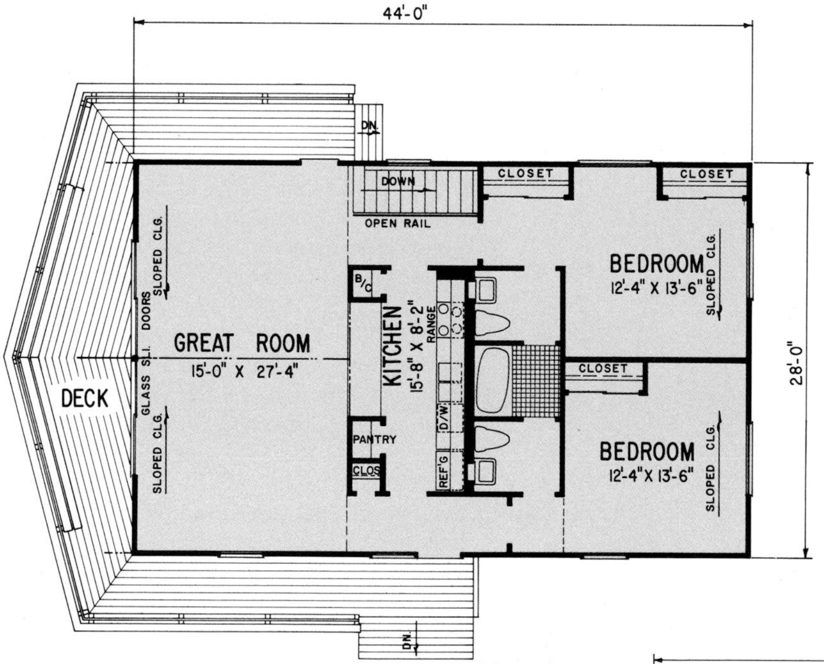

44'-0"
DN
DOWN
CLOSET
CLOSET
OPEN RAIL
B/C
BEDROOM
12'-4" X 13'-6"
SLOPED CLG.
SLOPED CLG.
GLASS SLI. DOORS
GREAT ROOM
15'-0" X 27'-4"
KITCHEN
15'-8" X 8'-2"
RANGE
CLOSET
DECK
28'-0"
SLOPED CLG.
PANTRY
D/W
CLOS
REF'G
BEDROOM
12'-4" X 13'-6"
SLOPED CLG.
DN

● Good things come in small packages, too! The size and shape of this design will help hold down construction costs without sacrificing livability. The enormous great room is a multi-purpose living space with room for a dining area and several seating areas. Also notice the sloped ceilings. Sliding glass doors provide access to the wraparound deck and sweeping views of the outdoors. The well-equipped kitchen includes a pass-through and pantry. Two bedrooms, each with sloped ceilings, and compartmented bath round out the plan.

Design V44027

Square Footage: 1,232

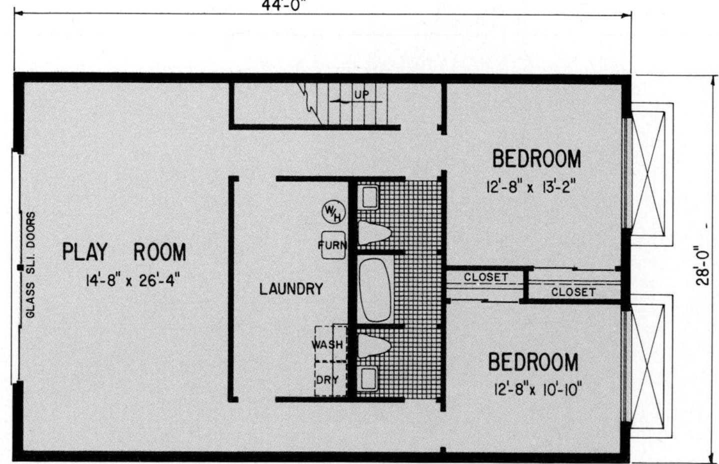

Optional Basement

57 - 0

BEDROOM
11 - 0 x 15 - 0

CLOSET
CLOSET

BEDROOM
11 - 0 x 10 - 6

BEDROOM
11 - 0 x 10 - 6

CLOSET
CLOSET

BEDROOM
11 - 0 x 15 - 0

PORCH

CLOSET

COATS

COUNTER

SINK
D.W.

KITCHEN
12 - 8 x 12 - 6

REF'G.
RANGE
OVEN

STORAGE
GRILLE

DINING ROOM
10 - 8 x 10 - 8

PORCH

DOWN
DOWN

50 - 8

LIVING ROOM
21 - 8 x 15 - 0

GLASS SLIDING DOORS

WOOD DECK

Design V44015

Square Footage: 1,420

● The perfect vacation home combines open, informal living spaces with lots of sleeping space. Study this plan carefully. The spacious living room has a warming fireplace and sliding glass doors onto the deck. Convenient to the dining room, the efficient kitchen is carefully placed so as not to interfere with the living room. Notice the four spacious bedrooms — there's plenty of room for accommodating guests. Two of the bedrooms boast private porches.

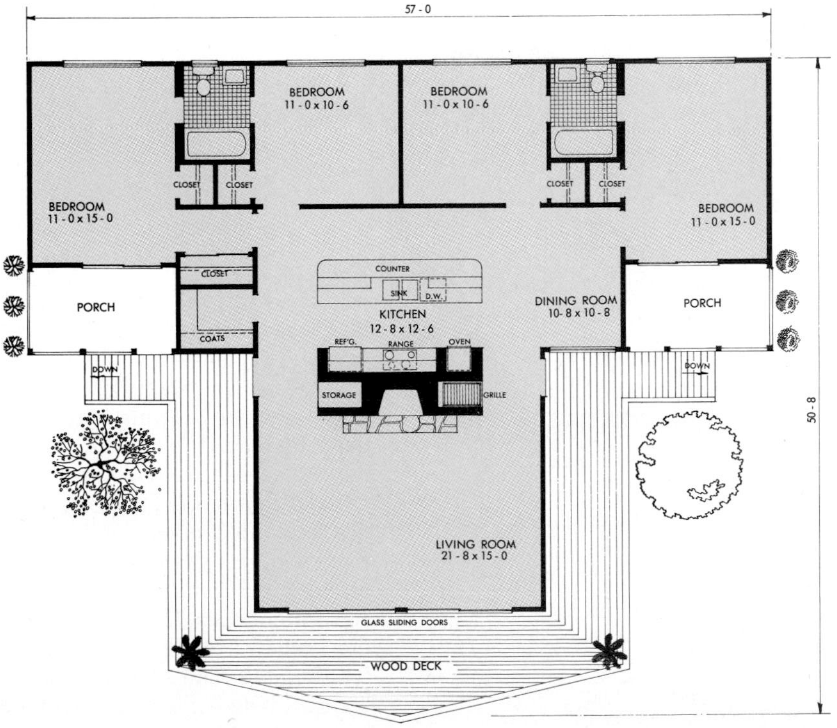

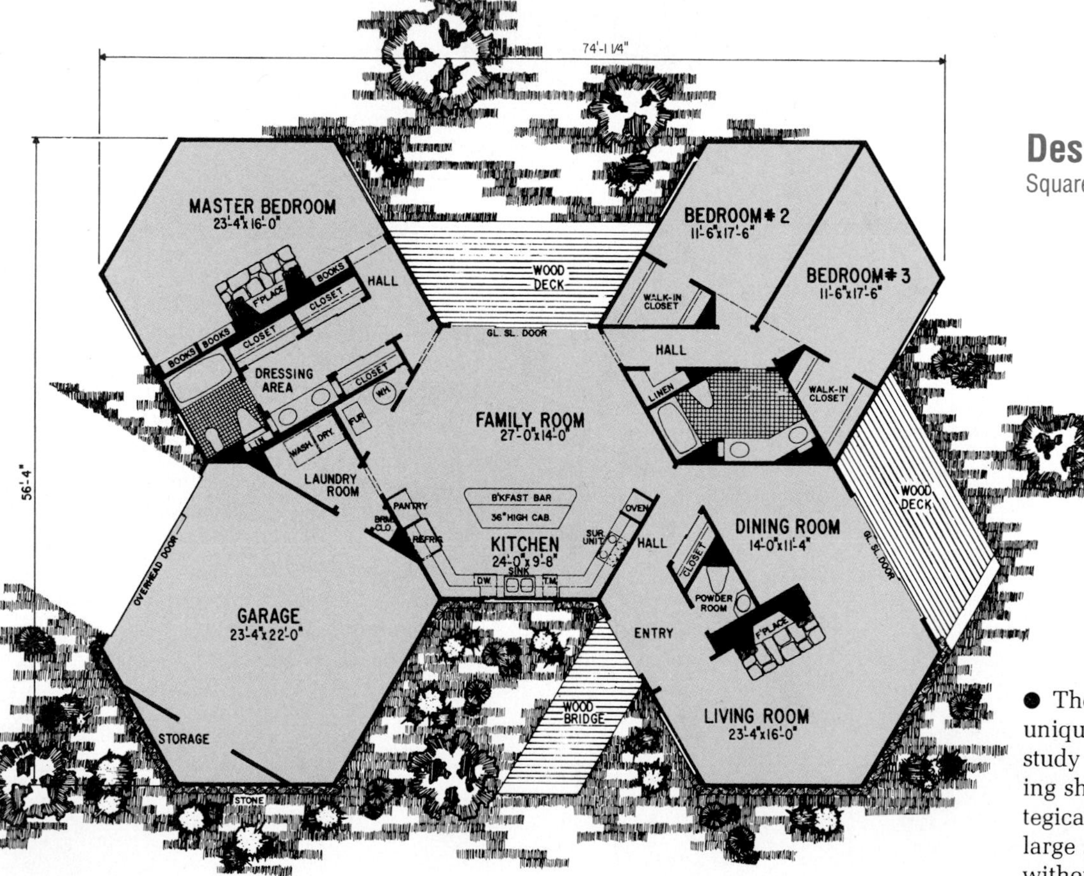

Design V44302

Square Footage: 2,457

● Those in search of a truly unique vacation home should study this plan carefully. Interesting shapes are the rule here. Strategically placed features divide large spaces into smaller ones without sacrificing openness. Notice how the fireplace and powder room separate the living room and dining room from the entry. A convenient breakfast bar separates the kitchen from the spacious family room. The sleeping quarters are split between two wings. Two bedrooms and a shared bath occupy one; a master bedroom with fireplace is housed in the other. Notice the decks.

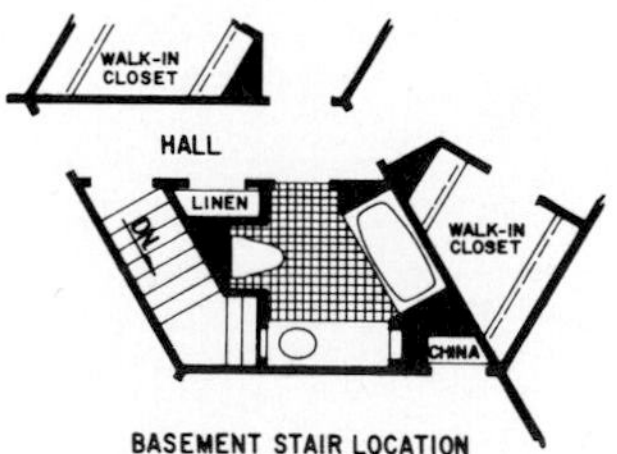

BASEMENT STAIR LOCATION

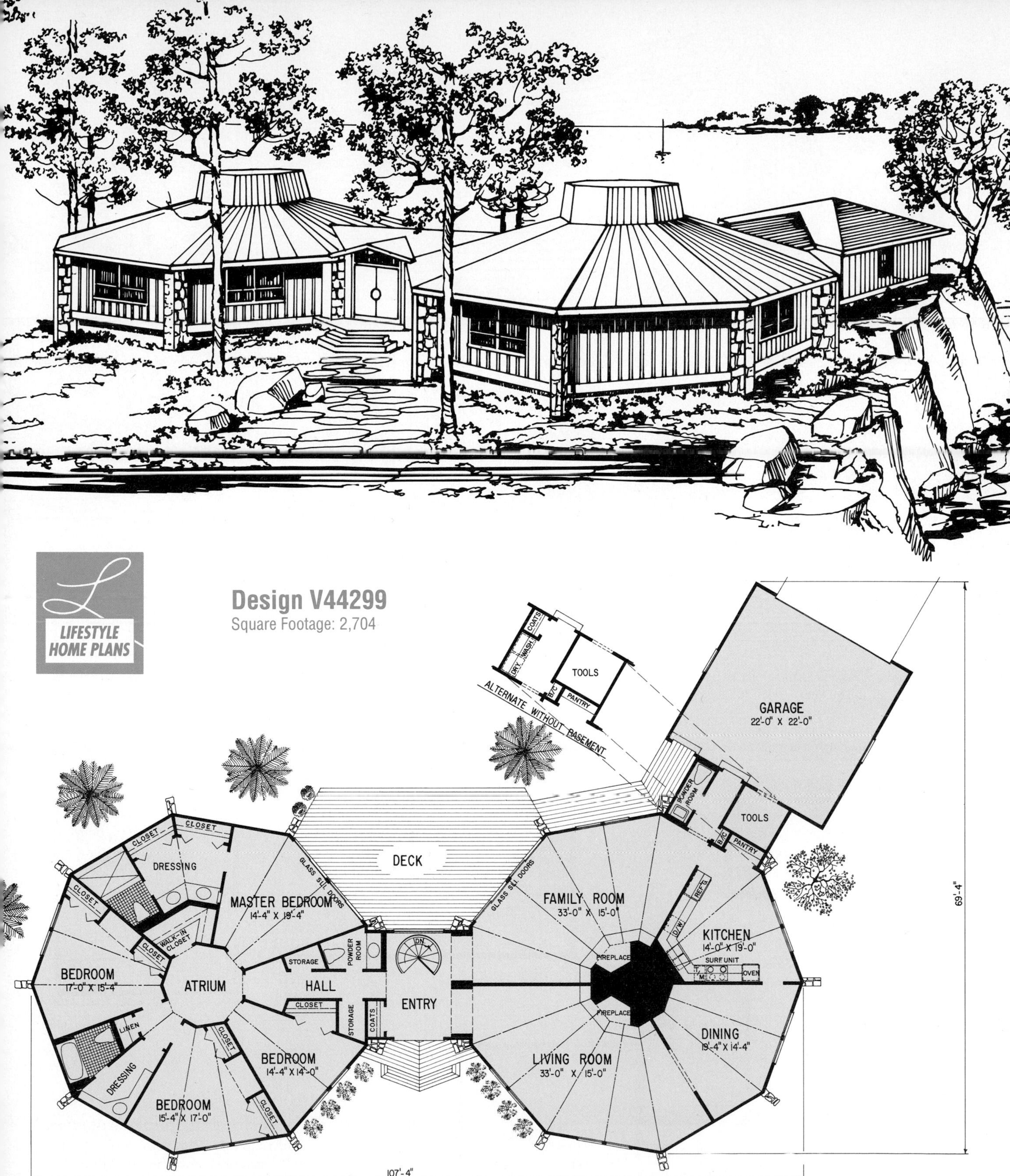

● Dramatic geometric design makes for a striking home both inside and out. To the right of the entry is the living area with its rooms flowing around the central fireplaces. The living room, dining room, and family room provide space for all activities. Convenient to all three rooms is a spacious kitchen. Across the entry hall is the sleeping wing with rooms radiating off of a central atrium. This area houses four large bedrooms, two baths, and plenty of closet space. Sliding glass doors in the master bedroom and family room open onto an enormous deck — perfect for sunning or enjoying the view.

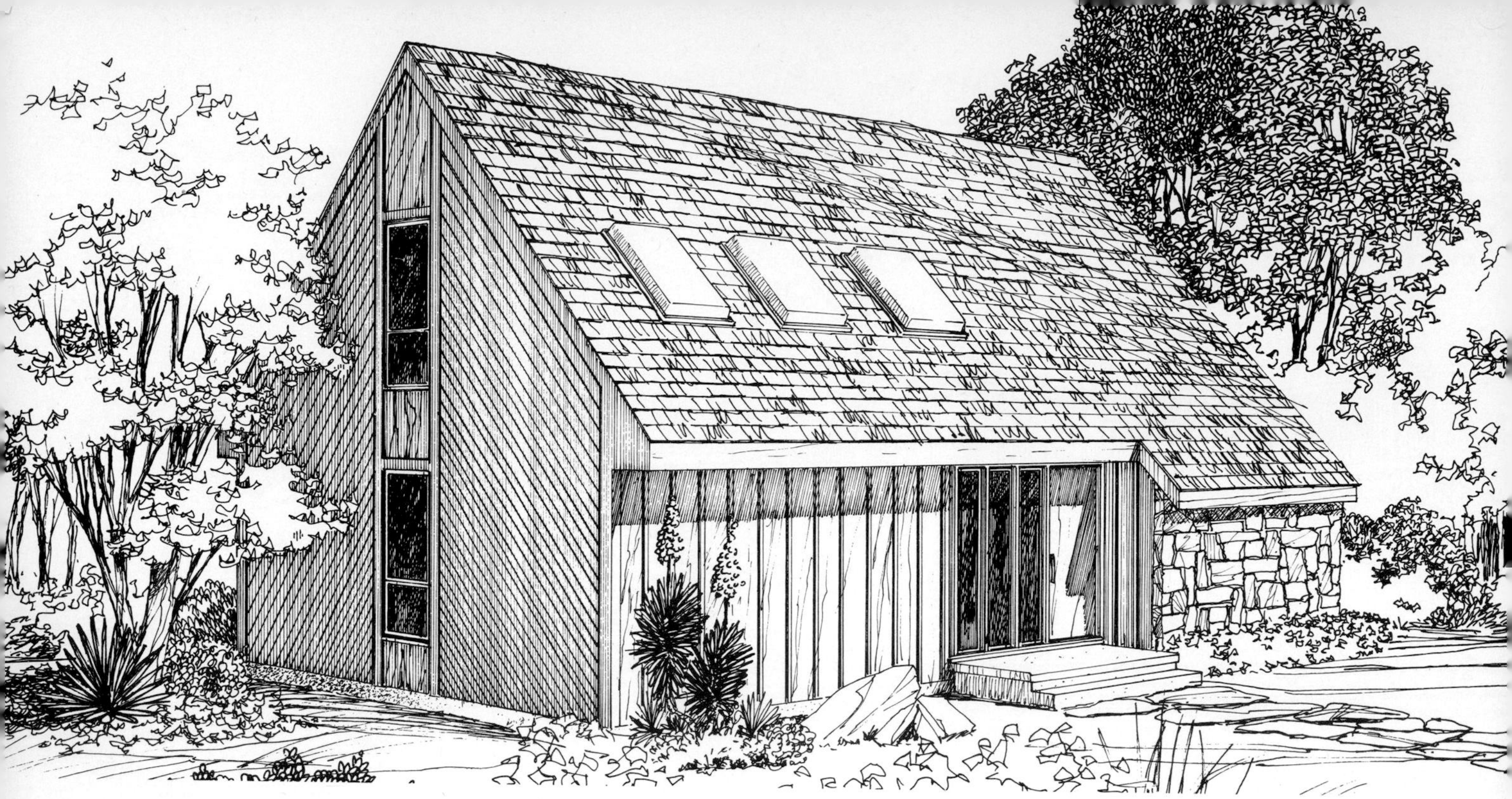

Design V44153 First Floor: 893 square feet
Second Floor: 549 square feet; Total: 1,442 square feet

L D

LIFESTYLE
HOME PLANS

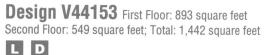

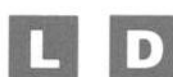

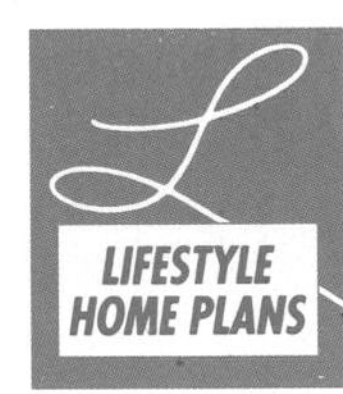

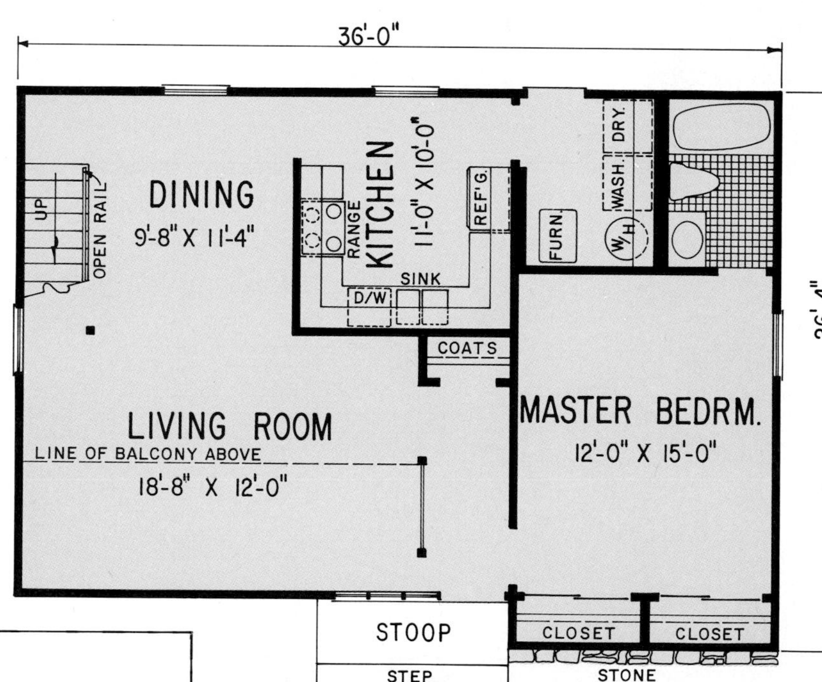

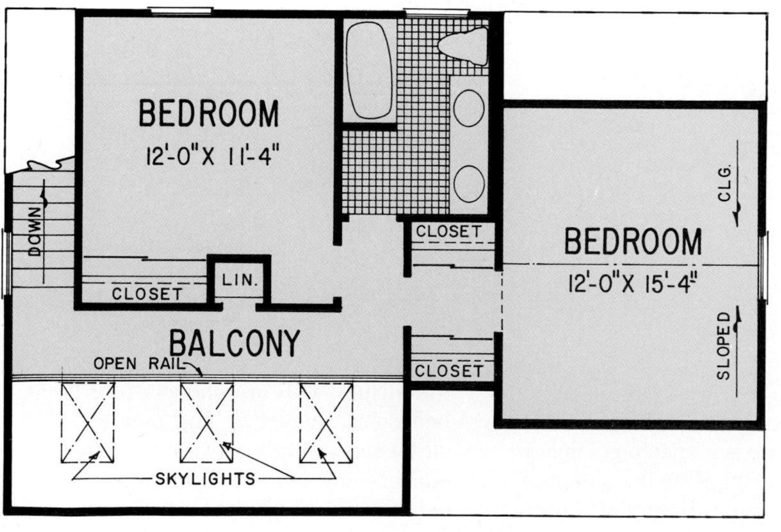

● The rectangular shape of this design will make it an economical and easy-to-build choice for those wary of high construction costs. The first floor benefits from the informality of open planning; the living room and dining room combine to make one large living space. The partitioned kitchen is conveniently adjacent yet keeps the cooking process out of the living area. Also downstairs is the master bedroom and bath. The second floor houses two large bedrooms, a full bath, and a balcony over the living room. Notice the skylights.

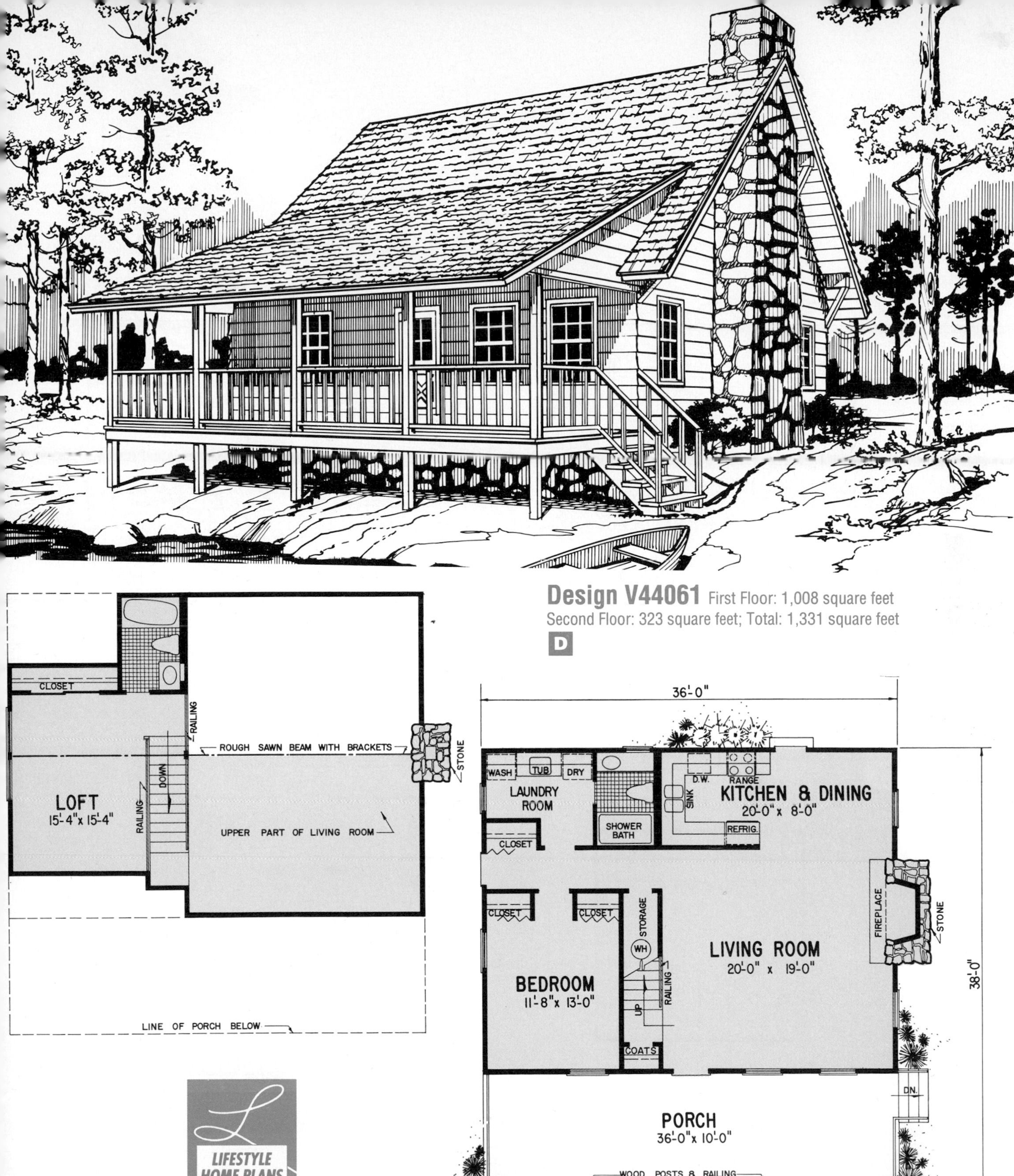

Design V44061 First Floor: 1,008 square feet
Second Floor: 323 square feet; Total: 1,331 square feet
D

● This charming farmhouse design will be economical to build and a pleasure to occupy. Like most vacation homes, this design features an open plan. The large living area includes a living room and dining room and a massive stone fireplace. A partition separates the kitchen from the living room. Also downstairs are a bedroom, full bath, and laundry room. Upstairs is a spacious sleeping loft overlooking the living room. Don't miss the large front porch — this will be a favorite spot for relaxing.

Design V44319

First Floor: 900 square feet
Second Floor: 144 square feet
Total: 1,044 square feet

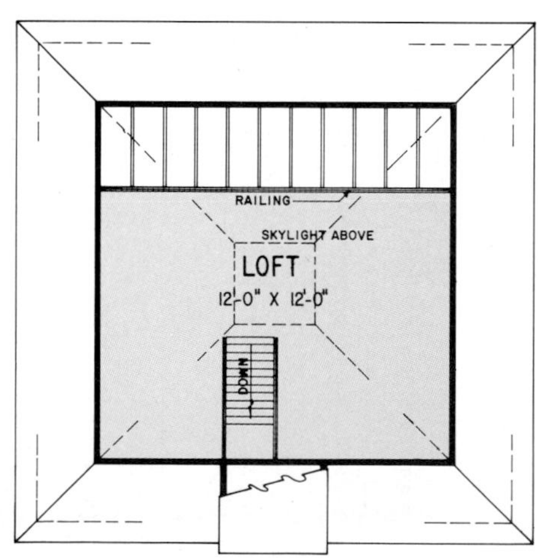

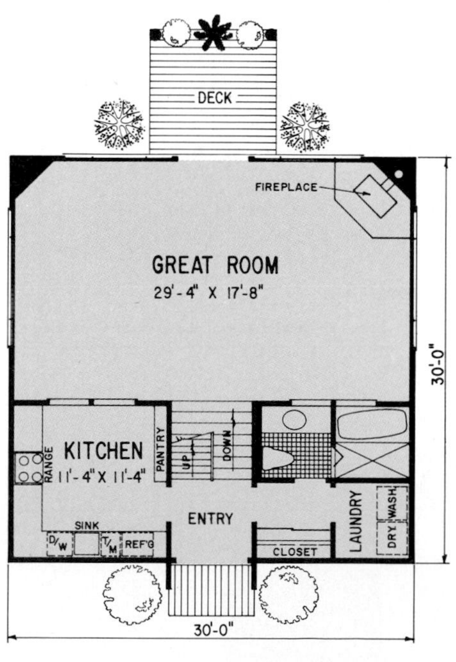

● This plan seems ideal for a water-side lot with a rear deck extending into the water and doubling as a dock. Inside, this compact design is perfect for those who wish to leave behind the formality of everyday living. The enormous great room functions well as a multi-purpose living space. Note the corner fireplace. An upstairs loft accommodates sleeping arrangements.

BEST LEISURE LIVING DESIGNS . . . *comprise a col-*

ection of some of our finest and most popular plans for relaxed living. With living areas beginning at 1,040 square feet, these homes repre-ent one-, two-, and multi-level variations in both traditional and contemporary exteriors to make the most of the perfect get-away.

Design V42488 First Floor: 1,113 square feet; Second Floor: 543 square feet; Total: 1,656 square feet

D

CUSTOMIZABLE

Custom Alterations? See page 251 for customizing this plan to your specifications.

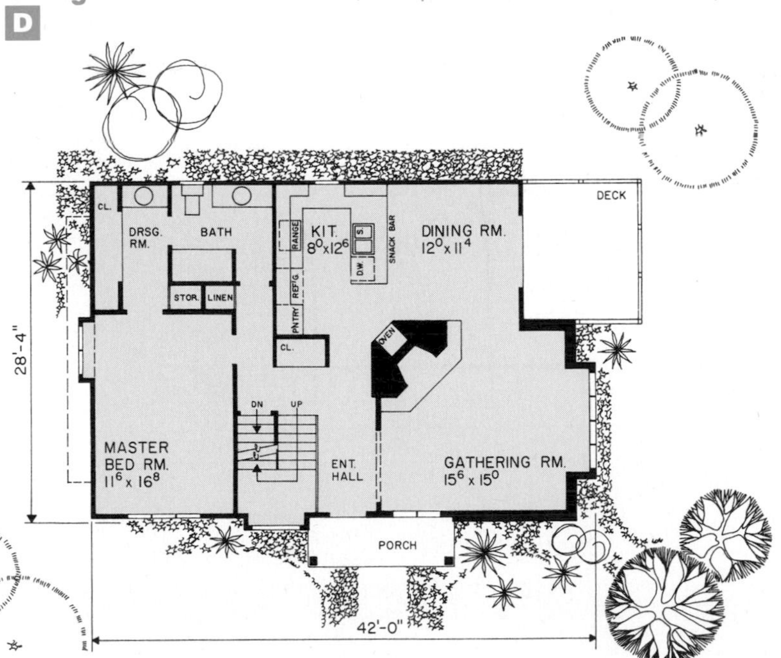

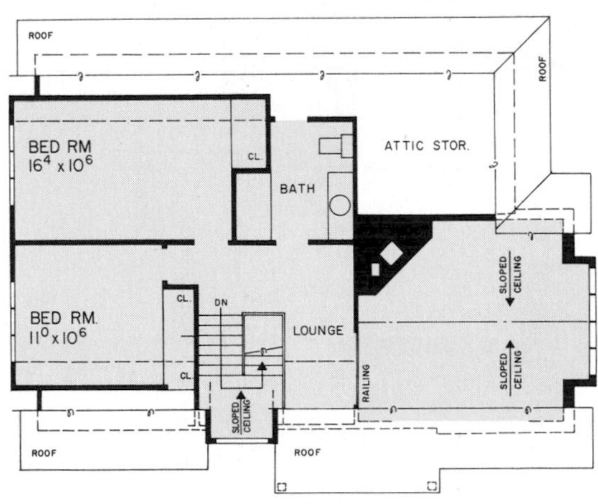

● A cozy cottage for the young at heart! Whether called upon to serve the young active family as a leisure-time retreat at the lake, or the retired couple as a quiet haven in later years, this charming design will perform well. As a year round second home, the upstairs with its two sizable bedrooms, full bath and lounge area looking down into the gathering room below, will ideally accommodate the younger generation. When called upon to function as a retirement home, the second floor will cater to the visiting family members and friends. Also, it will be available for use as a home office, study, sewing room, music area, the pursuit of hobbies, etc. Of course, as an efficient, economical home for the young, growing family, this design will function well.

Design V42486 First Floor: 1,124 square feet; Second Floor: 528 square feet; Total: 1,652 square feet

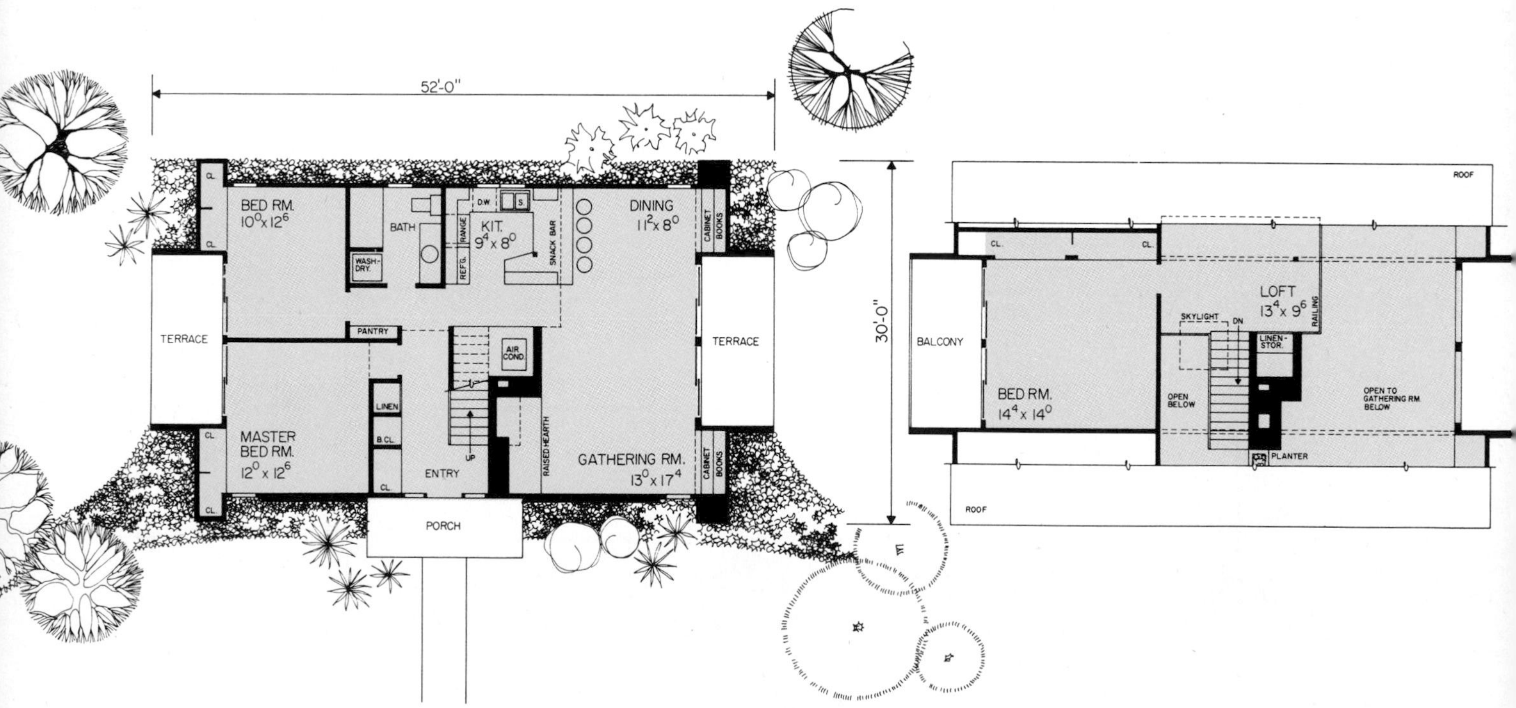

● A two-story vacation home with a distinctive and appealing exterior. Surely the family will welcome the change of pace this retreat represents. It just spells, informality. The living area features a generous 25 foot long gathering room/dining area and a high spacious two-story ceiling. A snack bar and huge counter separate the dining and kitchen areas. Downstairs there are two bedrooms, while upstairs there is a big 14 x 14 foot bedroom plus a loft. A skylight provides plenty of natural light to this area. This compact plan offers fine storage facilities. Even space for a stacked or combination washer and dryer. For indoor-outdoor living there are two terraces and a balcony. This will be a fine family investment which will appreciate in value, as well as memories, as the years pass.

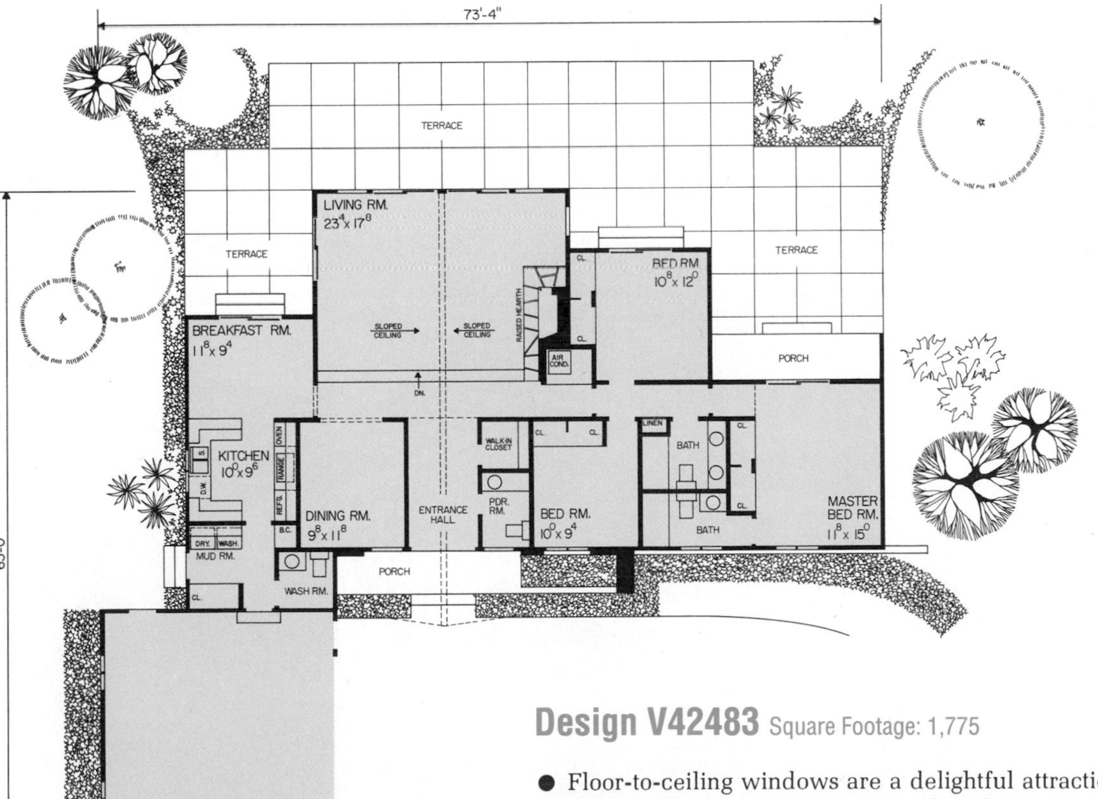

Design V42483 Square Footage: 1,775

● Floor-to-ceiling windows are a delightful attraction in the living room. Good looking and a way to take advantage of the beautiful outdoor scenery. For more good looks, sloped ceilings and a raised hearth fireplace plus a terrace that runs the length of the house. A formal dining room is convenient to the efficient U-shaped kitchen with a separate breakfast nook. The laundry/mud room will allow immediate clean-up after a day spent fishing or on the beach. Three bedrooms! Including one with a private bath.

Design V42478

First Floor: 1,137 square feet
Second Floor: 257 square feet
Total: 1,394 square feet

● An appealing geometric exterior with a fine floor plan for informal family living. Note the three decks, the big family room, the spacious kitchen, the two fireplaces and the upstairs dormitory.

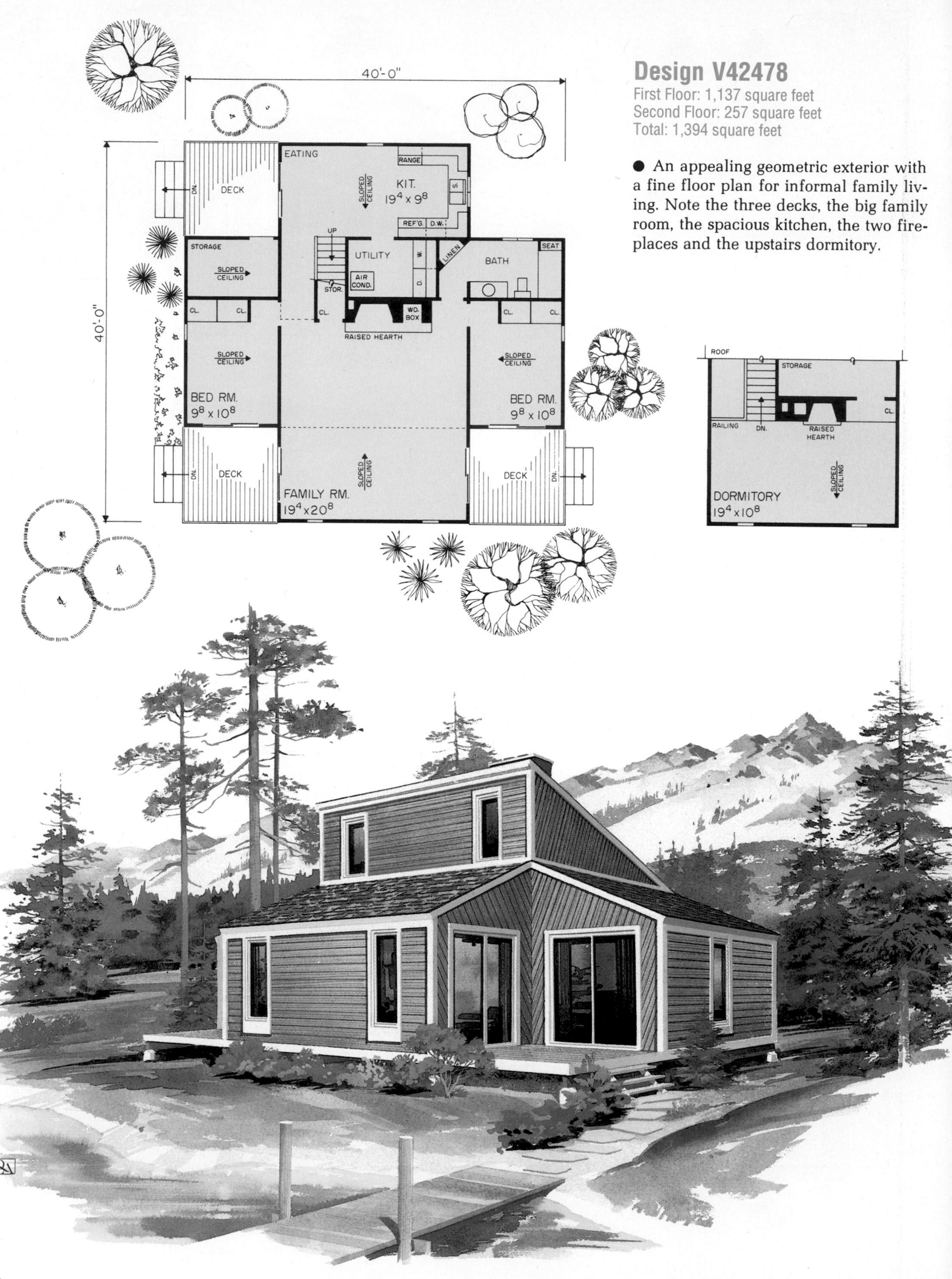

Design V42480

First Floor: 826 square feet
Second Floor: 553 square feet
Total: 1,359 square feet

● This distinctive contemporary two-story leisure-time home provides excellent living patterns for all. Observe the efficient kitchen, separate laundry, sloped-ceiling living room, two baths and three bedrooms.

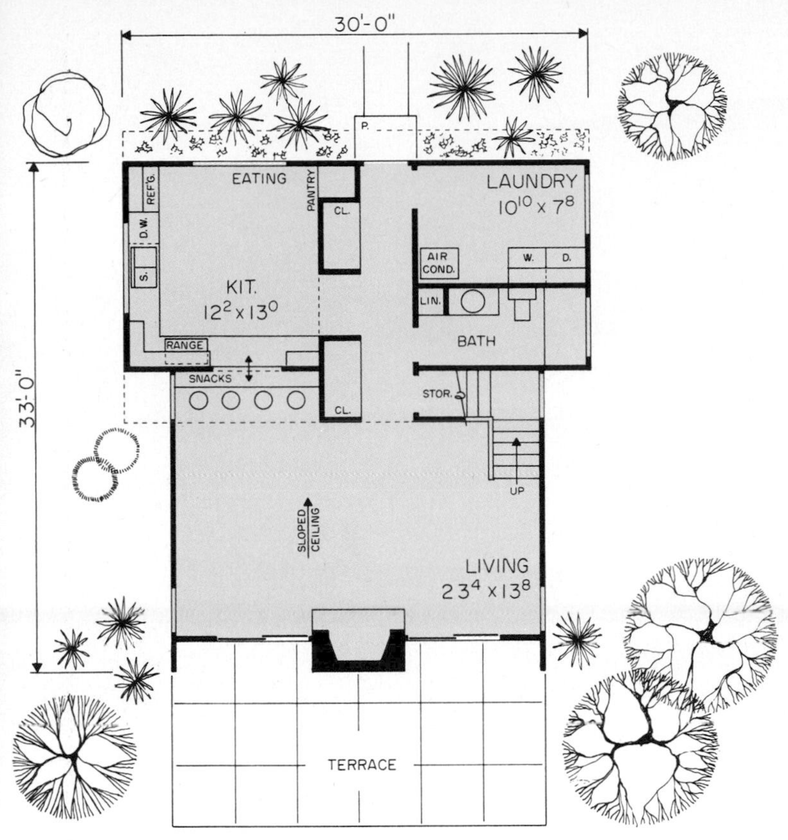

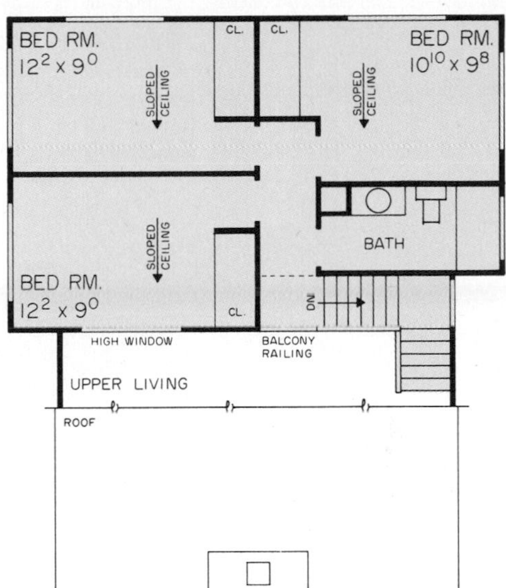

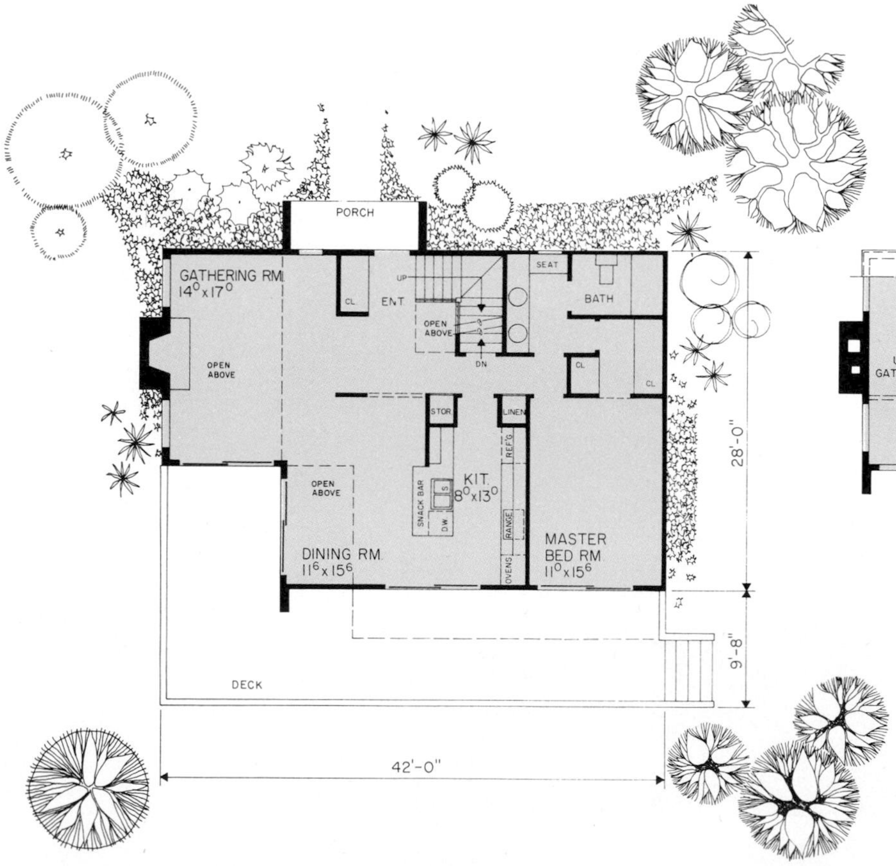

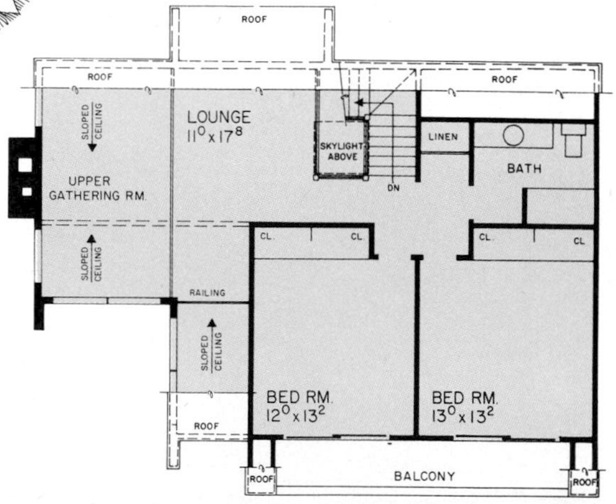

Design V42489

First Floor: 1,076 square feet
Second Floor: 693 square feet
Total: 1,769 square feet

● Outdoors-oriented families will appreciate the dramatic sliding glass doors and the sweeping decks that make this contemporary perfect. The plan of the first floor features a spacious two-story gathering room with sloping ceiling, a large fireplace and access to the large deck which runs the full length of the house. Also having direct access to the deck is the dining room which is half-open to the second floor above. A snack bar divides the dining room from the compact kitchen. The master bedroom is outstanding with its private bath, walk-in closet and sliding glass door. The second floor is brightened by a skylight and houses two bedrooms, lounge and full bath.

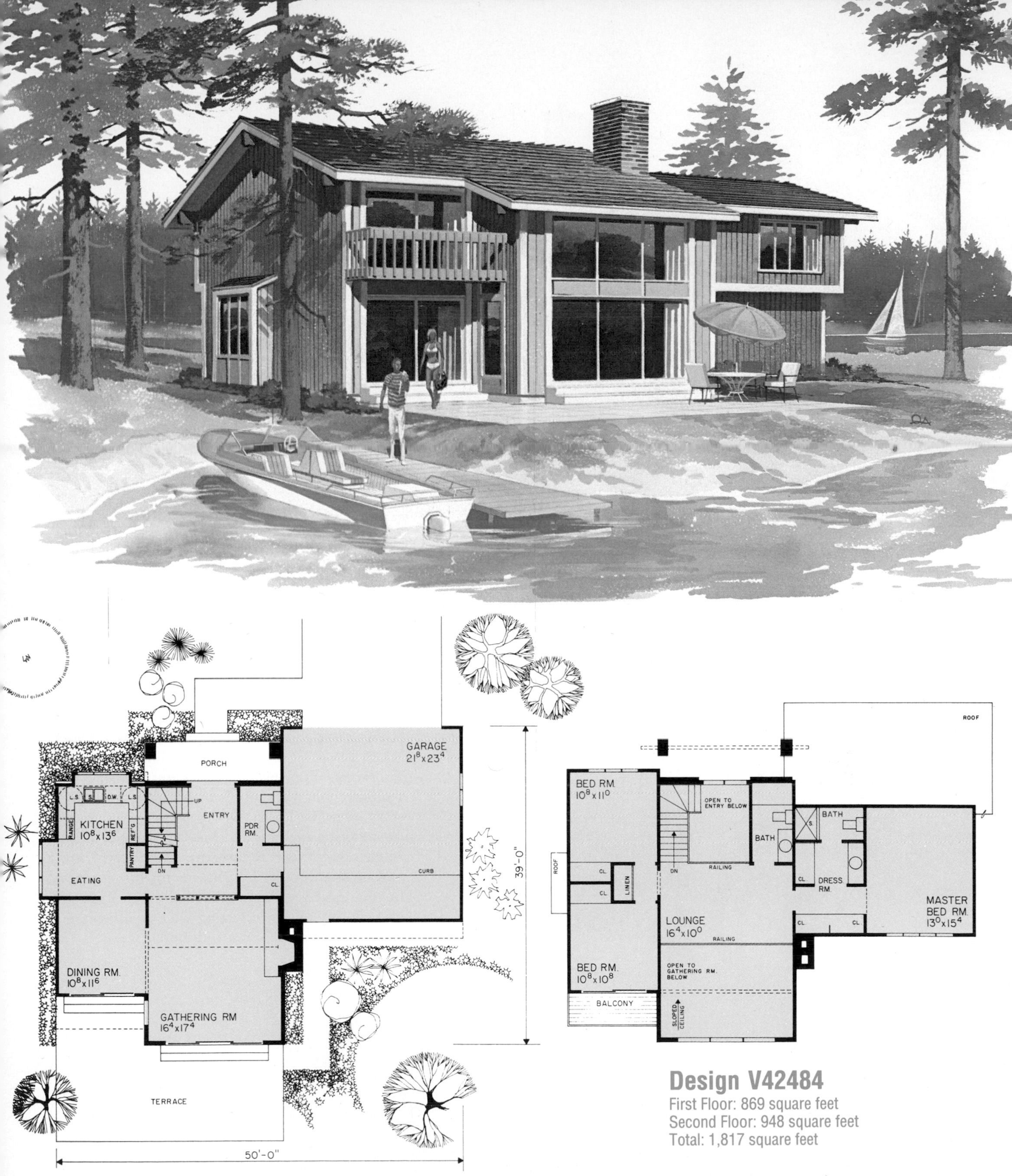

Design V42484

First Floor: 869 square feet
Second Floor: 948 square feet
Total: 1,817 square feet

● A two-story leisure-time house with all the comforts of home and maybe even a few more. Yet, the enviroment, the atmosphere and the living patterns will be entirely different. Imagine the fun everybody will have during their visits to this delightfully contemporary retreat. The large glass areas preserve the view from the rear. The upstairs lounge looks down into the gathering room. There are two eating areas adjacent to the U-shaped kitchen which could hardly be more efficient. There are 2½ baths, a fireplace, an attached garage and a basement. If you wish to forego the basement, locate the heating equipment where the basement stairs and pantry are located.

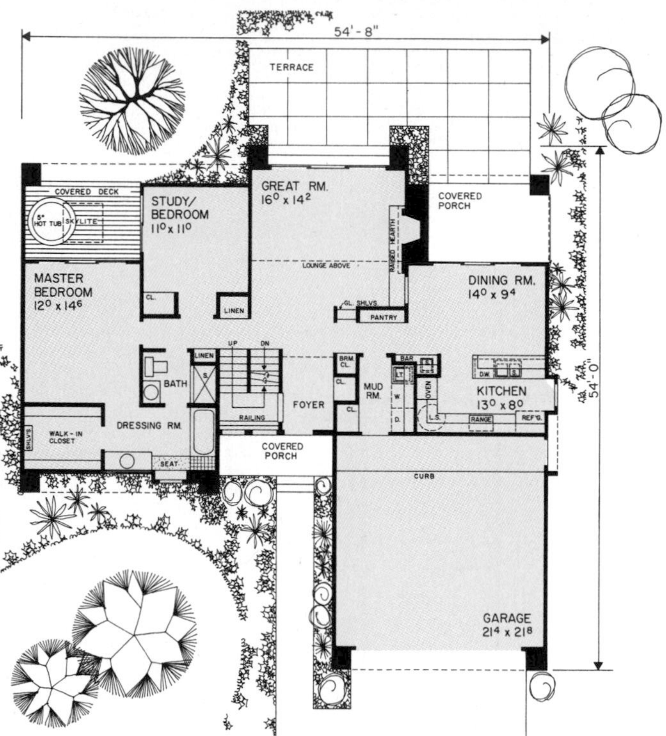

UPPER GREAT RM.
RAILING
LOUNGE / HOBBIES $16^0 x 9^2$
CL.
DN
RAILING
STOR./ BATH
UPPER FOYER
RAILING

Design V42822

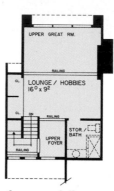

First Floor: 1,363 square feet
Second Floor: 351 square feet
Total: 1,714 square feet

● Here is a truly unique house whose interior was designed with the current decade's economies, lifestyles and demographics in mind. While functioning as a one-story home, the second floor provides an extra measure of livability when required. In addition, this two-story section adds to the dramatic appeal of both the exterior and the interior. Within only 1,363 square feet, this contemporary delivers refreshing and outstanding living patterns for those who are buying their first home, those who have raised their family and are looking for a smaller home and those in search of a retirement home.

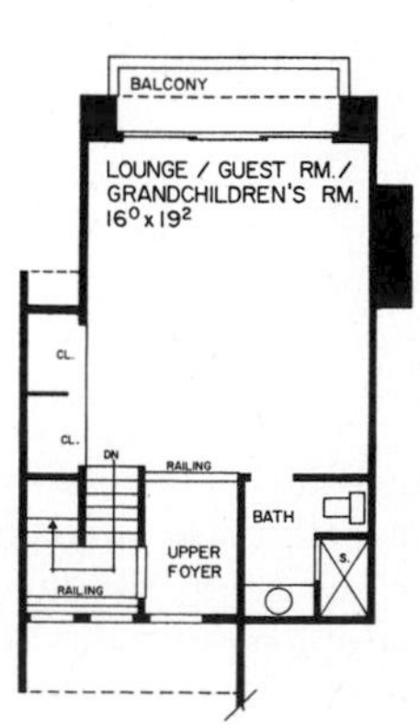

ALTERNATE SECOND FLOOR

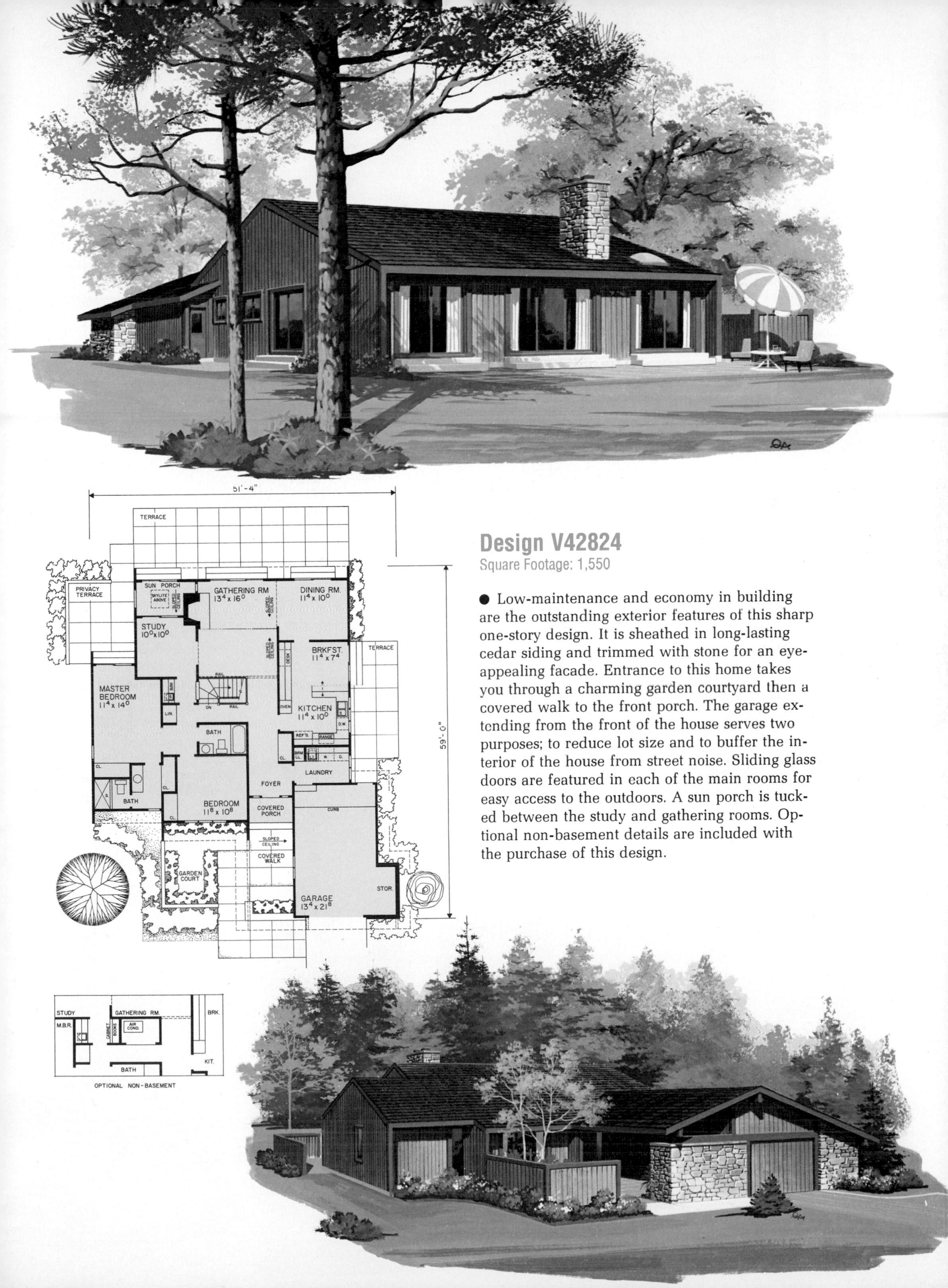

Design V42824

Square Footage: 1,550

● Low-maintenance and economy in building are the outstanding exterior features of this sharp one-story design. It is sheathed in long-lasting cedar siding and trimmed with stone for an eye-appealing facade. Entrance to this home takes you through a charming garden courtyard then a covered walk to the front porch. The garage extending from the front of the house serves two purposes; to reduce lot size and to buffer the interior of the house from street noise. Sliding glass doors are featured in each of the main rooms for easy access to the outdoors. A sun porch is tucked between the study and gathering rooms. Optional non-basement details are included with the purchase of this design.

Design V42247

Main Level: 979 square feet
Upper Level: 1,049 square feet
Lower Level: 915 square feet
Total: 2,940 square feet

Design V42434 Square Footage: 1,376

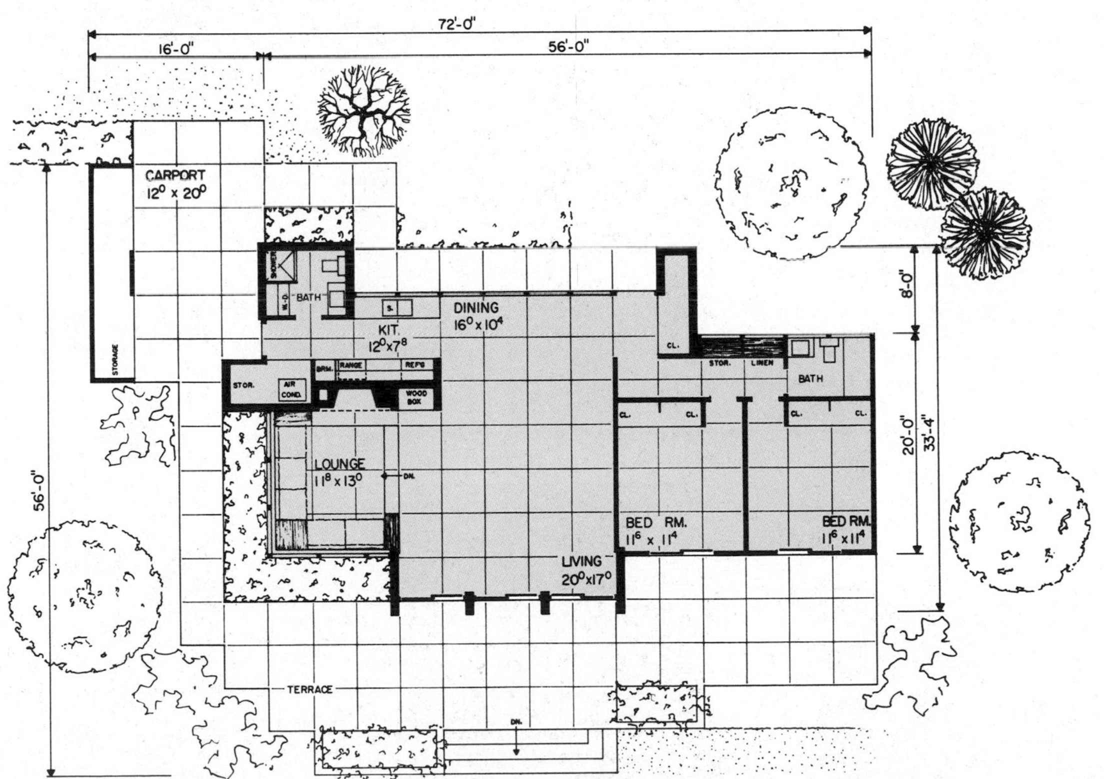

● It should be easy to visualize the fun and frolic you, your family, your guests and your neighbors will have in this home. The setting does not have to be near a bubbling brook, either. It can be almost any place where the pressures of urban life are far distant. The flat roof planes, the vertical brick piers, the massive chimney and the strategic glass areas are among the noteworthy elements of this design. Inside, there is space galore. The huge living-dining area flows down into the cozy, sunken lounge. The sleeping area of two bedrooms, a bath and good storage facilities is a zone by itself. The kitchen is efficient and has the bath and laundry equipment nearby. Imagine the spacious living area that runs from the front to the back of the house.

Design V42416

Square Footage: 1,051

● As viewed from the lake, the adjoining ski slope or down the path apiece, the front exterior of this design is highlighted by the dramatic glass gable. The wide overhanging roof and the masses of masonry add their note of distinction to this three bedroom second home. All the elements are present to permit year 'round living. The raised-hearth fireplace, along with the wall of glass sliding doors, makes the living area an outstanding one. The kitchen has all the conveniences of home.

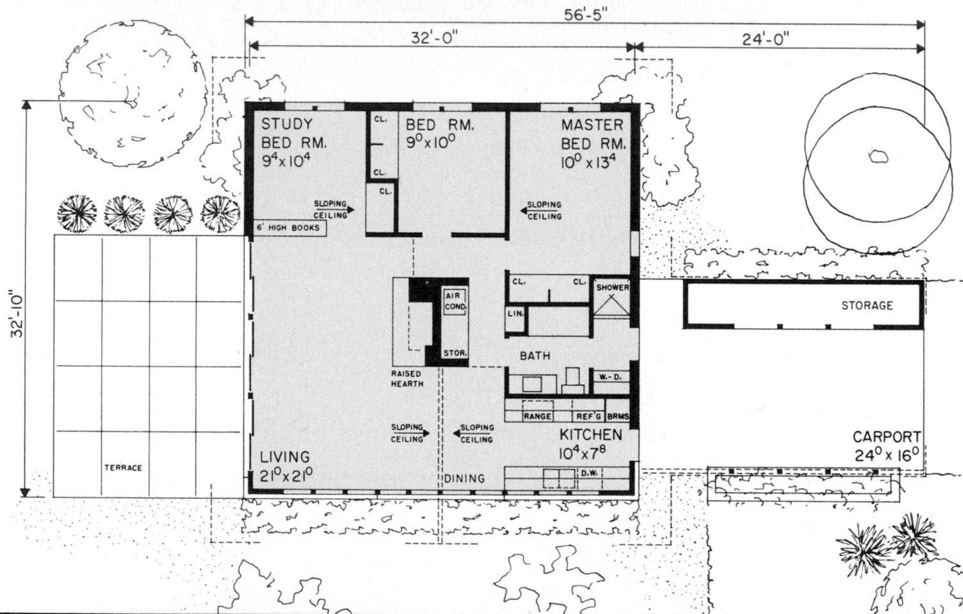

Design V41438

Square Footage: 1,040

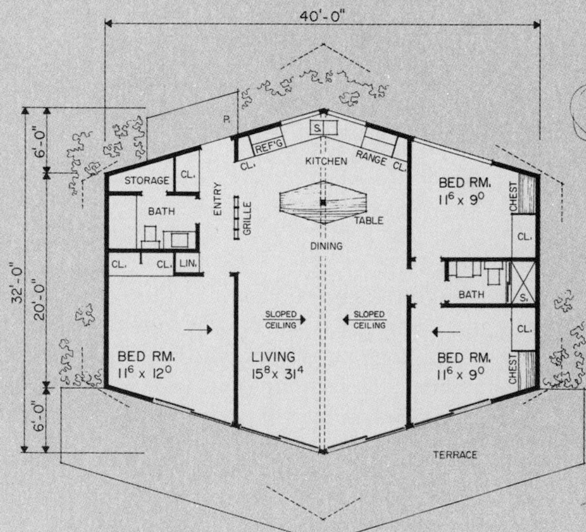

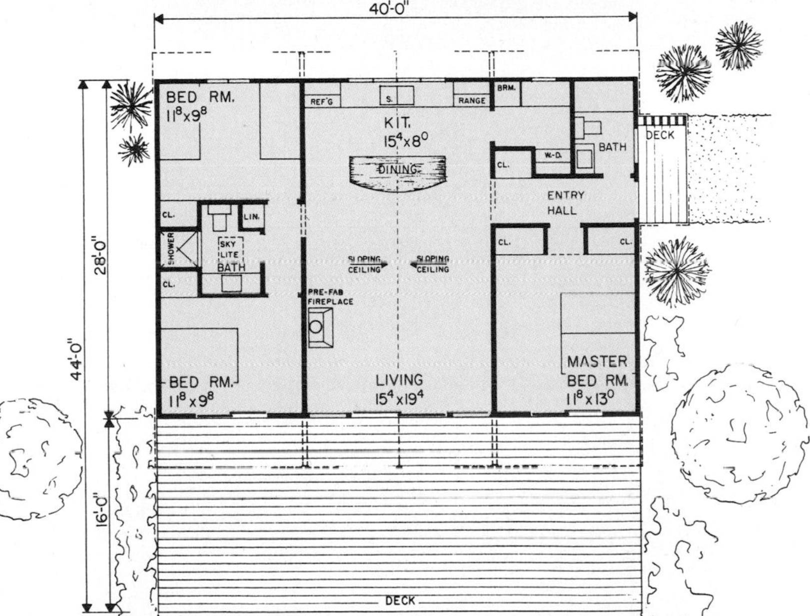

Design V42428

Square Footage: 1,120

● This delightfully different vacation home will provide you with years of complete satisfaction. Your investment will deliver to you and your family a constant pride of ownership. As you sit upon the wood deck enjoying the view, at your back will be a distinctive exterior with an equally unique interior. A front-to-rear living area separates the children's bedrooms from the parents' master bedroom. There are two full baths - one with a tub, the other with a stall shower. The living area with its glass gable, high sloping ceiling, free-standing fireplace and large built-in dining surface, is exciting, indeed. Notice the skylight in the children's bathroom.

Design V42462

Square Footage: 1,256

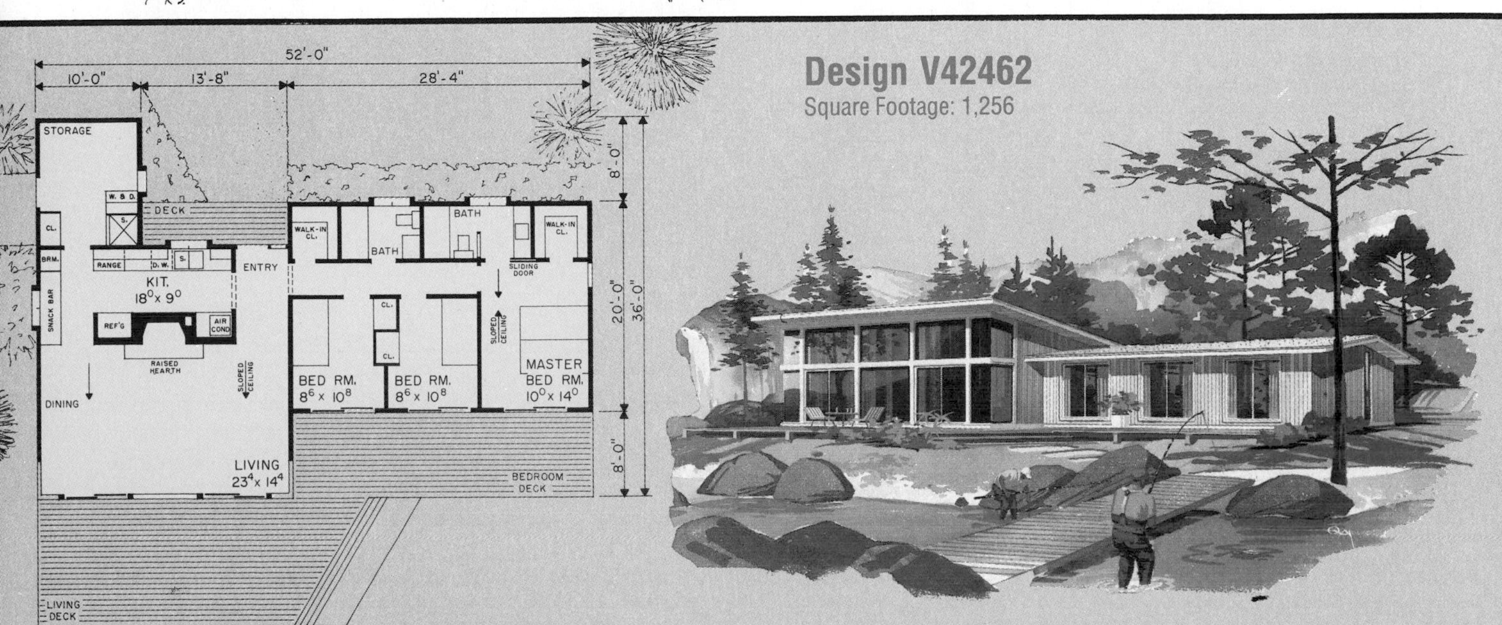

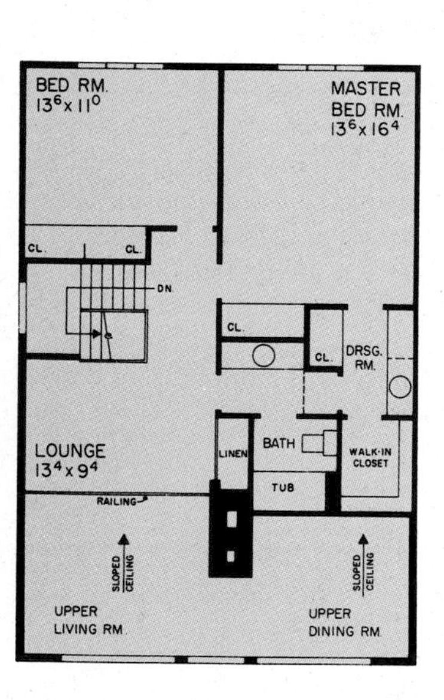

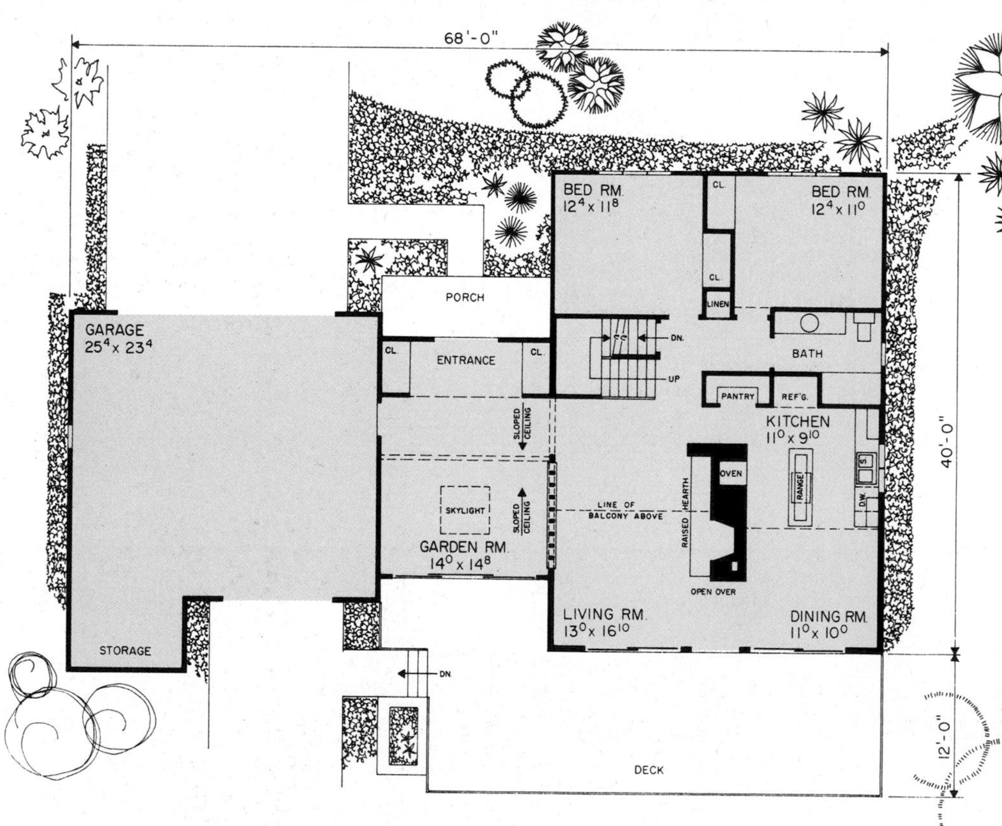

Design V42487 First Floor: 1,407 square feet; Second Floor: 833 square feet; Total: 2,240 square fee

● This contemporary vacation home will be distinctive at any location. The exterior is highlighted by angled roofs and sweeping expanses of wood and glass. Entrance to the home is through a skylight garden room with sloped ceiling. The living area is adjacent including a living room, dining room and kitchen. A massive raised hearth fireplace attractively divides the living area from the work center. Access to the large deck will be achieved through sliding glass doors in the garden, living and dining rooms. Two bedrooms and a bath are in the rear of the plan. The second floor master bedroom, an additional bedroom and lounge, which overlooks the living areas below, create the final finishing touch to this design. Make this your holiday or everyday home.

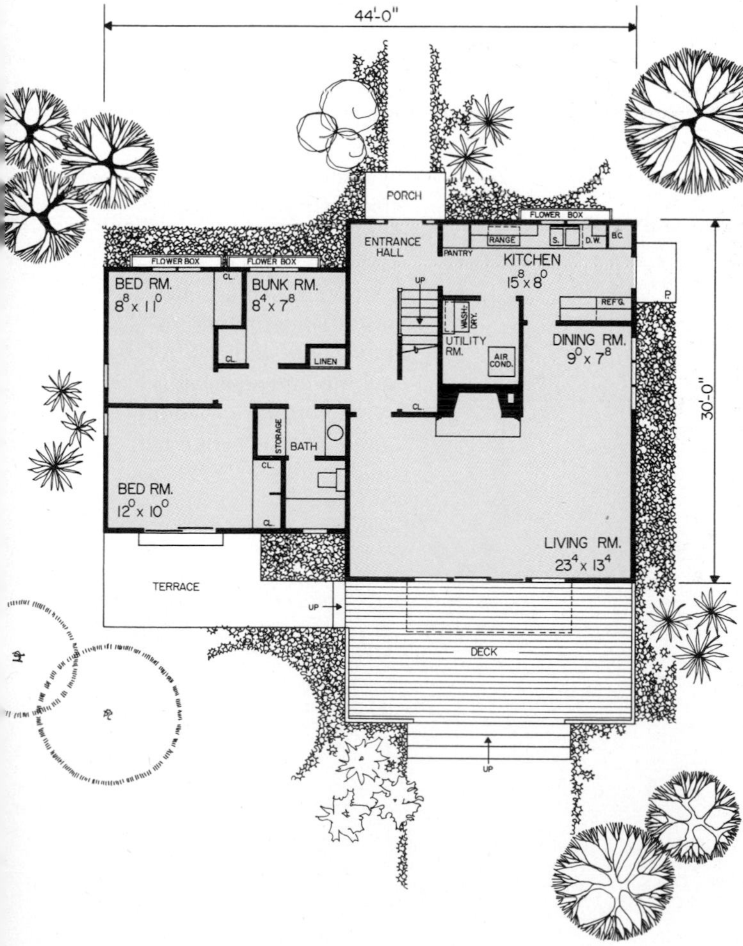

Design V42481

First Floor: 1,160 square feet
Second Floor: 828 square feet
Total: 1,988 square feet

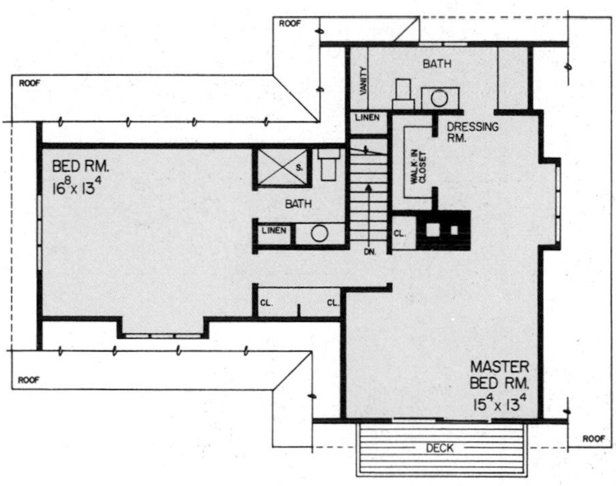

● Five rooms for sleeping! A complete master suite plus three bedrooms and a bunk room. Three full baths, one on the first floor and two upstairs. The living room will enjoy easy access to a large deck plus a fireplace. The dining room is conveniently located between the living area and the efficient kitchen which has a pantry and nearby laundry/utility room. Surely a great planned work center for a vacation home.

ONE-STORY RETIREMENT and SECOND HOMES . . .

provide a portfolio of designs that can function well as either a primary residence for empty-nesters or retirees, or as a cozy second home. The compact nature of these homes is enhanced by open gathering areas and there is sufficient sleeping room for visiting grandchildren or out-of-town guests.

Design V42947

Square Footage: 1,830

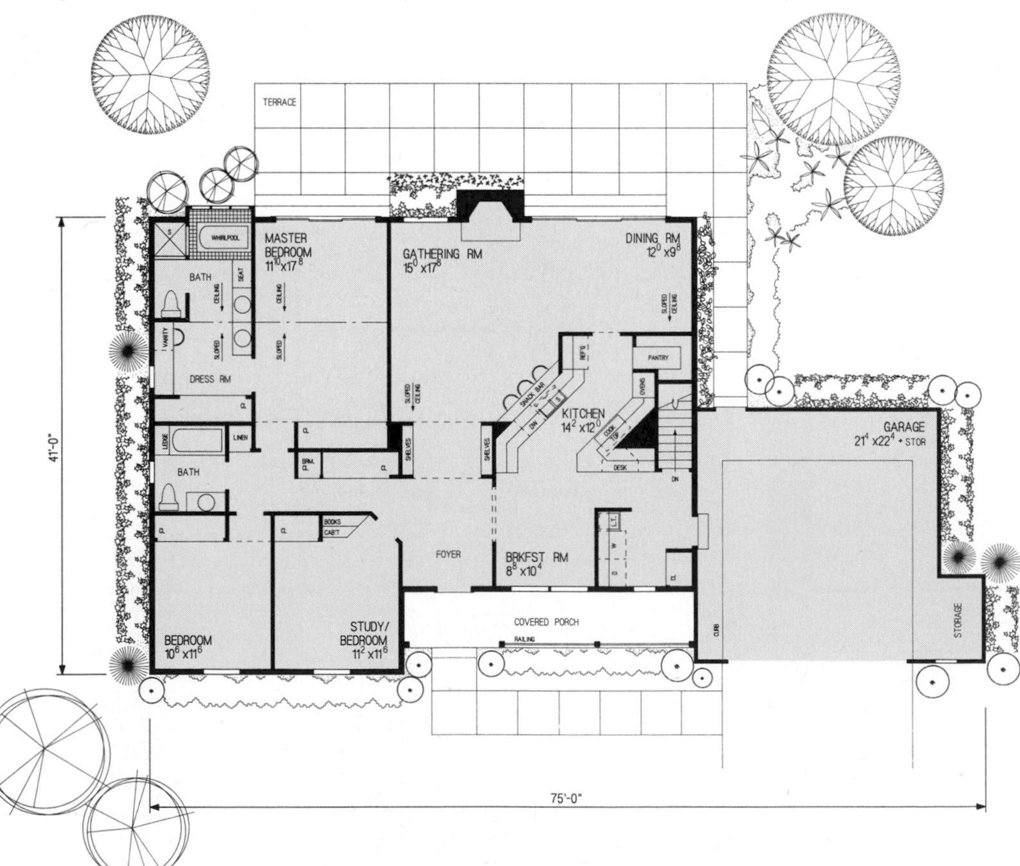

● This charming one-story Traditional home greets visitors with a covered porch. A galley-style kitchen shares a snack bar with the spacious gathering room where a fireplace is the focal point. An ample master suite includes a luxury bath with whirlpool tub and separate dressing room. Two additional bedrooms, one that could double as a study, are located at the front of the home.

Custom Alterations? See page 251 for customizing this plan to your specifications.

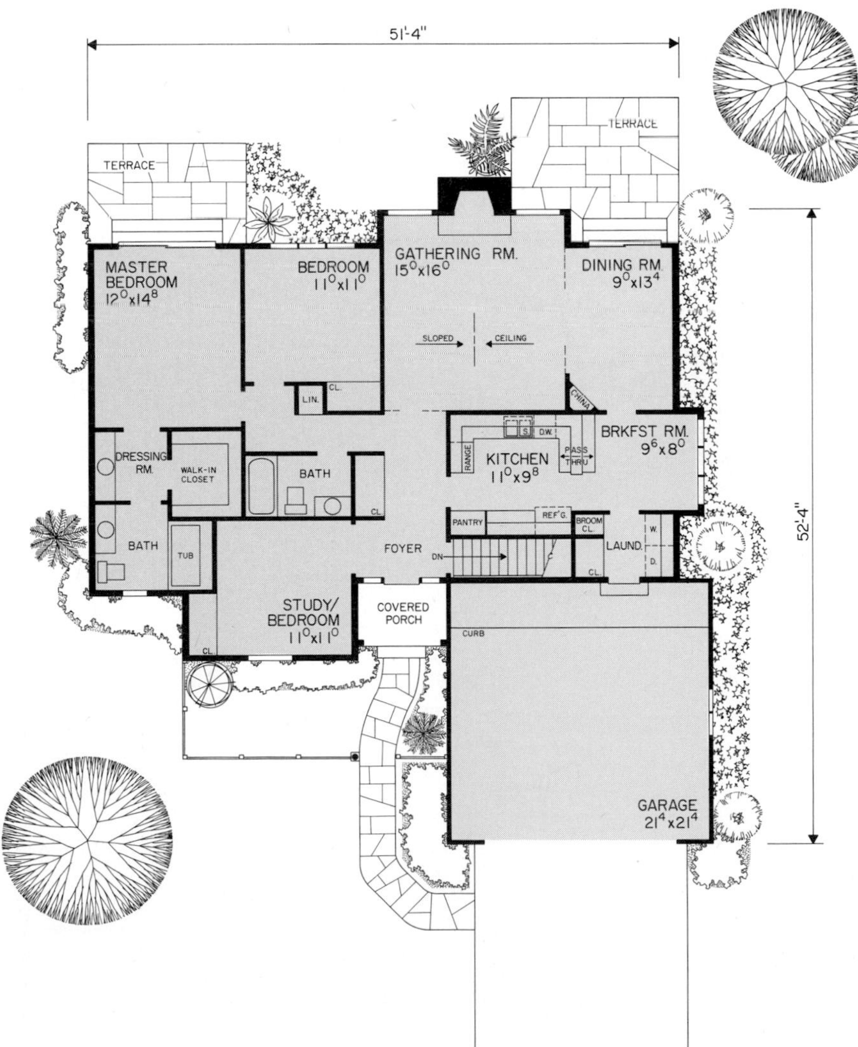

Design V42878

Square Footage: 1,521

L D

● This charming one-story Traditional design offers plenty of livability in a compact size. Thoughtful zoning puts all bedroom sleeping apart from household activity in the living and service area. The home includes a spacious gathering room with sloped ceiling, in addition to formal dining room and separate breakfast room. There's also a handy pass-thru between the breakfast room and an efficient, large kitchen. The laundry is strategically located adjacent to garage and breakfast/kitchen areas for handy access. A master bedroom enjoys its own suite with private bath and walk-in closet. A third bedroom can double as a sizable study just off the central foyer. This design offers the elegance of Traditional styling with the comforts of modern lifestyle.

Custom Alterations? See page 251 for customizing this plan to your specifications.

Design V42426

Square Footage: 1,521

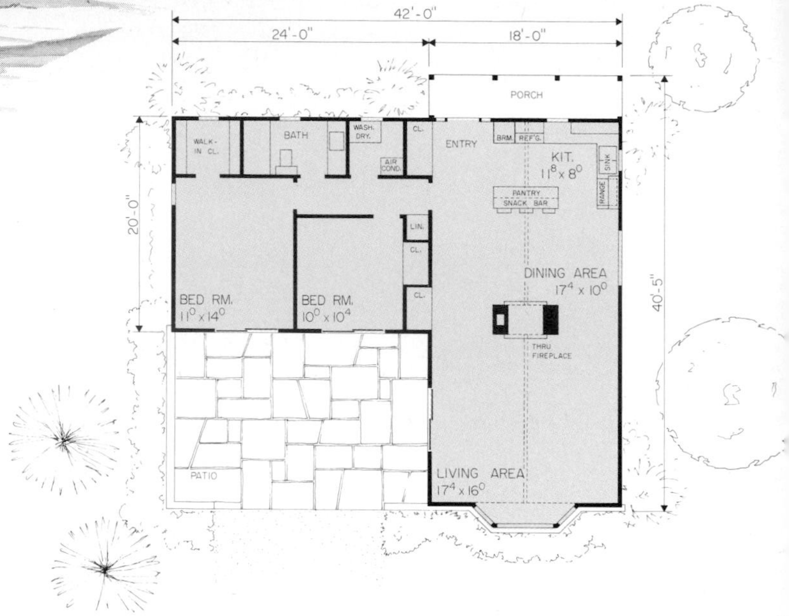

● A touch of traditional pervades the environment around this L-shaped, frame leisure-time home. The narrow horizontal siding, the delicate window treatment and the prudent use of fieldstone, all help set the character. Inside, the floor plan offers wonderful livability. The huge living and dining areas are separated by an appealing thru fireplace. Don't miss the efficient kitchen.

Design V41477

Square Footage: 1,446

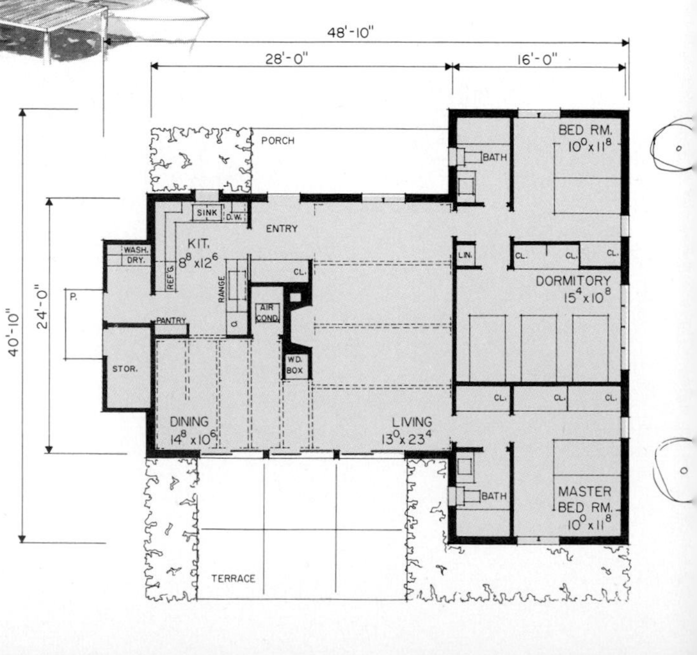

● Who said you can't have a vacation home with French Provincial flair? The intriguing thought of having your own villa is certainly within the realm of distinct possibility. Call it what you like, this hip-roofed, brick veneer summer house has an inviting warmth you will love. Inside, there is space galore. List the outstanding highlights.

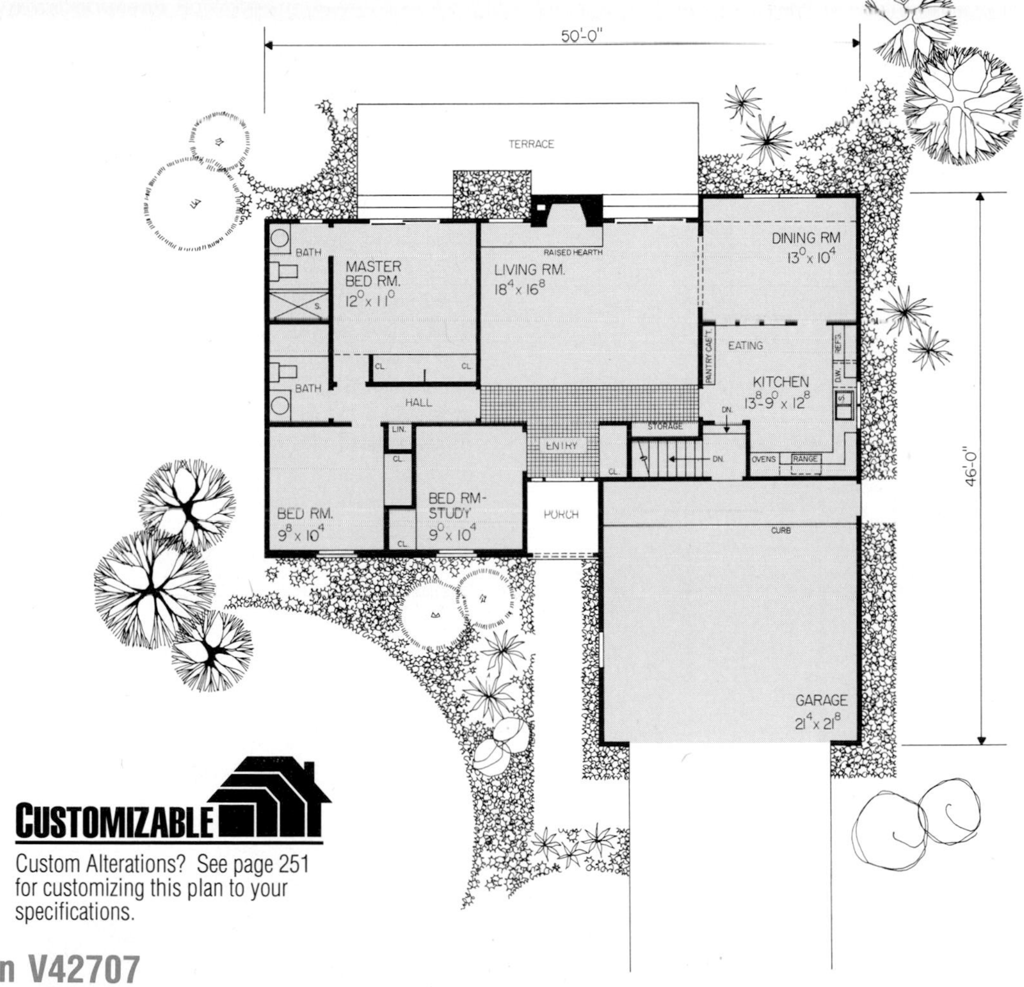

CUSTOMIZABLE

Custom Alterations? See page 251 for customizing this plan to your specifications.

Design V42707

Square Footage: 1,267

● Here is a charming Early American adaptation that will serve as a picturesque and practical retirement home. Also, it will serve admirably those with a small family in search of an efficient, economically built home. The living area, highlighted by the raised hearth fireplace, is spacious. The kitchen features eating space and easy access to the garage and basement. The dining room is adjacent to the kitchen and views the rear yard. Then, there is the basement for recreation and hobby pursuits. The bedroom wing offers three bedrooms and two full baths. Don't miss the sliding doors to the terrace from the living room and the master bedroom. Storage units are plentiful including a pantry cabinet in the eating area of the kitchen. This plan will be efficient and livable.

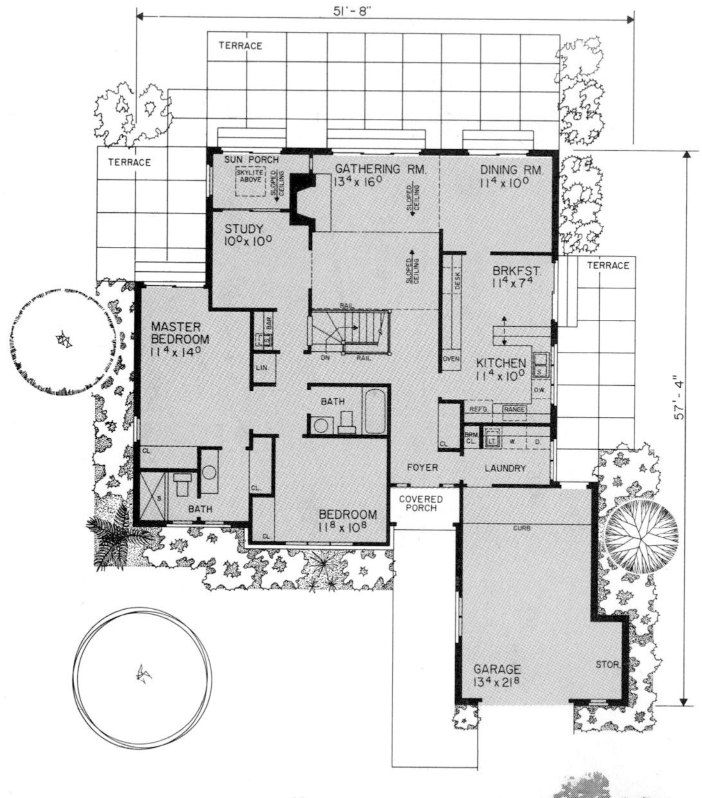

Design V42825

Square Footage: 1,584

● With today's tight economy, this house will be a real bargain. It has all of the necessary features to insure gracious living yet keep costs down - generous living space, packed with amenities and constructed with durable materials. Locating the garage to the front of this design is practical because it makes the overall width only 51' so it will fit on a narrow lot and it will act as a buffer against street noise. The interior of this home will be interesting. Three sets of sliding glass doors at the rear of the plan will flood the interior with natural light. Since it is a modified open plan it will allow the sunlight to penetrate deep into the interior. The gathering room which seems expanded by the cathedral ceiling has a fireplace.

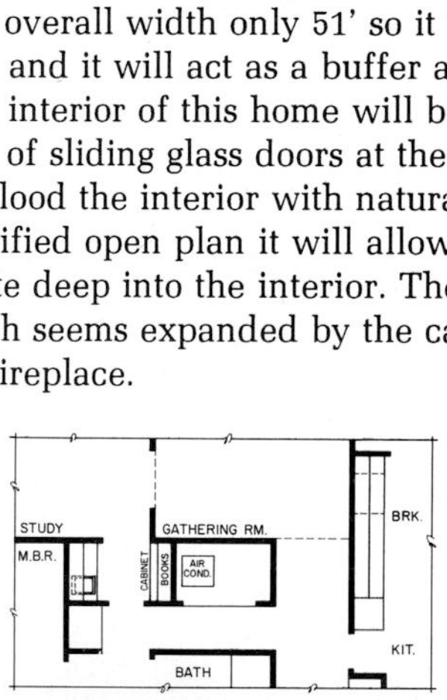

OPTIONAL NON-BASEMENT

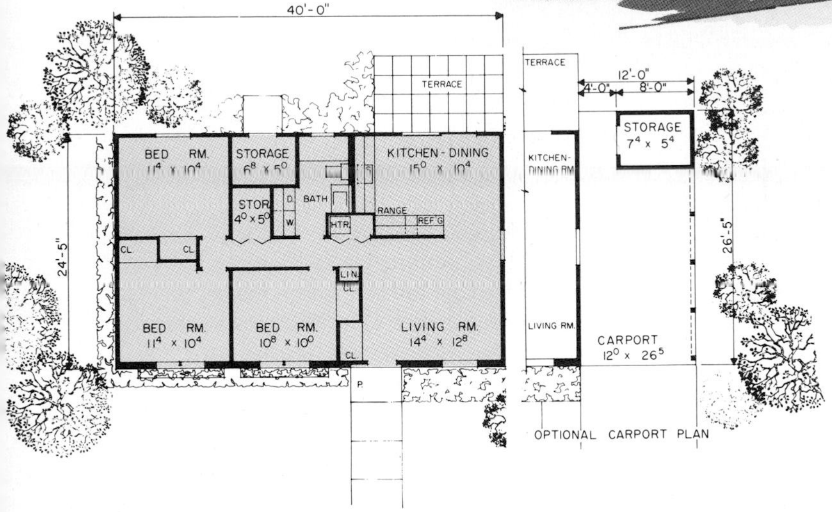

Design V43221

Square Footage: 976

● This hip-roof home has a wide overhang. The plan features excellent storage facilities. The kitchen-dining area is spacious and overlooks the rear yard. Note the optional carport with storage area.

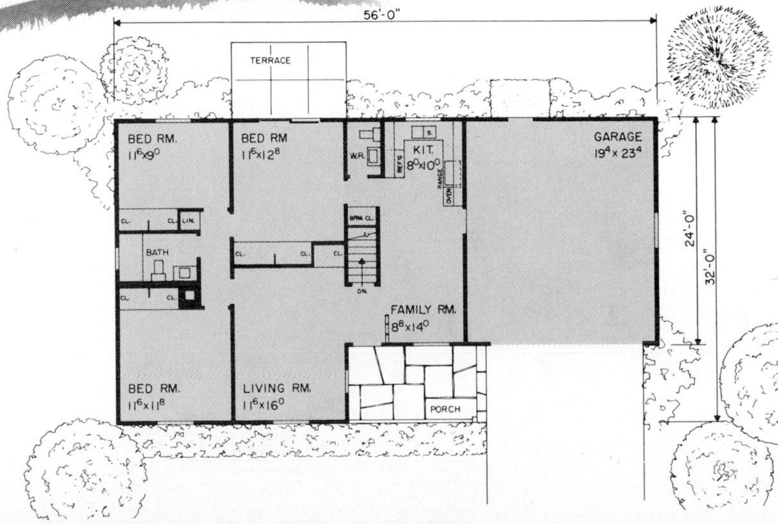

Design V41301

Square Footage: 1,056

● Charming is just the word to describe this L-shaped traditional home. Note formal living and informal family rooms, U-shaped kitchen and extra washroom.

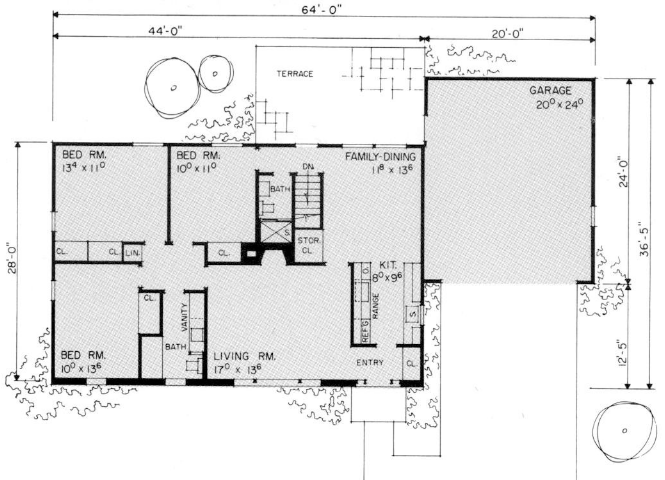

Design V41024

Square Footage: 1,252

● "Charming," is but one of the many words that could be chosen to describe this traditional home. While essentially a frame house, the front exterior features natural quarried stone. Below the overhanging roof, the window and door treatment is most pleasing. The board fence with its lamp post completes a delightful picture. Highlighting the interior is the living room with its raised-hearth fireplace.

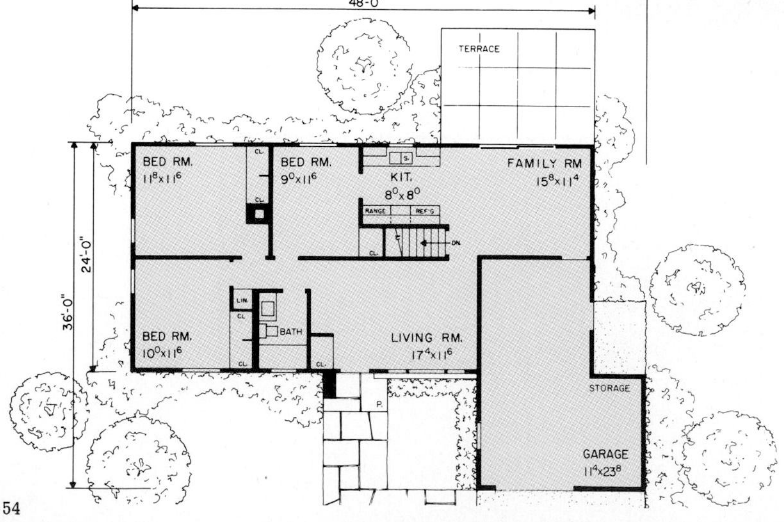

Design V41300

Square Footage: 1,008

● The projecting garage with its bulk storage area adds a full measure of design distinction. Behind the garage is a family room which functions with the kitchen.

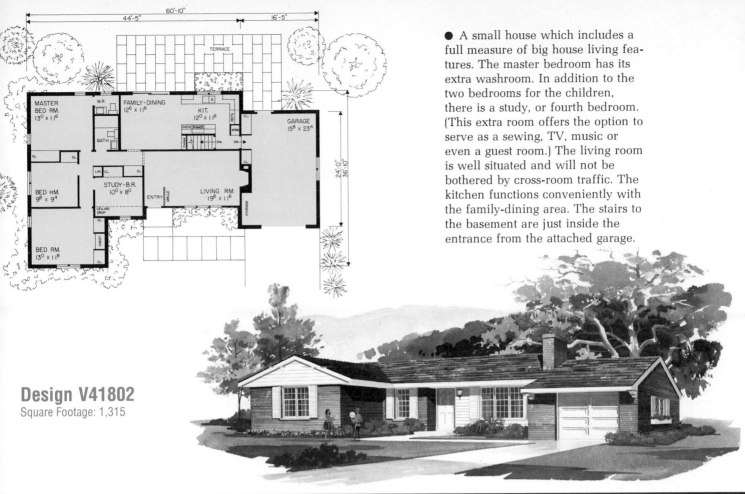

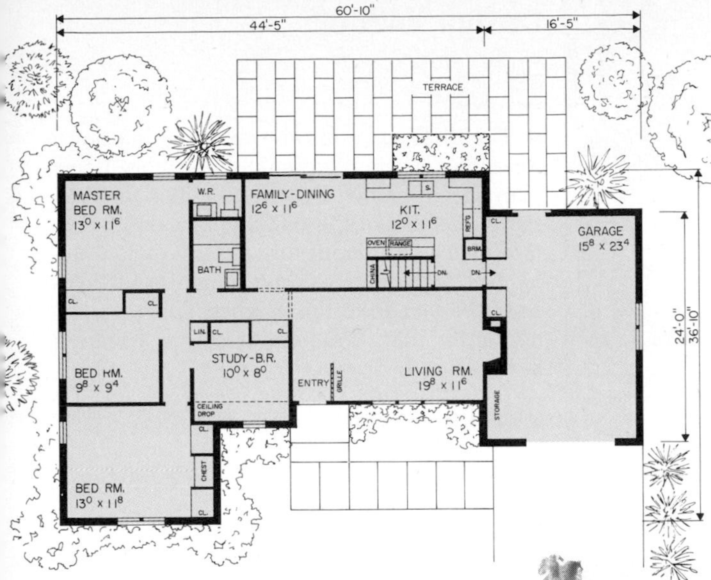

● A small house which includes a full measure of big house living features. The master bedroom has its extra washroom. In addition to the two bedrooms for the children, there is a study, or fourth bedroom. (This extra room offers the option to serve as a sewing, TV, music or even a guest room.) The living room is well situated and will not be bothered by cross-room traffic. The kitchen functions conveniently with the family-dining area. The stairs to the basement are just inside the entrance from the attached garage.

Design V41802

Square Footage: 1,315

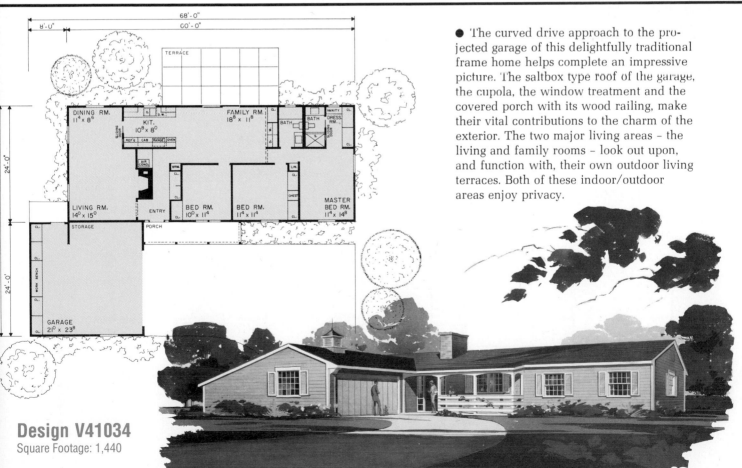

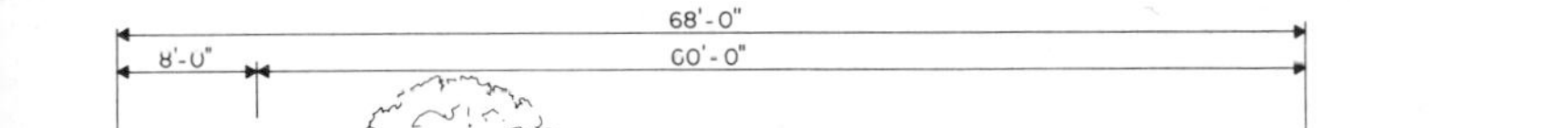

● The curved drive approach to the projected garage of this delightfully traditional frame home helps complete an impressive picture. The saltbox type roof of the garage, the cupola, the window treatment and the covered porch with its wood railing, make their vital contributions to the charm of the exterior. The two major living areas - the living and family rooms - look out upon, and function with, their own outdoor living terraces. Both of these indoor/outdoor areas enjoy privacy.

Design V41034

Square Footage: 1,440

Design V42802

Square Footage: 1,729

L D

● The three exteriors shown at the left house the same, efficiently planned one-story floor plan shown below. Be sure to notice the design variations in the window placement and roof pitch. The Tudor design to the left is delightful. Half-timbered stucco and brick comprise the facade of this English Tudor variation of the plan. Note authentic bay window in the front bedroom.

Design V42803

Square Footage: 1,679

L D

● Housed in varying facades, this floor plan is very efficient. The front foyer leads to each of the living areas. The sleeping area of two, or optional three, bedrooms is ready to serve the family. Then there is the gathering room. This room is highlighted by its size, 16 x 20 feet. A contemporary mix of fieldstone and vertical wood siding characterizes this exterior. The absence of columns or posts gives a modern look to the covered porch.

Design V42804

Square Footage: 1,674

L D

● Stuccoed arches, multi-paned windows and a gracefully sloped roof accent the exterior of this Spanish-inspired design. Like the other two designs, the interior kitchen will efficiently serve the dining room, covered dining porch and breakfast room with great ease. Blueprints for all three designs include details for an optional non-basement plan.

Custom Alterations? See page 251 for customizing this plan to your specifications.

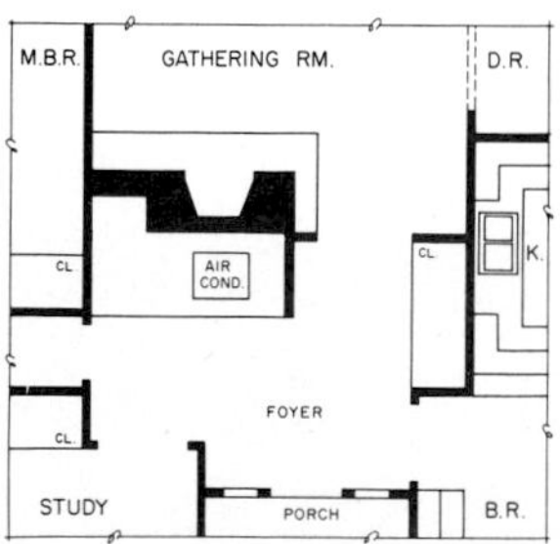

OPTIONAL NON-BASEMENT

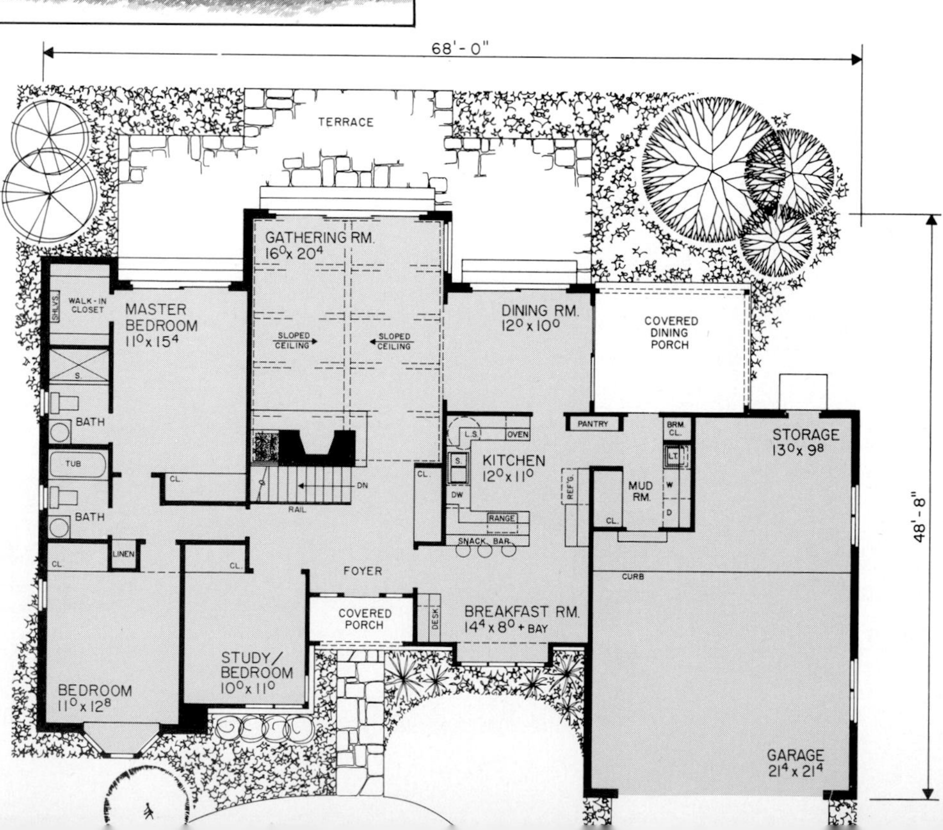

Design V42805

Square Footage: 1,547

● Three completely different exterior facades share one compact, practical and economical floor plan. The major design variations are roof pitch, window placement and garage openings. Each design will hold its own when comparing the three exteriors. The design to the right is a romantic stone-and-shingle cottage design. This design, along with the other two designs presented here, is outstanding.

Design V42806

Square Footage: 1,584

● Even though these exteriors are different in their styling and have a few design variations, their floor plans are identical. Each will provide the family with a livable plan. In this brick and half-timbered stucco Tudor version, the living-dining room expands across the rear of the plan and has direct access to the covered porch. Notice the built-in planter adjacent to the open staircase leading to the basement.

Design V42807

Square Footage: 1,576

● Along with the living-dining areas of the other two plans, this sleek contemporary styled home's breakfast room also will have a view of the covered porch. A desk, snack bar and mud room housing the laundry facilities are near the U-shaped kitchen. Clustering these work areas together is very convenient. The master bedroom has a private bath.

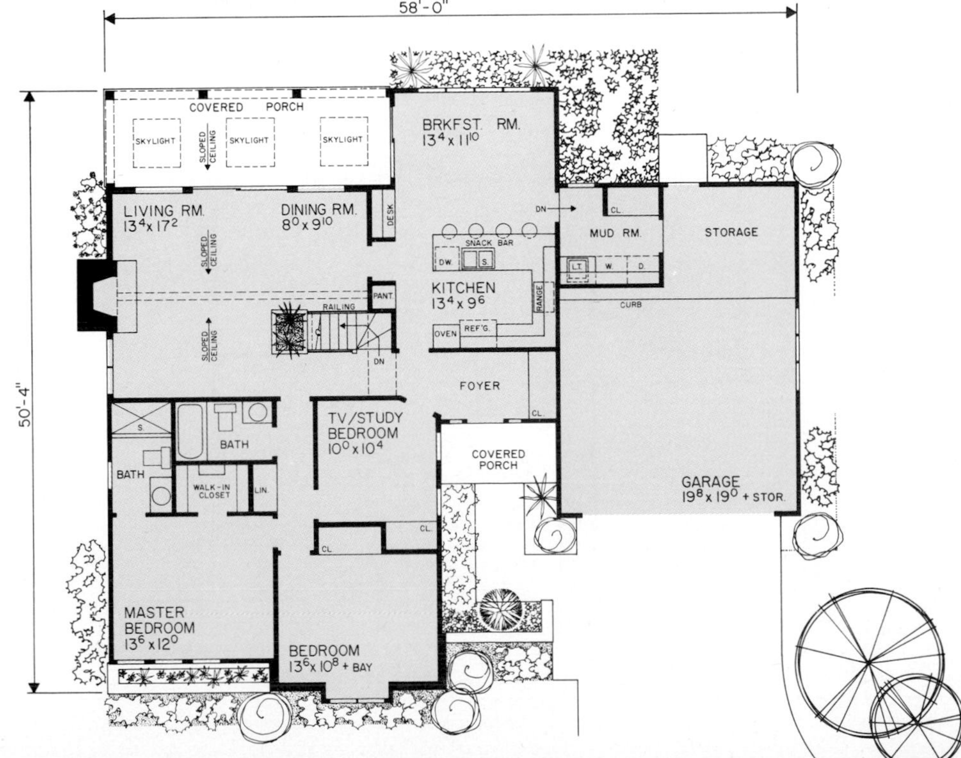

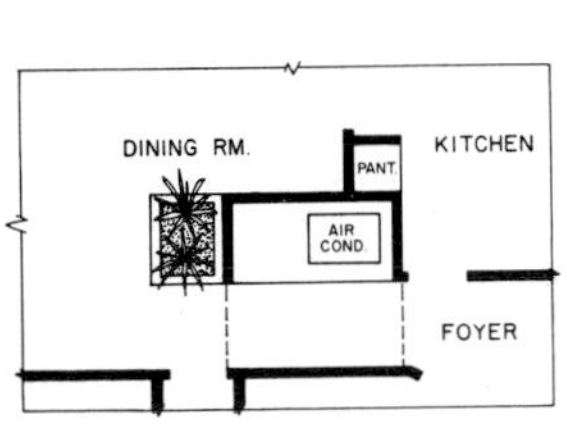

OPTIONAL NON-BASEMENT

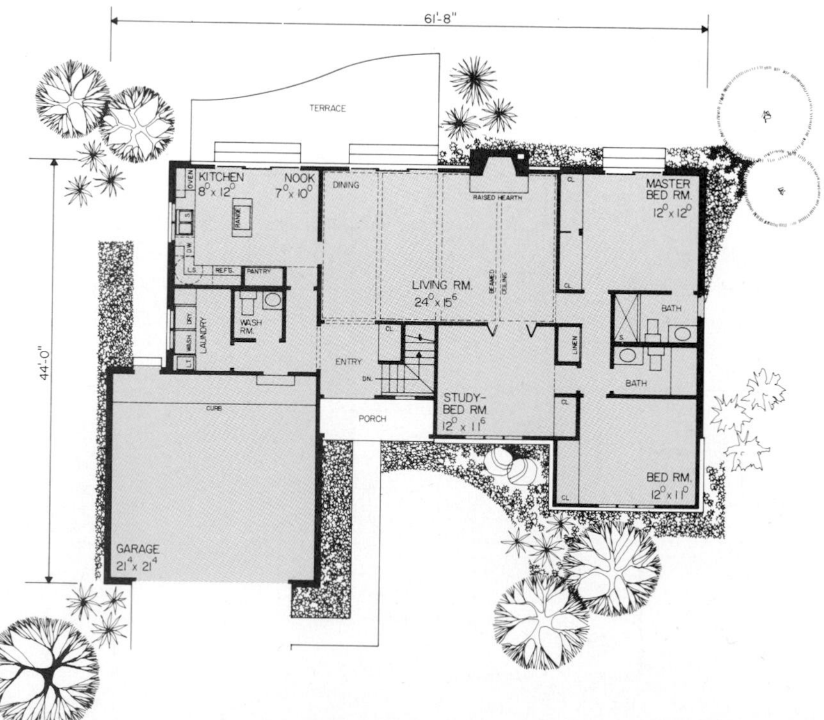

Design V42565

Square Footage: 1,540

L **D**

● This modest sized floor plan has much to offer in the way of livability. It may function as either a two or three bedroom home. The living room is huge and features a fine, raised hearth fireplace. The open stairway to the basement is handy and will lead to what may be developed as the recreation area. In addition to the two full baths, there is an extra washroom. Adjacent is the laundry room and the service entrance from the garage. The blueprints you order for this design will show details for each of the three delightful elevations above. Which is your favorite? The Tudor, the Colonial, or the Contemporary?

Custom Alterations? See page 251 for customizing this plan to your specifications.

Design V42505

Square Footage: 1,366

L **D**

● This design offers you a choice of three distinctively different exteriors. Which is your favorite? Blueprints show details for all three optional elevations. A study of the floor plan reveals a fine measure of livability. In less than 1,400 square feet there are features galore. An excellent return on your construction dollar. In addition to the two eating areas and the open planning of the gathering room, the indoor-outdoor relationships are of great interest. The basement may be developed for recreational activities. Be sure to note the storage potential, particularly the linen closet, the pantry, the china cabinet and the broom closet.

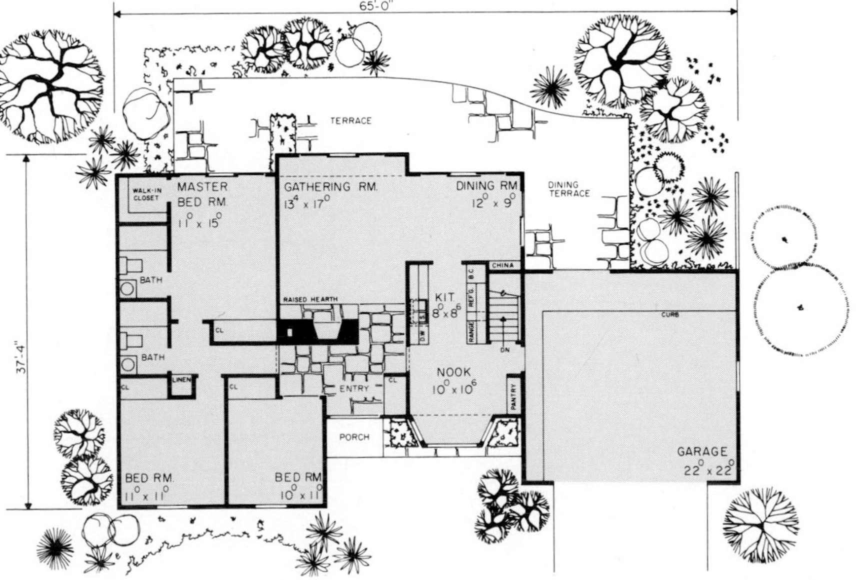

The Bungalow

This once-popular home design is

Design V43314

Square Footage: 1,951

● Scaled down but definitely upscale, this plan leaves nothing out. Two verandas, front and back, provide outdoor enjoyment along with a screened porch that extends the formal and casual eating areas. A galley kitchen serves both areas. The glow from the fireplace in the gathering room warms any gathering, three bedrooms (one a large master) have a full bath nearby.

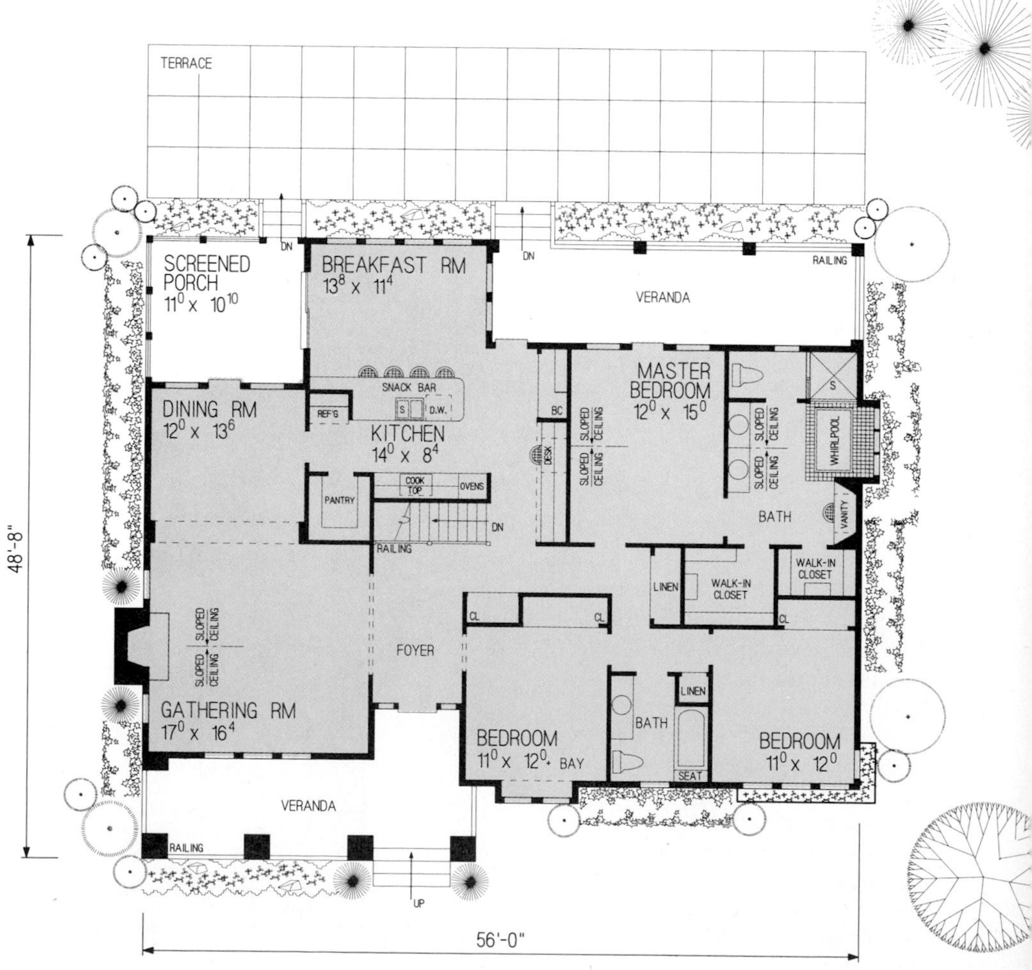

Is Back!

making an exciting resurgence.

Design V43315

Lounge: 330 square feet
Total: 3,248 square feet

● This three-bedroom bungalow is right in step with modern floor planning. The large gathering/dining room area is thoughtfully placed to the back of the home and has an overhanging loft for quiet relaxing. Verandas both front and back are cool spots to take in a breath of fresh air.

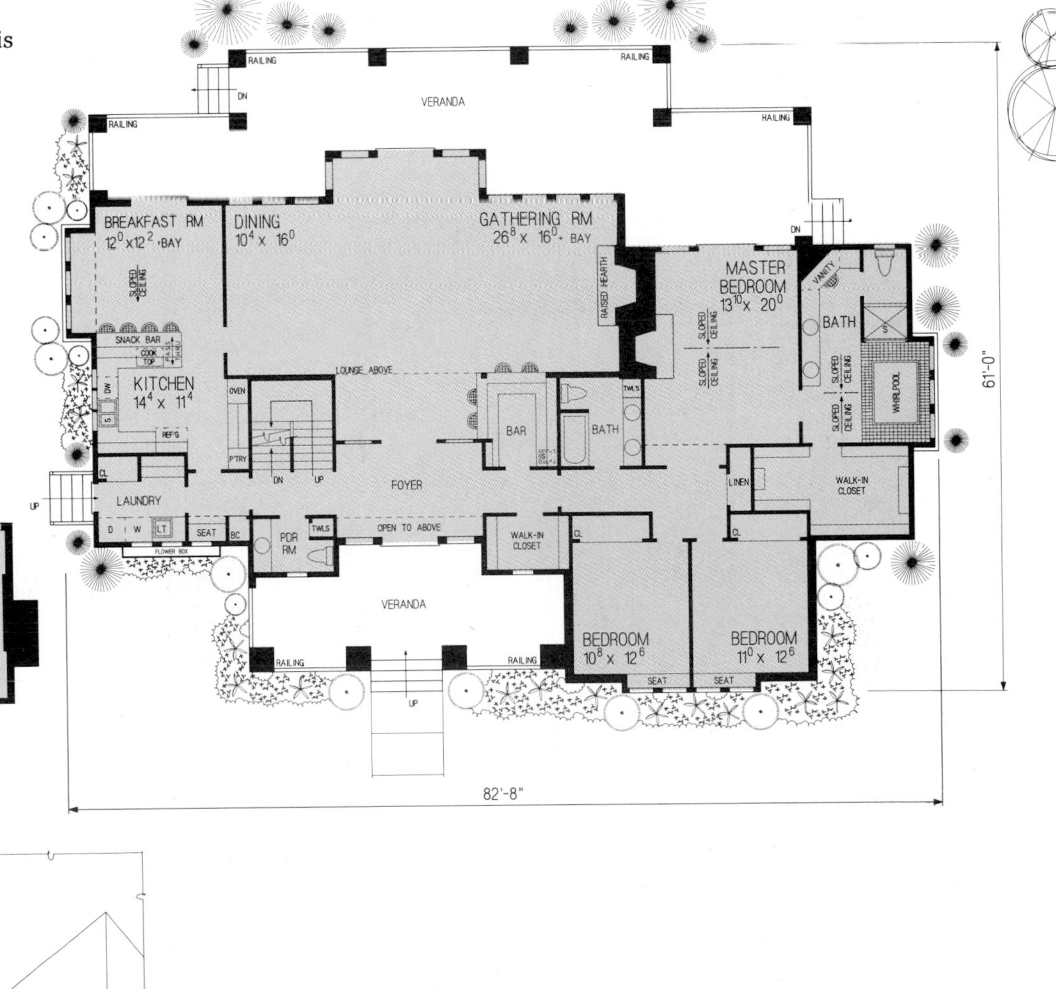

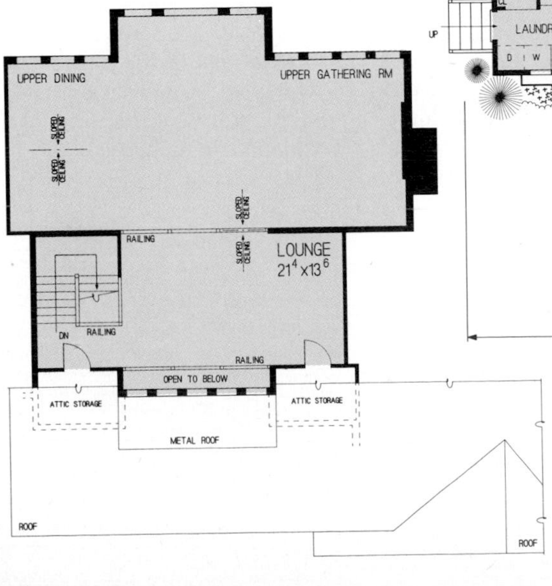

CUSTOMIZABLE

Custom Alterations? See page 251 for customizing this plan to your specifications.

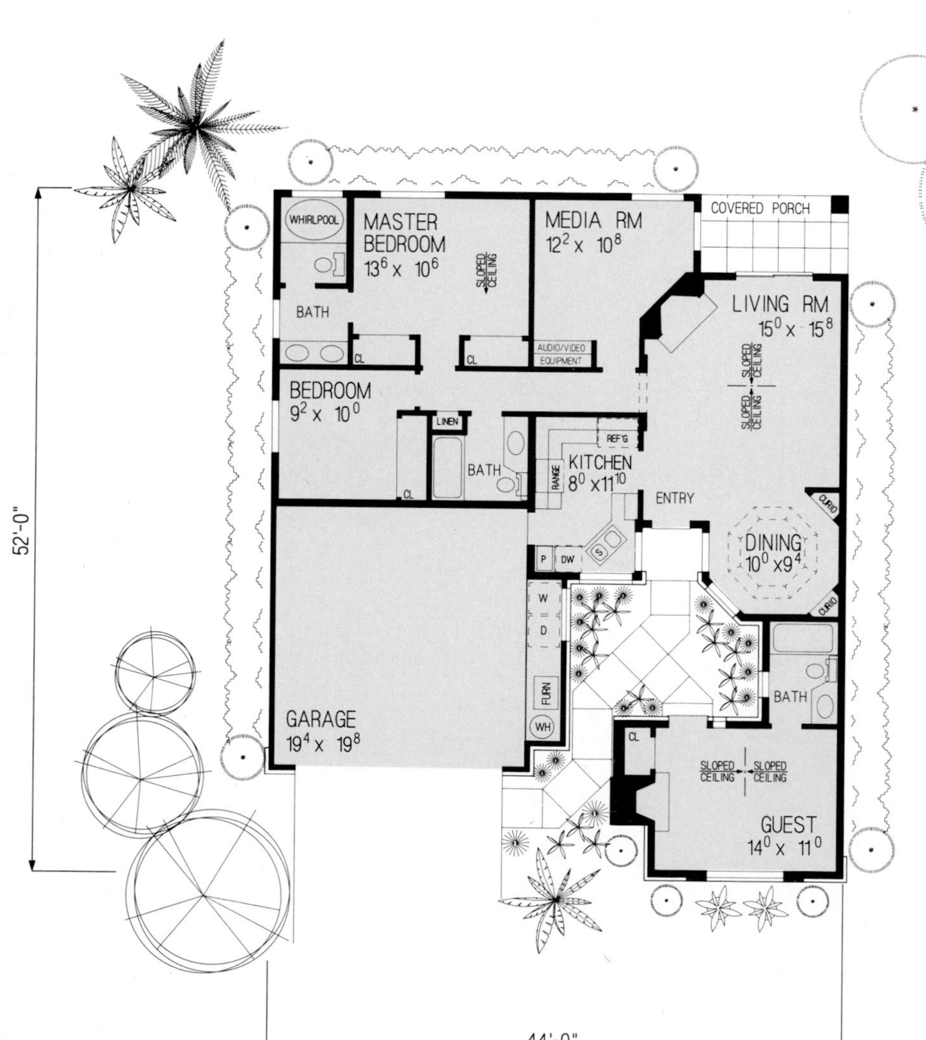

Design V43416

Square Footage: 1,375

● Here's a Southwestern design that will be economical to build and a pleasure to occupy. The front door opens into a spacious living room with corner fireplace and dining room with coffered ceiling. The nearby kitchen serves both easily. A few steps away is the cozy media room with built-in space for audio-visual equipment. Down the hall are two bedrooms and two baths; the master features a whirlpool. A guest room is found across the entry court and includes a fireplace and sloped ceiling.

Design V43419

Square Footage: 1,965

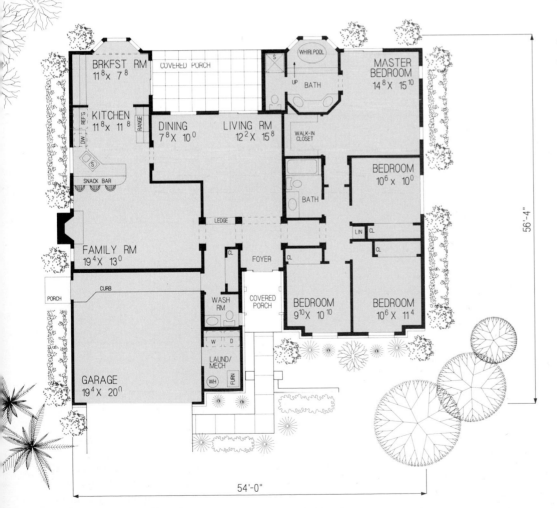

BRKFST RM 11^8 X 7^8
COVERED PORCH
KITCHEN 11^8 X 11^8
REF'G
DW
RANGE
SNACK BAR
DINING 7^8 X 10^0
LIVING RM 12^2 X 15^8
WHIRLPOOL
BATH
UP
MASTER BEDROOM 14^8 X 15^{10}
WALK-IN CLOSET
BEDROOM 10^6 X 10^0
BATH
LEDGE
LIN
CL
FAMILY RM 19^4 X 13^0
FOYER
CURB
PORCH
WASH RM
COVERED PORCH
BEDROOM 9^{10} X 10^{10}
BEDROOM 10^6 X 11^4
W
D
LAUND/ MECH
WH
FURN
GARAGE 19^4 X 20^0
56'-4"
54'-0"

● This attractive, multi-gabled exterior houses a compact, livable interior. The entry foyer effectively routes traffic to all areas: left to the family room and kitchen, straight back to the dining room and living room, and right to the four-bedroom sleeping area. The spacious family room provides an informal gathering space while the living and dining rooms are perfect for formal occasions. The highlight of the sleeping area is the master bedroom with its whirlpool, walk-in closet and view of the back yard.

Custom Alterations? See page 251 for customizing this plan to your specifications.

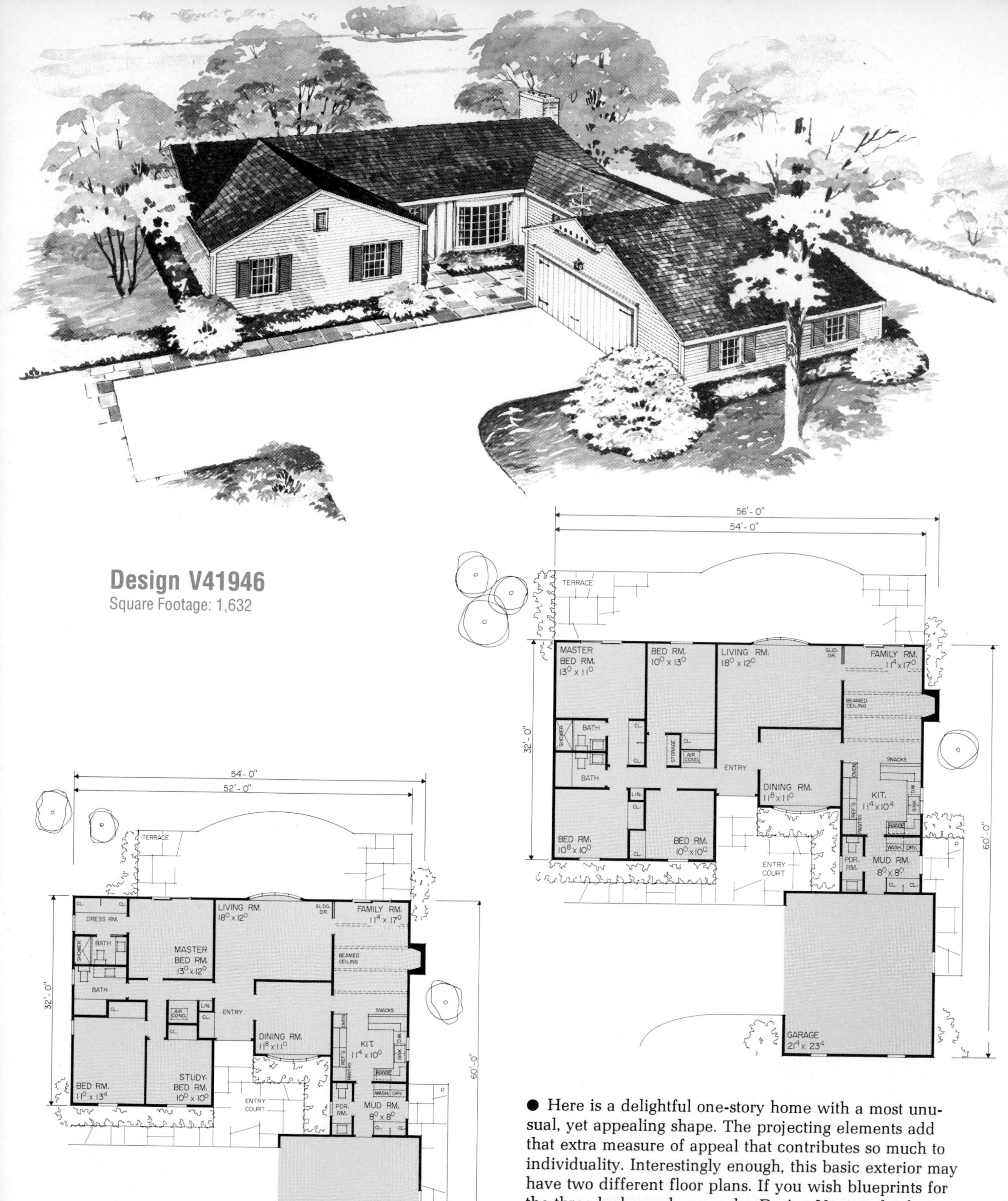

Design V41946

Square Footage: 1,632

Design V41945

Square Footage: 1,568

● Here is a delightful one-story home with a most unusual, yet appealing shape. The projecting elements add that extra measure of appeal that contributes so much to individuality. Interestingly enough, this basic exterior may have two different floor plans. If you wish blueprints for the three bedroom home order Design V41945: for four bedroom blueprints, order Design V41946. Whichever you select, you will enjoy the efficiency of the remainder of the plan. There are formal living and dining rooms, an informal family room with a beamed ceiling, a U-shaped kitchen and a strategically placed mud room with an adjacent powder room for easy convenience.

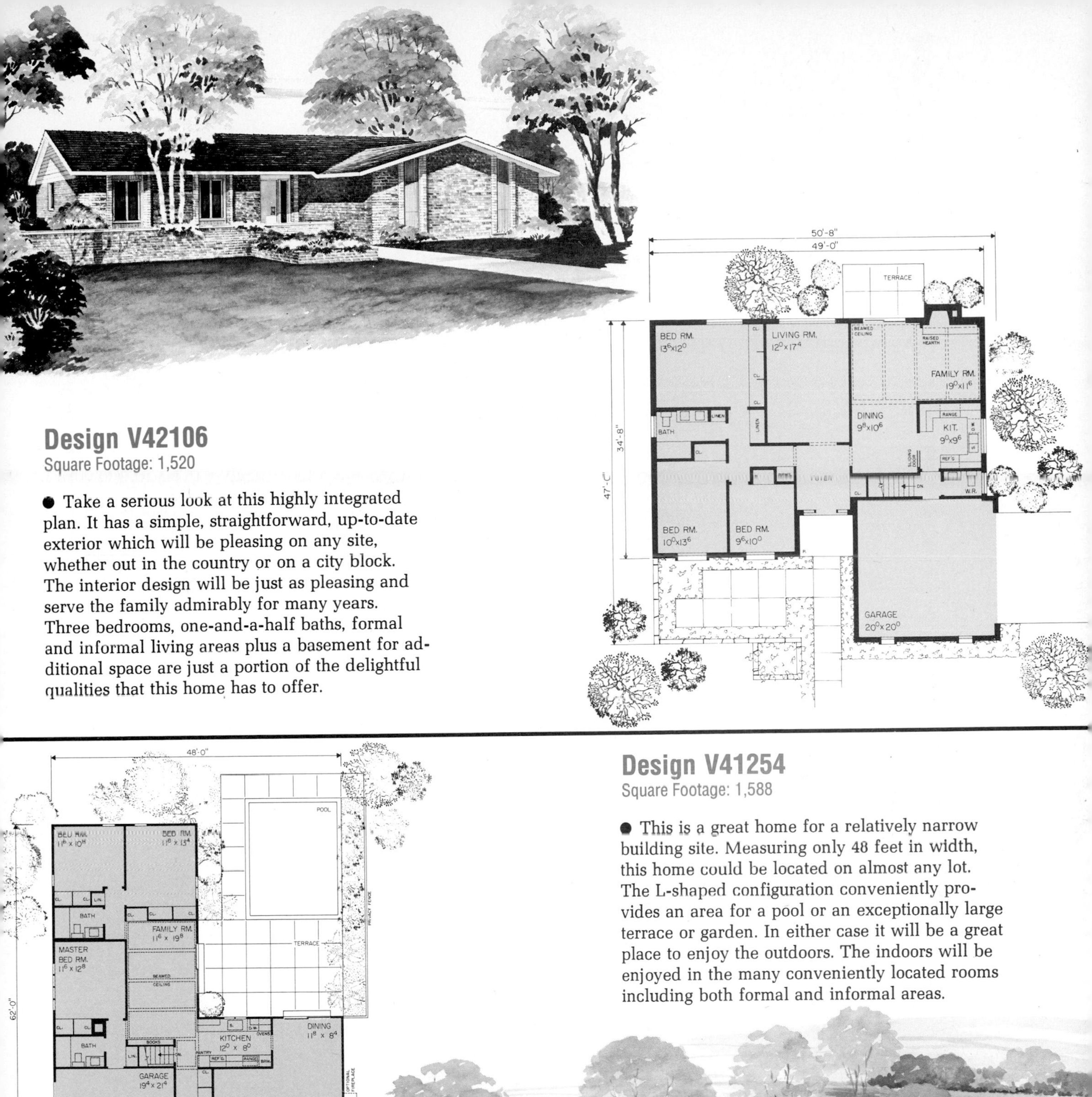

Design V42106

Square Footage: 1,520

● Take a serious look at this highly integrated plan. It has a simple, straightforward, up-to-date exterior which will be pleasing on any site, whether out in the country or on a city block. The interior design will be just as pleasing and serve the family admirably for many years. Three bedrooms, one-and-a-half baths, formal and informal living areas plus a basement for additional space are just a portion of the delightful qualities that this home has to offer.

Design V41254

Square Footage: 1,588

● This is a great home for a relatively narrow building site. Measuring only 48 feet in width, this home could be located on almost any lot. The L-shaped configuration conveniently provides an area for a pool or an exceptionally large terrace or garden. In either case it will be a great place to enjoy the outdoors. The indoors will be enjoyed in the many conveniently located rooms including both formal and informal areas.

Design V43373

Square Footage: 1,378

L D

Design V43374

Square Footage: 1,378

L D

Design V43375

Square Footage: 1,378

L D

● This charmingly compact plan has three facades from which to choose: Greek Revival (V43373), Tudor (V43374) or Southwestern (V43375). The interior plan contains a large living room/dining room combination, a media room, a U-shaped kitchen with breakfast room and two bedrooms. If the extra space is needed, the media room could serve as a third bedroom. Note the terrace to the rear of the plan off the dining room and the sloped ceilings throughout.

Design V43460

Square Footage: 1,346

● A double dose of charm, this special farmhouse plan offers two elevations in its blueprint package. Though rooflines and porch options are different, the floor plan is basically the same and very livable. A formal living room/dining room combination has a warming fireplace and delightful bay window. The kitchen separates this area from the more casual family room. Three bedrooms include two family bedrooms served by a full, shared bath, and a lovely master suite with its own private bath.

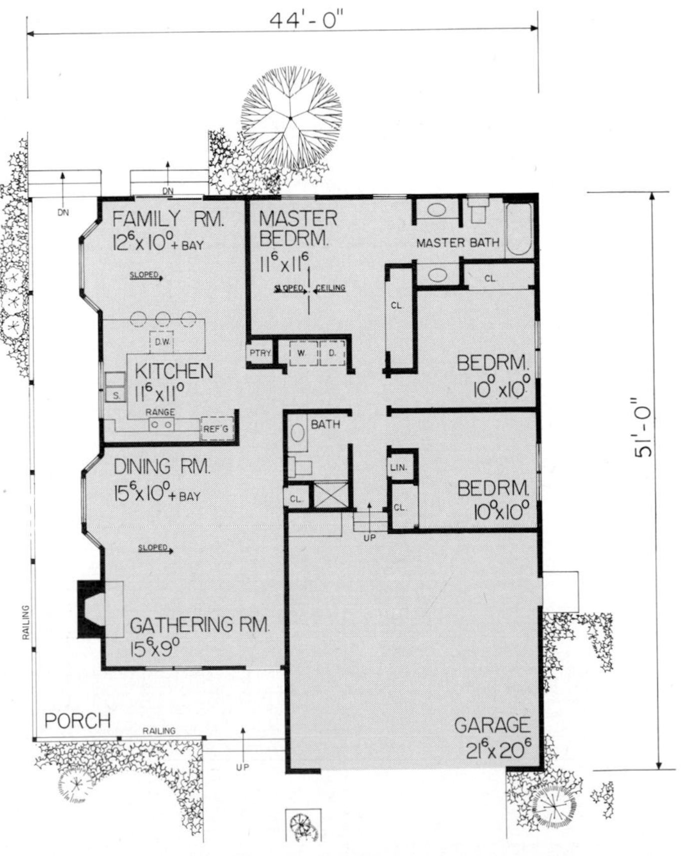

Design V41342

Square Footage: 1,560

● A well-planned, medium-sized contemporary home with plenty of big-house features. The brick line of the projected bedroom wing extends toward the projected two-car garage to form an attractive front court. The large glass panels below the overhanging roof are a dramatic feature. In addition to the two full baths, there is an extra washroom easily accessible from the kitchen/family room area as well as the outdoors. The laundry equipment is strategically located.

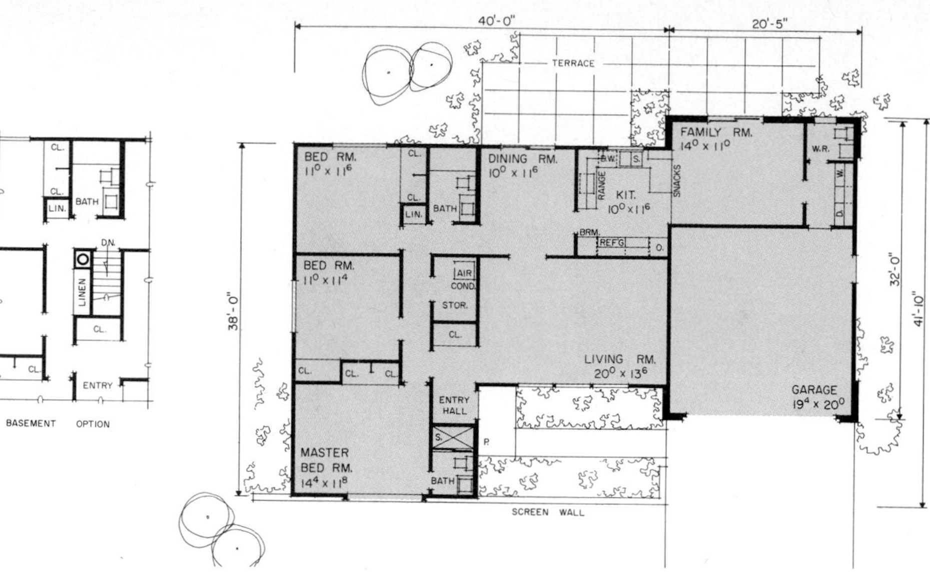

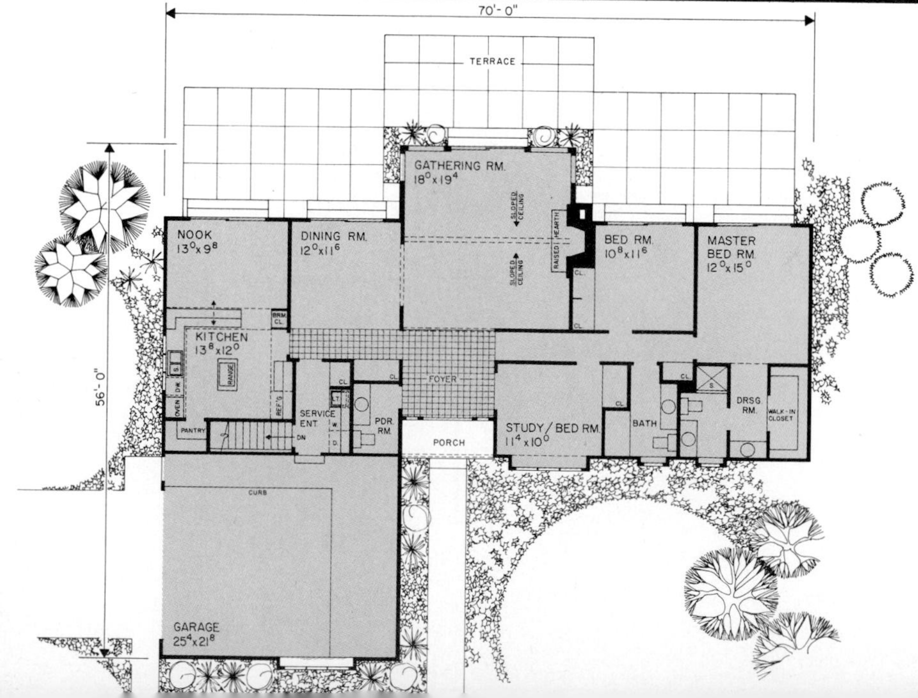

Design V42792

Square Footage: 1,944

● Indoor-outdoor living hardly could be improved upon in this contemporary design. All of the rear rooms have sliding glass doors to the large terrace. Divide the terrace in three parts and the nook and dining room have access to a dining terrace, the gathering room to a living terrace and two bedrooms to a lounging terrace. A delightful way to bring the outdoors view inside. Other fine features include the efficient kitchen which has plenty of storage space and an island range, a first floor laundry with stairs to the basement and a powder room adjacent to the front door.

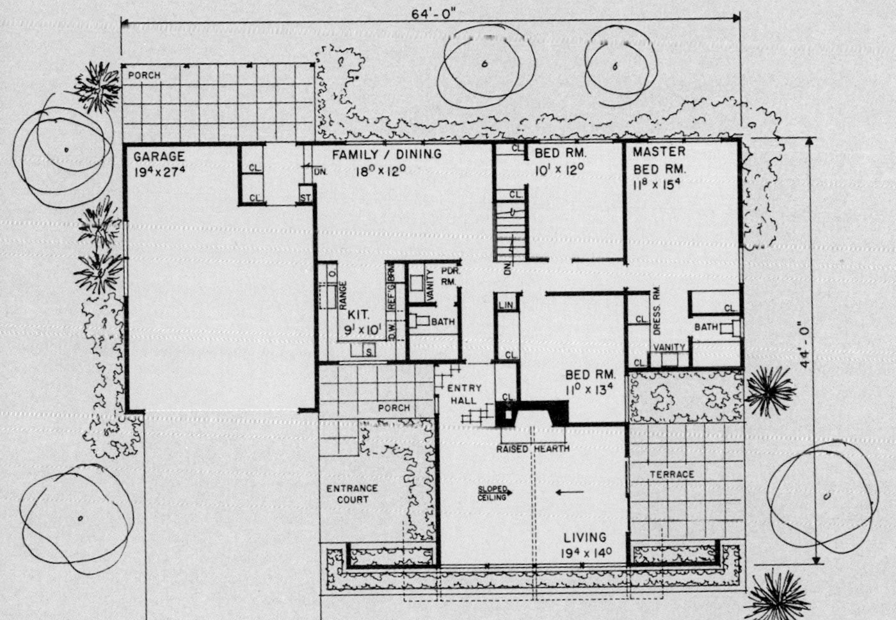

Design V41065

Square Footage: 1,492

● Here is a refreshing design that reflects all that is so appealing in good up-to-date exterior detailing and practical, efficient floor planning. The low pitched, wide overhanging roof, the glass gabled end with exposed rafters, the raised planter and the extended wing walls are all delightful exterior features. Of particular interest, is the formation of the front entrance court and side terrace resulting from the extension of the front living room wall. Inside, there is much to excite the new occupants. The quietly, formal living room will have plenty of light. The strategically located kitchen is ideal to view approaching callers. Master bedroom with bath, vanity and dressing room housing two closets will be welcomed by the parents.

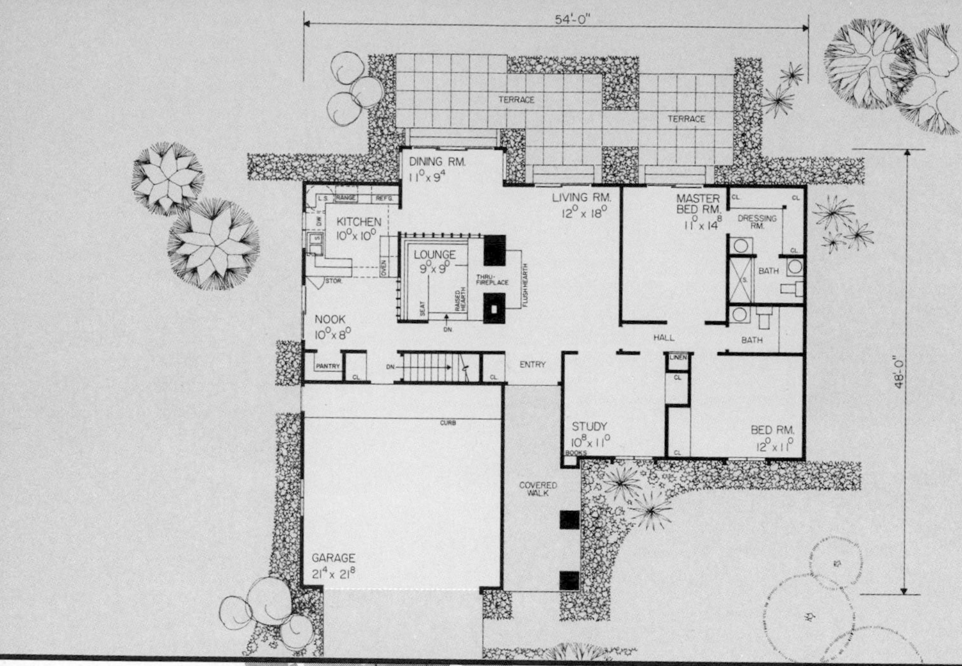

Design V42703

Square Footage: 1,445

D

● This modified, hip-roofed contemporary design will be the answer for those who want something both practical, yet different, inside and out. The covered front walk sets the stage for entering a modest sized home with tremendous livability. The focal point will be the pleasant conversation lounge. It is sunken, partially open to the other living areas and shares the enjoyment of the thru-fireplace with the living room. There are two bedrooms, two full baths and a study. The kitchen is outstanding.

Design V42753

Square Footage: 1,539

D

● In this day and age of expensive building sites, projecting the attached garage from the front line of the house makes a lot of economic sense. It also lends itself to interesting roof lines and plan configurations. Here, a pleasing covered walkway to the front door results. A privacy wall adds an extra measure of design appeal and provides a sheltered terrace for the study/bedroom. You'll seldom find more livability in 1,539 square feet. Imagine, three bedrooms, two baths, a spacious living/dining area and a family room.

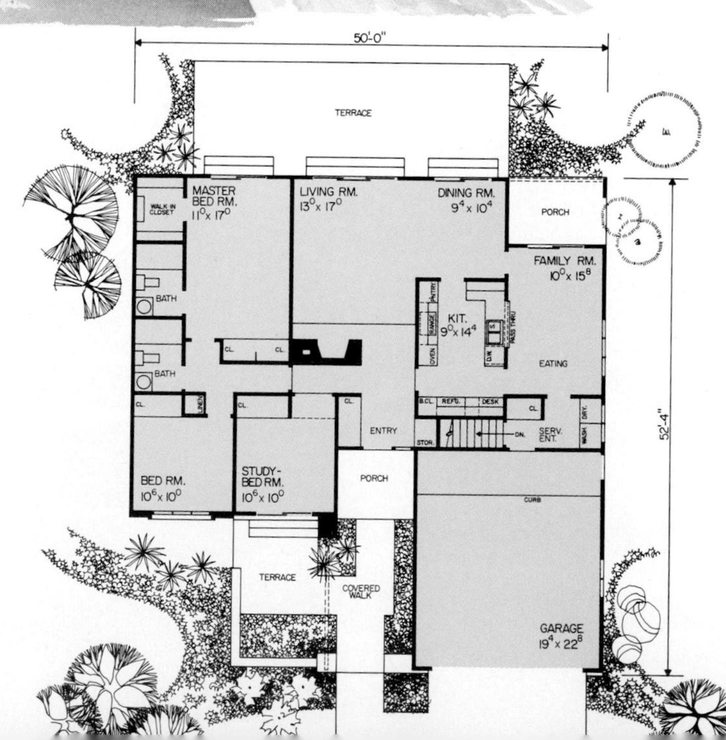

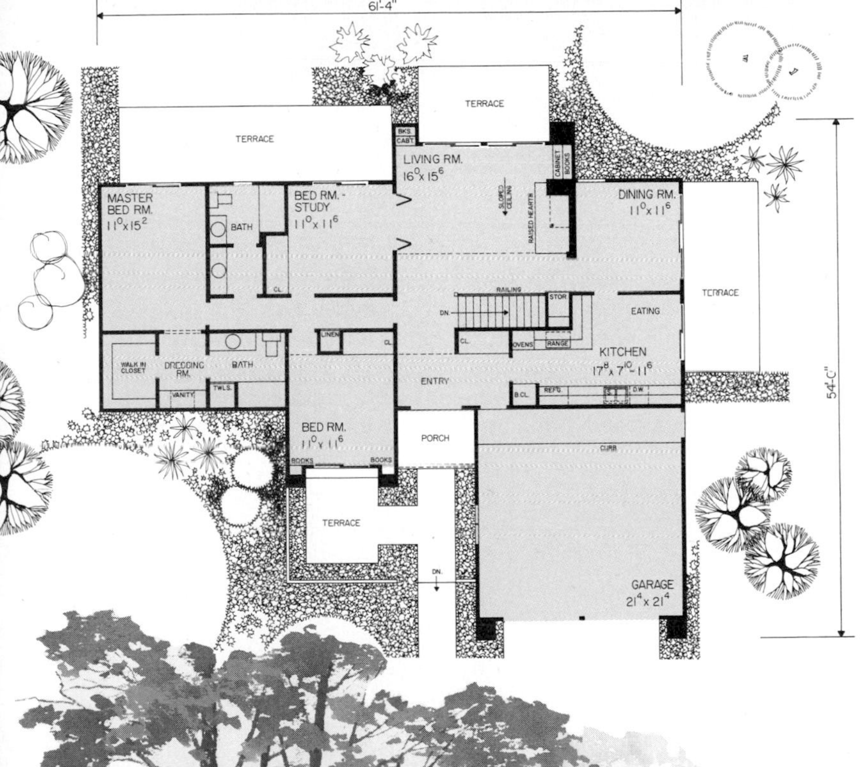

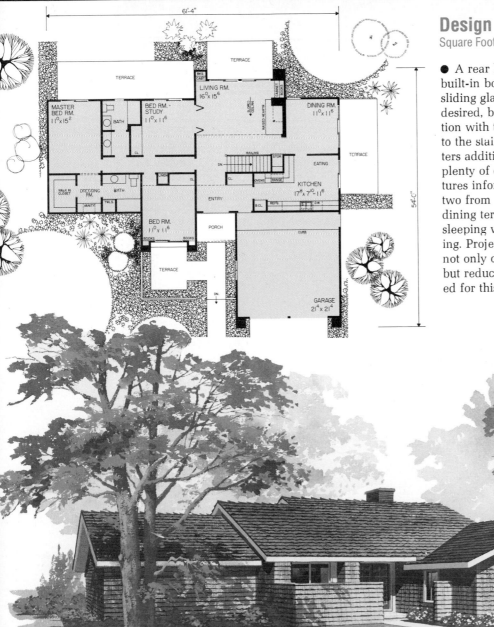

Design V42702

Square Footage: 1,636

● A rear living room with a sloping ceiling, built-in bookcases, a raised hearth fireplace and sliding glass doors to the rear living terrace. If desired, bi-fold doors permit this room to function with the adjacent study. Open railing next to the stairs to the basement recreation area fosters additional spaciousness. The kitchen has plenty of cabinet and cupboard space. It features informal eating space and is but a step or two from the separate dining room. Note side dining terrace. Each of the three rooms in the sleeping wing has direct access to outdoor living. Projecting the two-car garage to the front not only contributes to an interesting exterior, but reduces the size of the building site required for this home.

TWO-STORY RETIREMENT and SECOND HOMES . . .

are larger versions of their one-story cousins, and consequently allow more room for active lifestyles. In some cases, the second floor provides additional bedrooms, a lounge, or a play or hobby room—or it may be dominated by an expansive master suite. Any one of the two-stories in this section would be a fine consideration as an empty-nester or second-home option.

● A country-style home is part of America's fascination with the rural past. This home's emphasis of the traditional country home is in its historic gambrel roof, dormers and fanlight windows. Having a traditional exterior from the street view, this two-story home has large window walls and a greenhouse, which opens the house to the outdoors in a thoroughly contemporary manner. The interior of this design was planned to meet the requirements of today's active family. Like the country houses of the past, this home has a large gathering room for family get-togethers or entertaining. Note its L-shape which accommodates a music alcove. This area is large enough for a grand piano and storage for TV/Stereo equipment.

Design V42883

First Floor: 1,919 square feet
Second Floor: 895 square feet
Total: 2,814 square feet

The adjacent two-story greenhouse doubles as the dining room. There is a pass-thru snack bar to the country kitchen here. This country kitchen just might be the heart of the house with its two areas - the work zone and the sitting room. A front study is ready for those more quiet retreats.

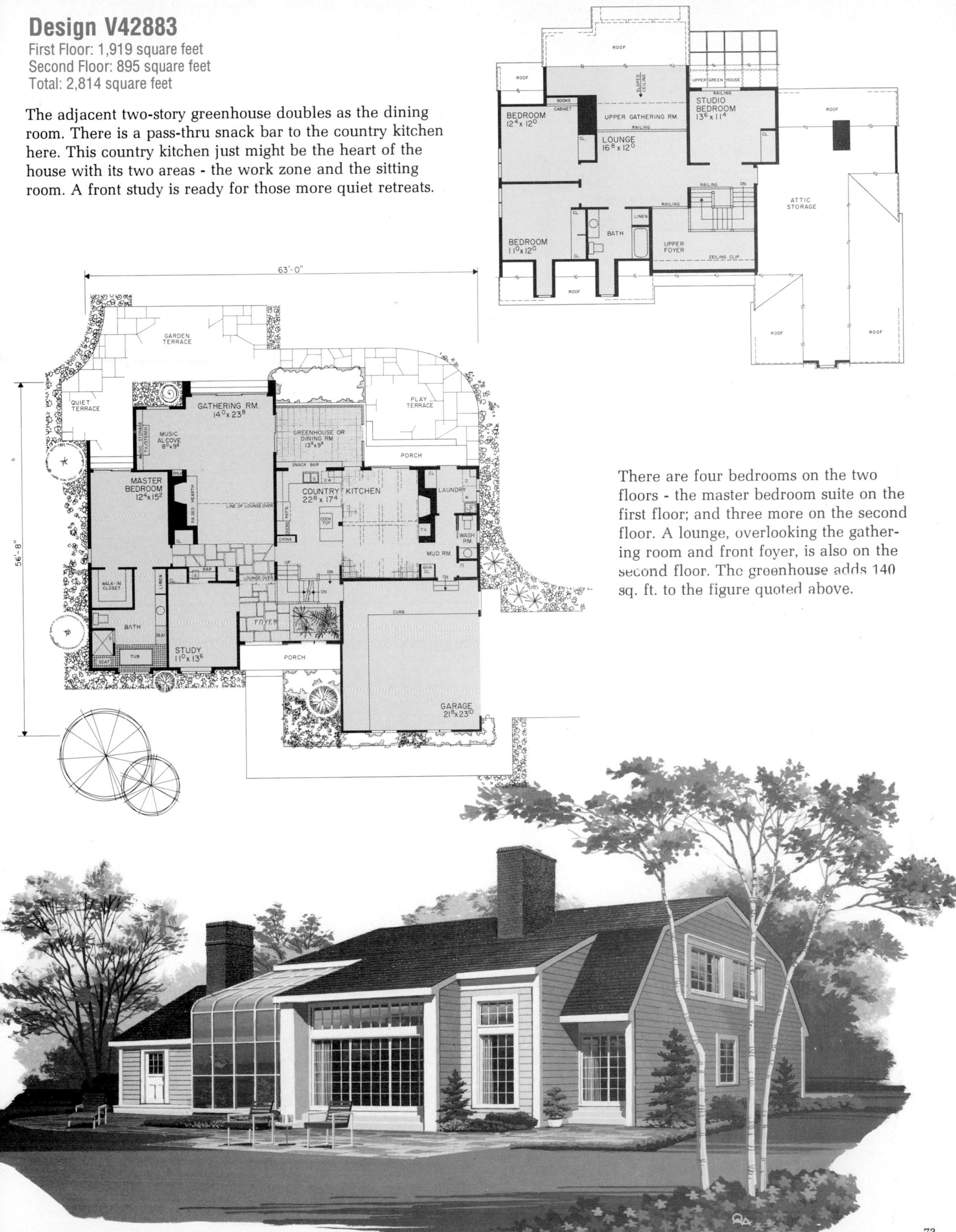

There are four bedrooms on the two floors - the master bedroom suite on the first floor; and three more on the second floor. A lounge, overlooking the gathering room and front foyer, is also on the second floor. The greenhouse adds 140 sq. ft. to the figure quoted above.

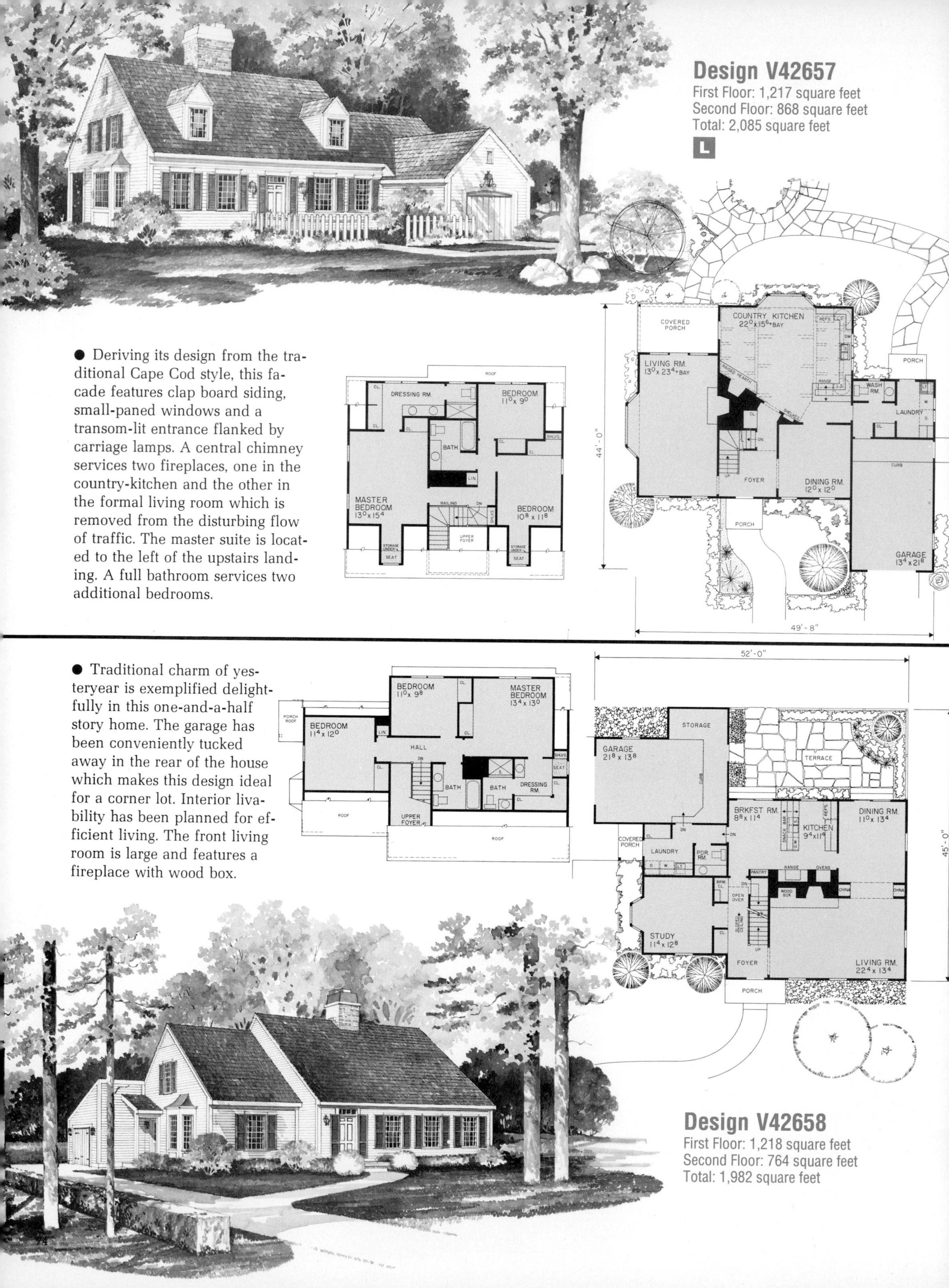

Design V42657

First Floor: 1,217 square feet
Second Floor: 868 square feet
Total: 2,085 square feet

L

● Deriving its design from the traditional Cape Cod style, this facade features clap board siding, small-paned windows and a transom-lit entrance flanked by carriage lamps. A central chimney services two fireplaces, one in the country-kitchen and the other in the formal living room which is removed from the disturbing flow of traffic. The master suite is located to the left of the upstairs landing. A full bathroom services two additional bedrooms.

● Traditional charm of yesteryear is exemplified delightfully in this one-and-a-half story home. The garage has been conveniently tucked away in the rear of the house which makes this design ideal for a corner lot. Interior livability has been planned for efficient living. The front living room is large and features a fireplace with wood box.

Design V42658

First Floor: 1,218 square feet
Second Floor: 764 square feet
Total: 1,982 square feet

Design V42852 First Floor: 919 square feet; Second Floor: 535 square feet; Total: 1,454 square feet

L D

● Compact enough for even the smallest lot, this cozy design provides comfortable living space for a small family. At the heart of the plan is a spacious country kitchen. It features a cooking island, snack bar, and a dining area that opens to a house-wide rear terrace. The nearby dining room also opens to the terrace. At the front of the plan is a living room, warmed by a fireplace. Across the central foyer is a cozy study. Two second-floor bedrooms are serviced by two baths. Note the first-floor powder room and storage closet located next to the side entrance. The charm and warmth of this Cape Cod cottage design will be a delight to the family and a practical investment.

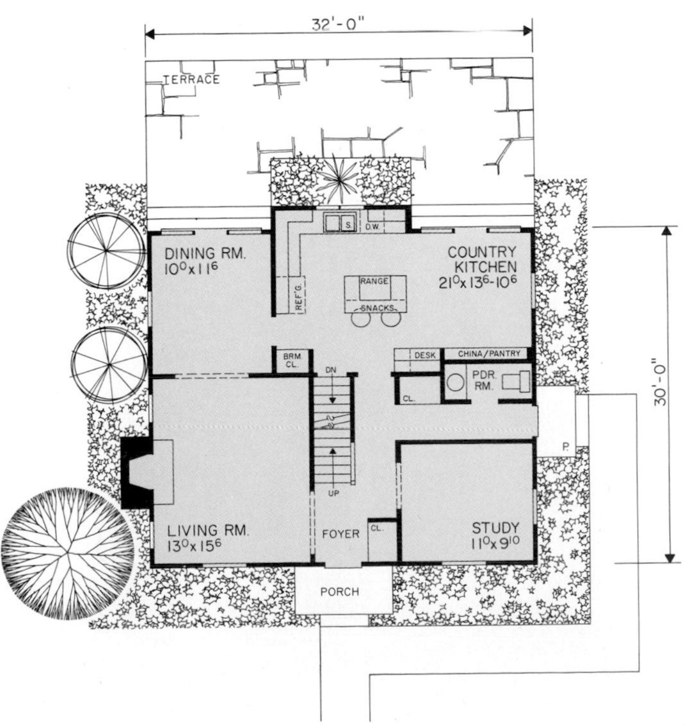

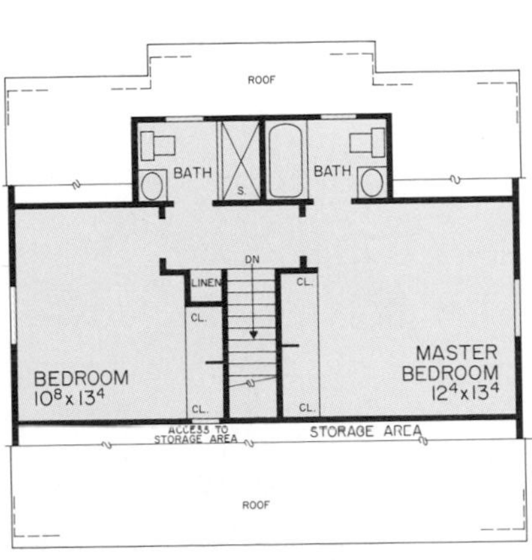

Expanding the Half-House

Design V42682 First Floor (Basic Plan): 976 square feet
First Floor (Expanded Plan): 1,230 square feet; Second Floor (Both Plans): 744 square feet
Total (Basic Plan): 1,720 square feet; Total (Expanded Plan): 1,974 square feet

L D

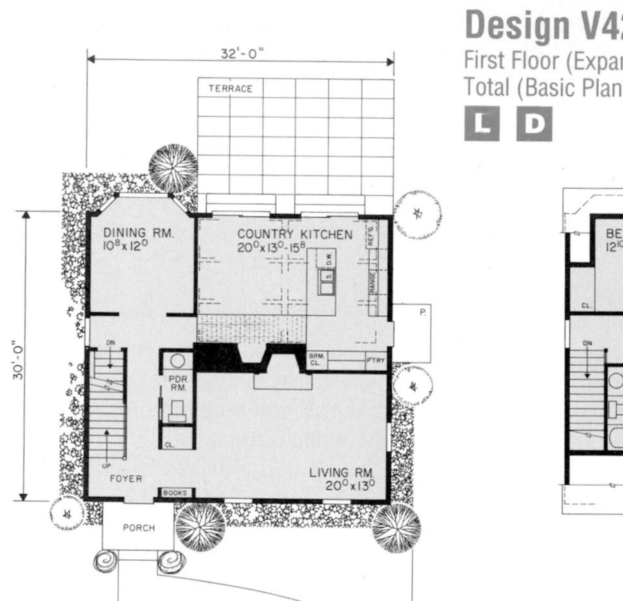

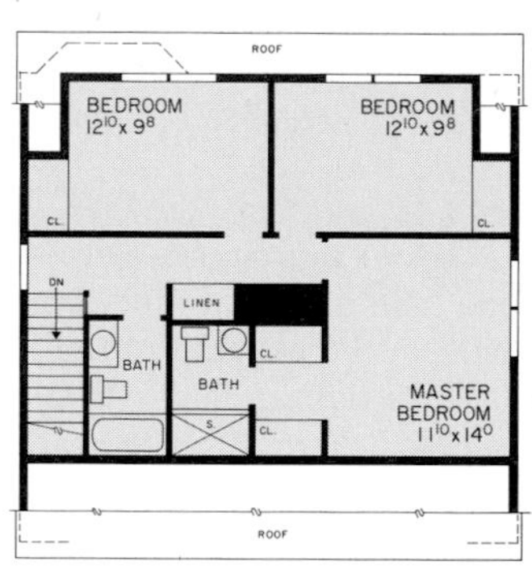

● Here is an expandable Colonial with a full measure of Cape Cod Charm. For those who wish to build the basic house, there is an abundance of low-budget livability. Twin fireplaces serve the formal living room and the informal country kitchen. Note the spaciousness of both areas. A dining room and powder room are also on the first floor of this basic plan. Upstairs three bedrooms and two full baths.

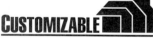

Custom Alterations? See page 251 for customizing this plan to your specifications.

Build Small and Add On Later

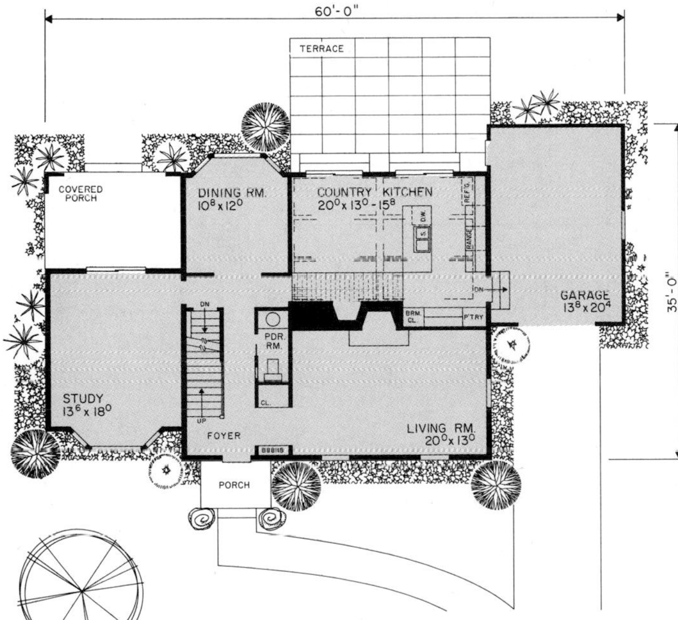

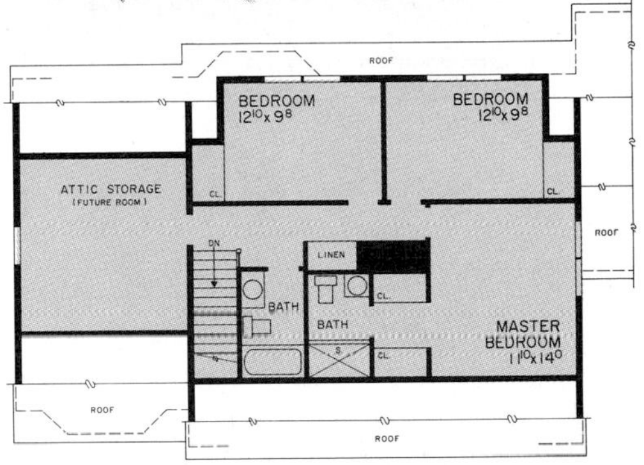

● This expanded version of the basic house on the opposite page is equally as reminiscent of Cape Cod. Common in the 17th-Century was the addition of appendages to the main structure. This occurred as family size increased or finances improved. This version provides for the addition of wings to accommodate a large study and a garage. Utilizing the alcove behind the study results in a big, covered porch. Certainly a charming design whichever version you decide to build for your family.

Design V41372

First Floor: 768 square feet
Second Floor: 432 square feet
Total: 1,200 square feet

● Low cost livability could hardly ask for more. Here, is an enchanting exterior and a four bedroom floor plan. Note stairs to basement.

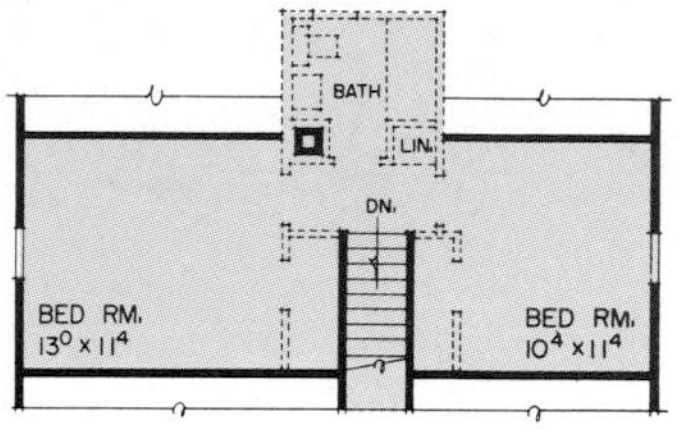

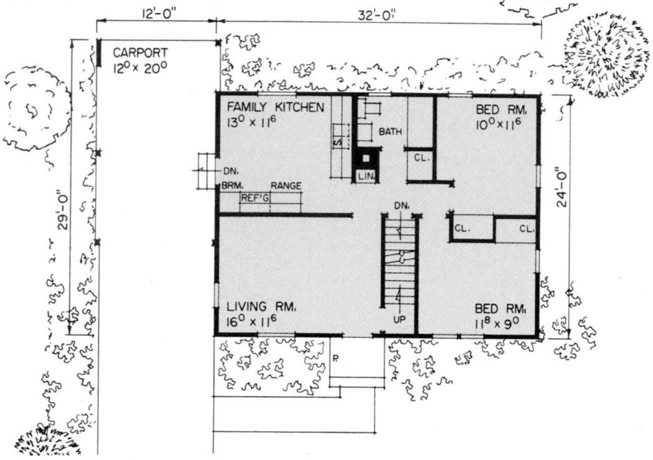

Design V42162

First Floor: 741 square feet
Second Floor: 504 square feet
Total: 1,245 square feet

L D

● This economical design delivers great exterior appeal and fine livability. In addition to kitchen eating space there is a separate dining room.

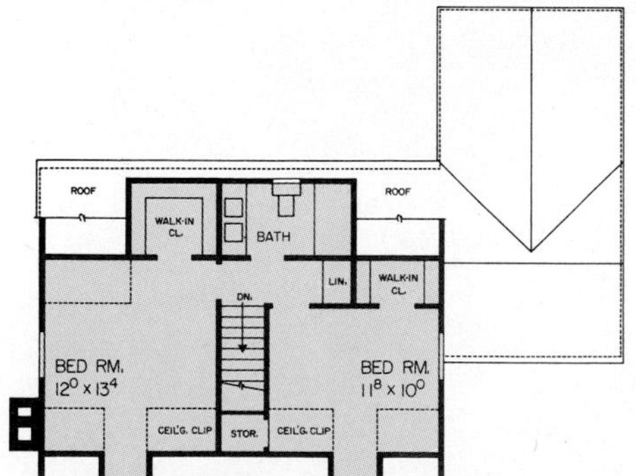

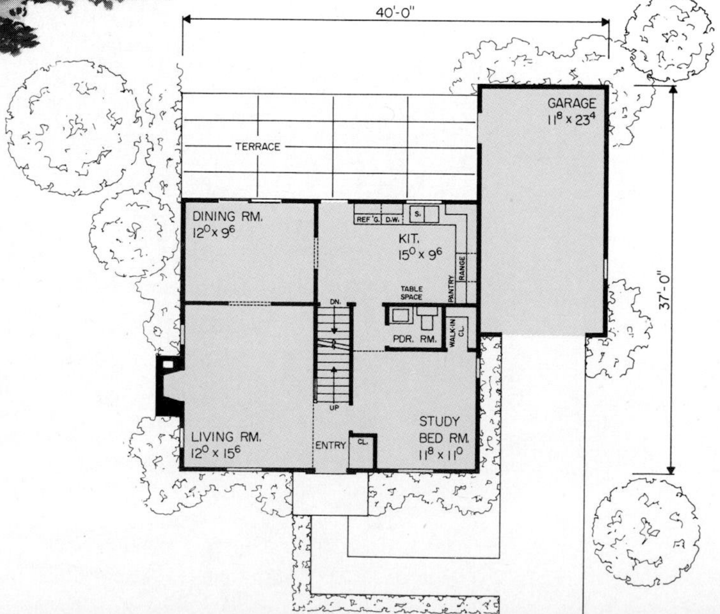

Design V41394

First Floor: 832 square feet
Second Floor: 512 square feet
Total: 1,344 square feet

● The growing family with a restricted building budget will find this a great investment - a convenient living floor plan inside an attractive facade.

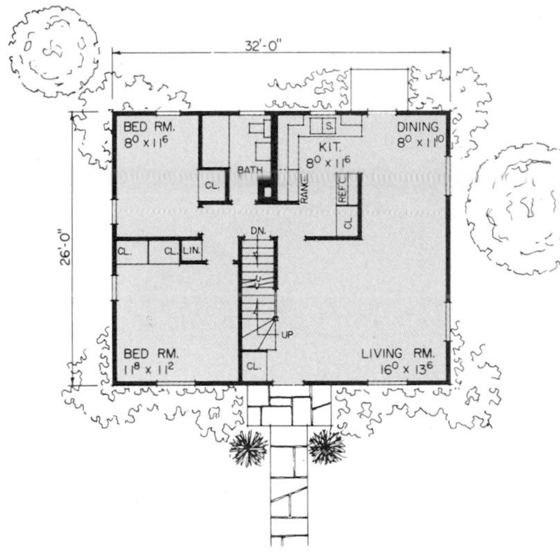

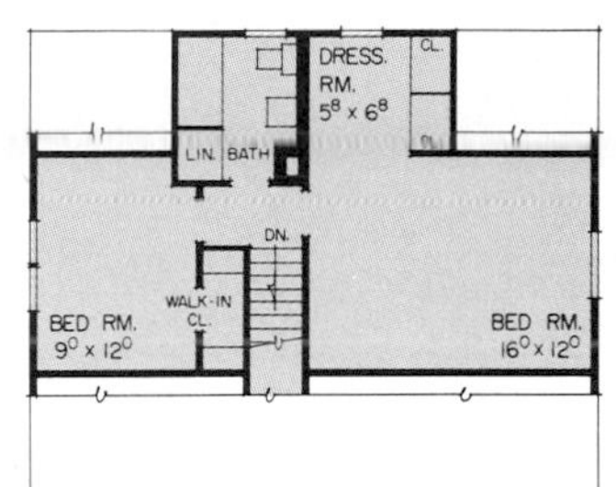

Design V42510

First Floor: 1,191 square feet
Second Floor: 533 square feet
Total: 1,724 square feet

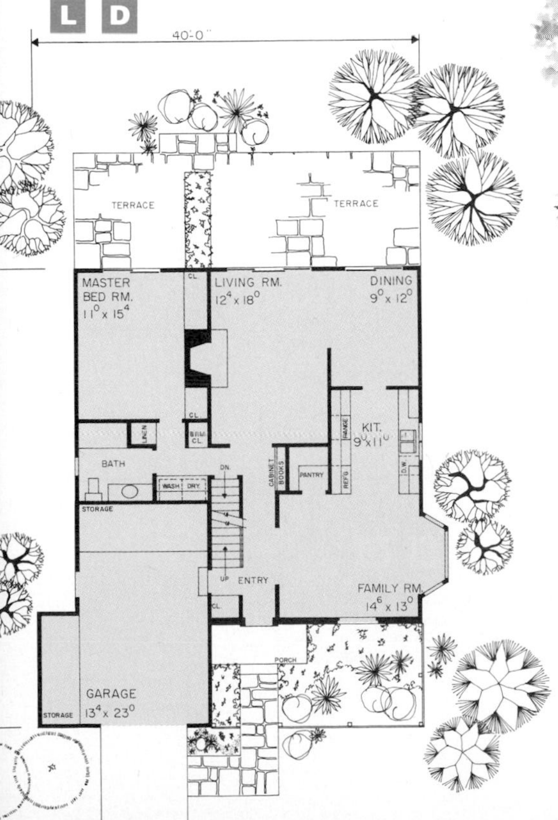

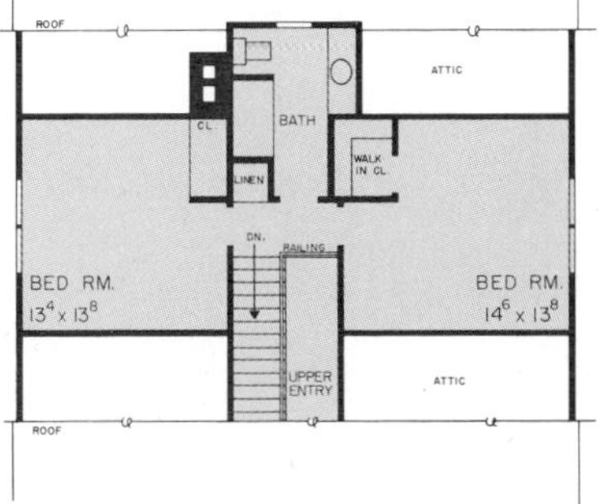

● The pleasant in-line kitchen is flanked by a separate dining room and a family room. The master bedroom is on the first floor with two more bedrooms upstairs.

CUSTOMIZABLE

Custom Alterations? See page 251 for customizing this plan to your specifications.

Design V43302

First Floor: 1,326 square feet
Second Floor: 542 square feet
Total: 1,868 square feet

● A cottage fit for a king! Appreciate the highlights: a two-story foyer, a rear living zone (gathering room, terrace, and dining room), pass-through snack bar in kitchen, a two-story master bedroom. Two upstairs bedrooms share a full bath.

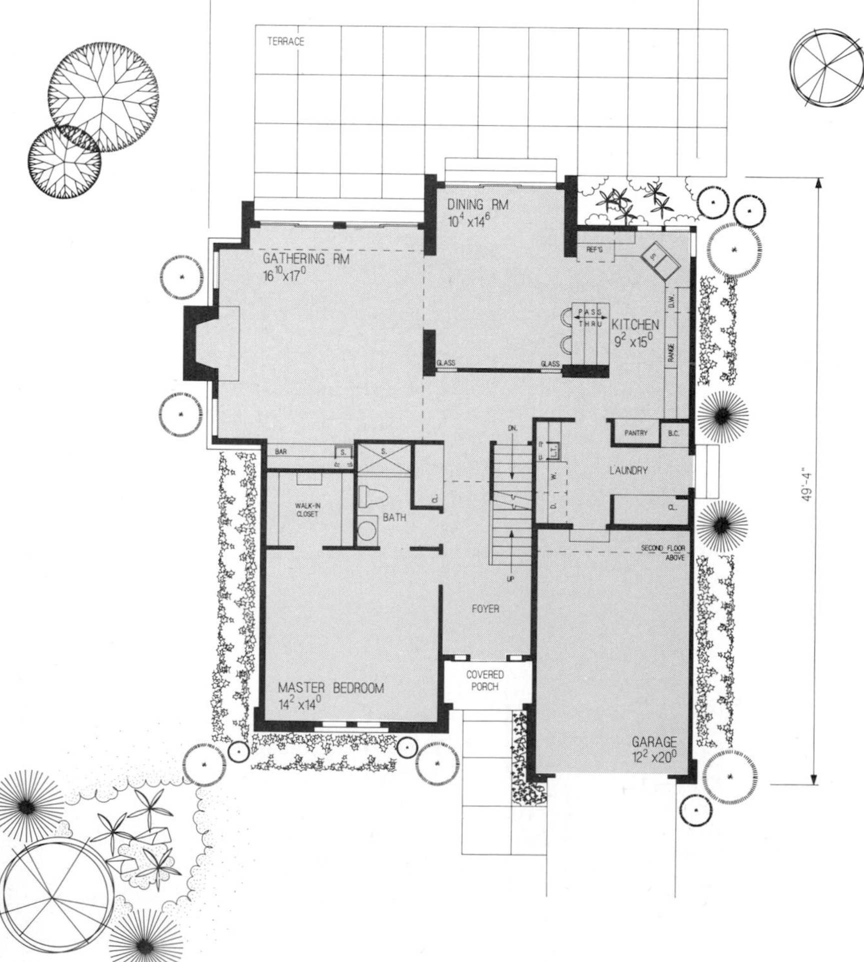

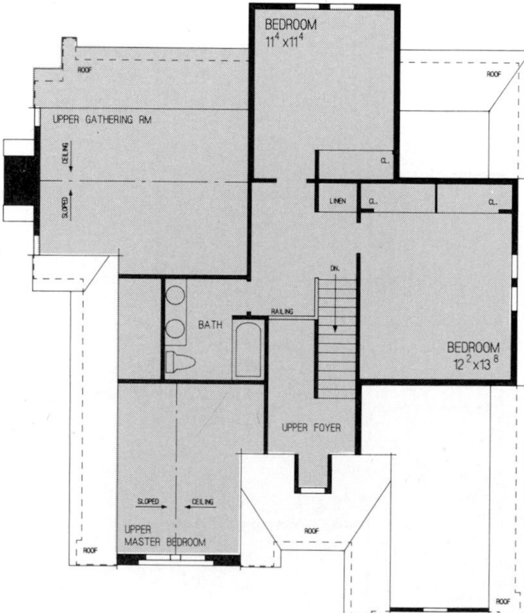

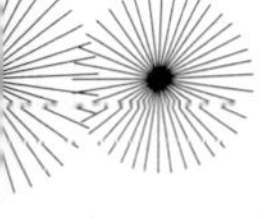

Design V43331

First Floor: 1,115 square feet
Second Floor: 690 square feet
Total: 1,805 square feet

● Who could guess that this compact design contains three bedrooms and two full baths? The kitchen has indoor eating space in the dining room and outdoor eating space in an attached deck. A fireplace in the two-story gathering room welcomes company.

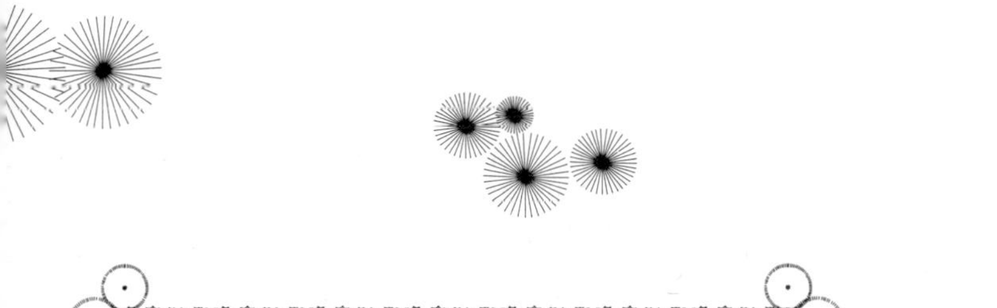

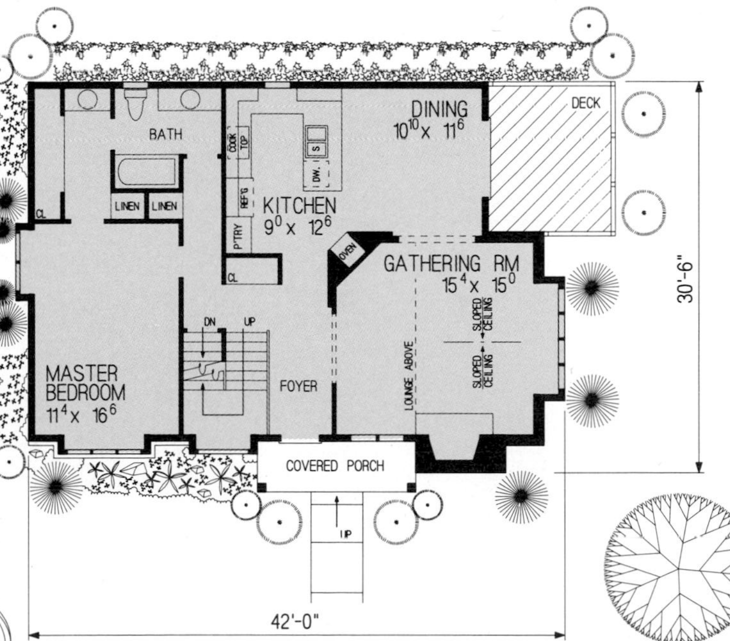

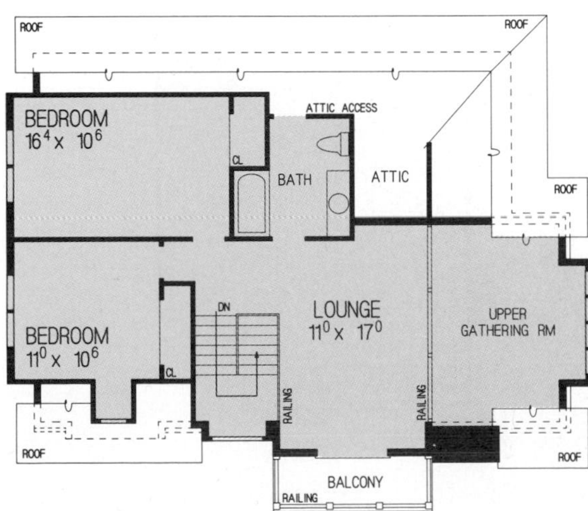

Design V43313

First Floor: 1,482 square feet
Second Floor: 885 square feet
Total: 2,367 square feet

● Cozy living abounds in a first-floor living room and family room, dining room, and kitchen with breakfast room. Two fireplaces keep things warm. Three bedrooms upstairs have more than adequate closet space.

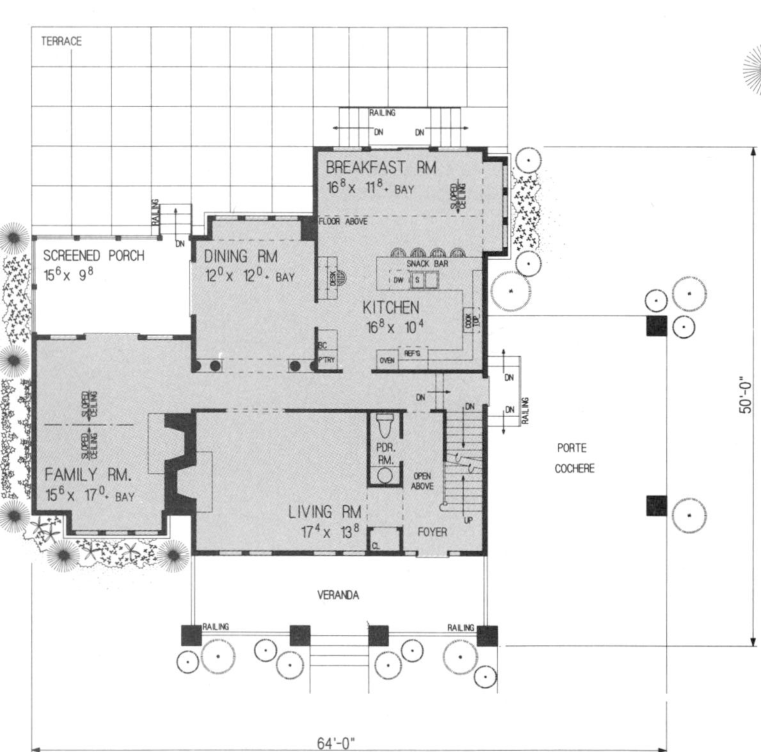

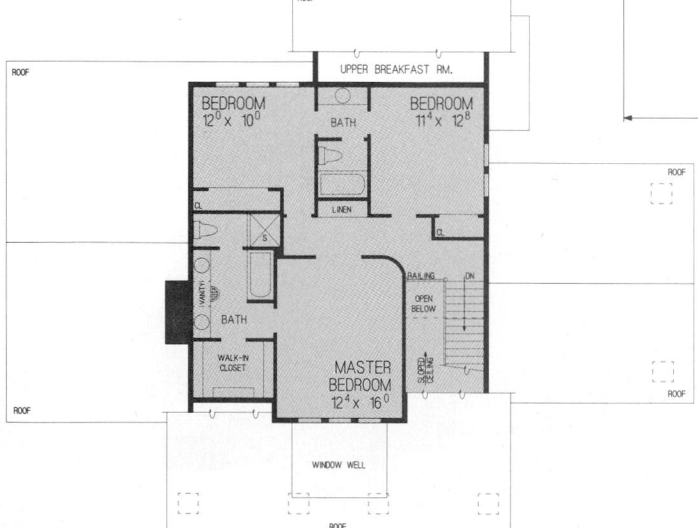

Design V43316

First Floor: 1,111 square feet
Second Floor: 886 square feet
Total: 1,997 square feet

● Don't be fooled by a small-looking exterior. This plan offers three bedrooms and plenty of living space. Notice that the screened porch leads to a rear terrace with access to the breakfast room. A living room/dining room combination adds spaciousness to the first floor.

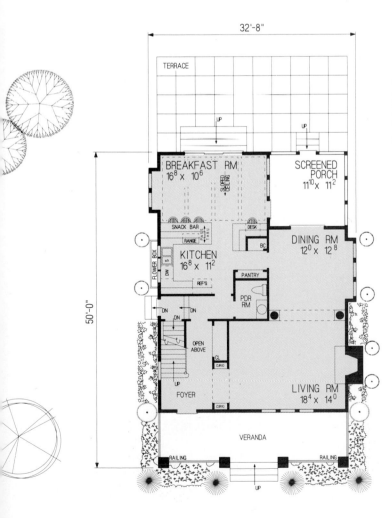

32'-8"
50'-0"
TERRACE
UP
UP
BREAKFAST RM
$16^8 \times 10^6$
SLOPED CEILING
SCREENED PORCH
$11^{10} \times 11^2$
SNACK BAR
DESK
RANGE
PASS THRU
KITCHEN
$16^8 \times 11^2$
FLOWER BOX
DW
S
REF'G
BC
DINING RM
$12^0 \times 12^8$
PANTRY
PDR RM
DN
DN
DN
OPEN ABOVE
CL
CURIO
UP
FOYER
LIVING RM
$18^4 \times 14^0$
CURIO
VERANDA
RAILING
RAILING
UP

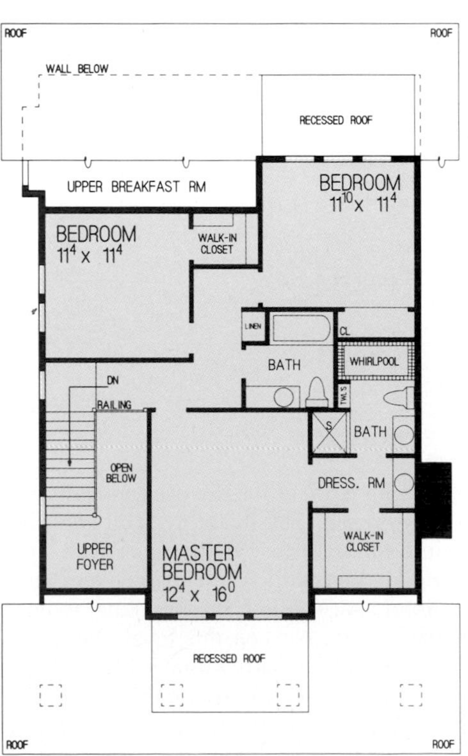

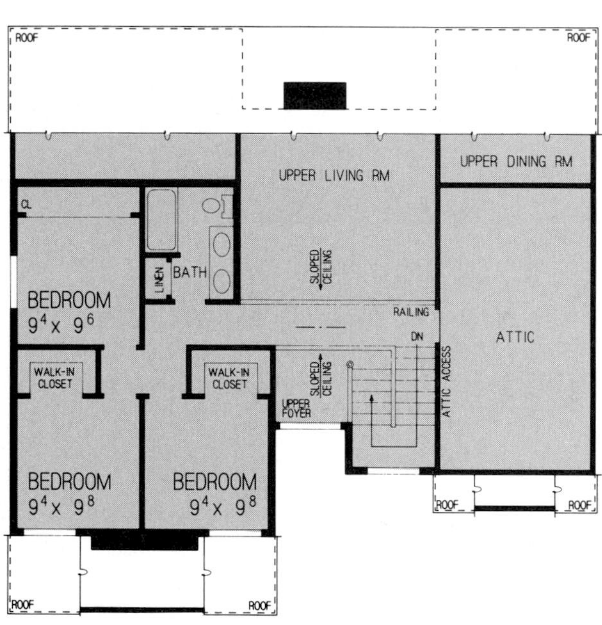

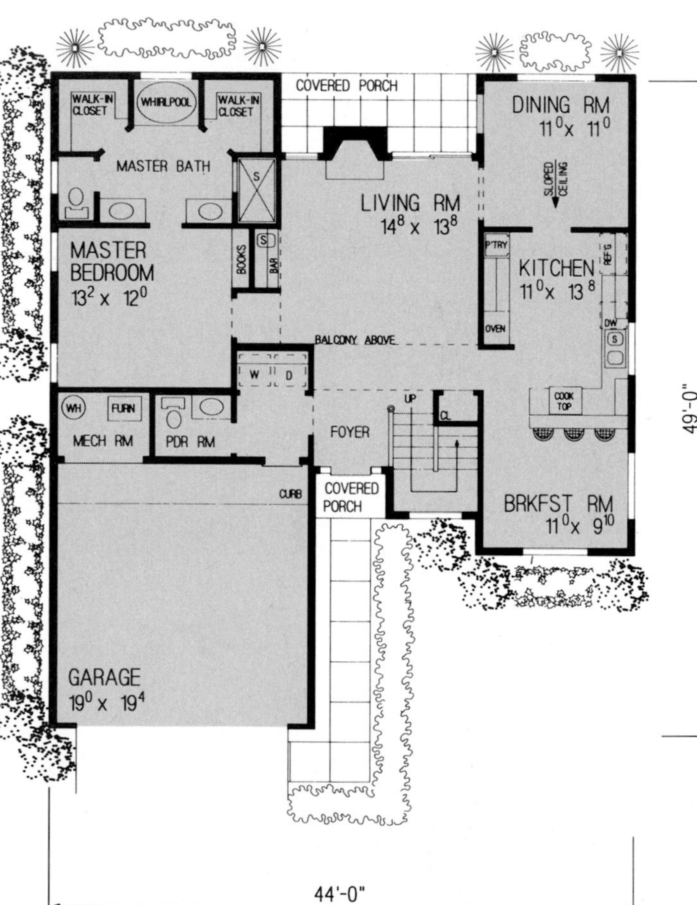

Design V43418

First Floor: 1,283 square feet
Second Floor: 552 square feet
Total: 1,835 square feet

● This home is ideal for the economically minded who don't want to sacrifice livability. The entry foyer opens directly into the two-story living room with fireplace. To the right, the kitchen with peninsula cooktop and snack bar conveniently serves both the breakfast room and the formal dining room. Also on this level, the master bedroom boasts an enormous bath with a whirlpool and His and Hers walk-in closets. Three other bedrooms are located upstairs to ensure peace and quiet. Also notice the abundant storage space in the attic.

Custom Alterations? See page 251 for customizing this plan to your specifications.

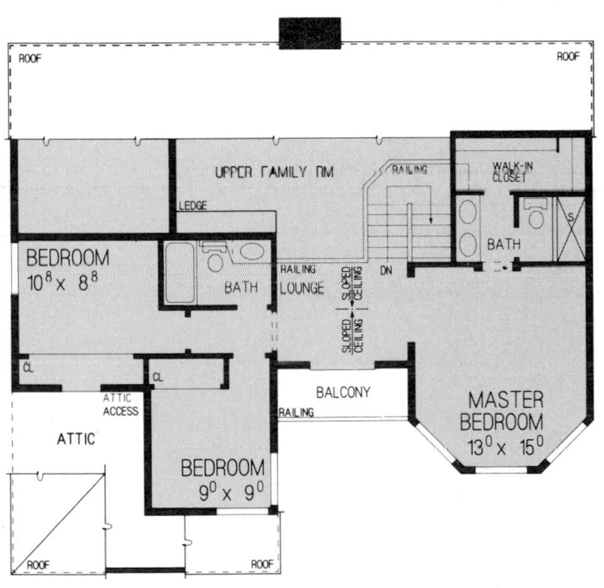

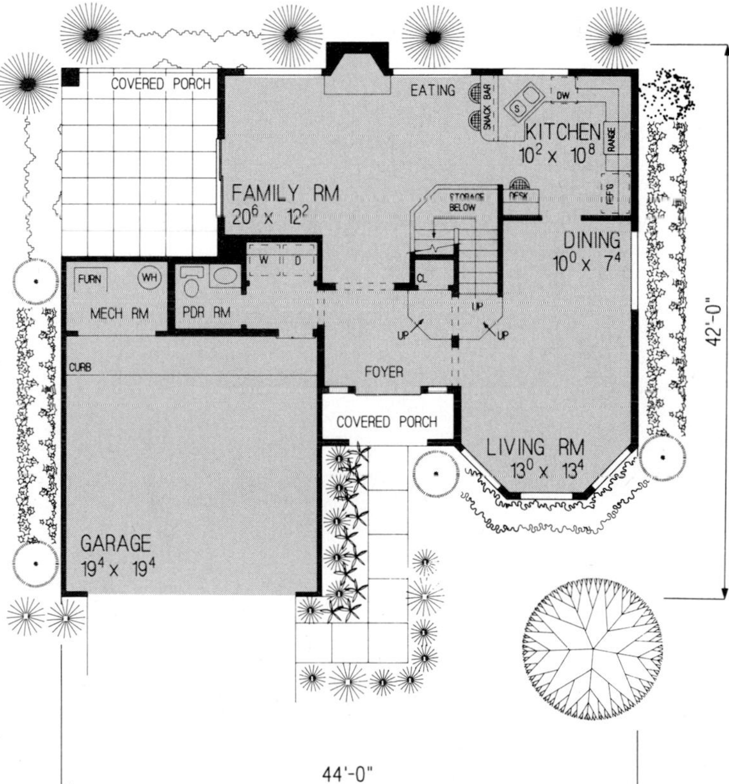

Design V43417 First Floor: 875 square feet
Second Floor: 731 square feet; Total: 1,606 square feet

● Perfect for a starter home, this design is compact yet features great livability. The plan provides both formal and informal living areas. There's a living room with bay window and adjacent dining area. Open to the kitchen, the spacious family room is large enough to accommodate an informal eating area. The second floor boasts a balcony lounge overlooking the family room, master bedroom with bay window and two smaller family bedrooms.

Custom Alterations? See page 251 for customizing this plan to your specifications.

Design V41354

First Floor: 644 square feet
Second Floor: 572 square feet
Total: 1,216 square feet

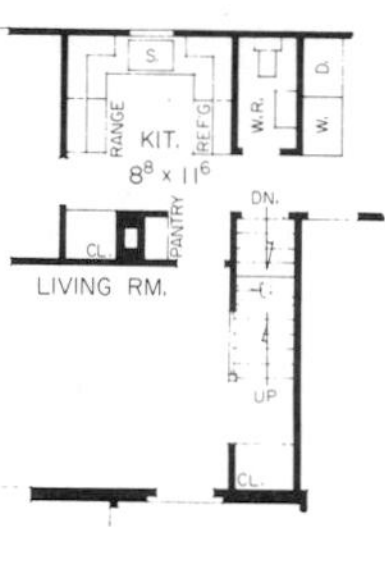

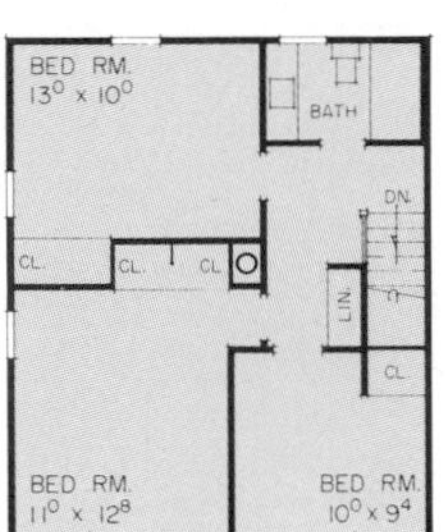

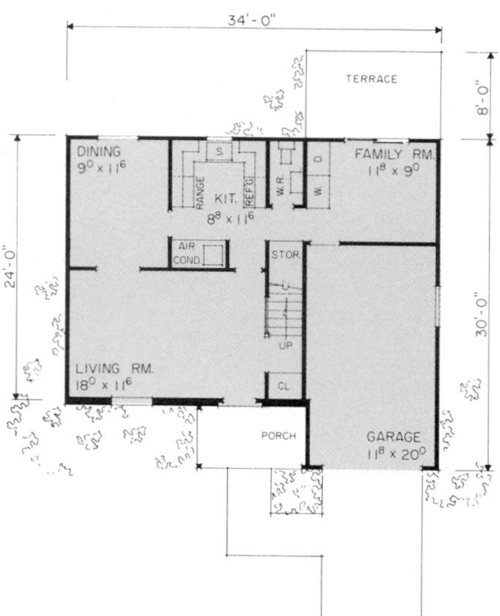

Design V41913

First Floor: 740 square feet
Second Floor: 728 square feet
Total: 1,468 square feet

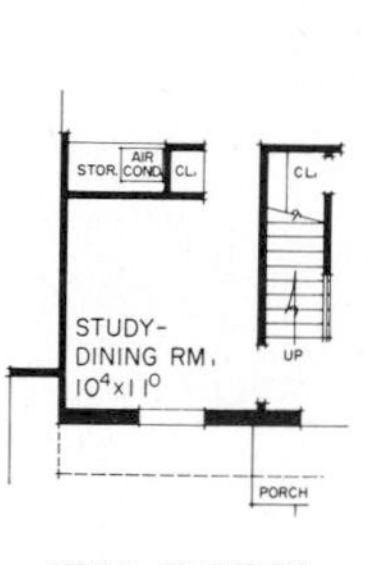

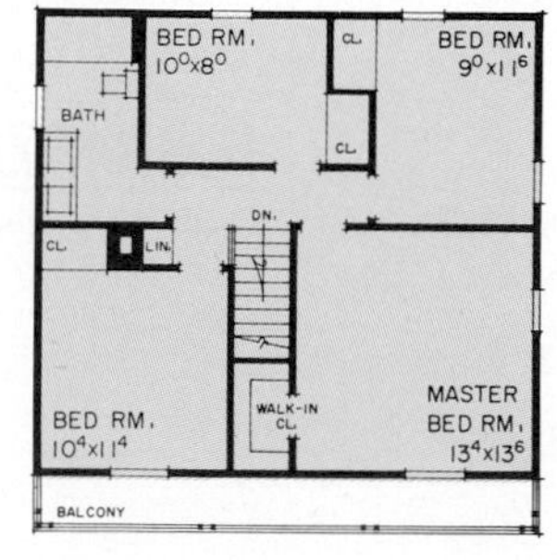

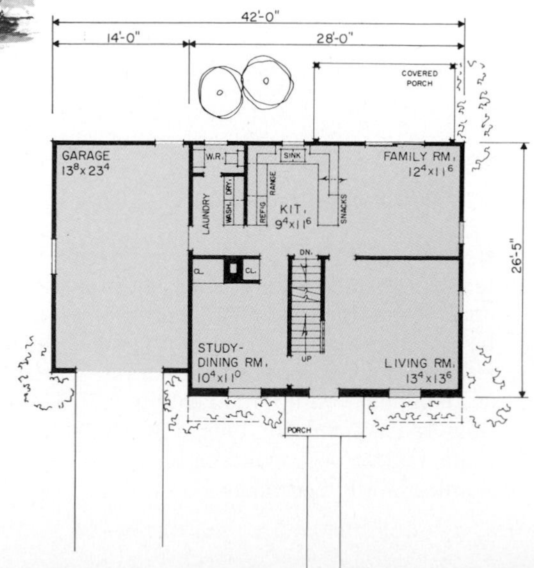

Design V43501

First Floor: 960 square feet
Second Floor: 762 square feet
Total: 1,722 square feet

● This efficient Saltbox design includes three bedrooms and two full baths plus a handy powder room on the first floor. A large living room in the front of the home features a fireplace. The rear of the home is left open, with room for a kitchen with snack bar, breakfast area with fireplace and dining room with outdoor access. If you wish, use the breakfast area as an all-purpose dining room and turn the dining room into a library or sitting room.

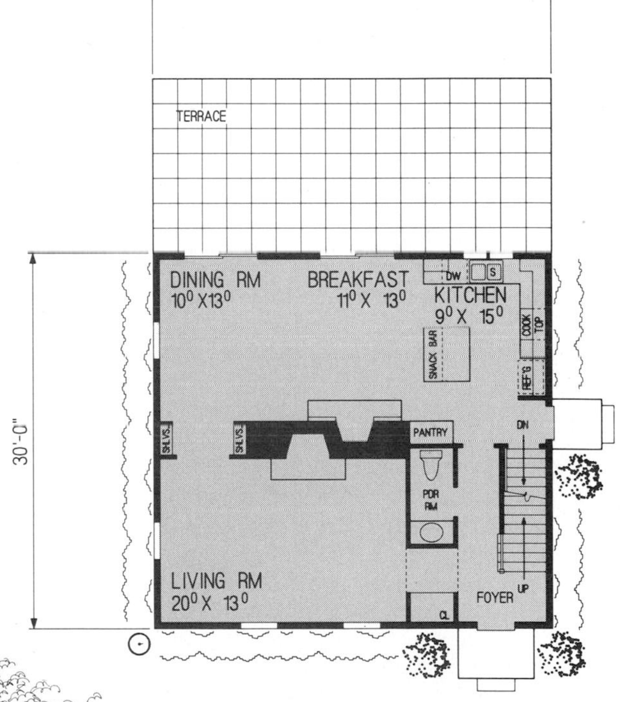

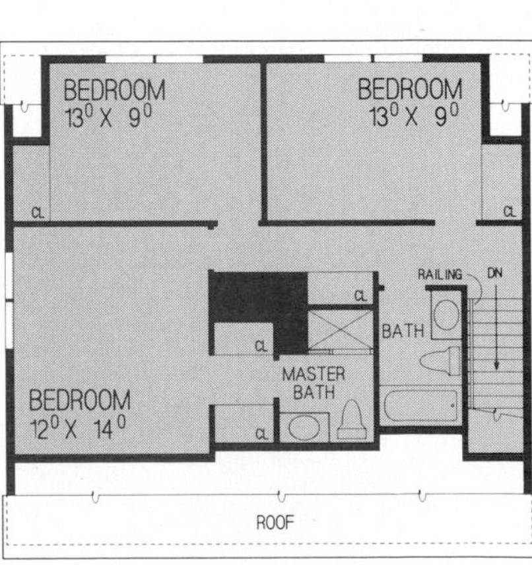

Design V42923

First Floor: 1,100 square feet
Second Floor: 970 square feet
Total: 2,070 square feet

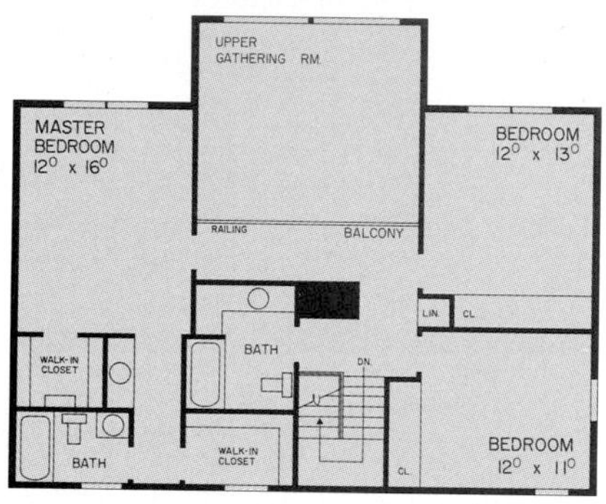

● This Trend Home is as charming on the outside as it is comfortable on the inside. Note the Early American window treatments, second-story overhang, central fireplace, and textured look of stone and board siding. Inside one finds a large rear gathering room with fireplace, efficient U-shaped kitchen, formal dining room, study, and foyer on the first floor. Upstairs are three bedrooms plus an upper gathering room. The two-car garage includes storage space. Note the view windows and covered porch in the rear.

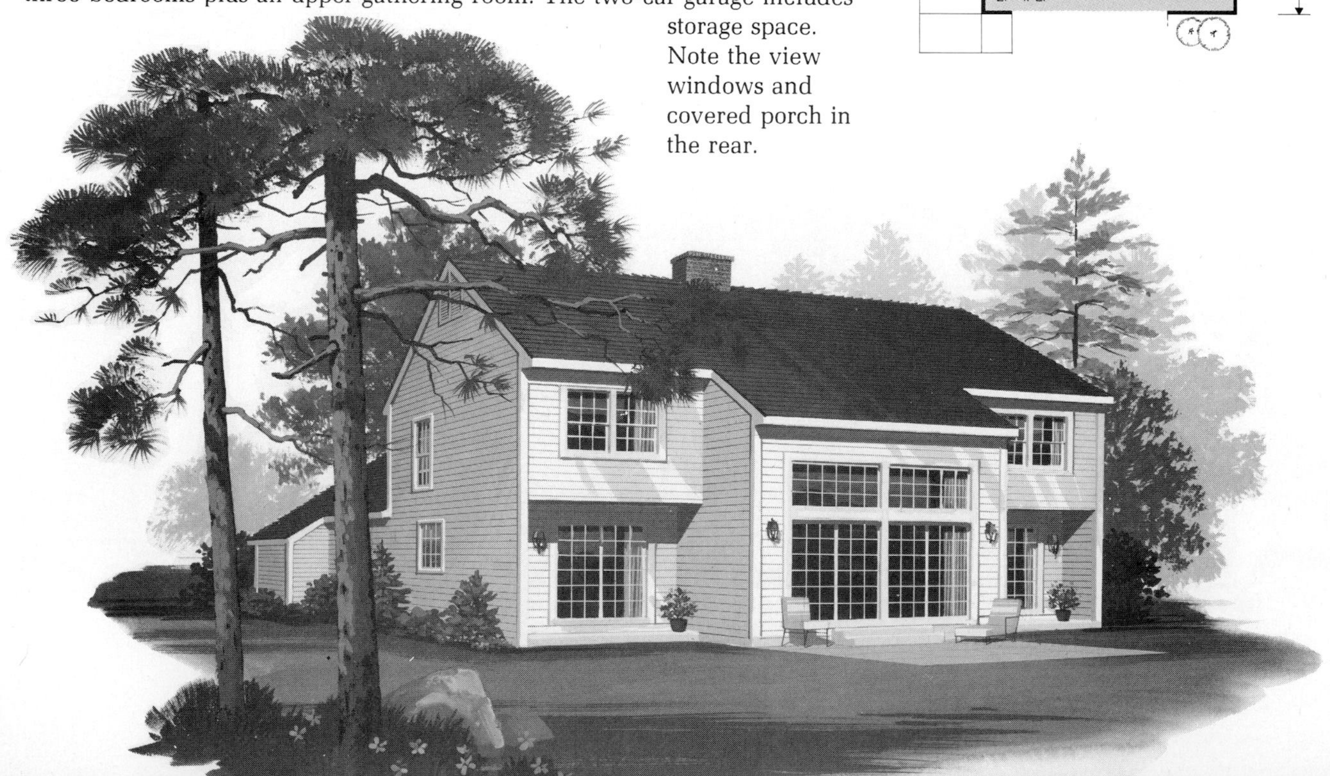

CUSTOMIZABLE

Custom Alterations? See page 251 for customizing this plan to your specifications.

Design V42826

First Floor: 1,112 square feet
Second Floor: 881 square feet
Total: 1,993 square feet

D

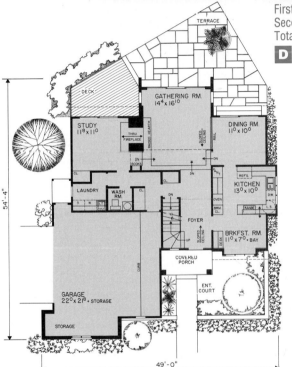

TERRACE
DECK
GATHERING RM. 14^4 x 16^{10}
STUDY 11^8 x 11^0
DINING RM. 11^0 x 10^0
KITCHEN 13^0 x 10^0
LAUNDRY
WASH RM.
FOYER
BRKFST. RM. 11^0 x 7^0 + BAY
COVERED PORCH
ENT. COURT
GARAGE 22^0 x 21^8 + STORAGE
STORAGE
54'-4"
49'-0"

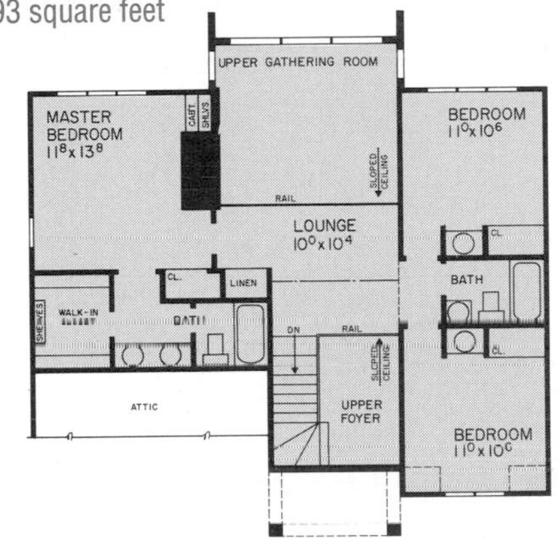

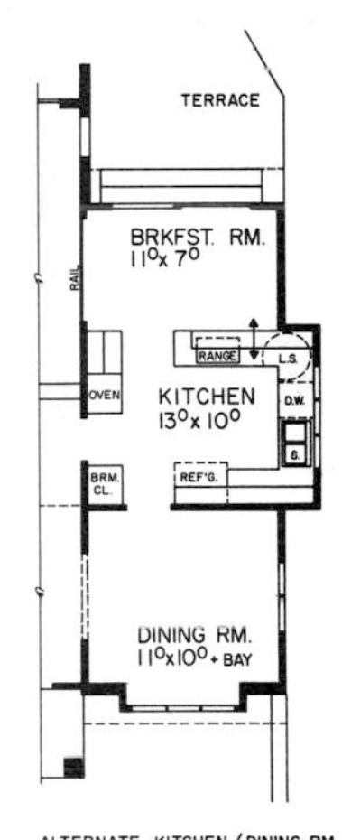

ALTERNATE KITCHEN/DINING RM/ BREAKFAST RM. FLOOR PLAN

● This is an outstanding example of the type of informal, traditional-style architecture that has captured the modern imagination. The interior plan houses all the features that people want most - a spacious gathering room, formal and informal dining areas, efficient, U-shaped kitchen, master bedroom, two children's bedrooms, second-floor lounge, entrance court and rear terrace and deck. Study all areas of this plan carefully.

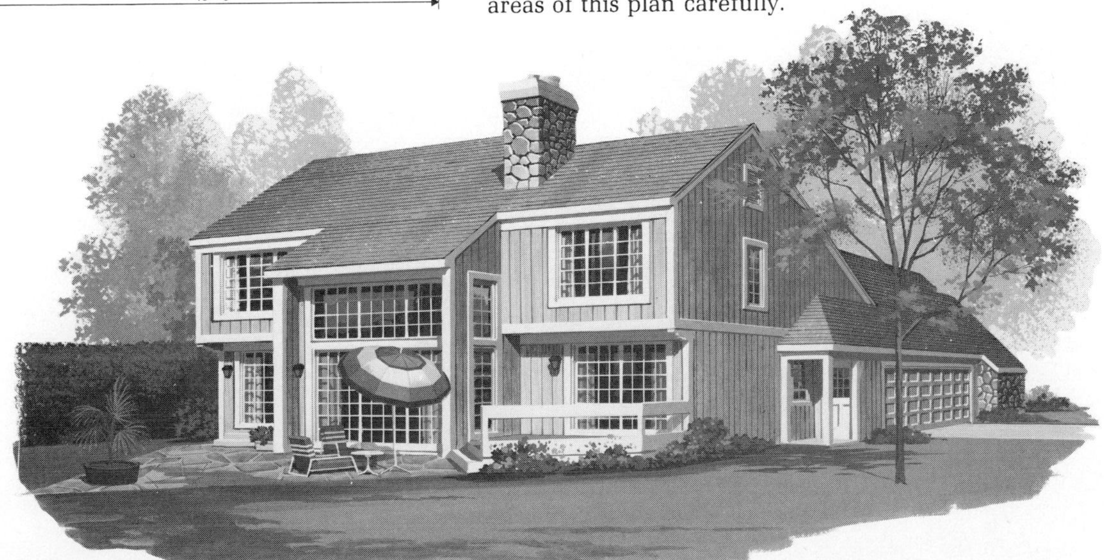

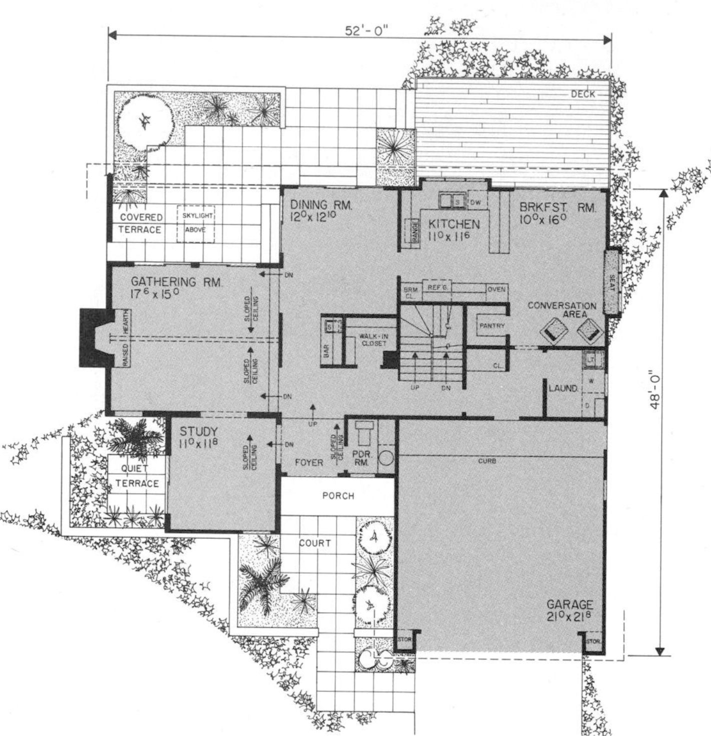

Design V42823

First Floor: 1,370 square feet
Second Floor: 927 square feet
Total: 2,297 square feet

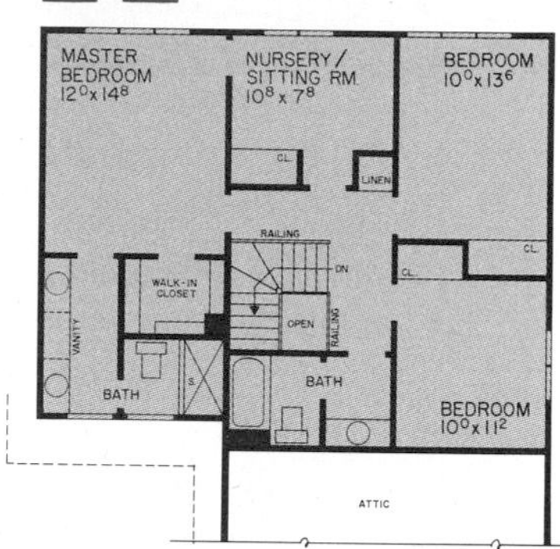

● The street view of this contemporary design features a small courtyard entrance as well as a private terrace off the study. Inside the livability will be outstanding. This design features spacious first floor activity areas that flow smoothly into each other. In the gathering room a raised hearth fireplace creates a dramatic focal point. An adjacent covered terrace, featuring a skylight, is ideal for outdoor dining and could be screened in later for an additional room.

CUSTOMIZABLE

Custom Alterations? See page 251 for customizing this plan to your specifications.

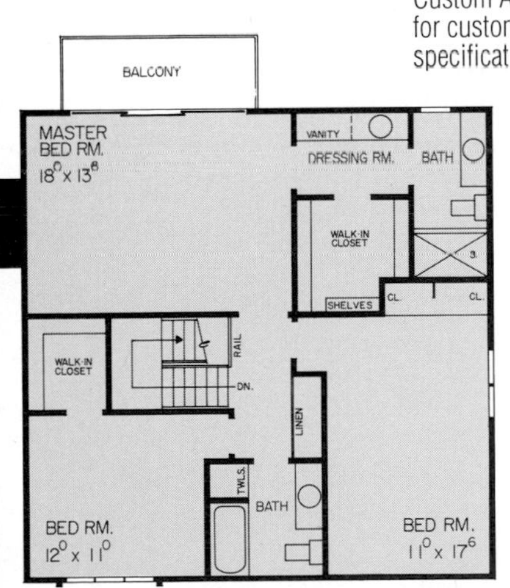

Design V42711

First Floor: 975 square feet
Second Floor: 1,024 square feet
Total: 1,999 square feet

L **D**

● Special features! A complete master suite with a private balcony plus two more bedrooms and a bath upstairs. The first floor has a study with a storage closet. A convenient snack bar between kitchen and dining room. The kitchen offers many built-in appliances. Plus a gathering room and dining room that measures 31 feet wide. Note the curb area in the garage and fireplace in gathering room.

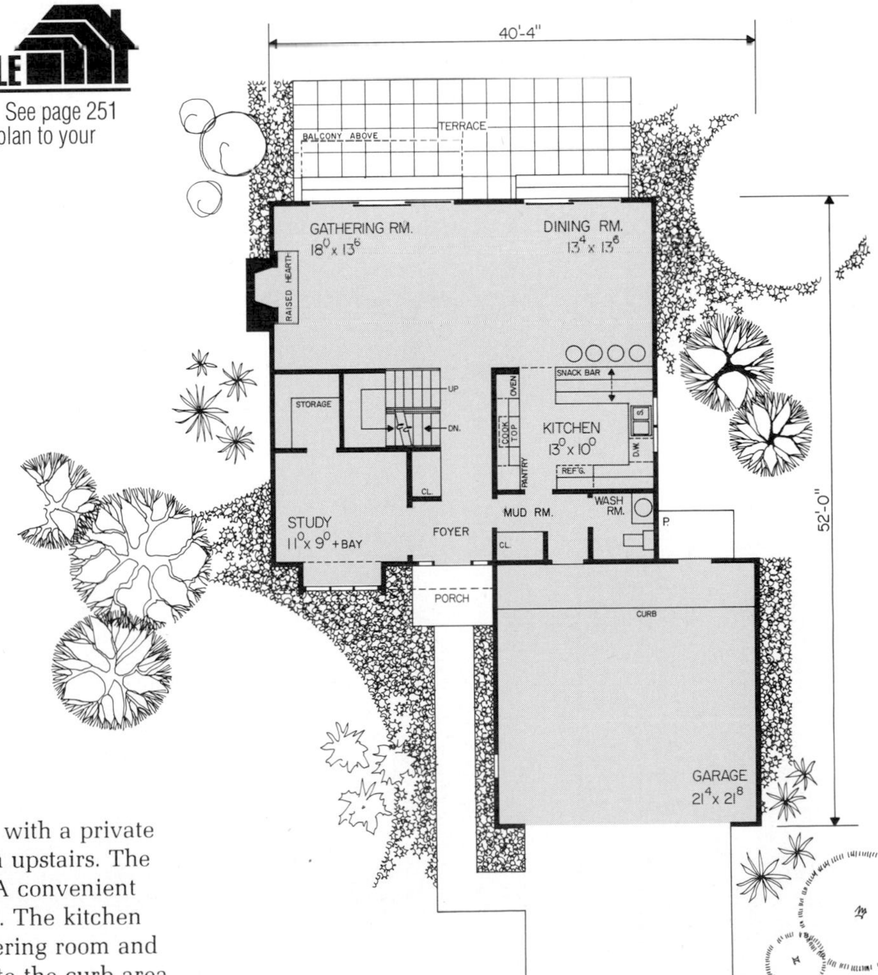

Design V42493

First Floor: 1,387 square feet
Second Floor: 929 square feet
Total: 2,316 square feet

● Perfect for a narrow lot, this shingle-and stone-sided Nantucket Cape caters to the casual lifestyle. The side entrance gives direct access to the wonderfully open living areas: gathering room with fireplace, kitchen with angled, pass-through snack bar, dining area with sliding glass doors to a covered eating area. Note also the large deck that further extends the living potential. Also on this floor is a large master suite. Upstairs is a convenient guest suite with private balcony. It is complemented by two smaller bedrooms.

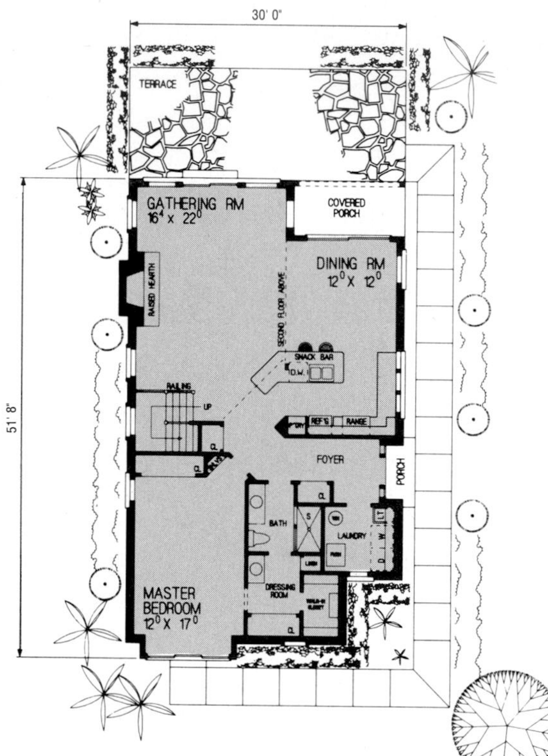

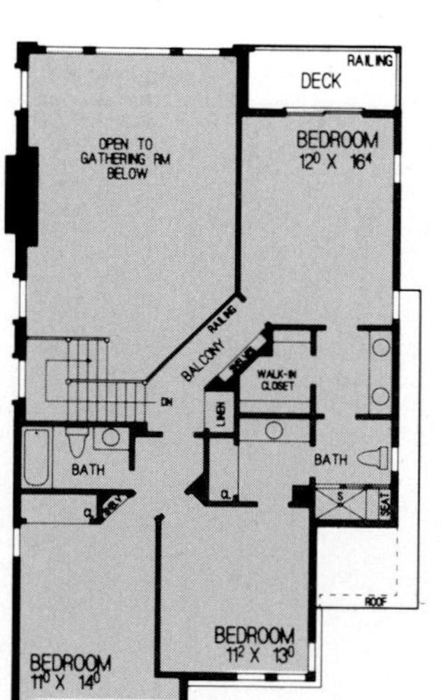

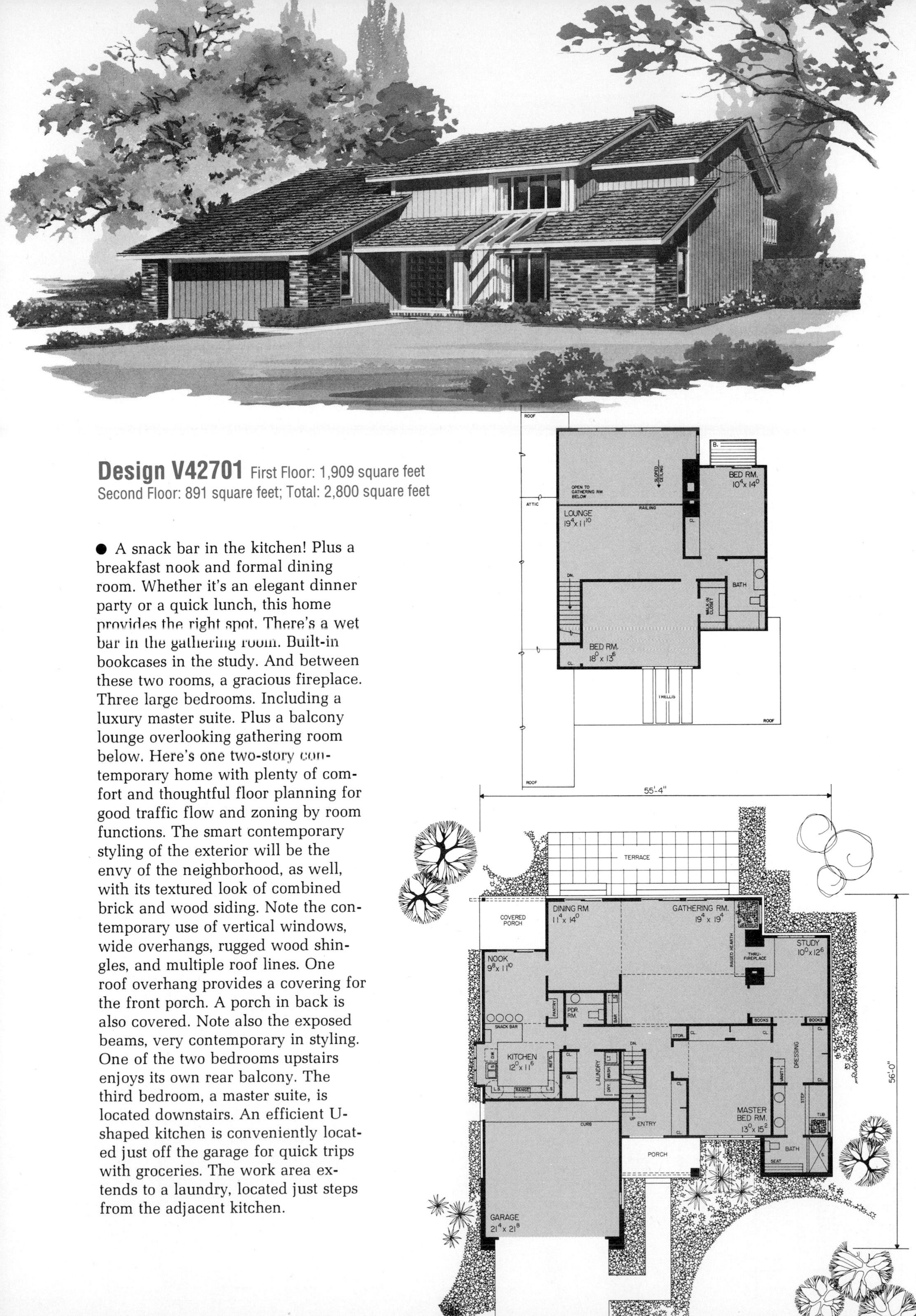

Design V42701 First Floor: 1,909 square feet

Second Floor: 891 square feet; Total: 2,800 square feet

● A snack bar in the kitchen! Plus a breakfast nook and formal dining room. Whether it's an elegant dinner party or a quick lunch, this home provides the right spot. There's a wet bar in the gathering room. Built-in bookcases in the study. And between these two rooms, a gracious fireplace. Three large bedrooms. Including a luxury master suite. Plus a balcony lounge overlooking gathering room below. Here's one two-story contemporary home with plenty of comfort and thoughtful floor planning for good traffic flow and zoning by room functions. The smart contemporary styling of the exterior will be the envy of the neighborhood, as well, with its textured look of combined brick and wood siding. Note the contemporary use of vertical windows, wide overhangs, rugged wood shingles, and multiple roof lines. One roof overhang provides a covering for the front porch. A porch in back is also covered. Note also the exposed beams, very contemporary in styling. One of the two bedrooms upstairs enjoys its own rear balcony. The third bedroom, a master suite, is located downstairs. An efficient U-shaped kitchen is conveniently located just off the garage for quick trips with groceries. The work area extends to a laundry, located just steps from the adjacent kitchen.

Design V42780

First Floor: 2,006 square feet
Second Floor: 718 square feet
Total: 2,724 square feet

● This 1½-story contemporary has more fine features than one can imagine. The livability is outstanding and can be appreciated by the whole family. Note the fine indoor-outdoor living relationships.

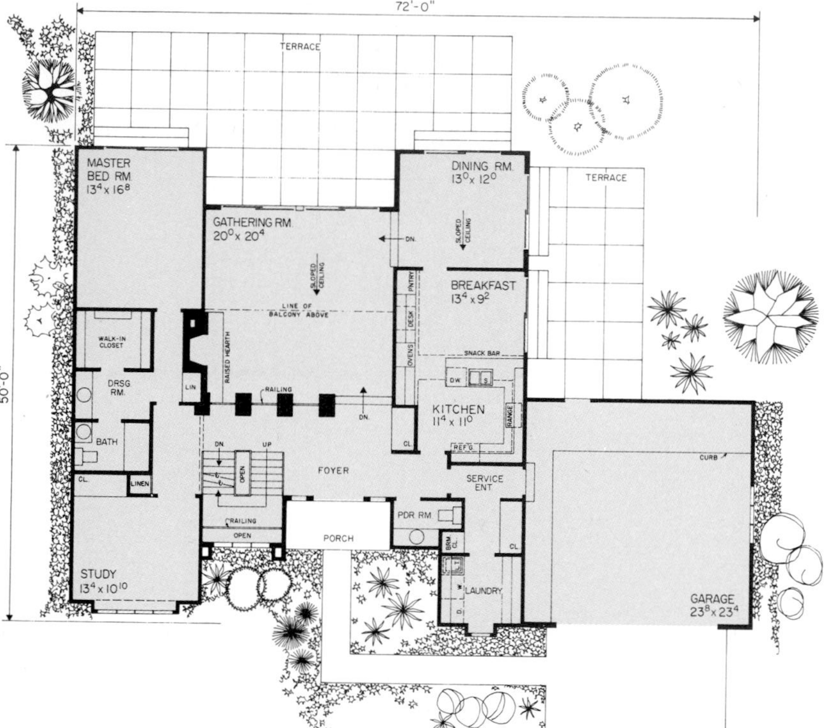

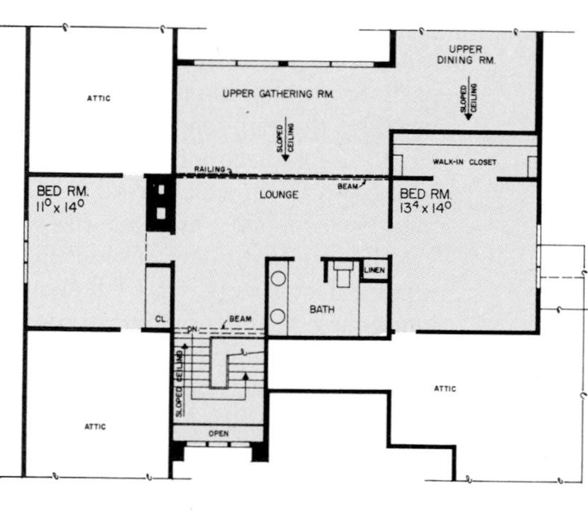

Design V42772

First Floor: 1,579 square feet
Second Floor: 1,240 square feet; Total: 2,819 square feet

● This four-bedroom two-story contemporary design is sure to suit your growing family needs. The rear U-shaped kitchen, flanked by the family and dining rooms, will be very efficient to the busy homemaker. Parents will enjoy all the convenience of the master bedroom suite.

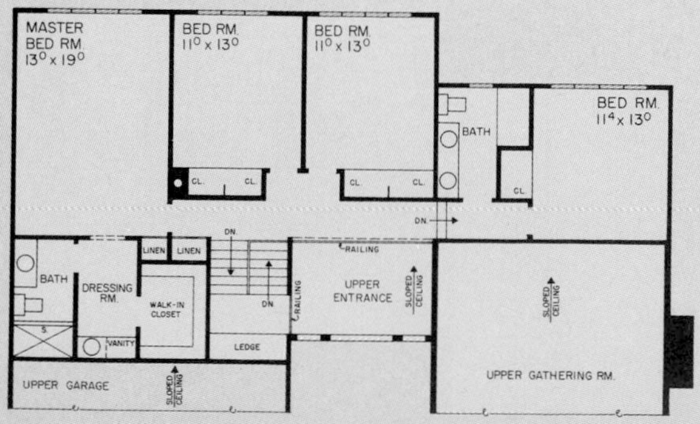

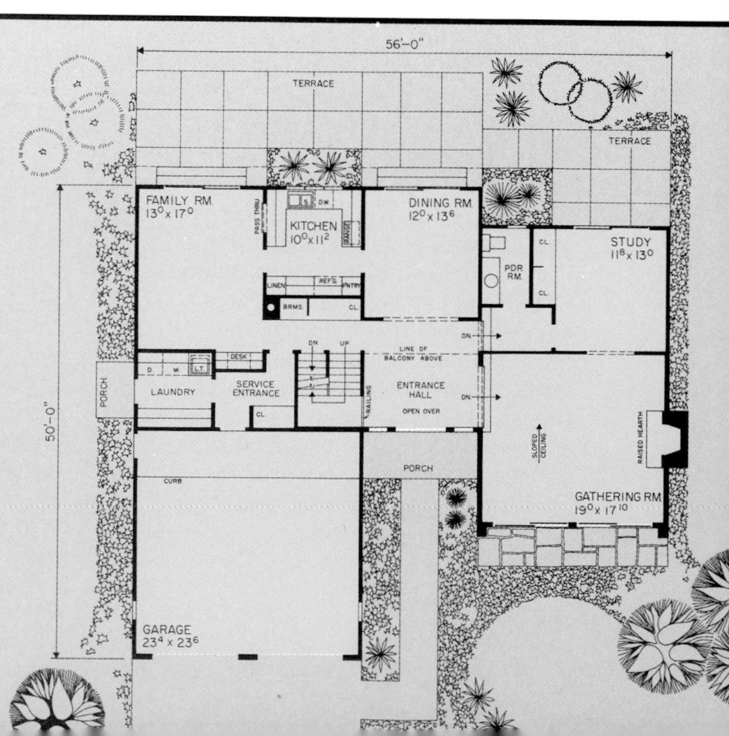

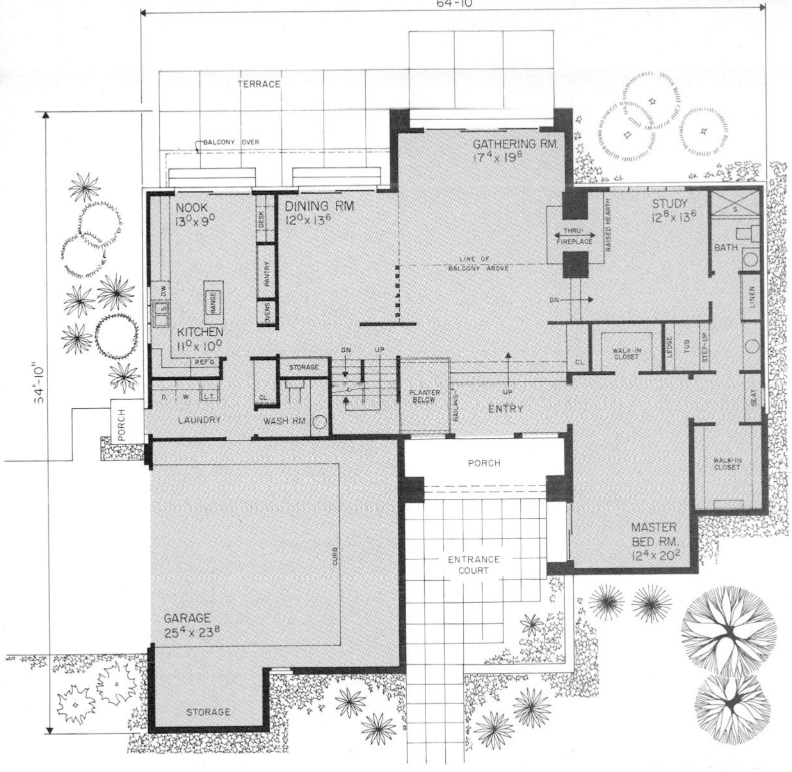

Design V42771

First Floor: 2,087 square feet
Second Floor: 816 square feet
Total: 2,903 square feet

● This design will provide an abundance of livability for your family. The second floor is highlighted by an open lounge which overlooks both the entry and the gathering room below.

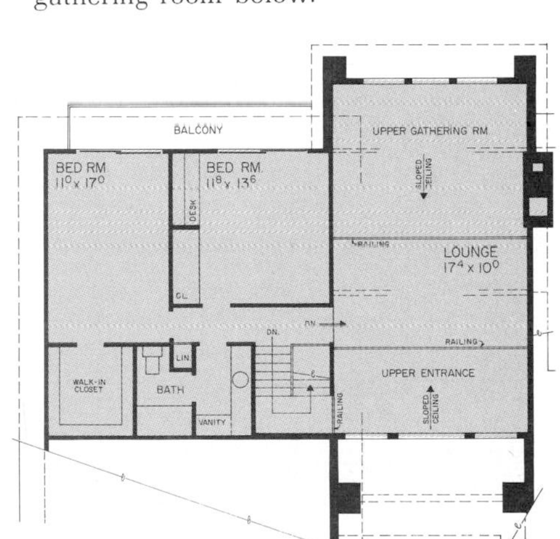

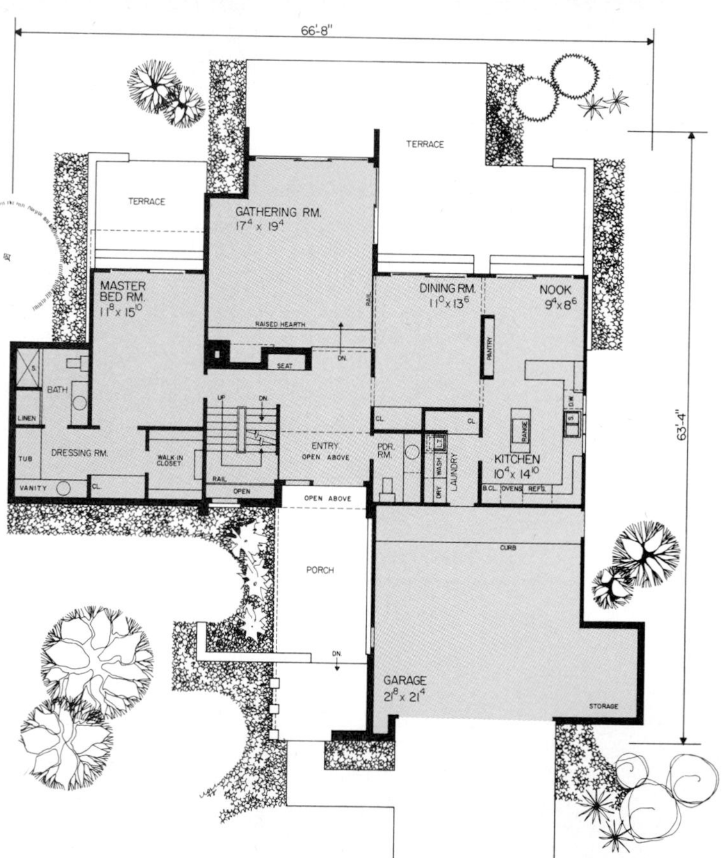

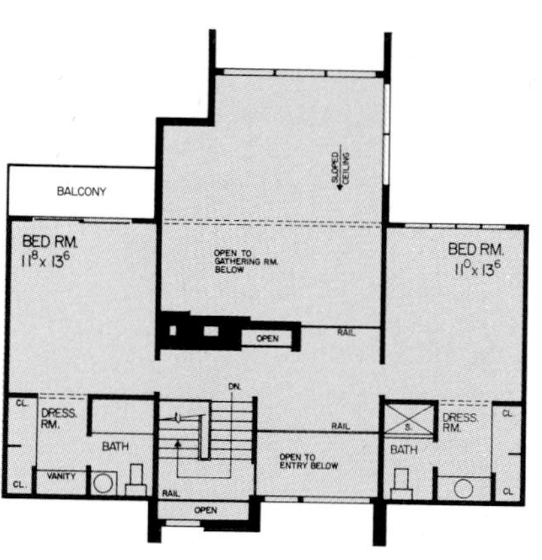

Design V42729

First Floor: 1,590 square feet
Second Floor: 756 square feet
Total: 2,346 square feet

● Entering this home will surely be a pleasure through the sheltered walk-way to the double front doors. And the pleasure and beauty does not stop there. The entry hall and sunken gathering room are open to the upstairs for added dimension. There's even a built-in seat in the entry area. The kitchen-nook area is very efficient with its many built-ins and the adjacent laundry room. There is a fine indoor-outdoor living relationship in this design. Note the private terrace off the luxurious master bedroom suite, a living terrace accessible from the gathering room, dining room and nook plus the balcony off the upstairs bedroom. Upstairs there is a total of two bedrooms, each having its own private bath and plenty of closets.

Design V42379 First Floor: 1,525 square feet; Second Floor: 748 square feet; Total: 2,273 square feet

L **D**

● A house that has "everything" may very well look just like this design. Its exterior is well-proportioned and impressive. Inside the inviting double front doors there are features galore. The living room and family room level are sunken. Separating these two rooms is a dramatic thru fireplace. A built-in bar, planter and beamed ceiling highlight the family room. Nearby is a full bath and a study which could be utilized as a fourth bedroom. The fine functioning kitchen has a pass-thru to the snack bar in the breakfast nook. The adjacent dining room overlooks the living room and has sliding doors to the covered porch. Upstairs three bedrooms, two baths and an outdoor balcony. Blueprints for this design include optional basement details.

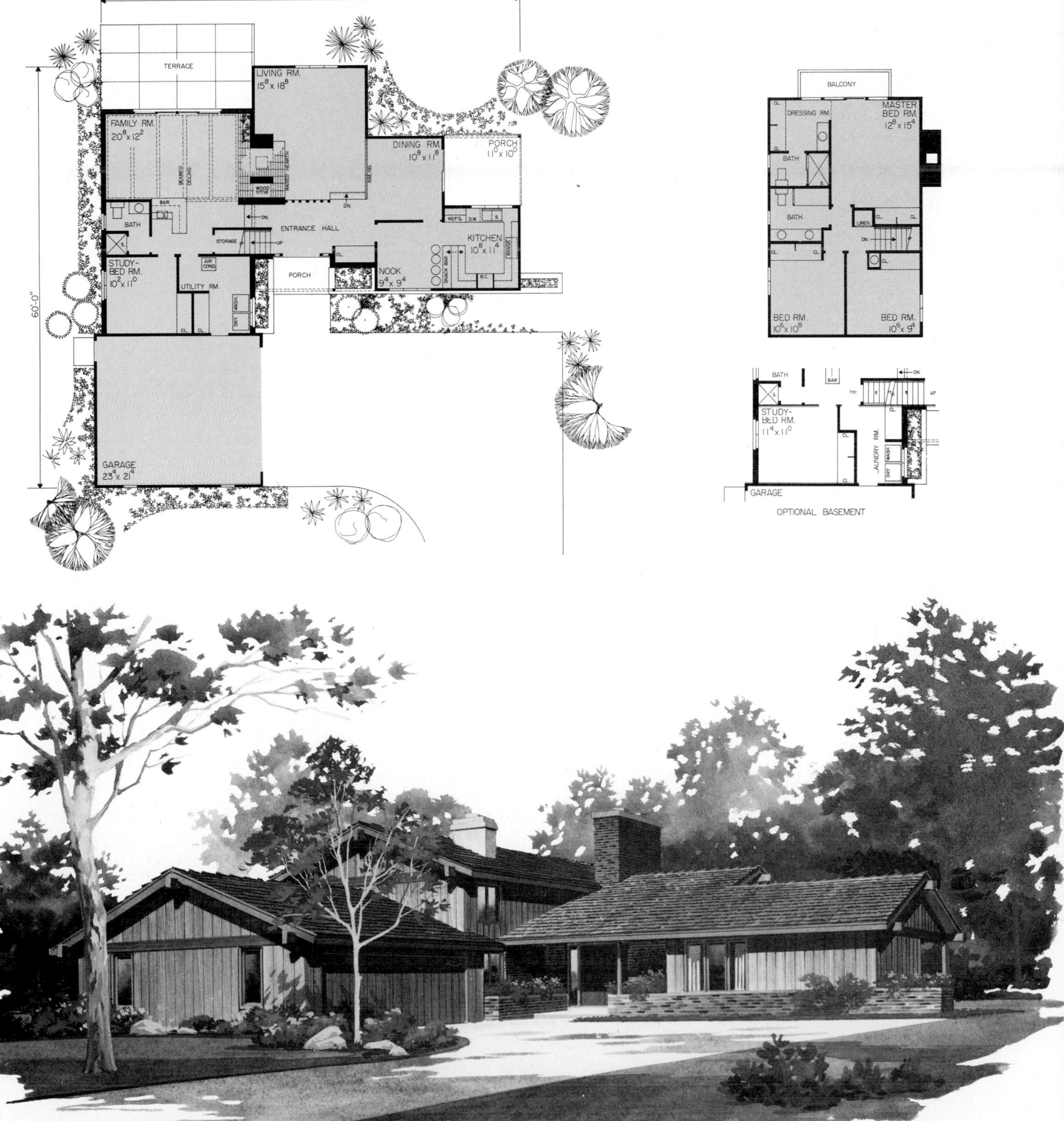

Second-Floor Space

Design V42821

First Floor: 1,363 square feet
Second Floor: 357 square feet
Total: 1,720 square feet

● Here is a truly unique house whose interior was designed with the current decade's economies, lifestyles and demographics in mind. While functioning as a one-story home, the second floor provides an extra measure of livability when required. In addition, this two-story section adds to the dramatic appeal of both the exterior and the interior. Within only 1,363 square feet, this contemporary delivers refreshing and outstanding living patterns for those who are buying their first home, those who have raised their family and are looking for a smaller home and those in search of a retirement home. The center entrance routes traffic effectively to each area. The great room with its raised-hearth fireplace, two-story arching and delightful glass areas is most distinctive. The kitchen is efficient and but a step from the dining room. The covered porch will provide an ideal spot for warm-weather, outdoor dining. The separate laundry room is strategically located. The sleeping area may consist of one bedroom and a study, or two bedrooms. Each room functions with the sheltered wood deck, a perfect location for a hot tub.

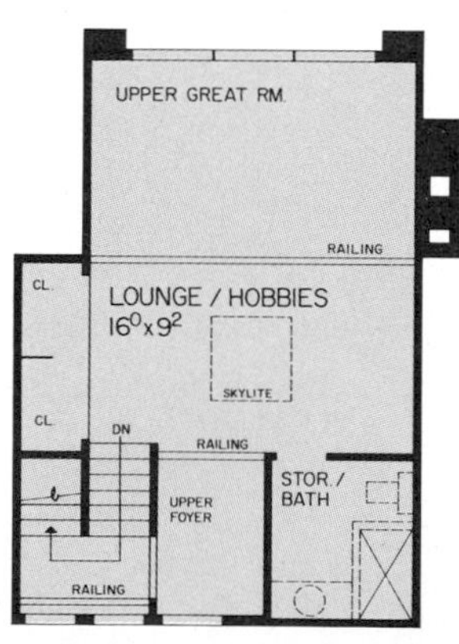

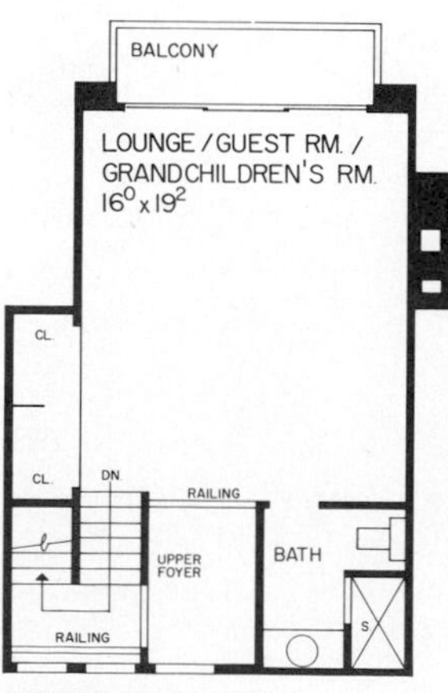

ALTERNATE SECOND FLOOR

With An Alternate Floor Plan

● The full bath is planned to have easy access to the master bedroom and living areas. Note the stall shower, tub, seat and vanity. The second floor offers two optional layouts. It may serve as a lounge, studio or hobby area overlooking the great room. Or, it may be built to function as a complete private guest room. It would be a great place for the visiting grandchildren. Don't miss the outdoor balcony. Additional livability and storage facilities may be developed in the basement. This is surely a modest-sized floor plan which will deliver new dimensions in small-family livability.

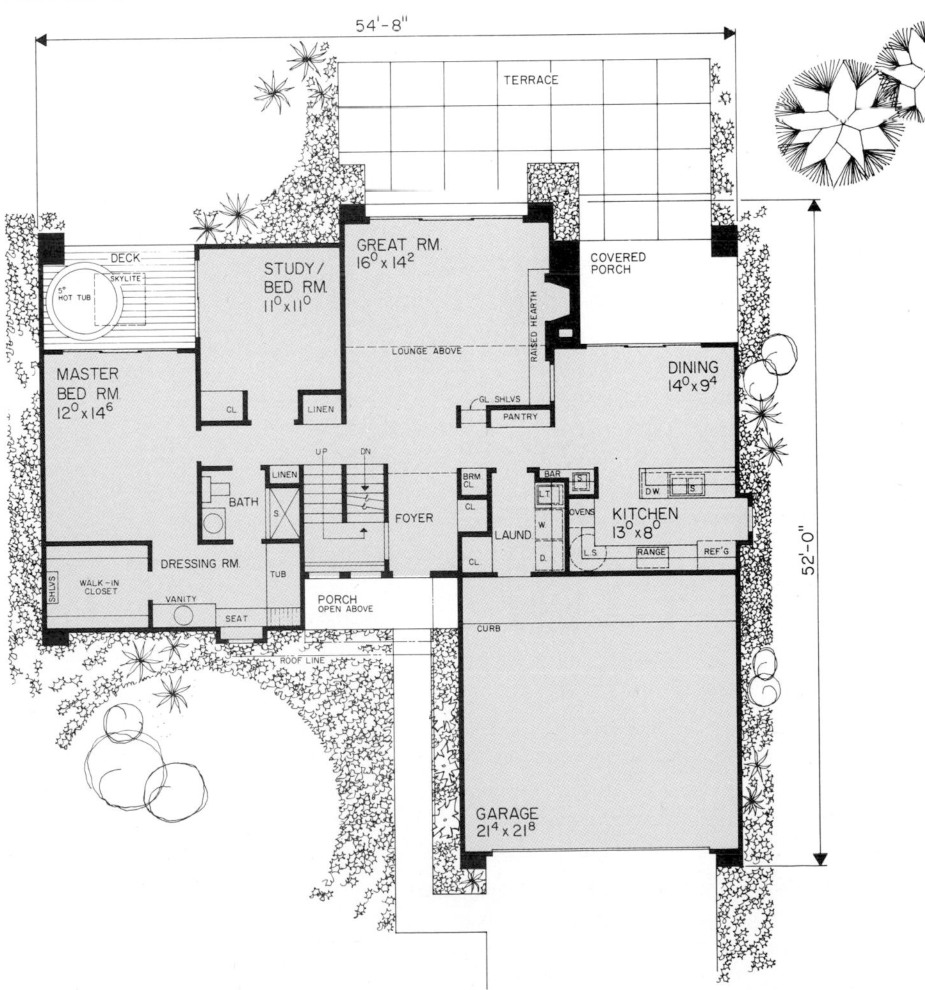

Great Views! Homes For View Lots

● Three levels of vacation living are contained in this interesting contemporary. At entry level, the great room and master bedroom share a full-width deck to the rear. The kitchen enjoys a window greenhouse. Under the long sloping roof are two more bedrooms with large walk-in closets and a full bath with twin commodes and vanities. The double garage, on the lower level, adjoins a large family room with covered patio.

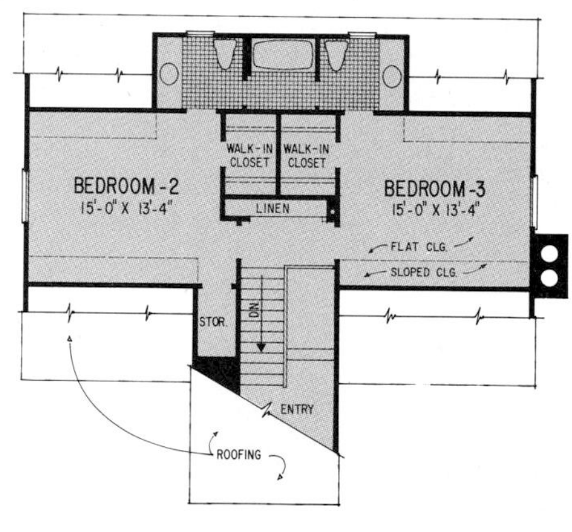

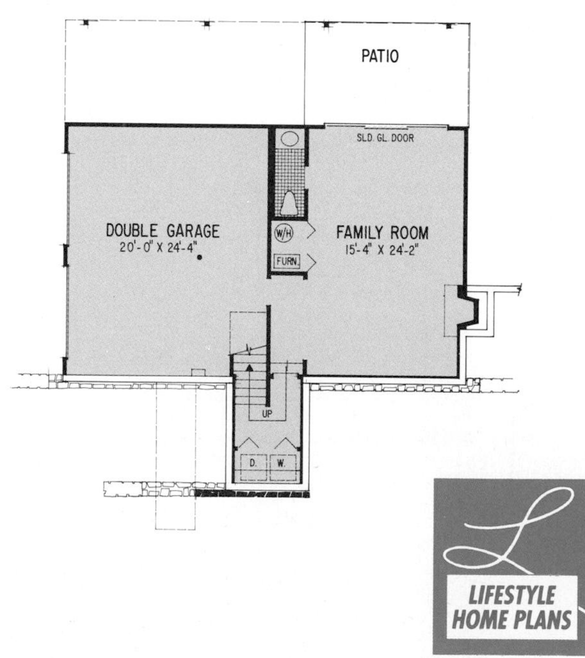

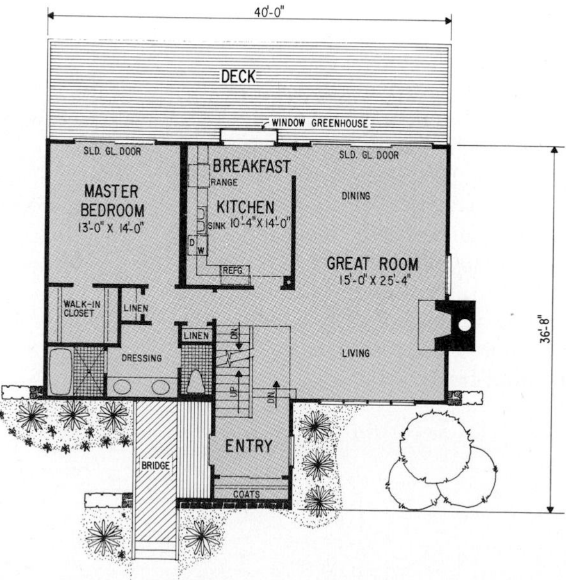

LIFESTYLE HOME PLANS

Design V44249 Main Level: 1,138 square feet
Upper Level: 693 square feet; Lower Level: 610 square feet
Total: 2,441 square feet

Design V44254

Main Level: 1,160 square feet
Upper Level: 715 square feet
Lower Level: 614 square feet
Total: 2,489 square feet

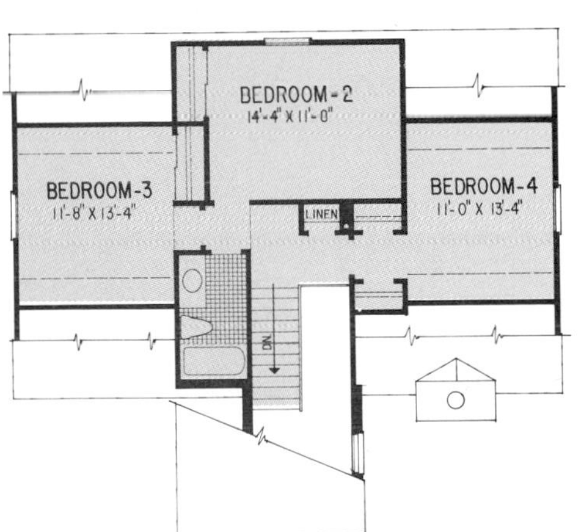

● Similar in floor plan to design V44249, this home adds a fourth bedroom on the second floor for those who need a little extra sleeping space. Also notice the altered placement of the chimney stack and fireplace and the covered porch entrance. Either plan, three- or four-bedroom, delivers an abundance of vacation-residence living.

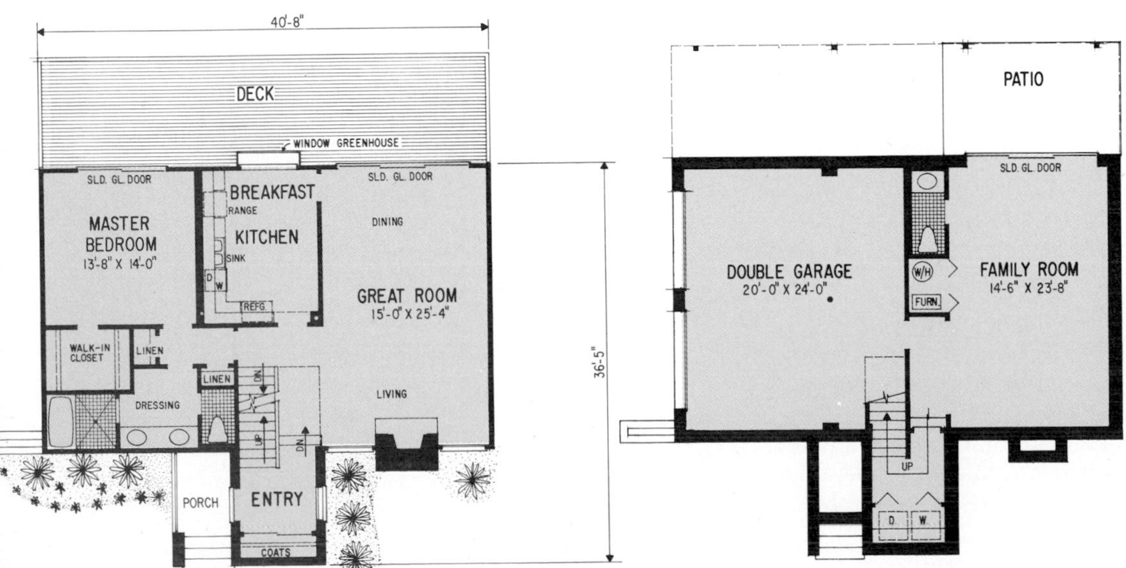

Design V44210

Entry Level: 768 square feet
Upper Level: 288 square feet
Total: 1,056 square feet

● This unusual contemporary design has a refreshingly simple interior layout, with deck access at three points. Two bedrooms, one upstairs and one down, round out a floor plan that has an L-shaped kitchen with pantry, and a hearth-warmed living room. Two full baths are conveniently located near the bedrooms.

Design V44317

Square Footage: 1,792

● There's a lot going on in this clever design that's not immediately evident from its facade. Beyond the side entry are four bedrooms, two full baths, and formal and informal living areas. Outdoor livability is a major focus with deck extensions from the family room, living room, master bedroom, kitchen, and entry. Note the garden atrium just off the dining room.

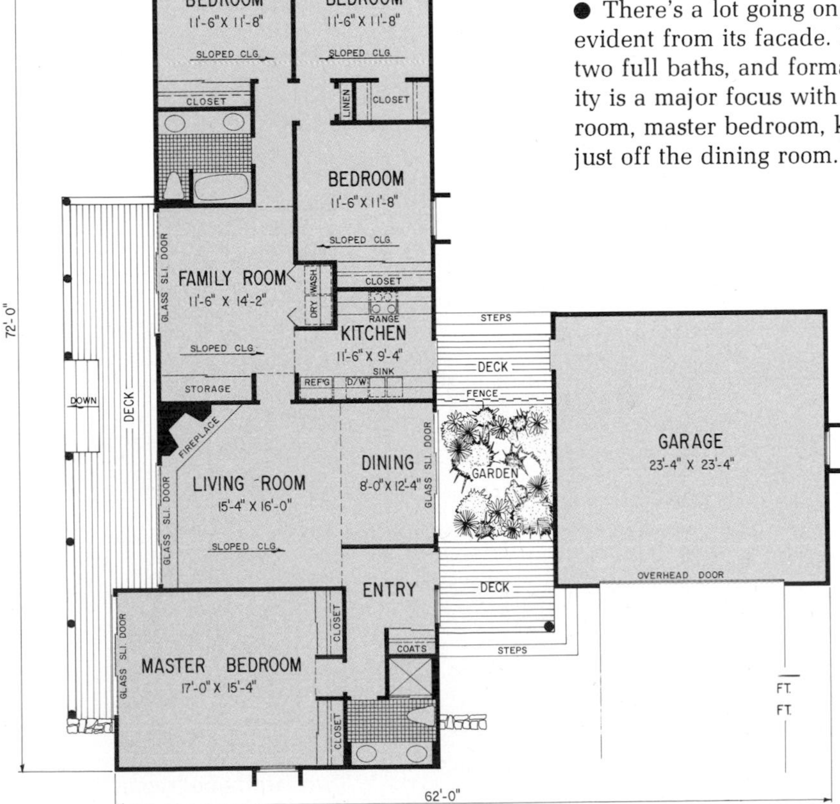

Design V44293 Square Footage: 1,873

D

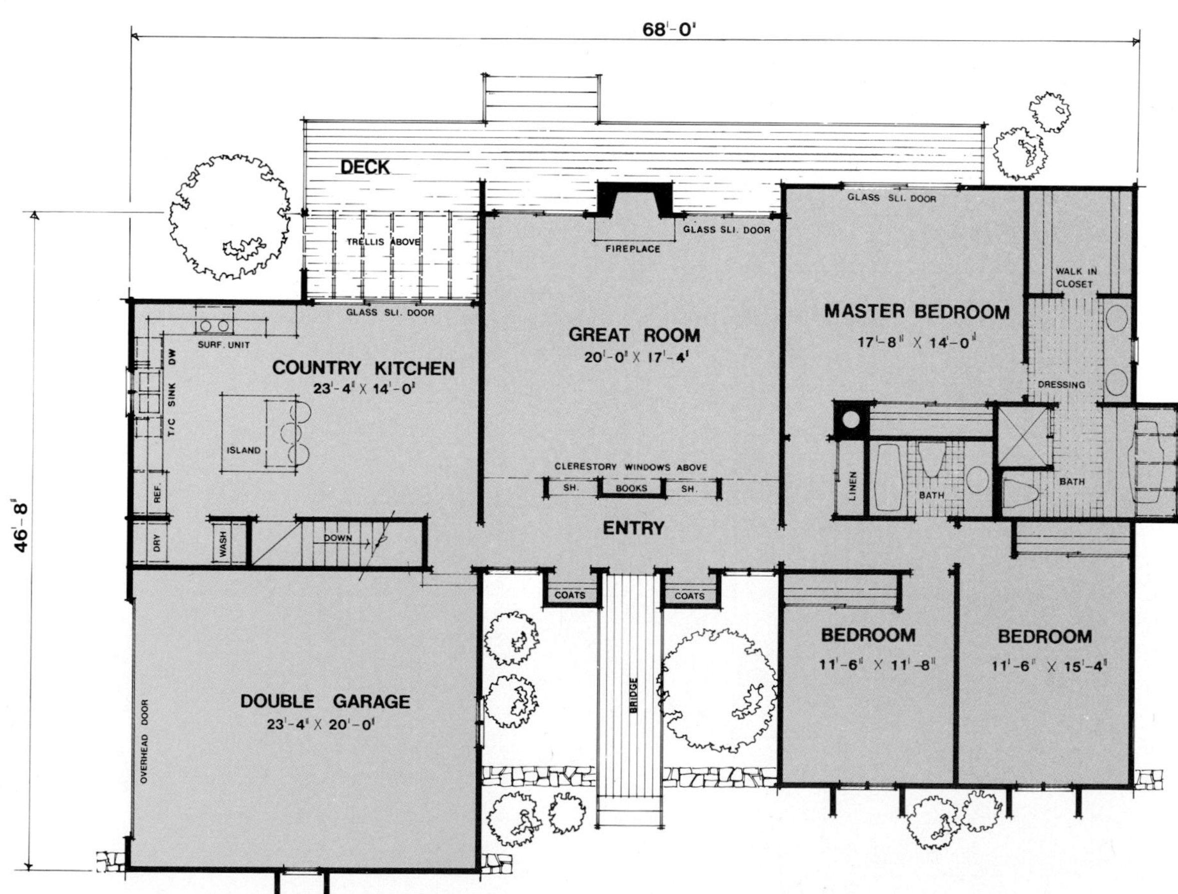

LIFESTYLE HOME PLANS

● Simple lines and a balanced sense of proportion dominate the look of this compact design. The open great room (note clerestory windows), country kitchen with island work area, and master bedroom all overlook a rear deck. Two family bedrooms, to the front of the home, have access to a full bath.

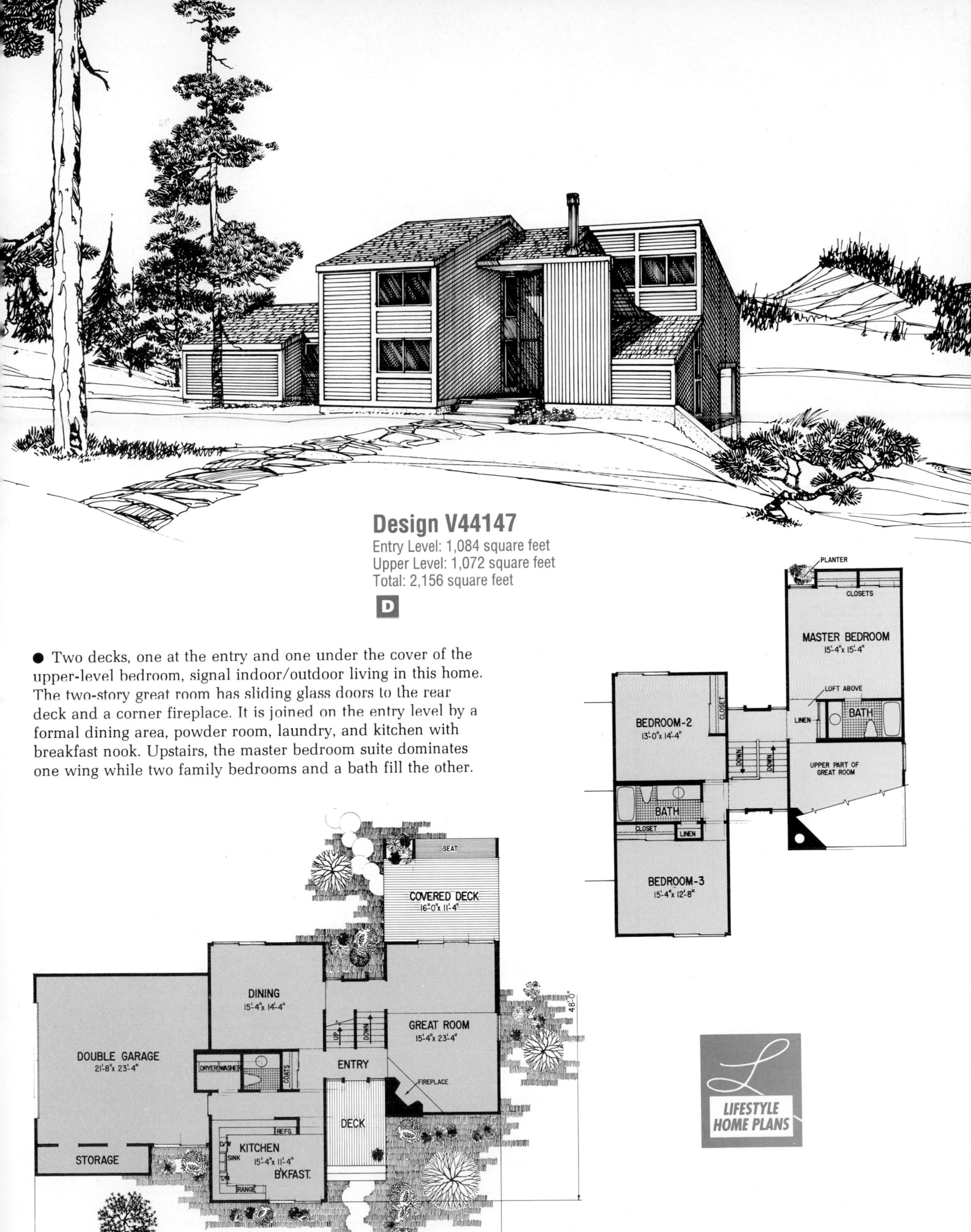

Design V44147

Entry Level: 1,084 square feet
Upper Level: 1,072 square feet
Total: 2,156 square feet

D

● Two decks, one at the entry and one under the cover of the upper-level bedroom, signal indoor/outdoor living in this home. The two-story great room has sliding glass doors to the rear deck and a corner fireplace. It is joined on the entry level by a formal dining area, powder room, laundry, and kitchen with breakfast nook. Upstairs, the master bedroom suite dominates one wing while two family bedrooms and a bath fill the other.

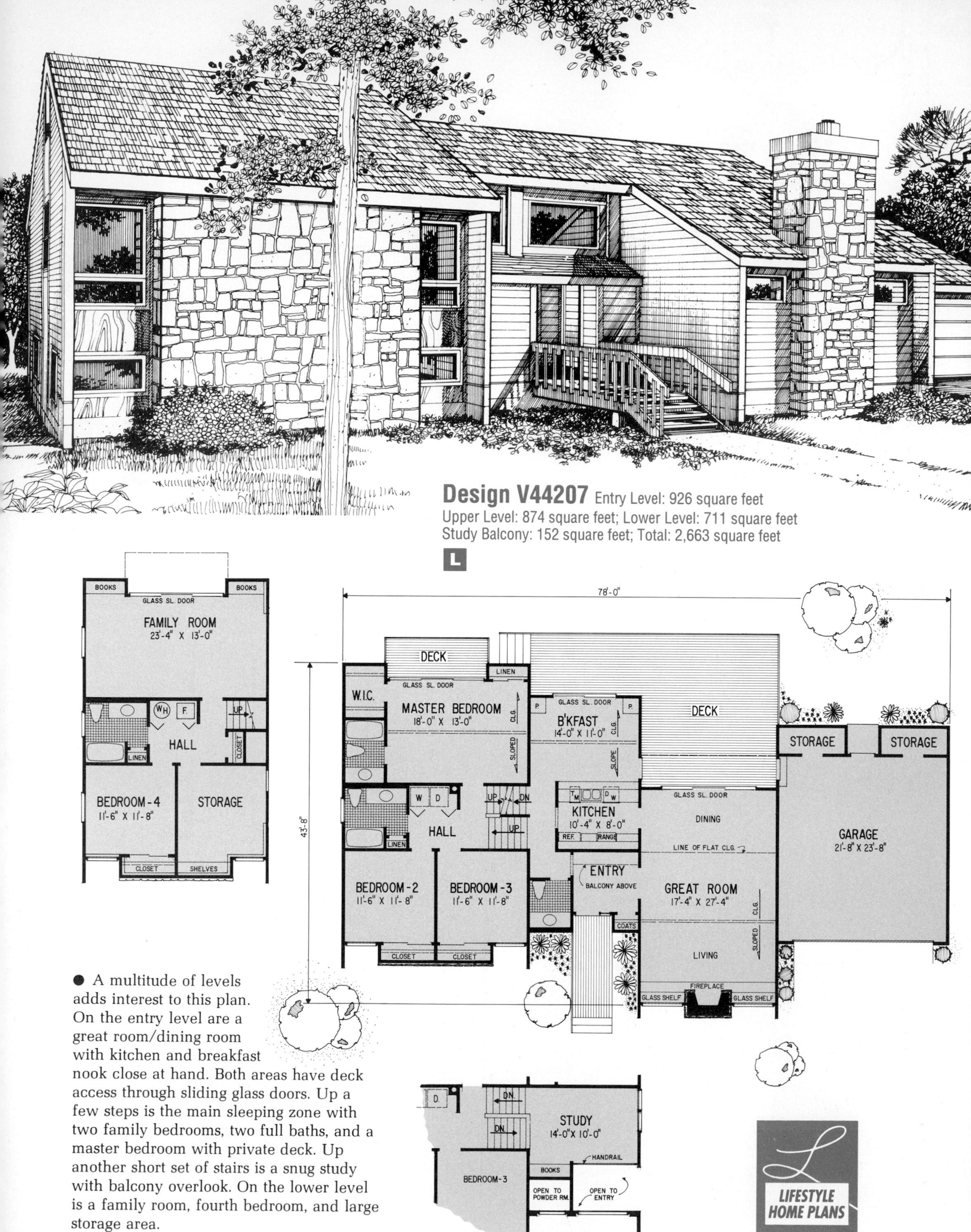

Design V44207 Entry Level: 926 square feet
Upper Level: 874 square feet; Lower Level: 711 square feet
Study Balcony: 152 square feet; Total: 2,663 square feet

L

● A multitude of levels adds interest to this plan. On the entry level are a great room/dining room with kitchen and breakfast nook close at hand. Both areas have deck access through sliding glass doors. Up a few steps is the main sleeping zone with two family bedrooms, two full baths, and a master bedroom with private deck. Up another short set of stairs is a snug study with balcony overlook. On the lower level is a family room, fourth bedroom, and large storage area.

Design V44115

Entry Level: 1,494 square feet
Upper Level: 597 square feet
Total: 2,091 square feet

● Interior spaces are dramatically proportioned because of the long and varied roof lines of this contemporary. The two-story living area has a sloped ceiling as does the master bedroom and two upper-level bedrooms. Two fireplaces, a huge rear wooden deck, a small upstairs sitting room, and a liberal number of windows make this a most comfortable vacation residence.

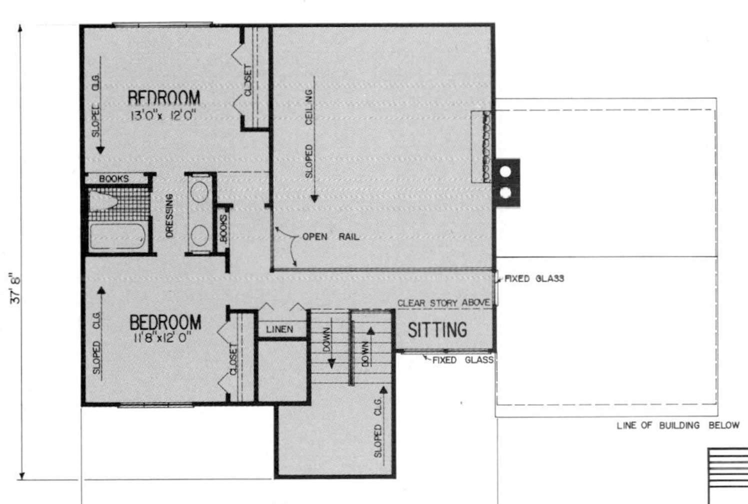

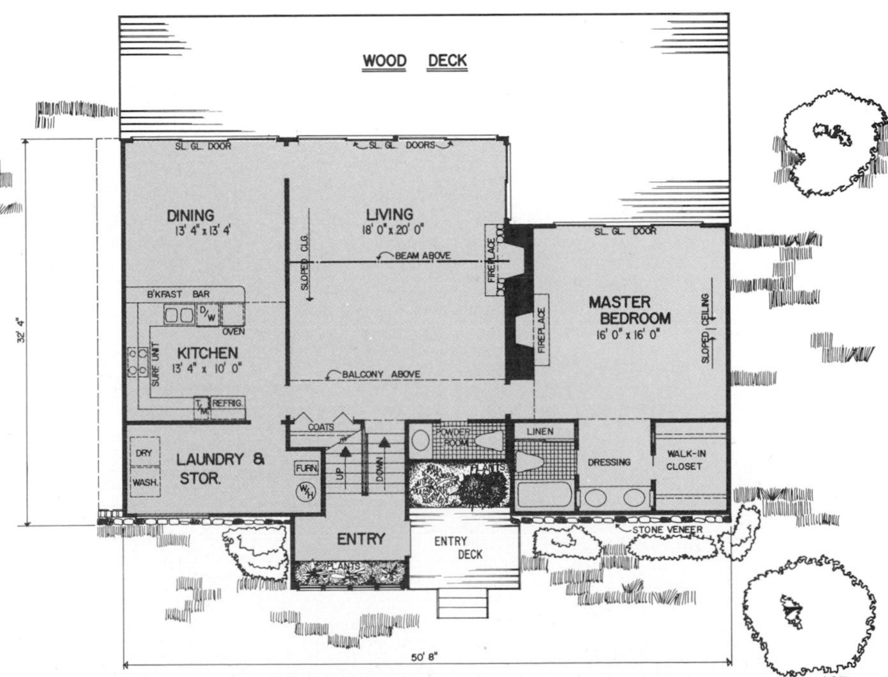

LIFESTYLE HOME PLANS

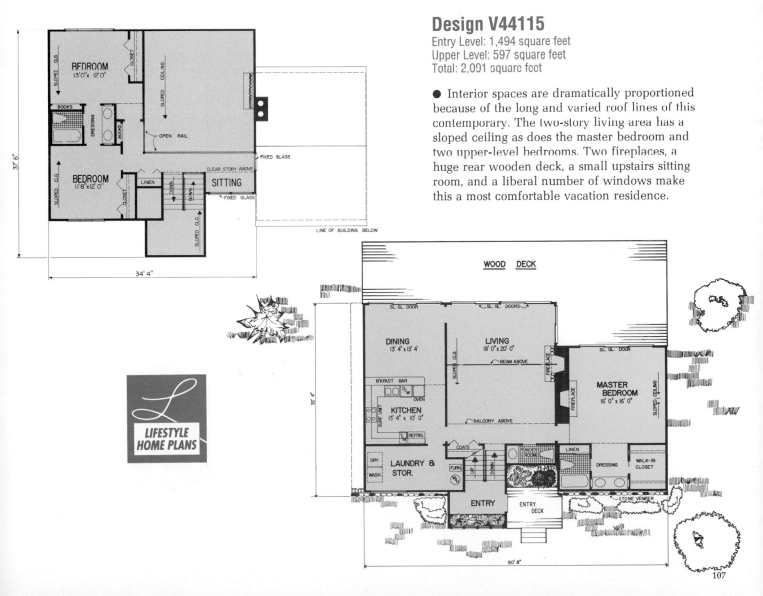

Design V44332

First Floor: 1,781 square feet
Second Floor: 677 square feet
Total: 2,458 square feet

● A pleasing mix of traditional and contemporary elements highlight this plan's exterior. And between the front covered deck and rear deck is a great floor plan. The living zone is contained in one wing in a family room, living room, dining room, and kitchen. Notice the through-fireplace, bay windows, and balcony overlooks. The master suite and den are in the opposite wing. Upstairs (note double stairwells) there are two sloped-ceiling bedrooms and a full bath.

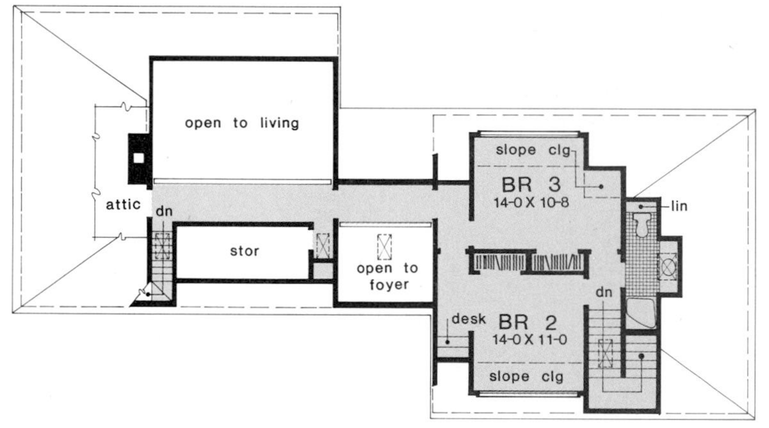

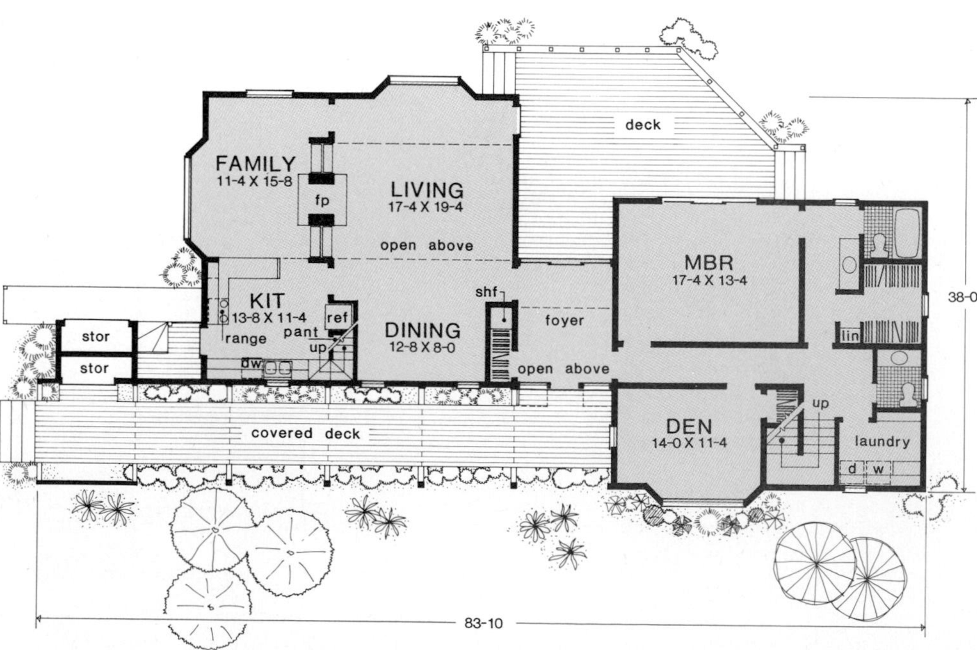

Design V42716 Main Level: 1,013 square feet

Upper Level: 885 square feet; Lower Level: 1,074 square feet; Total: 2,972 square feet

L

● A genuine master suite! It overlooks the gathering room through shuttered windows and includes a private balcony, a 9' by 9' sitting/dressing room and a full bath. There's more, a two-story gathering room with a raised hearth fireplace, sloped ceiling and sliding glass doors onto the main balcony. Plus, a family room and a study both having a fireplace. A kitchen with lots of built-ins and a separate dining nook.

Design V42842

Entrance Level: 156 square feet
Upper Level: 1,038 square feet
Lower Level: 1,022 square feet
Total: 2,216 square feet

D

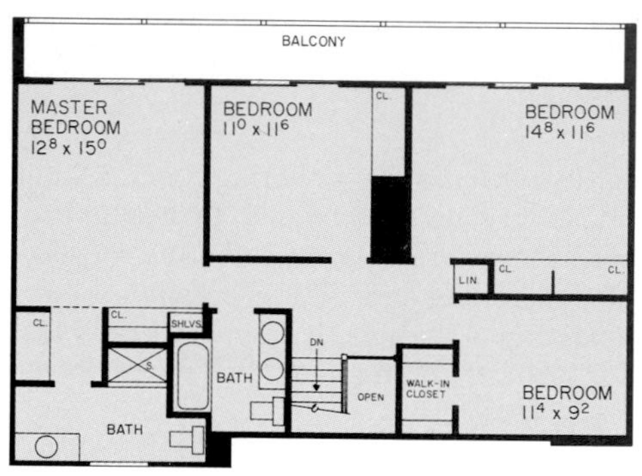

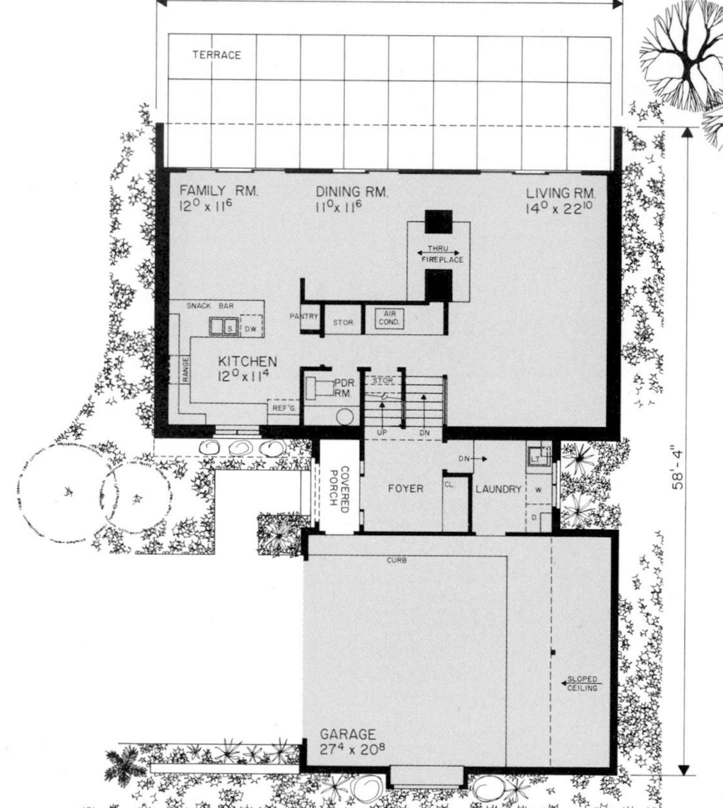

● This narrow, 42 foot width, house can be built on a narrow lot to cut down overall costs. Yet its dramatic appeal surely is worth a million. The projecting front garage creates a pleasing curved drive. One enters this house through the covered porch to the entrance level foyer. At this point the stairs lead down to the living area consisting of formal living room, family room, kitchen and dining area then up the stairs to the four bedroom-two bath sleeping area. The indoor-outdoor living relationship at the rear is outstanding.

Design V42827

Upper Level: 1,618 square feet
Lower Level: 1,458 square feet
Total: 3,076 square feet

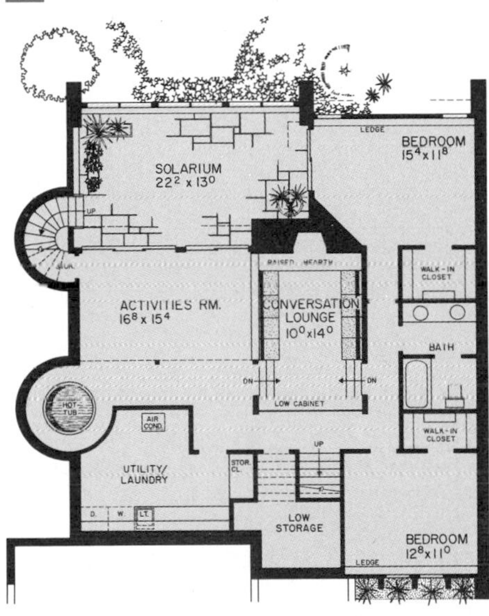

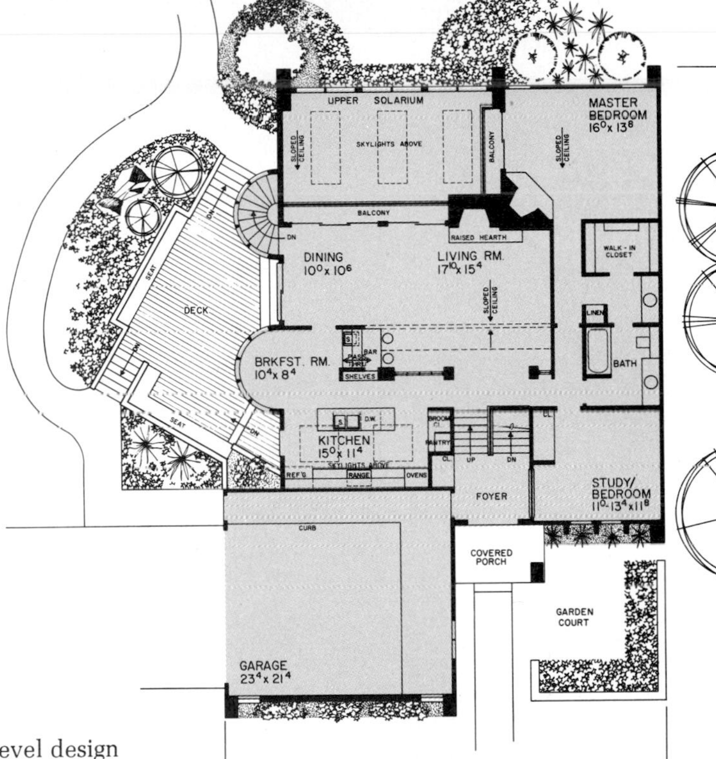

● The towering, two-story solarium in this bi-level design is its key to energy savings. Study the efficiency of this floor plan. The conversation lounge on the lower level is a unique focal point.

Design V42511

Main Level: 1,043 square feet
Upper Level: 703 square feet
Lower Level: 794 square feet
Total: 2,540 square feet

● Distinctive and newly fashioned, this geometric hillside home offers interesting living patterns. Its interior is as individualistic as its exterior. The main living level is delightfully planned with the efficient kitchen easily serving the snack bar and the dining room. The gathering room has a high ceiling and looks up at the upper level balcony. An angular deck provides the gathering and dining rooms with their outdoor living area. A study with adjacent full bath, provides the main level with an extra measure of living pattern flexibility. It has its own quiet outdoor balcony. Upstairs, a bunk room, a bedroom, and a full bath. Also, there is an exciting view through the gathering room windows. On the lower level an optional sleeping facility, the family's all-purpose activities room, a hobby room, and another full bath.

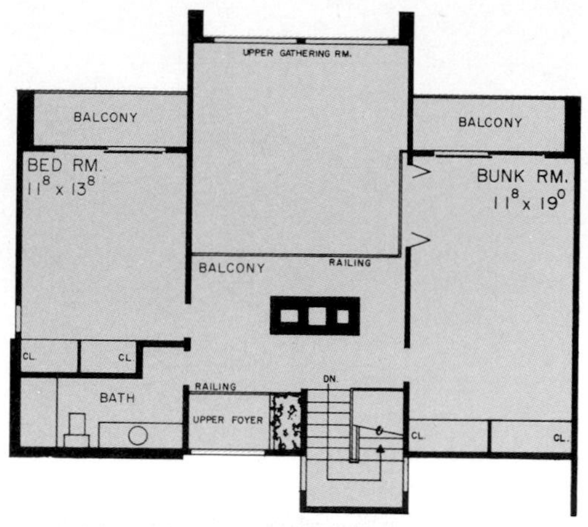

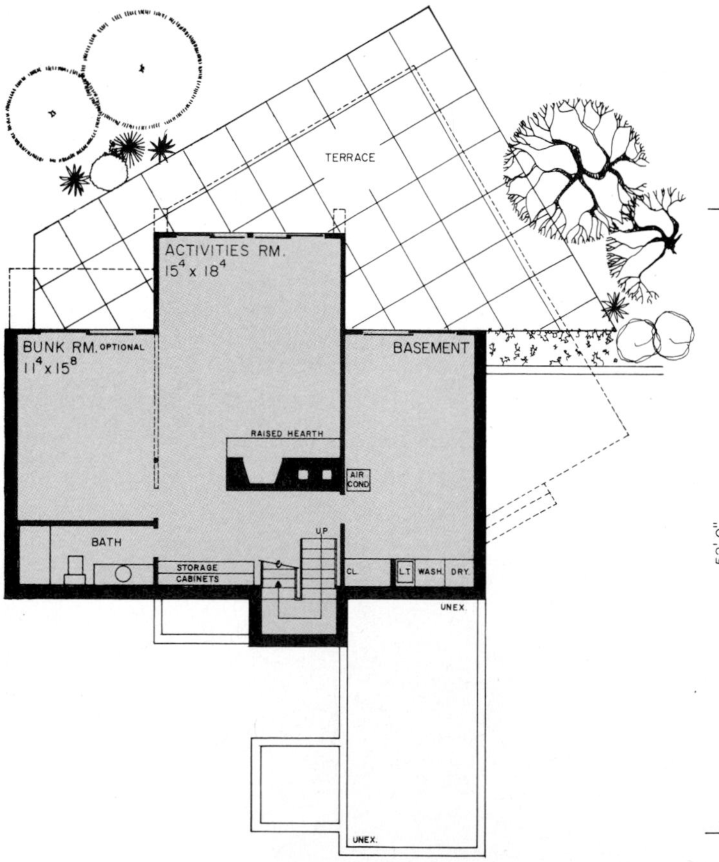

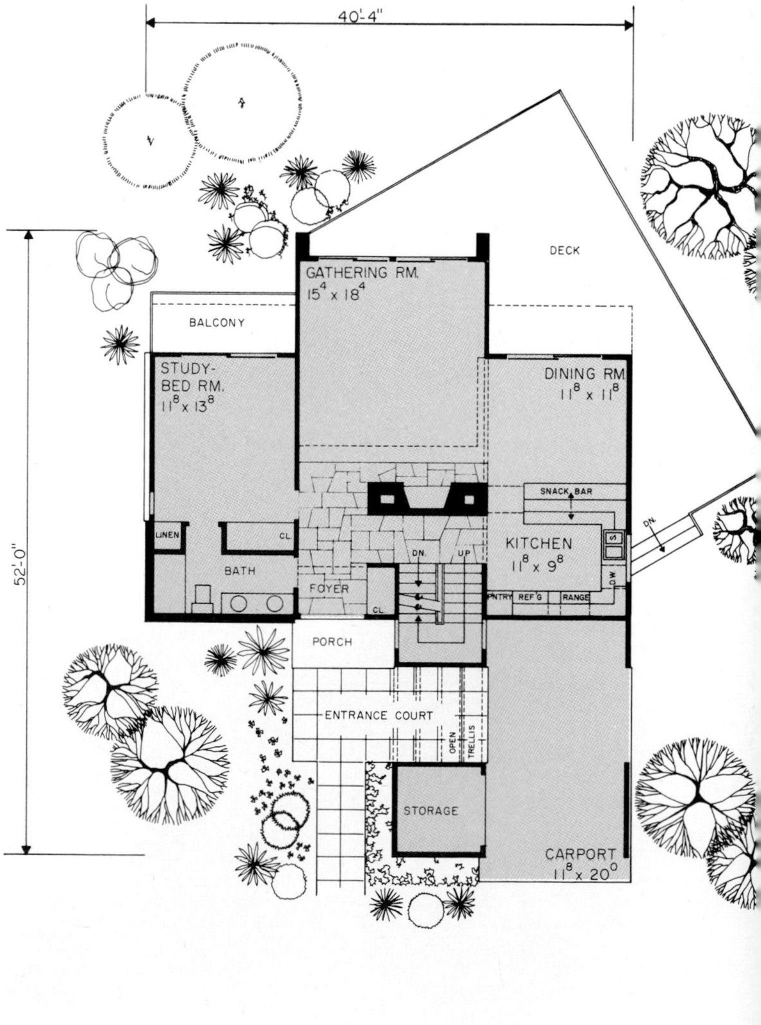

Design V42937

Main Level: 1,096 square feet
Upper Level: 1,115 square feet; Lower Level: 1,104 square feet
Total: 3,315 square feet

L

● This contemporary multi-level home features an extended rear balcony that covers a rear patio, plus a master bedroom suite, complete with whirlpool and raised-hearth pass-thru. Two other bedrooms and a second bath are on the upper level.

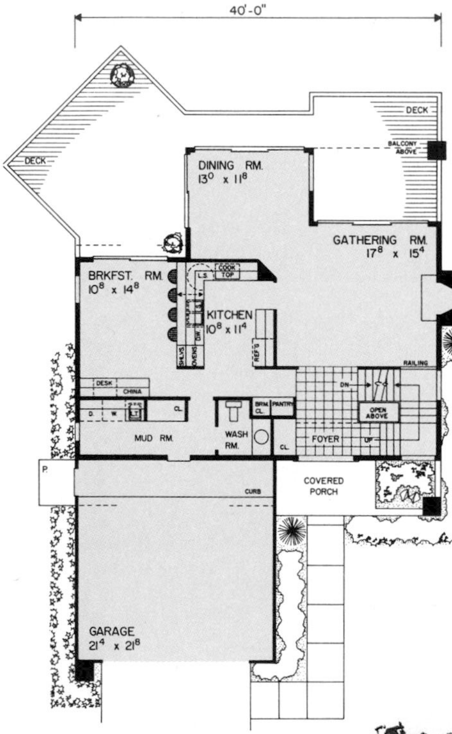

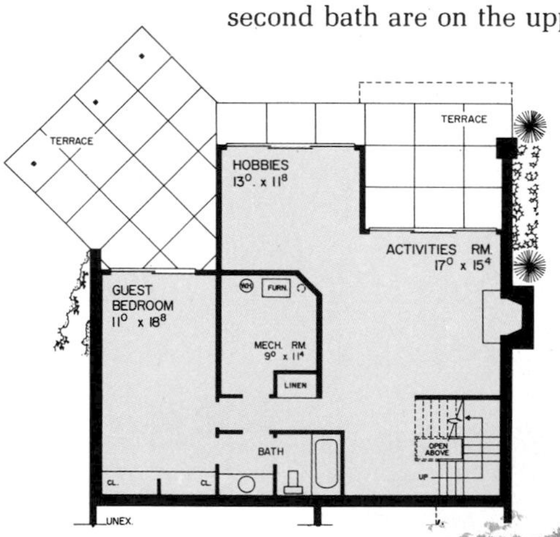

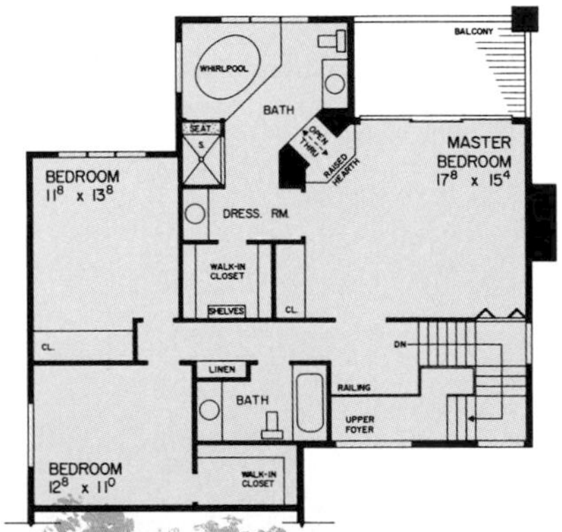

Design V42868 Upper Level: 1,203 square feet
Lower Level: 1,317 square feet; Total: 2,520 square feet

Common Living Areas – Sleeping Privacy

● Two couples sharing the expense of a house has got to be ideal and, of course, economical. The occupants of this house could do just that. The lower level, housing the kitchen, dining room, family and living rooms and the laundry facilities, is the common area to be shared by both couples. Centrally located, the kitchen and dining room act as a space divider to the living and family rooms so both couples can enjoy privacy.

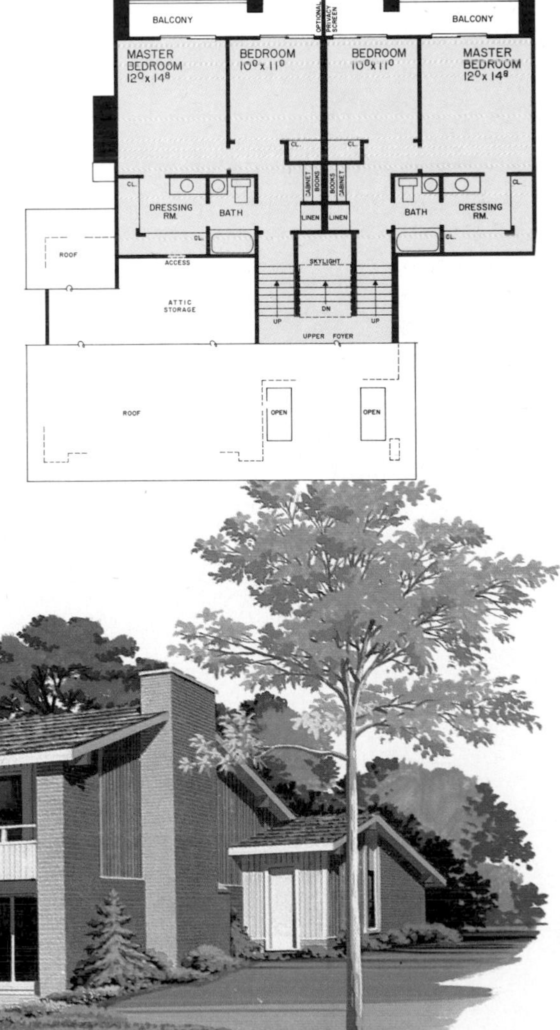

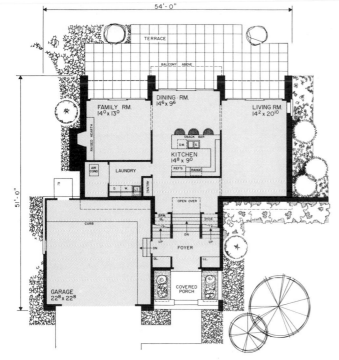

Separate stairways lead to the upper level from the skylit foyer. Each private area has two bedrooms, a dressing room and a full bath. Individual entrances can be locked for additional privacy. Sliding glass doors are in each of the rear rooms on both levels so the outdoors can be enjoyed to its fullest.

● This attractive, contemporary bi-level will overwhelm you with its features: two balconies, an open staircase with planter below, two lower level bedrooms, six sets of sliding glass doors and an outstanding master suite loaded with features. The occupants of this house will love the large exercise room. After a tough workout, you can relax in the whirlpool or the sauna or simply take a shower!

Design V42856 Upper Level: 1,801 square feet
Lower Level: 2,170 square feet; Total: 3,971 square feet

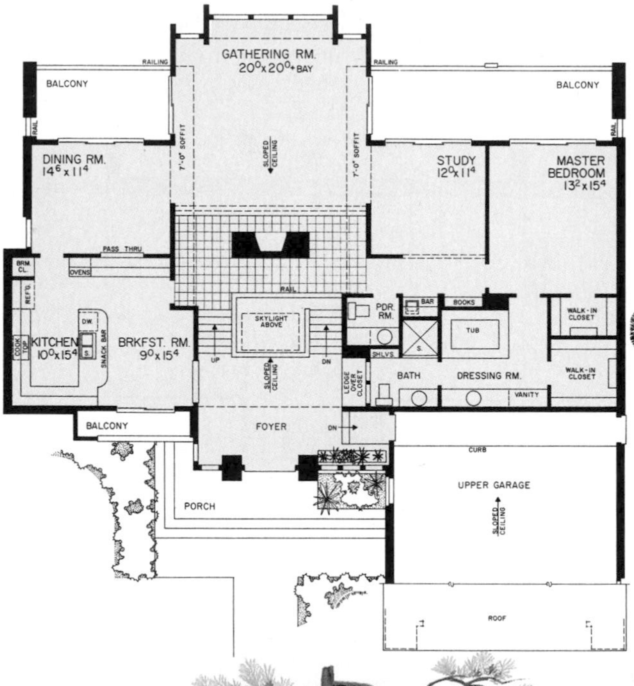

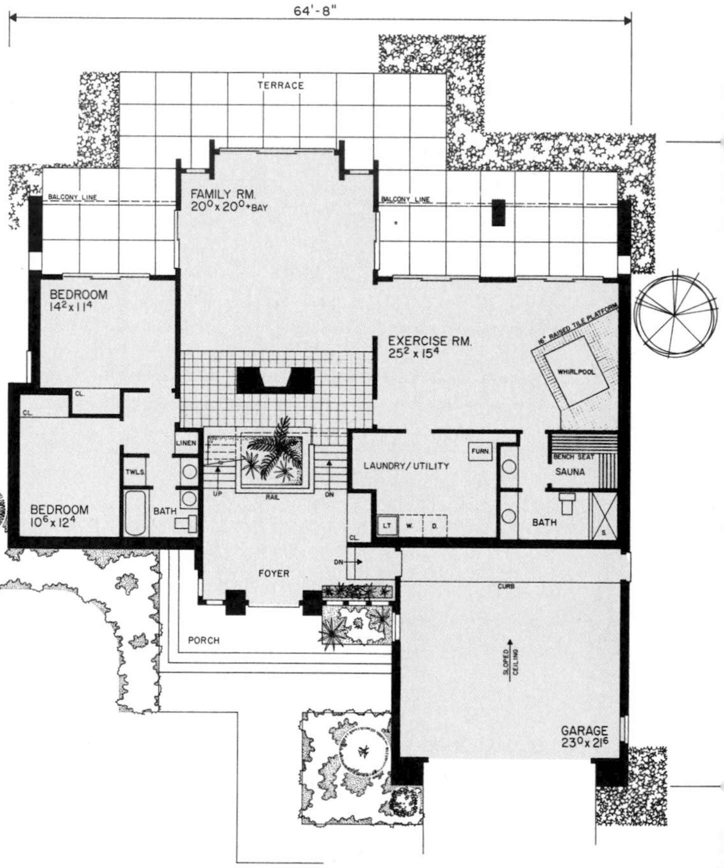

Design V42896 Main Level: 1,856 square feet
Lower Level: 1,454 square feet; Total: 3,310 square feet

● This contemporary, hillside home is very inviting. A large kitchen with an adjacent snack bar makes light meals a breeze. The adjoining breakfast room offers a scenic view through sliding glass doors. Notice the sloped ceiling in the dining and gathering rooms. A fireplace in the gathering room adds a cozy air. An interesting feature is the master bedroom's easy access to the study. Also, take note of the sliding doors in the master bedroom which lead to a private balcony. On the lower level, a large activities room will be a frequently used spot by family members. The fireplace and wet bar add a nice touch for entertaining friends. Take note of the two or optional three bedrooms - the choice is yours. Obviously, this house offers lots of livability and will be a joy to own.

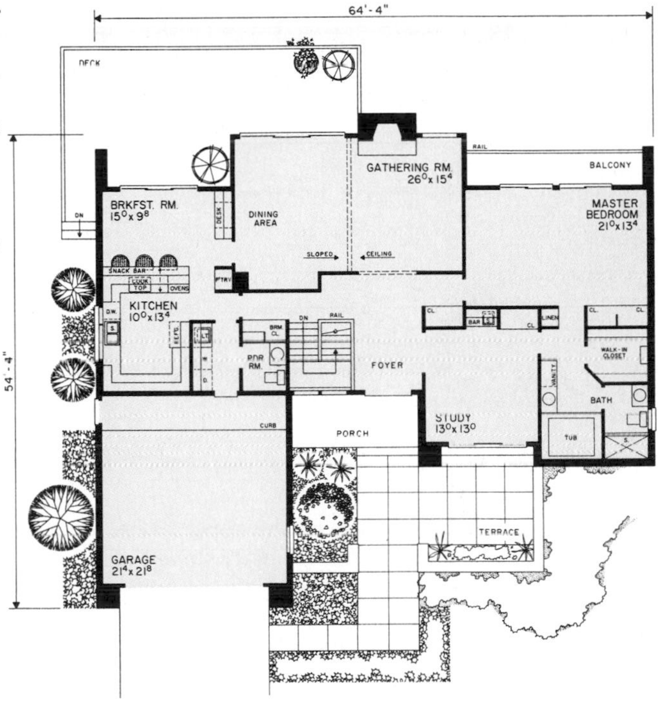

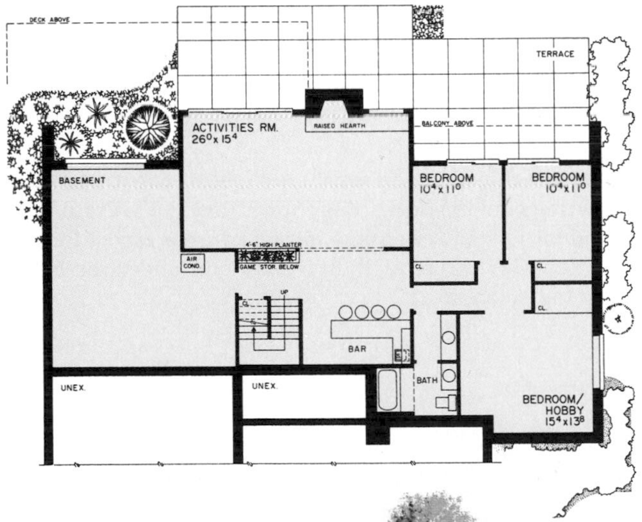

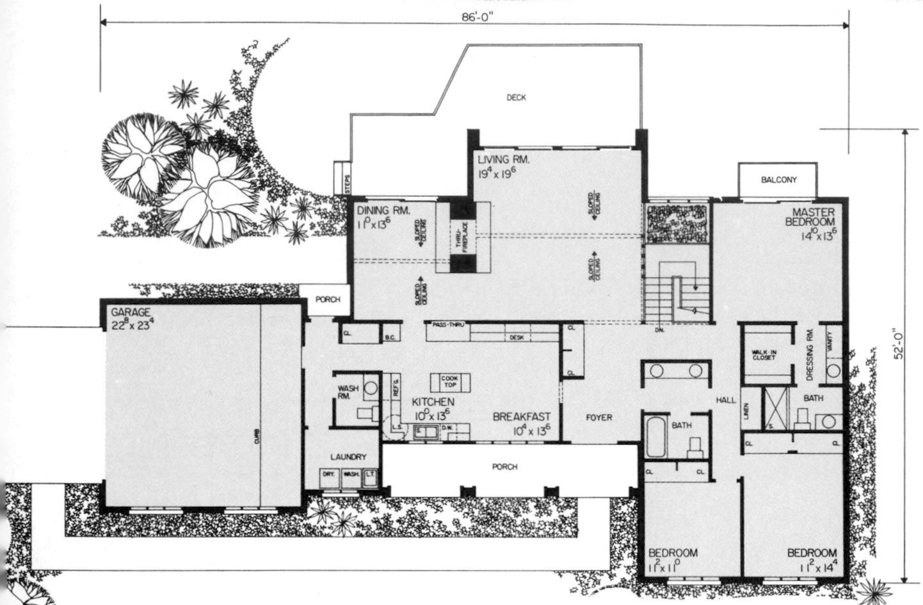

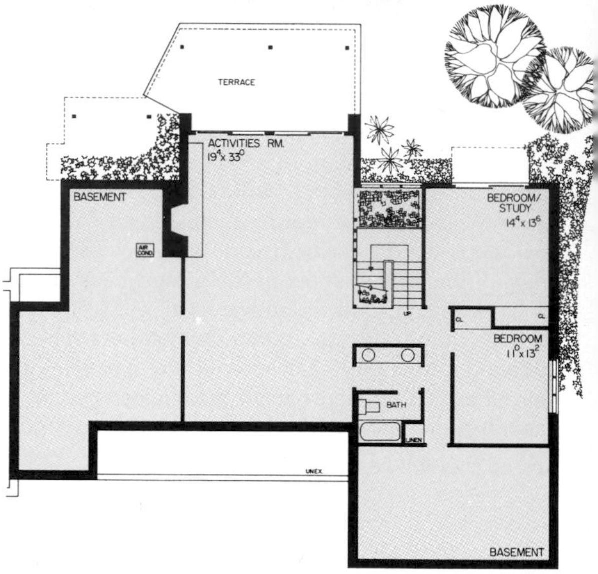

● This hillside home gives all the appearances of being a one-story ranch home; and what a delightful one at that! Should the contours of your property slope to the rear, this plan permits the exposing of the lower level. This results in the activities room and bedroom/study gaining direct access to outdoor living. Certainly a most desirable aspect for active, outdoor family living. The large and growing family will be admirably served with five bedrooms and three baths. An extra washroom and separate laundry add to the convenient living potential.

Design V42549

Main Level: 2,260 square feet
Lower Level: 1,406 square feet
Total: 3,666 square feet

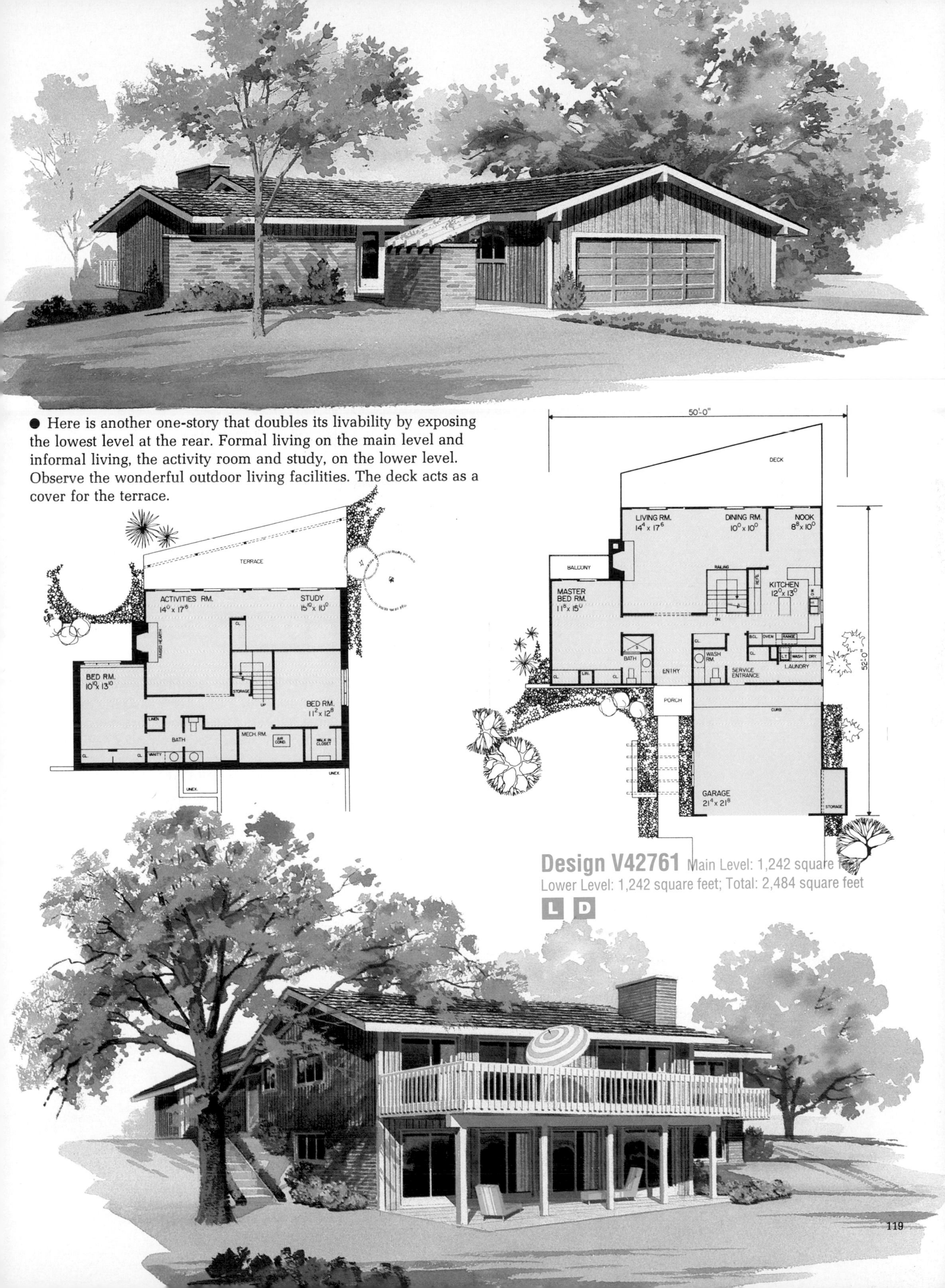

● Here is another one-story that doubles its livability by exposing the lowest level at the rear. Formal living on the main level and informal living, the activity room and study, on the lower level. Observe the wonderful outdoor living facilities. The deck acts as a cover for the terrace.

Design V42761 Main Level: 1,242 square feet
Lower Level: 1,242 square feet; Total: 2,484 square feet

L D

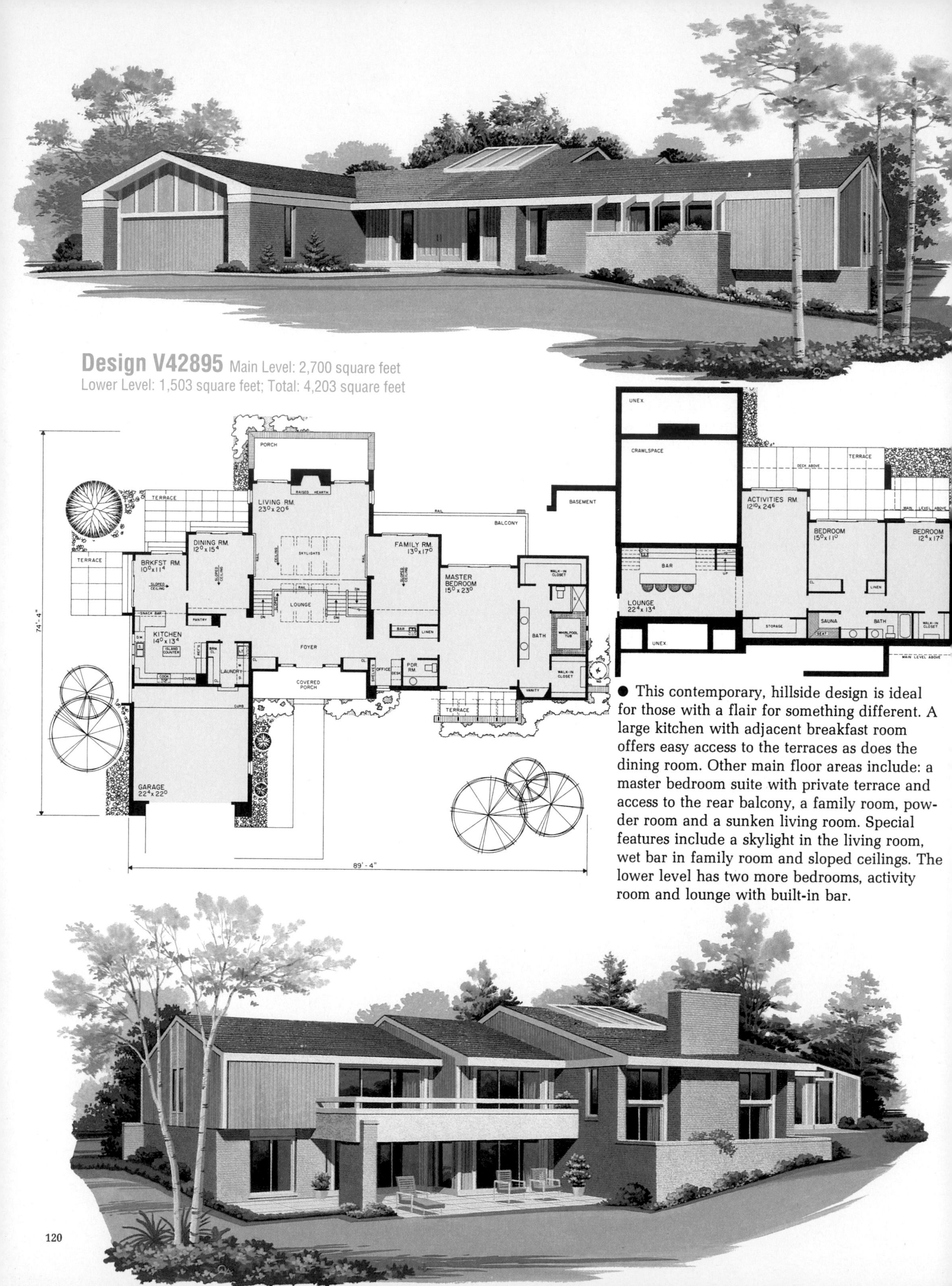

Design V42895 Main Level: 2,700 square feet

Lower Level: 1,503 square feet; Total: 4,203 square feet

● This contemporary, hillside design is ideal for those with a flair for something different. A large kitchen with adjacent breakfast room offers easy access to the terraces as does the dining room. Other main floor areas include: a master bedroom suite with private terrace and access to the rear balcony, a family room, powder room and a sunken living room. Special features include a skylight in the living room, wet bar in family room and sloped ceilings. The lower level has two more bedrooms, activity room and lounge with built-in bar.

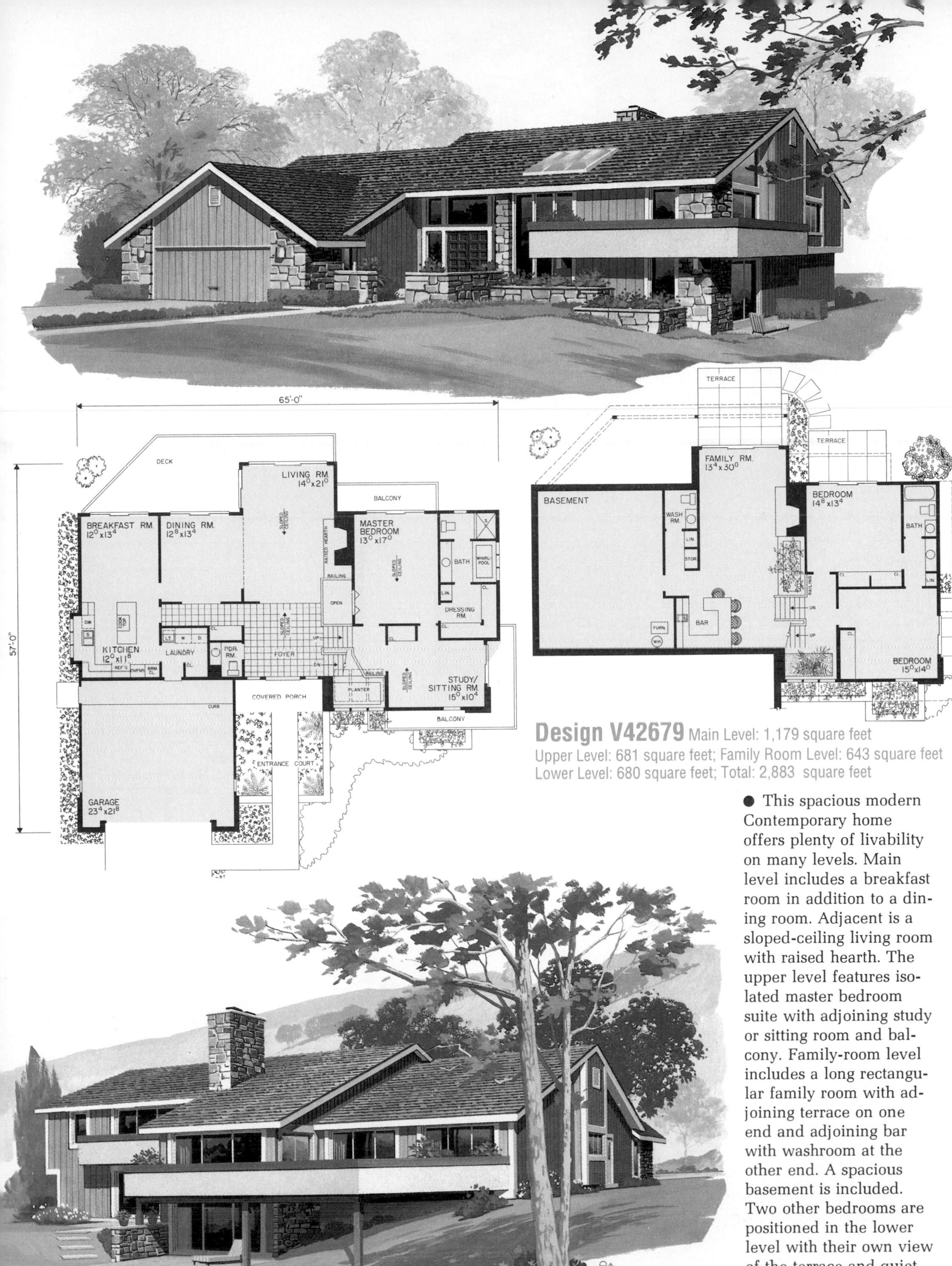

Design V42679 Main Level: 1,179 square feet
Upper Level: 681 square feet; Family Room Level: 643 square feet
Lower Level: 680 square feet; Total: 2,883 square feet

● This spacious modern Contemporary home offers plenty of livability on many levels. Main level includes a breakfast room in addition to a dining room. Adjacent is a sloped-ceiling living room with raised hearth. The upper level features isolated master bedroom suite with adjoining study or sitting room and balcony. Family-room level includes a long rectangular family room with adjoining terrace on one end and adjoining bar with washroom at the other end. A spacious basement is included. Two other bedrooms are positioned in the lower level with their own view of the terrace and quiet privacy. Note the rear deck.

Design V42847

Main Level: 1,874 square feet
Lower Level: 1,131 square feet; Total: 3,005 square feet

L D

● This is an exquisitely styled Tudor, hillside design, ready to serve its happy occupants for many years. The contrasting use of material surely makes the exterior eye-catching.

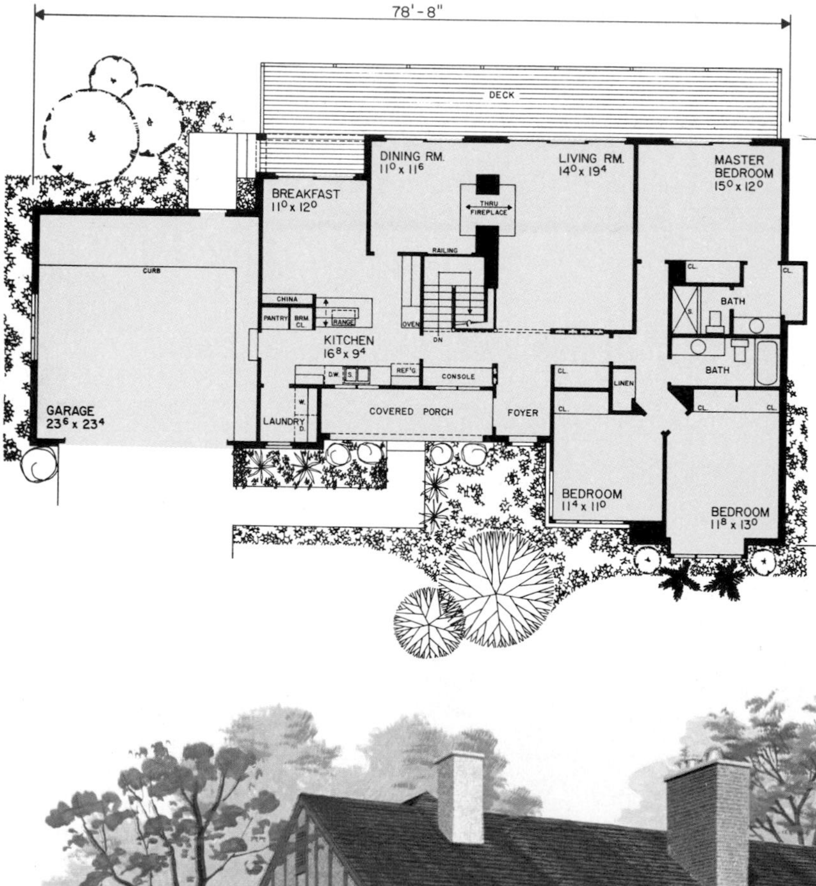

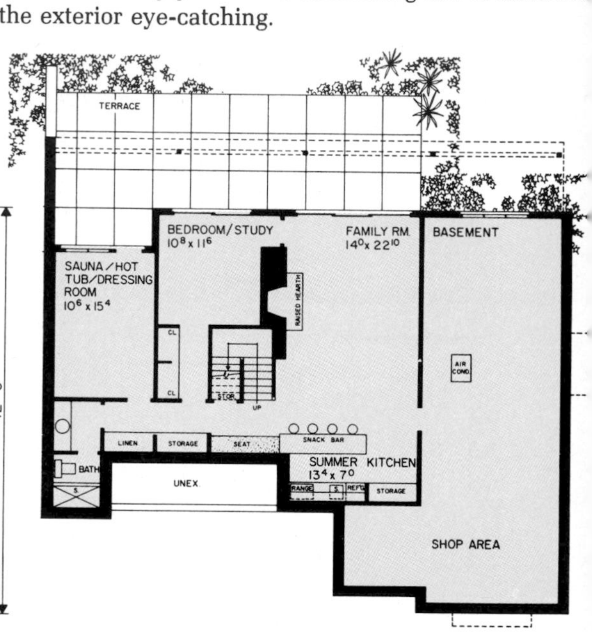

Design V42844

Upper Level: 1,882 square feet
Lower Level: 1,168 square feet; Total: 3,050 square feet

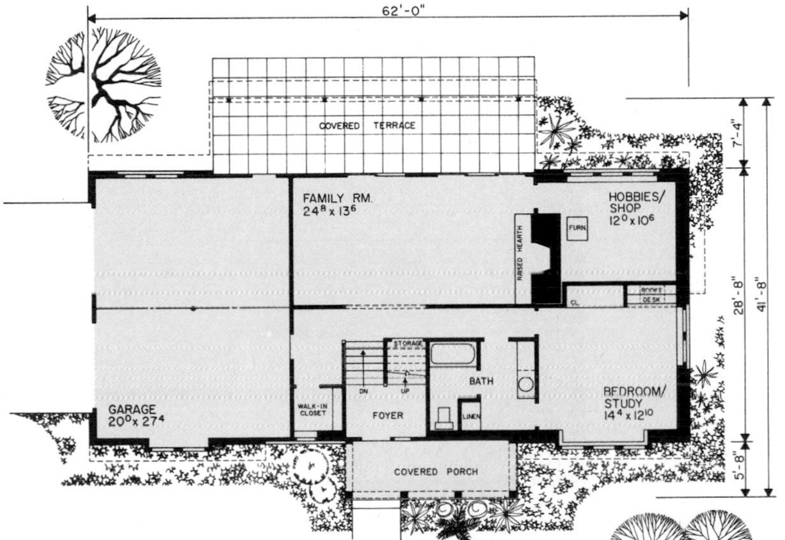

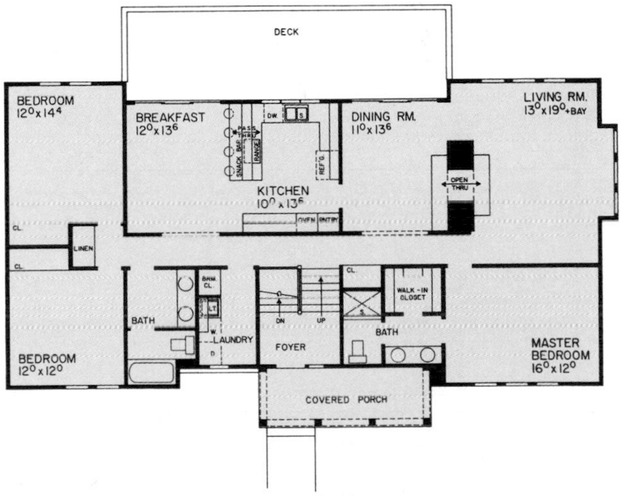

● Bi-level living will be enjoyed to the fullest in this Tudor design. Study each of the floor plans carefully. Both the upper and lower levels have been well planned. Note the seclusion of the master bedroom.

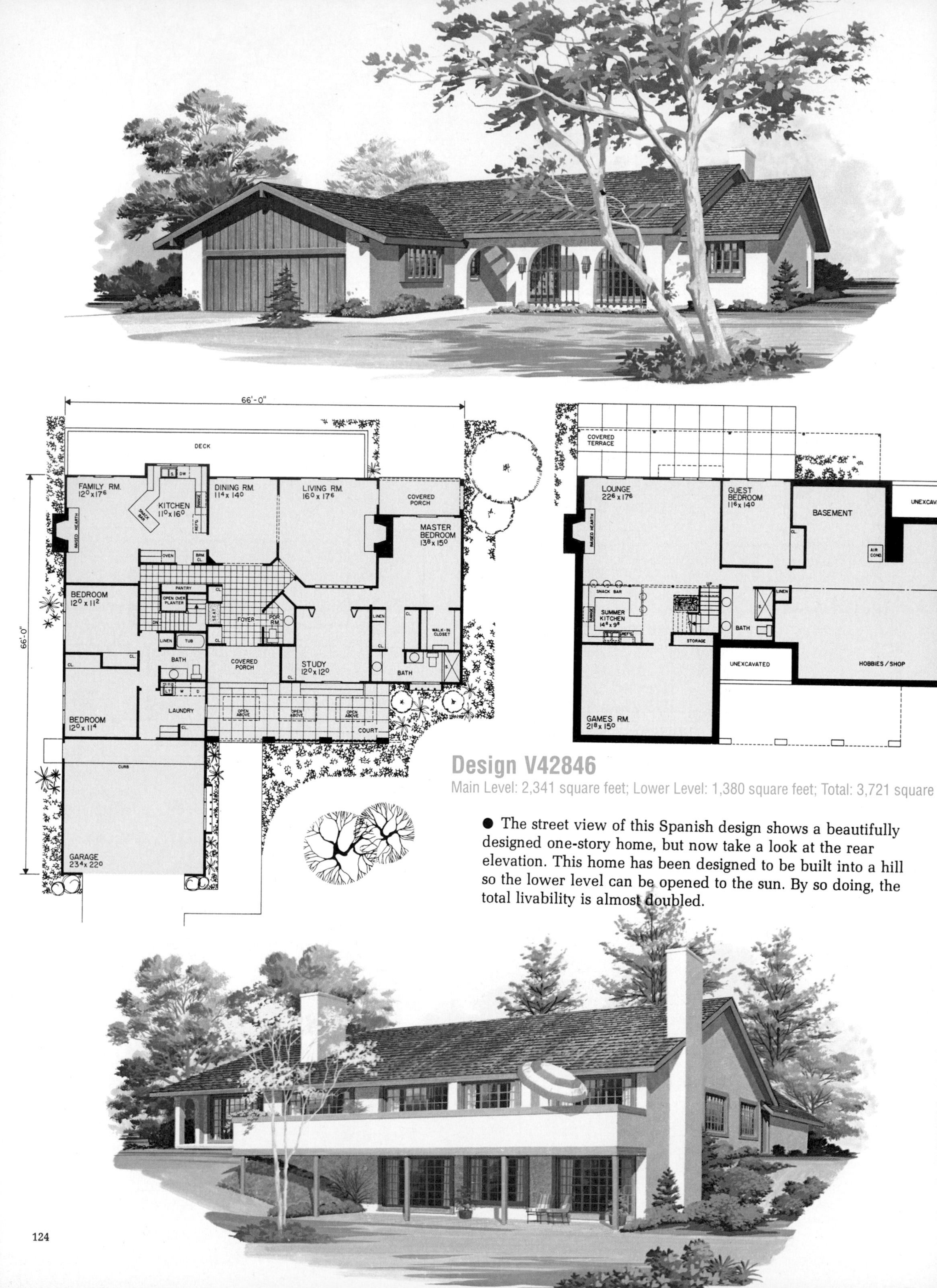

Design V42846

Main Level: 2,341 square feet; Lower Level: 1,380 square feet; Total: 3,721 square f

● The street view of this Spanish design shows a beautifully designed one-story home, but now take a look at the rear elevation. This home has been designed to be built into a hill so the lower level can be opened to the sun. By so doing, the total livability is almost doubled.

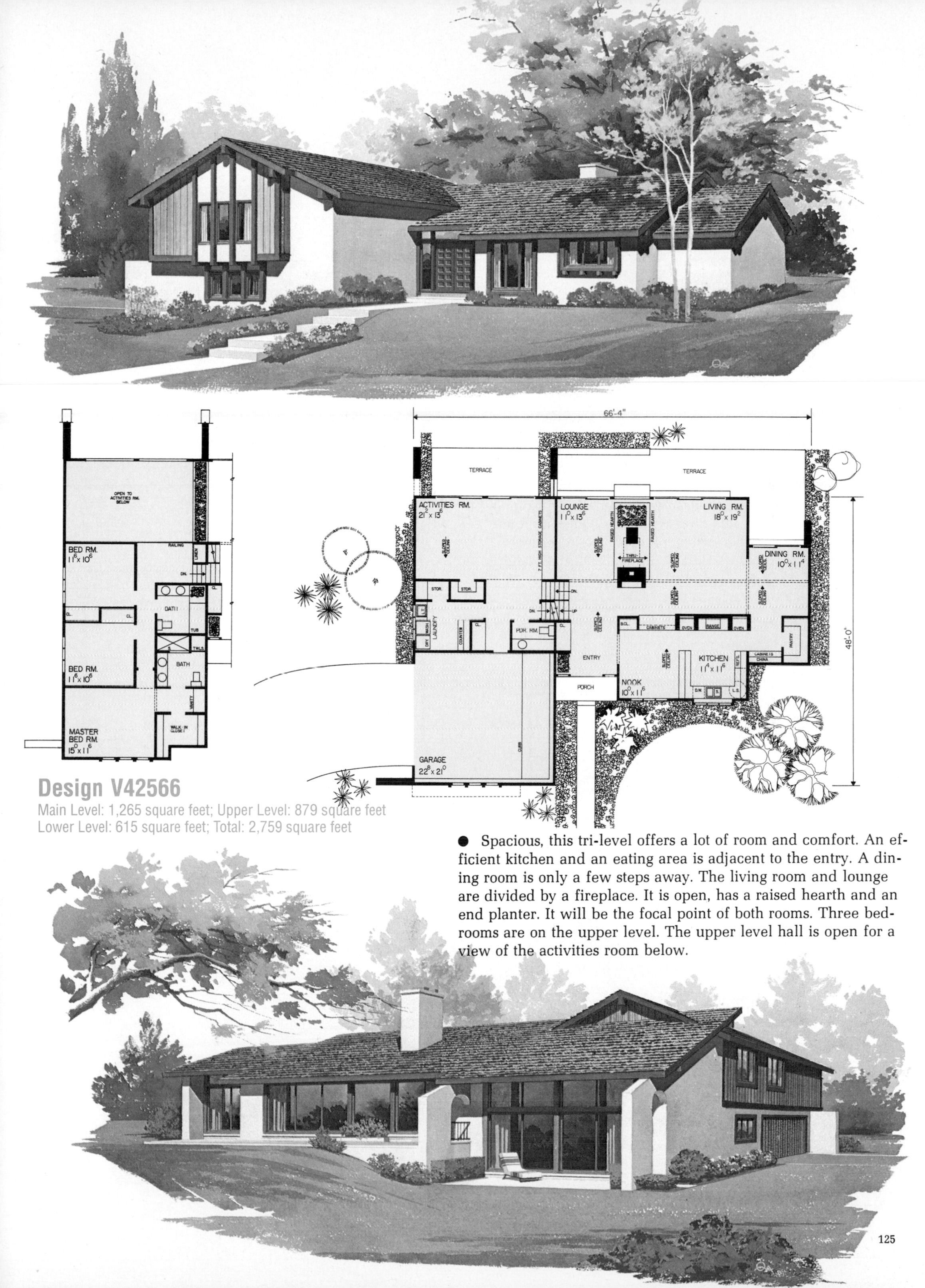

Design V42566

Main Level: 1,265 square feet; Upper Level: 879 square feet
Lower Level: 615 square feet; Total: 2,759 square feet

● Spacious, this tri-level offers a lot of room and comfort. An efficient kitchen and an eating area is adjacent to the entry. A dining room is only a few steps away. The living room and lounge are divided by a fireplace. It is open, has a raised hearth and an end planter. It will be the focal point of both rooms. Three bedrooms are on the upper level. The upper level hall is open for a view of the activities room below.

Design V41976 Main Level: 1,616 square feet; Lower Level: 1,472 square feet; Total: 3,088 square feet

● Here's a hillside design just patterned for the large, active family. Whatever the pursuits and interests of the various members, you'd have to guess there would be more than enough space to service one and all with plenty of room to spare. If the children were teenagers, just imagine the fun they would have with their bedrooms, their family room and their hobby room on the lower level. The parents would be equally thrilled with their adult facilities. A home to be enjoyed by all.

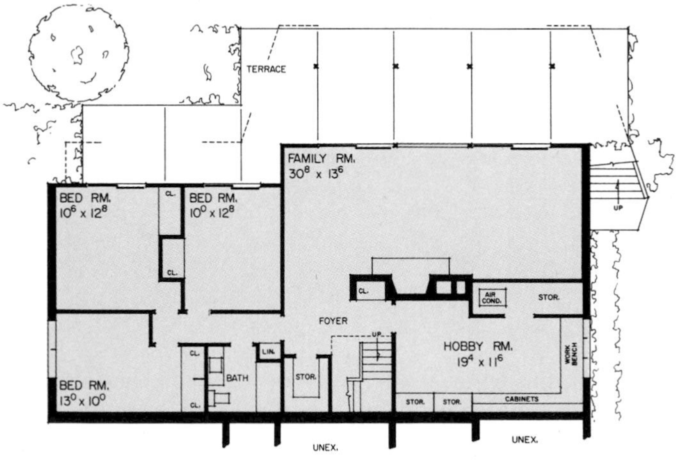

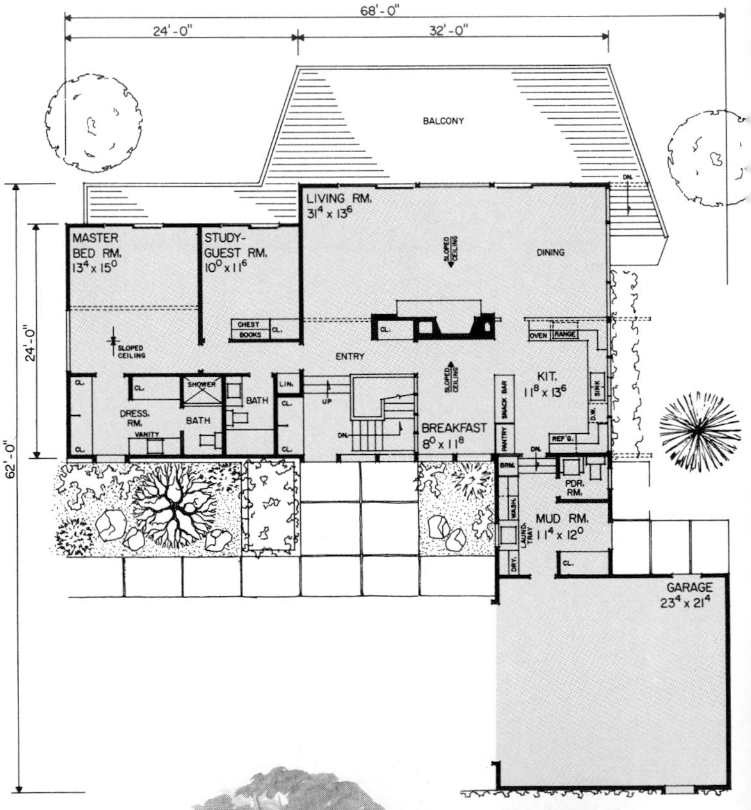

TERRACE
FAMILY RM. 30⁸ x 13⁶
BED RM. 10⁶ x 12⁸
BED RM. 10⁰ x 12⁸
BED RM. 13⁰ x 10⁰
FOYER
HOBBY RM. 19⁴ x 11⁶
BATH
STOR.
AIR COND.
WORK BENCH
CABINETS
UNEX.
UNEX.

68'-0"
24'-0"
32'-0"
BALCONY
LIVING RM. 31⁴ x 13⁶
DINING
MASTER BED RM. 13⁴ x 15⁰
STUDY-GUEST RM. 10⁰ x 11⁶
CHEST BOOKS
SLOPED CEILING
ENTRY
DRESS. RM.
VANITY
BATH
SHOWER
KIT. 11⁸ x 13⁶
OVEN
RANGE
BREAKFAST 8⁰ x 11⁸
SNACK BAR
PANTRY
PDR. RM.
MUD RM. 11⁴ x 12⁰
LAUND. TRAY
WASH.
DRY.
GARAGE 23⁴ x 21⁴
24'-0"
62'-0"

Design V41974 Main Level: 1,680 square feet; Lower Level: 1,344 square feet; Total: 3,024 square feet

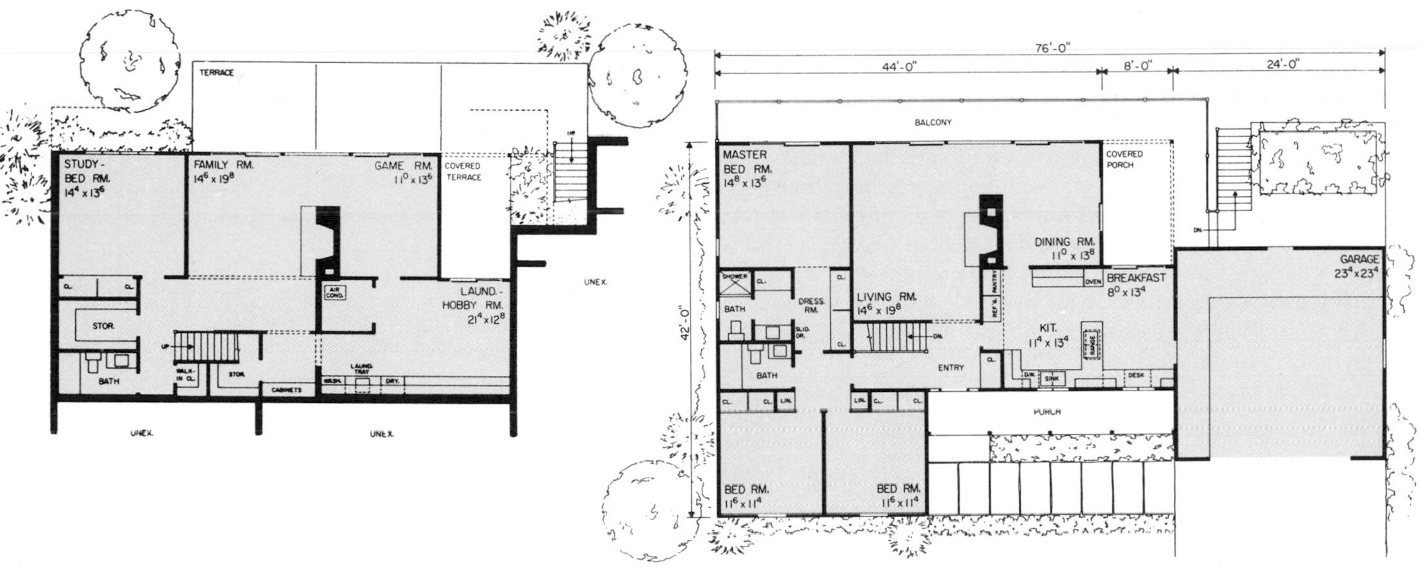

● You would never guess from looking at the front of this traditional design that it possessed such a strikingly different rear. From the front, you would guess that all of its livability is on one floor. Yet, just imagine the tremendous amount of livability that is added to the plan as a result of exposing the lower level - 1,344 square feet of it. Living in this hillside house will mean fun. Obviously, the most popular spot will be the balcony. Then again, maybe it could be the terrace adjacent to the family room. Both the terrace and the balcony have a covered area to provide protection against unfavorable weather. The interior of the plan also will serve the family with ease.

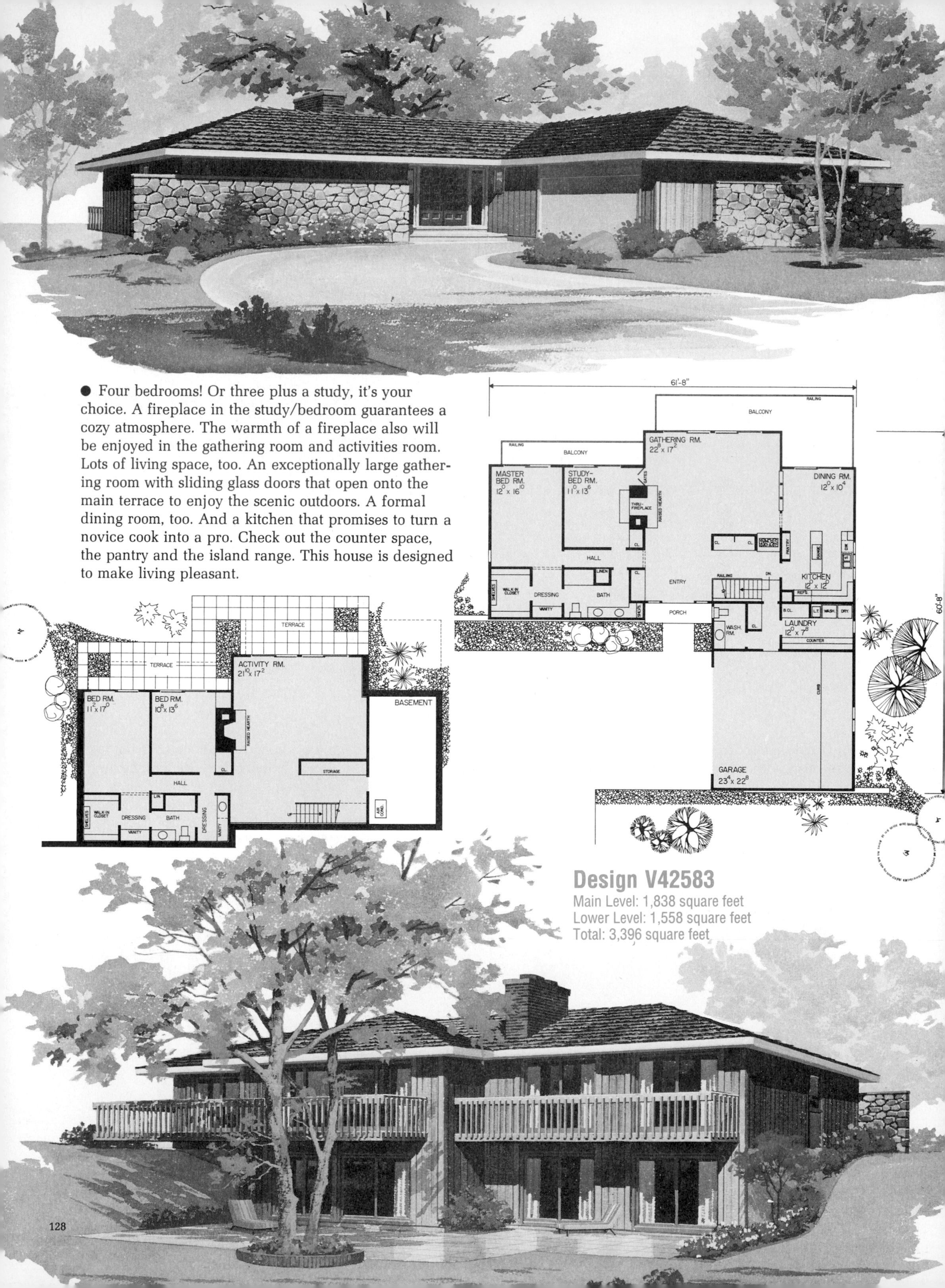

● Four bedrooms! Or three plus a study, it's your choice. A fireplace in the study/bedroom guarantees a cozy atmosphere. The warmth of a fireplace also will be enjoyed in the gathering room and activities room. Lots of living space, too. An exceptionally large gathering room with sliding glass doors that open onto the main terrace to enjoy the scenic outdoors. A formal dining room, too. And a kitchen that promises to turn a novice cook into a pro. Check out the counter space, the pantry and the island range. This house is designed to make living pleasant.

Design V42583

Main Level: 1,838 square feet
Lower Level: 1,558 square feet
Total: 3,396 square feet

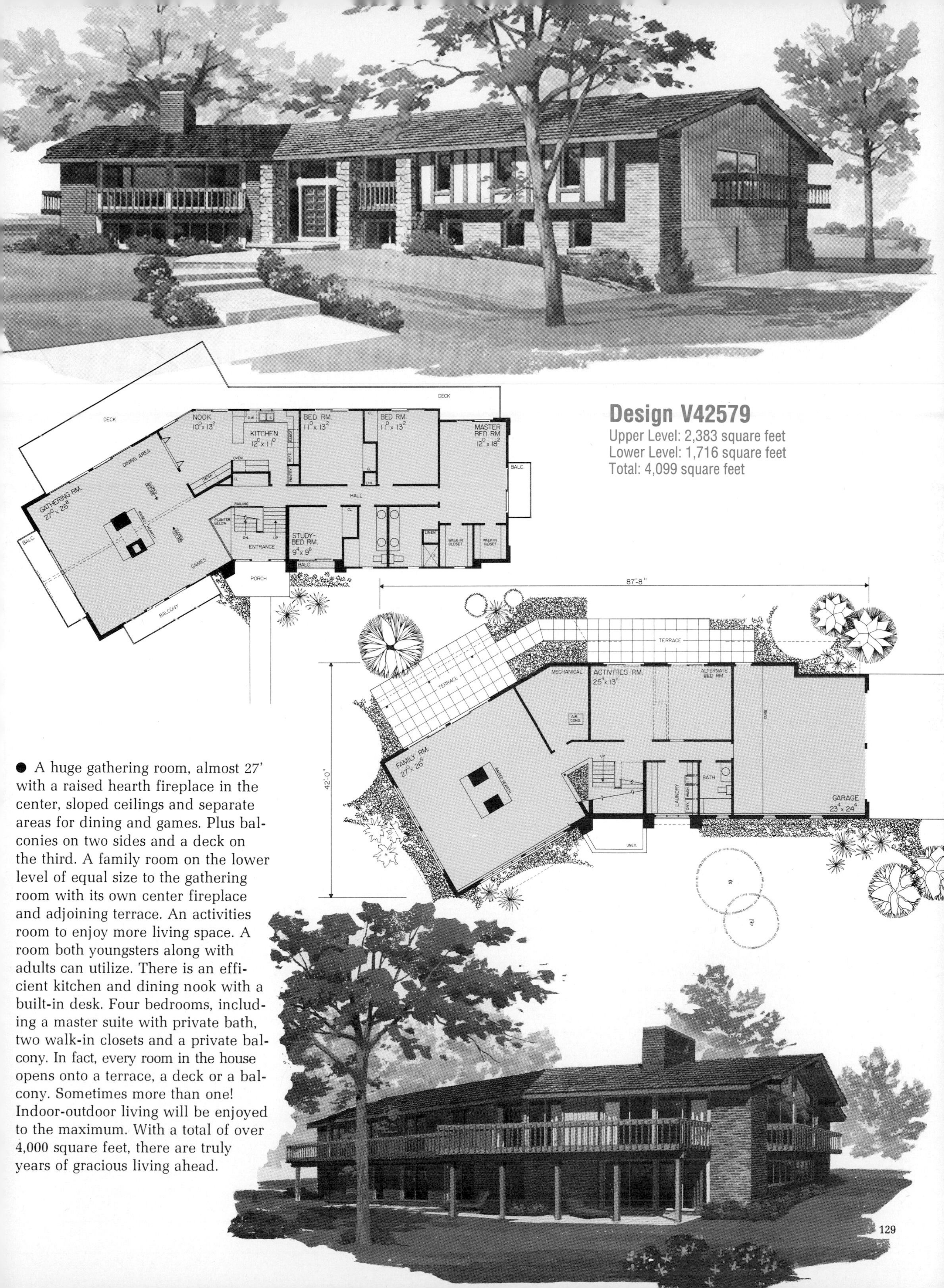

Design V42579

Upper Level: 2,383 square feet
Lower Level: 1,716 square feet
Total: 4,099 square feet

● A huge gathering room, almost 27' with a raised hearth fireplace in the center, sloped ceilings and separate areas for dining and games. Plus balconies on two sides and a deck on the third. A family room on the lower level of equal size to the gathering room with its own center fireplace and adjoining terrace. An activities room to enjoy more living space. A room both youngsters along with adults can utilize. There is an efficient kitchen and dining nook with a built-in desk. Four bedrooms, including a master suite with private bath, two walk-in closets and a private balcony. In fact, every room in the house opens onto a terrace, a deck or a balcony. Sometimes more than one! Indoor-outdoor living will be enjoyed to the maximum. With a total of over 4,000 square feet, there are truly years of gracious living ahead.

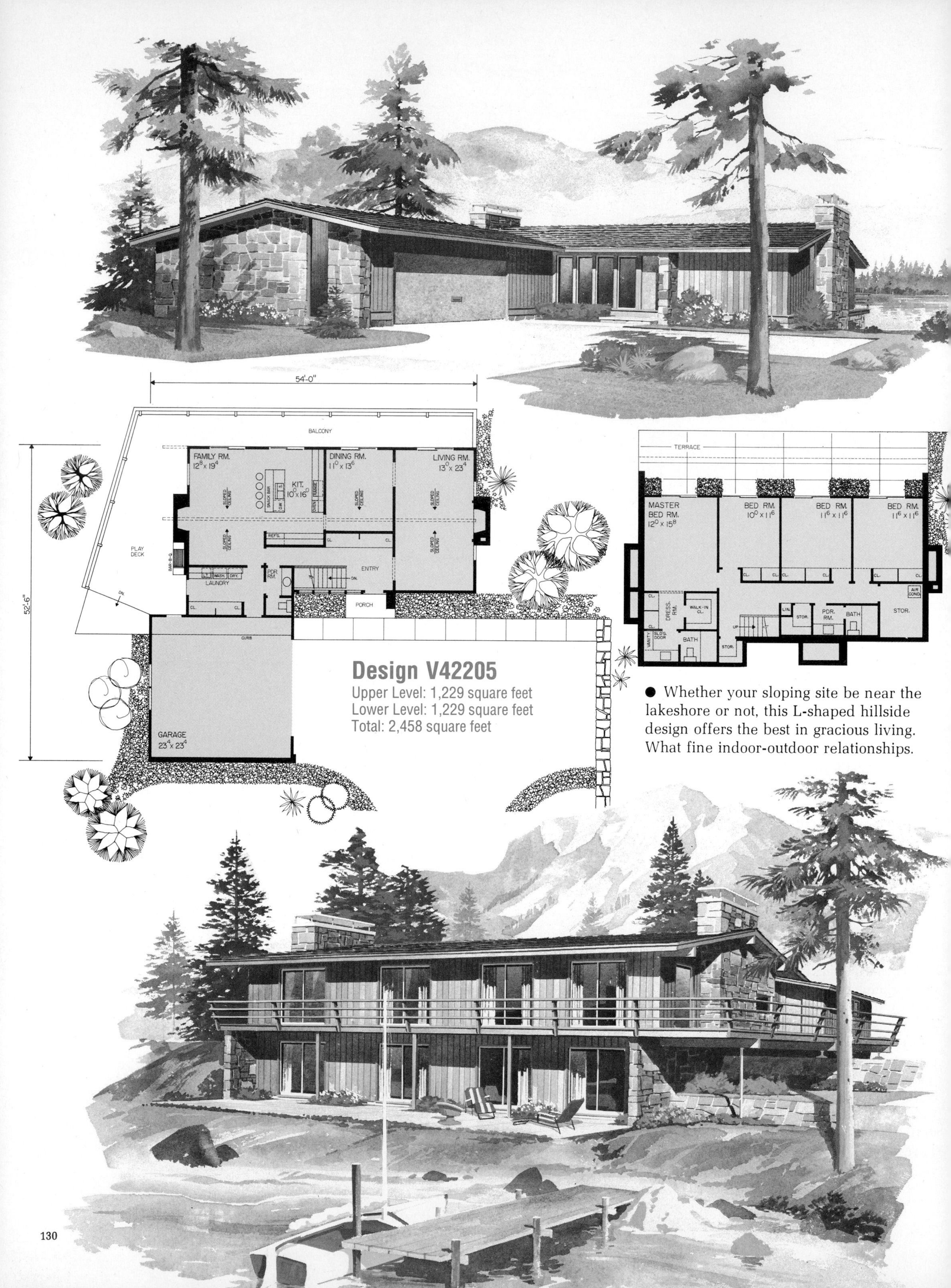

Design V42205

Upper Level: 1,229 square feet
Lower Level: 1,229 square feet
Total: 2,458 square feet

● Whether your sloping site be near the lakeshore or not, this L-shaped hillside design offers the best in gracious living. What fine indoor-outdoor relationships.

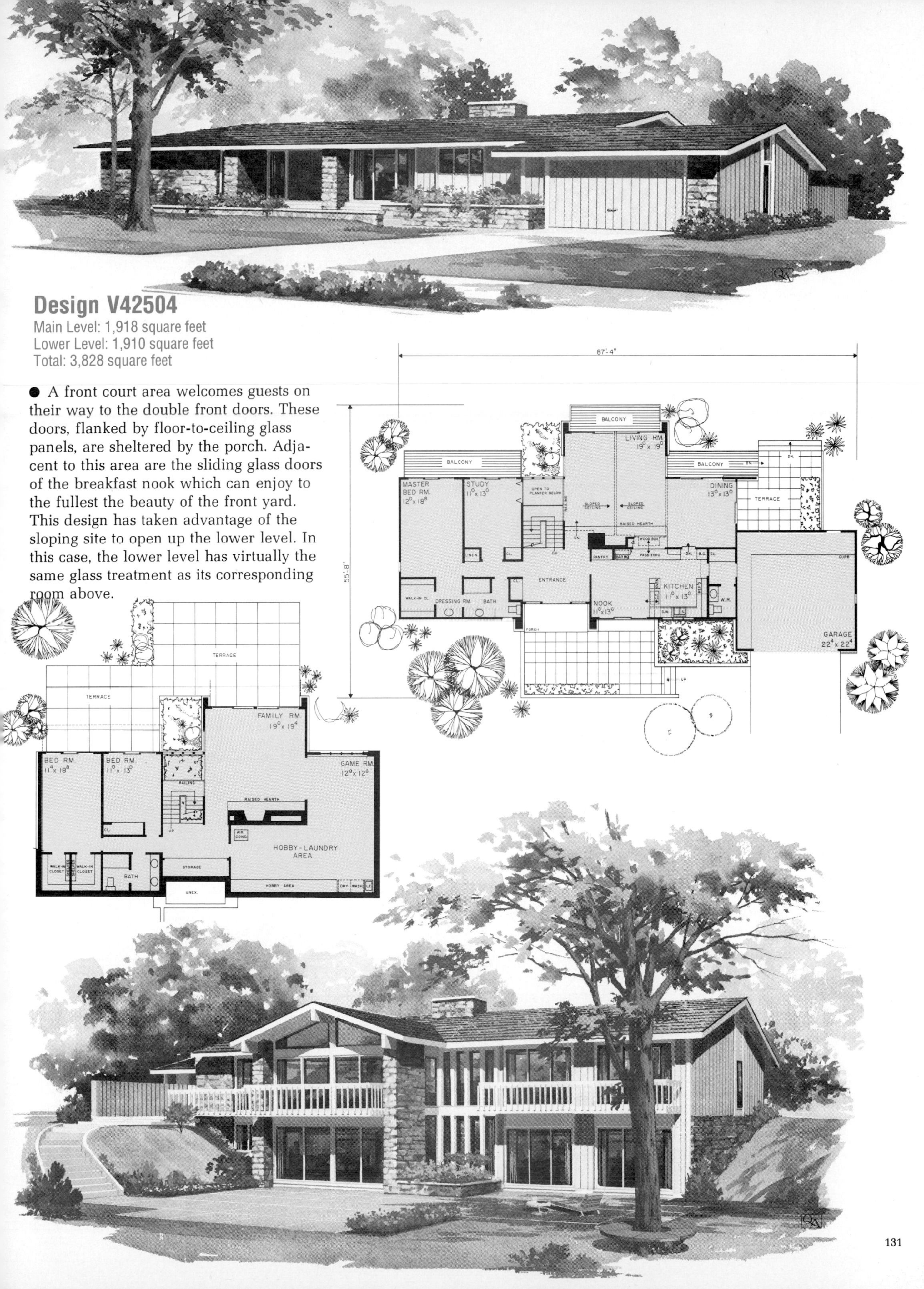

Design V42504

Main Level: 1,918 square feet
Lower Level: 1,910 square feet
Total: 3,828 square feet

● A front court area welcomes guests on their way to the double front doors. These doors, flanked by floor-to-ceiling glass panels, are sheltered by the porch. Adjacent to this area are the sliding glass doors of the breakfast nook which can enjoy to the fullest the beauty of the front yard. This design has taken advantage of the sloping site to open up the lower level. In this case, the lower level has virtually the same glass treatment as its corresponding room above.

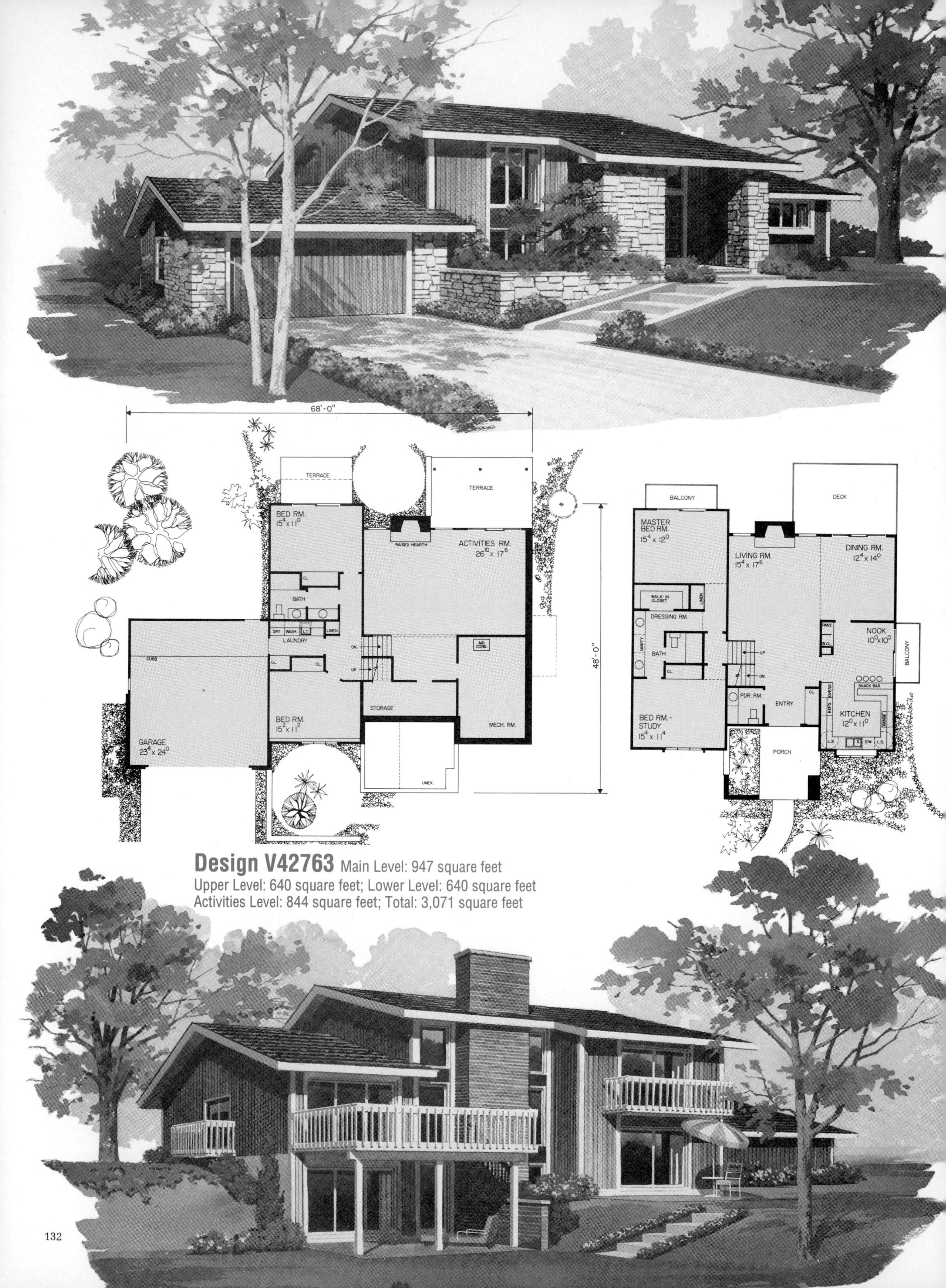

Design V42763 Main Level: 947 square feet
Upper Level: 640 square feet; Lower Level: 640 square feet
Activities Level: 844 square feet; Total: 3,071 square feet

ONE-STORY VACATION HOMES . . .

ffer the optimum in leisure living simplicity and convenience. Whatever your building budget, you'll find these designs offer open living reas and a feeling of spaciousness. Fireplaces, sloped ceilings, decks, and terraces are worthy of note. Sleeping accommodations range from ne-bedroom facilities to bunk space for many.

Design V41479

Square Footage: 1,360

● This unique plan is basically two 20 x 32 foot rectangles connected by an entrance hall, or passage unit. A sweeping wood deck provides the common outdoor living area. The sleeping unit has three bedrooms and two full baths. The ceiling of the master bedroom slopes.

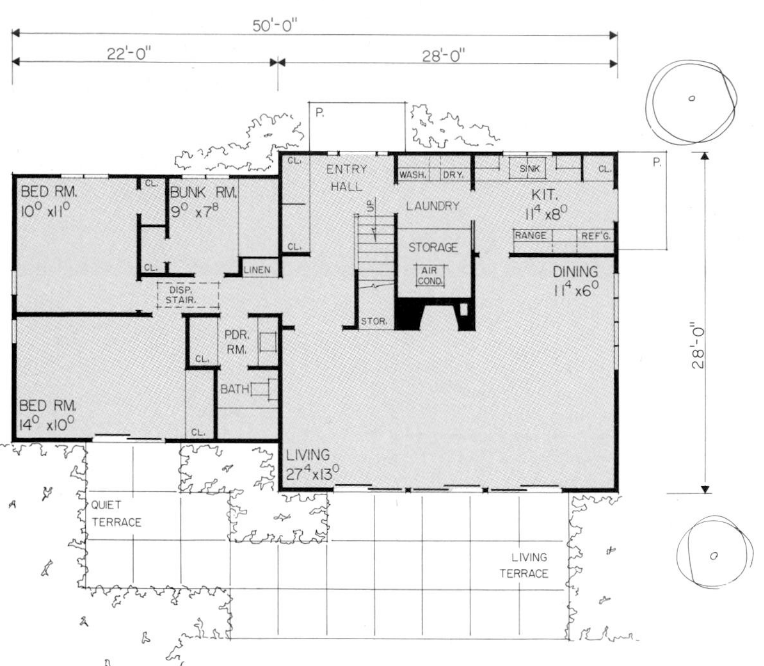

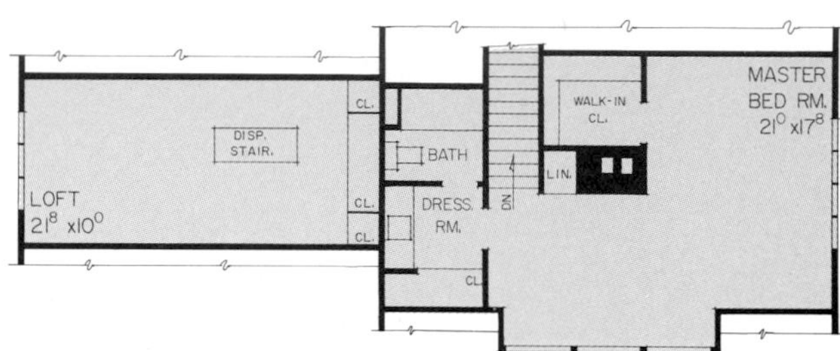

Design V41481

First Floor: 1,268 square feet
Second Floor: 700 square feet
Total: 1,968 square feet

● Here is a vacation home that retains much of the form, or shape, of traditional New England design to which present day window treatment has been added. The result is a pleasing mixture of the old and the new. Study the plans carefully. Livability is exceptional.

Design V41497

Square Footage: 1,292

● Another design whose general shape is most interesting and whose livability is truly refreshing. After a stay in this fine second home it will, indeed, be difficult to resume your daily activities in your first home. When you return from vacation you will miss the spaciousness of your living room, the efficiency of your work center, the pleasing layout of your master bedroom and all those glass sliding doors which mean you are usually but a step from the trouble-free out-of-doors.

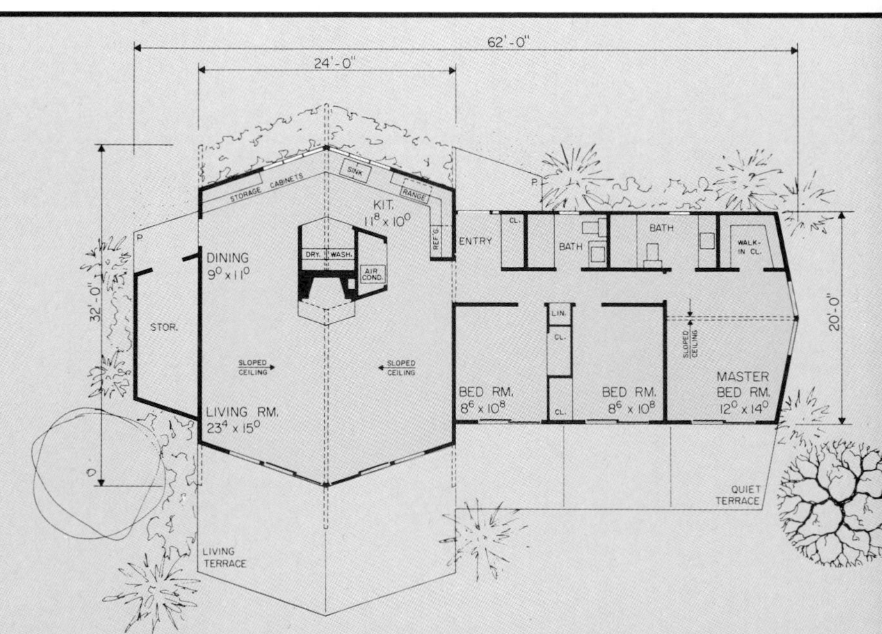

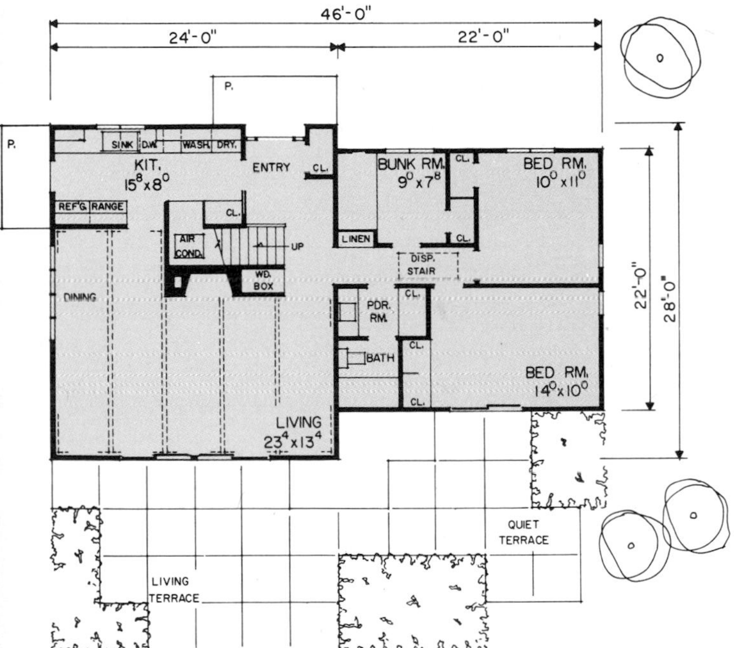

Design V41478

First Floor: 1,156 square feet
Second Floor: 596 square feet
Total: 1,752 square feet

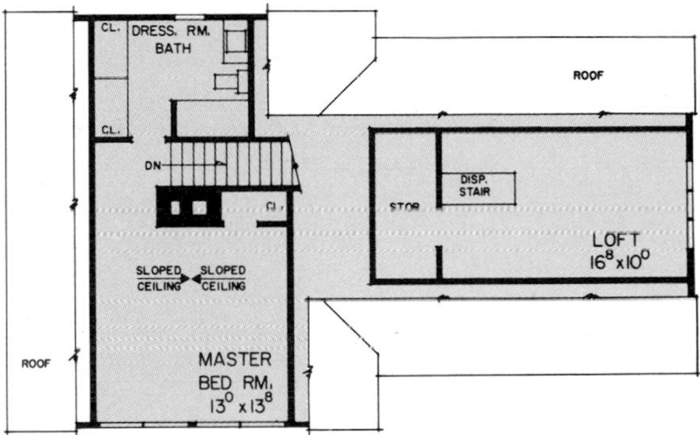

● Here is an abundance of vacation livability. Well zoned, there is a spacious beamed ceiling and dining area, an exceptional work center, a separate first floor sleeping wing. Upstairs there is the elegant master bedroom suite. For extra space don't miss the loft.

Design V42464

First Floor: 960 square feet
Second Floor: 448 square feet
Total: 1,408 square feet

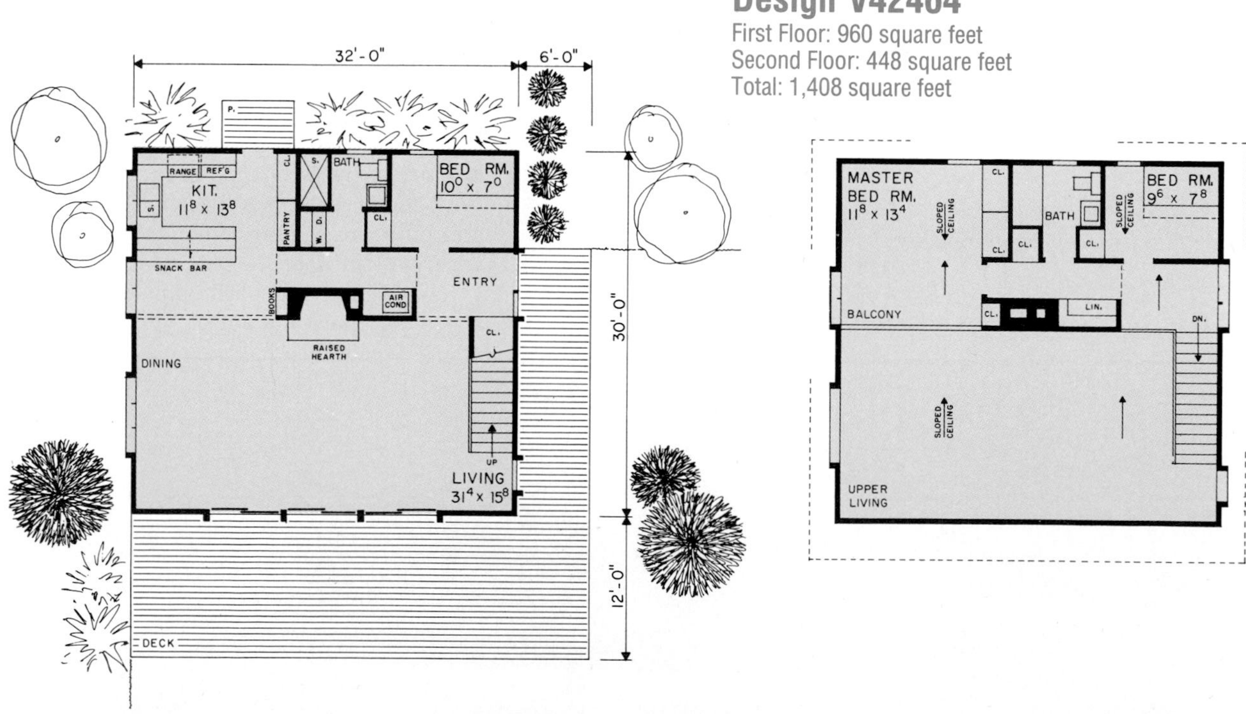

● Almost a perfect square (32 x 30 feet), this economically built leisure home has a wealth of features. The list is a long one and well might begin with that wood deck just outside the sliding glass doors of the 31 foot living area. And what an area it really is - 31 feet in length and with a sloped ceiling! The list of features continues with the U-shaped kitchen, the snack bar, the pantry and closet storage wall, the two full baths (one with stall shower), three bedrooms and raised hearth fireplace. Perhaps the favorite highlight will be the manner in which the second floor overlooks the first floor. The second floor balcony adds even a greater dimension of spaciousness and interior appeal. Don't miss side and rear entries. Observe coat closets placed nearby.

Design V41444

First Floor: 1,008 square feet
Second Floor: 624 square feet
Total: 1,632 square feet

● Everybody will have fun spending their vacations at this cottage. And why shouldn't they? The pleasant experiences of vacation living will be more than just sitting on the outdoor balconies of the second floor. They will include eating leisurely on the dining deck and lounging peacefully on the living deck. Further, they will encompass the relaxing hours spent before the cheerful fireplace in the living room on cool evenings.

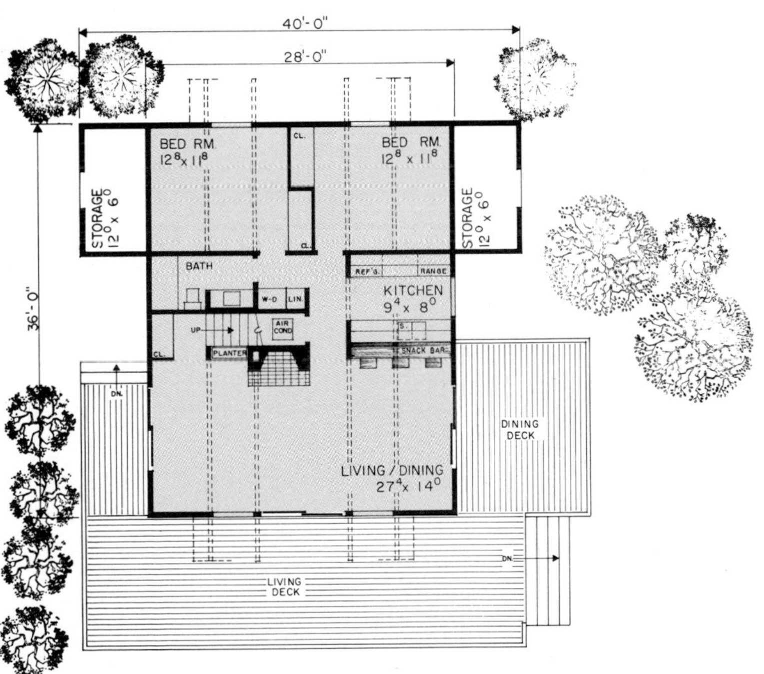

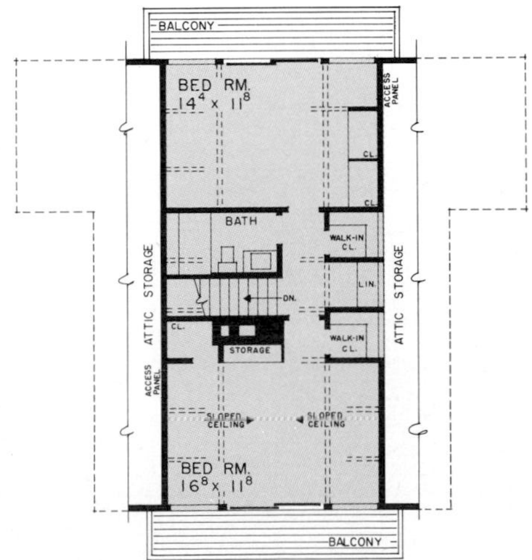

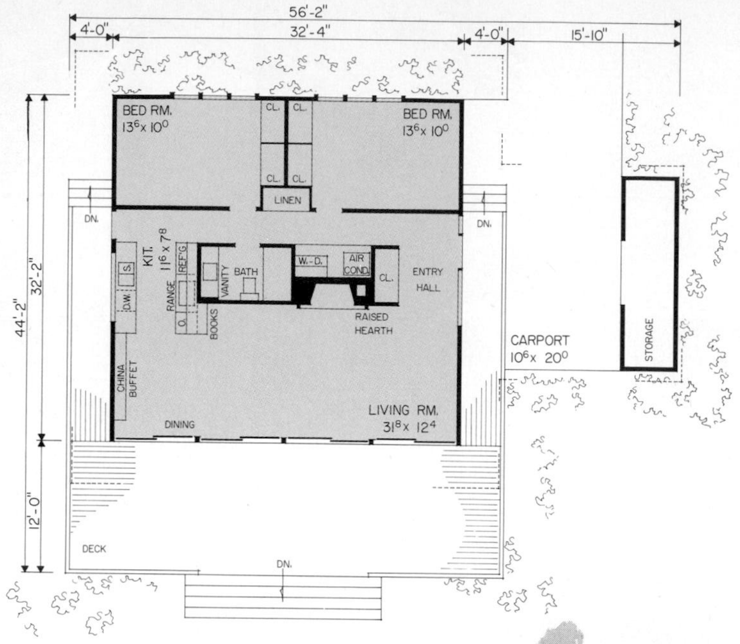

● This charming open-floor-plan vacation home features a host of special items: wide wrap-around deck, carport with storage space, raised-hearth fireplace, and built-ins. Two bedrooms have plenty of closet space and share a full bath. Take special note of the galley kitchen and convenient side entry.

Design V41419

Square Footage: 1,040

● A three-bedroom vacation home insures that everyone has a special get-away spot. This one boasts a true master suite with private bath. Also noteworthy are the laundry area in the central bath, wide front terrace, covered carport area, and abundant storage space.

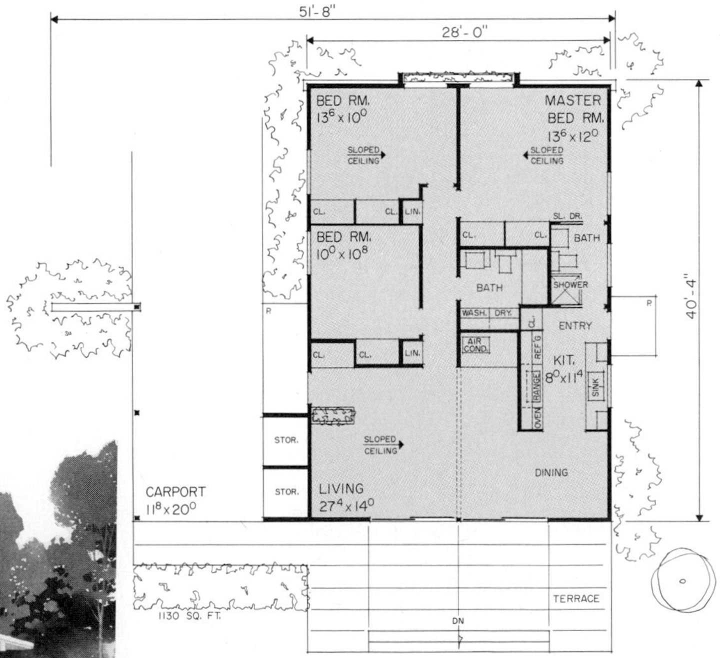

Design V42410

Square Footage: 1,130

Design V41471

Square Footage: 1,465

● A summer cottage which will surely play its part well. Although basically a two-bedroom house, its sleeping and living potential is much greater. The large screened porch offers a full measure of flexibility. It supplements the living room as an extra informal living area, while also permitting its use as a sleeping porch. Whatever its function, the screened porch certainly will be in constant use. Separating the living and dining rooms is the appealing raised hearth fireplace. A snack bar is handy to the kitchen which features a glass gable above the wall cabinets. This will be an efficient and cheerful place in which to work. A utility room houses the heating equipment and the combination washer-dryer. Sloping, beamed ceilings help maintain an aura of spaciousness throughout.

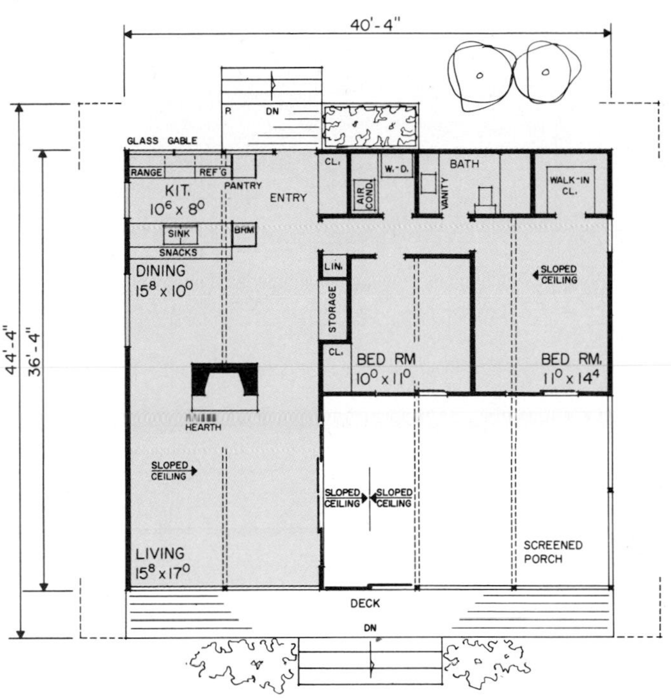

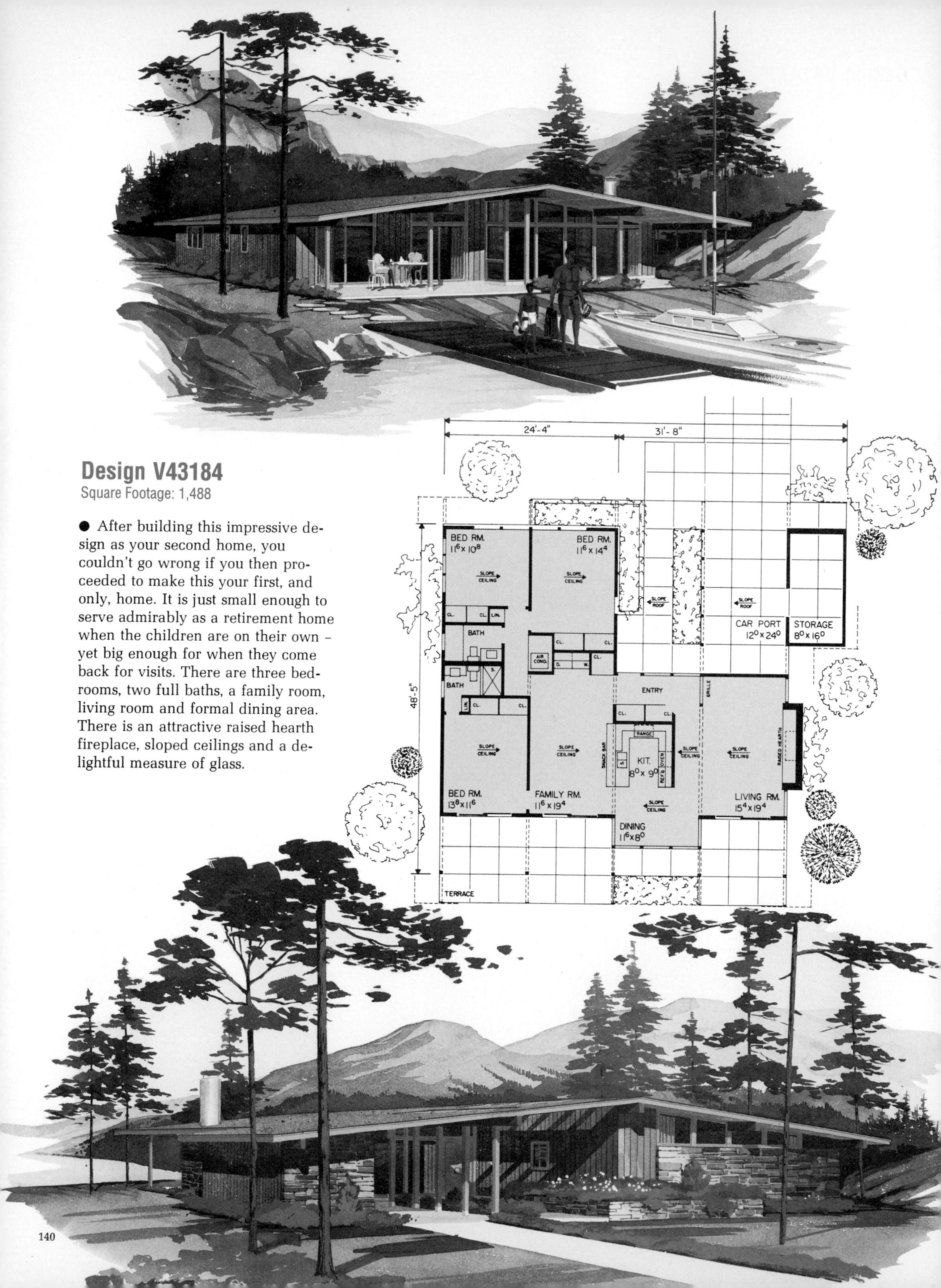

Design V43184

Square Footage: 1,488

● After building this impressive design as your second home, you couldn't go wrong if you then proceeded to make this your first, and only, home. It is just small enough to serve admirably as a retirement home when the children are on their own – yet big enough for when they come back for visits. There are three bedrooms, two full baths, a family room, living room and formal dining area. There is an attractive raised hearth fireplace, sloped ceilings and a delightful measure of glass.

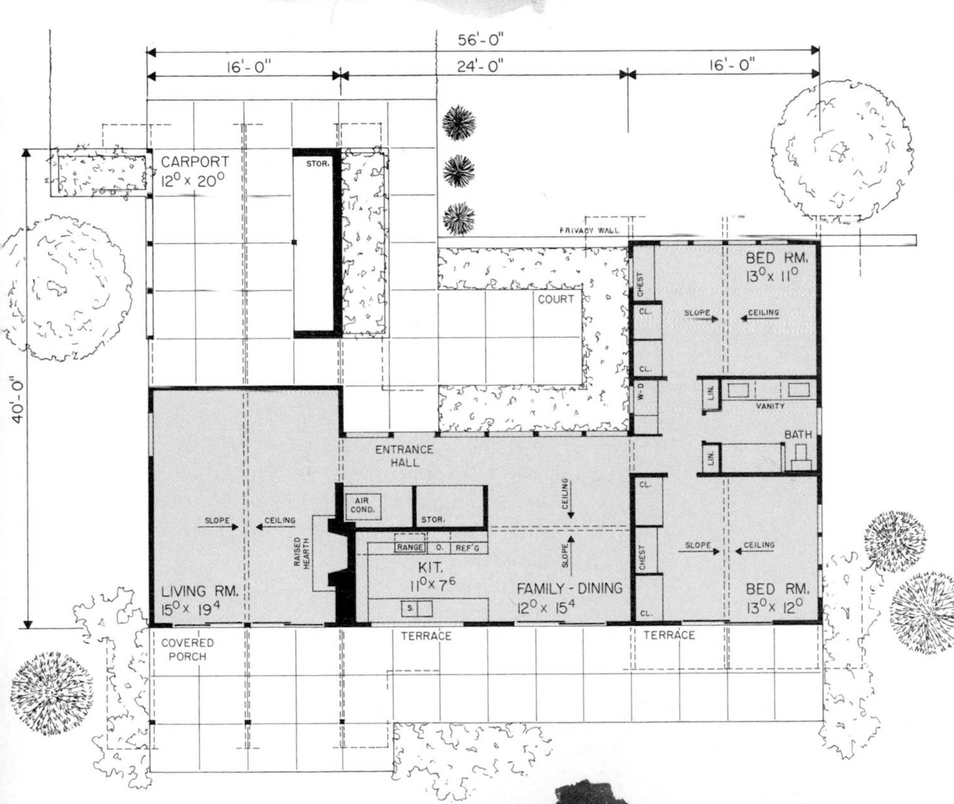

● The features of this two bedroom leisure-time home are legion. Its contemporary exterior, characterized by the low-pitched, wide overhanging roof, the masonry masses, the dramatic glass areas and the plan's irregular configuration, has a special appeal of its own. The front privacy wall helps form a delightful court. The development of this outdoor living area can be a pleasant summer-time project. Activities on and around the rear covered porch and terraces will be enjoyable ones, indeed. Inside, there is an atmosphere of spaciousness enhanced by the sloping ceilings.

Design V43185

Square Footage: 1,222

Design V42405

Square Footage: 874

● It's hard to imagine but in just over 800 square feet, this plan manages two bedrooms, a full bath, L-shaped kitchen and 24' wide living area. The carport has a huge storage room for sports equipment and games. Note the raised-hearth fireplace and sloped ceiling in the living room.

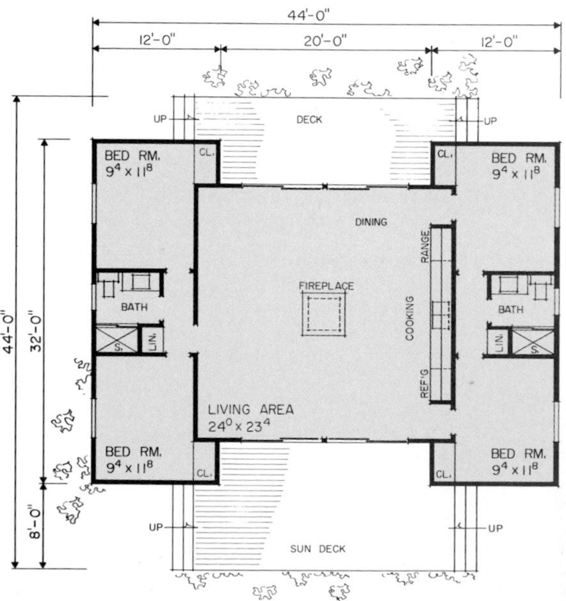

Design V41440

Square Footage: 1,248

● Here's a clever design that separates the sleeping areas into two wings, each with its own bath. The living area radiates around a central fireplace and has two deck options — one to the front, the other to the rear. Kitchen chores are accomplished along one long wall of the living area.

Design V42432

Square Footage: 984

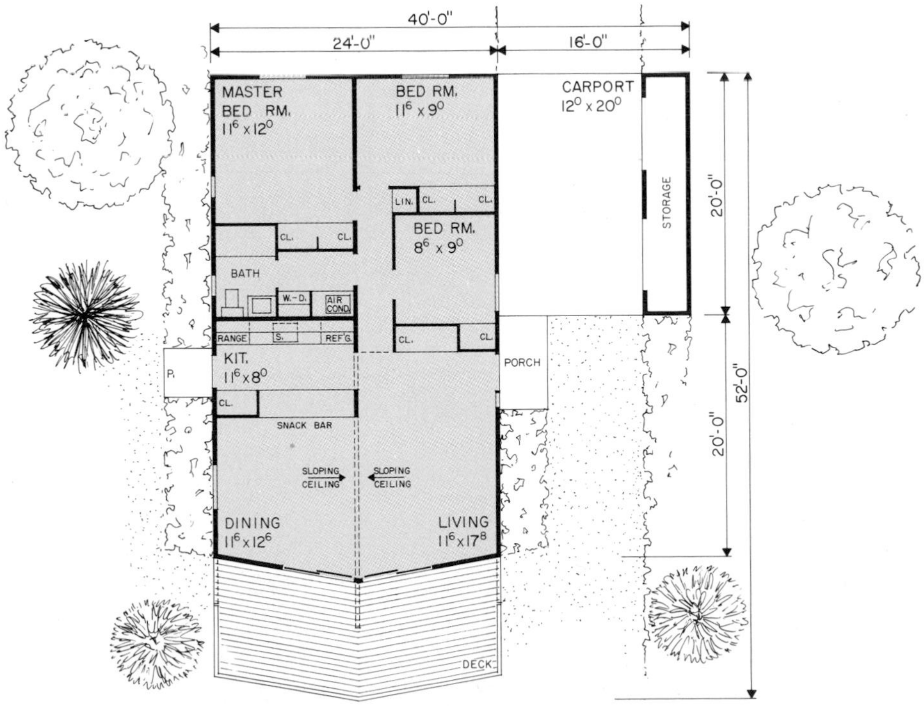

● Here is positive proof that even the most simple of floor plans can be long on livability and can be sheltered by a remarkably pleasing exterior. The 24 foot width of this second home is complemented by the 16 foot carport. The extension of the low-pitched roof to form the carport is a pleasing feature. The carport will double as a storage area for the boat while the storage wall will take care of all that fishing, boating, hunting and other recreational paraphernalia. The interior of this home is a model in the efficient use of space. None of it is wasted. There are plenty of closets; a fine, workable kitchen; a big counter snack bar; and sloping ceiling. You will cherish the hours spent on the wood deck. It is the ideal spot to sit back, relax and take in the beauty of the surroundings.

Design V41461

Square Footage: 1,844

● Let that vacation home of yours express that little extra "something" in the way of charm. Let it enjoy a character all of its own – one that is distinctively different. This large second home is impressive, indeed. It has all the comforts of most year 'round homes. Maybe even a few more. There are two big bedrooms, plus a study. There is a huge sunken living room with plenty of glass, sloping beamed ceiling and an attractive raised hearth fireplace. The separate dining room is a delightful area that looks down into the living room and out onto the terrace. The work center is certainly outstanding. It is highlighted by the mud room and extra washroom. Note powder room. The kitchen has a pass-thru to the snack bar and dining room.

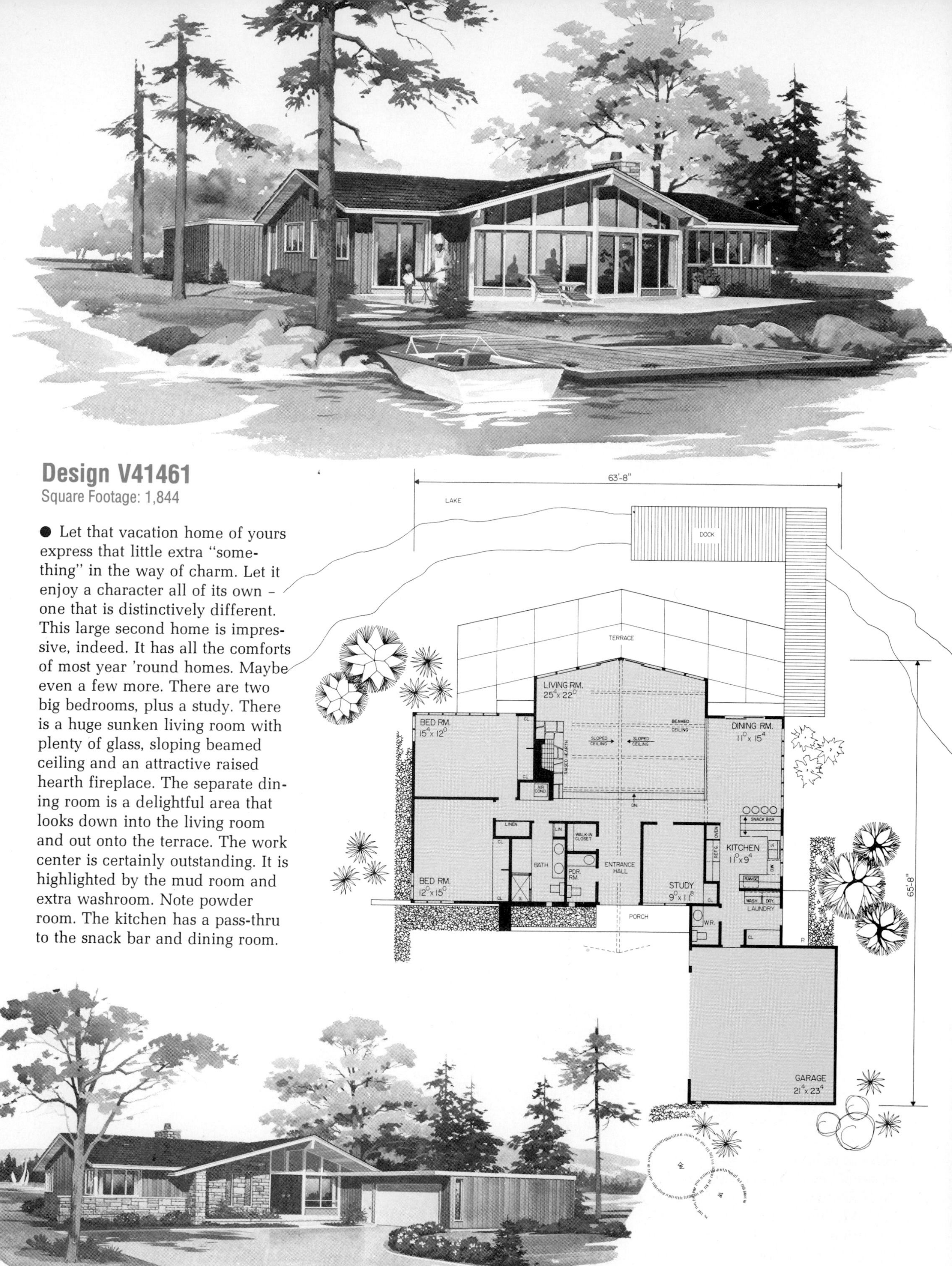

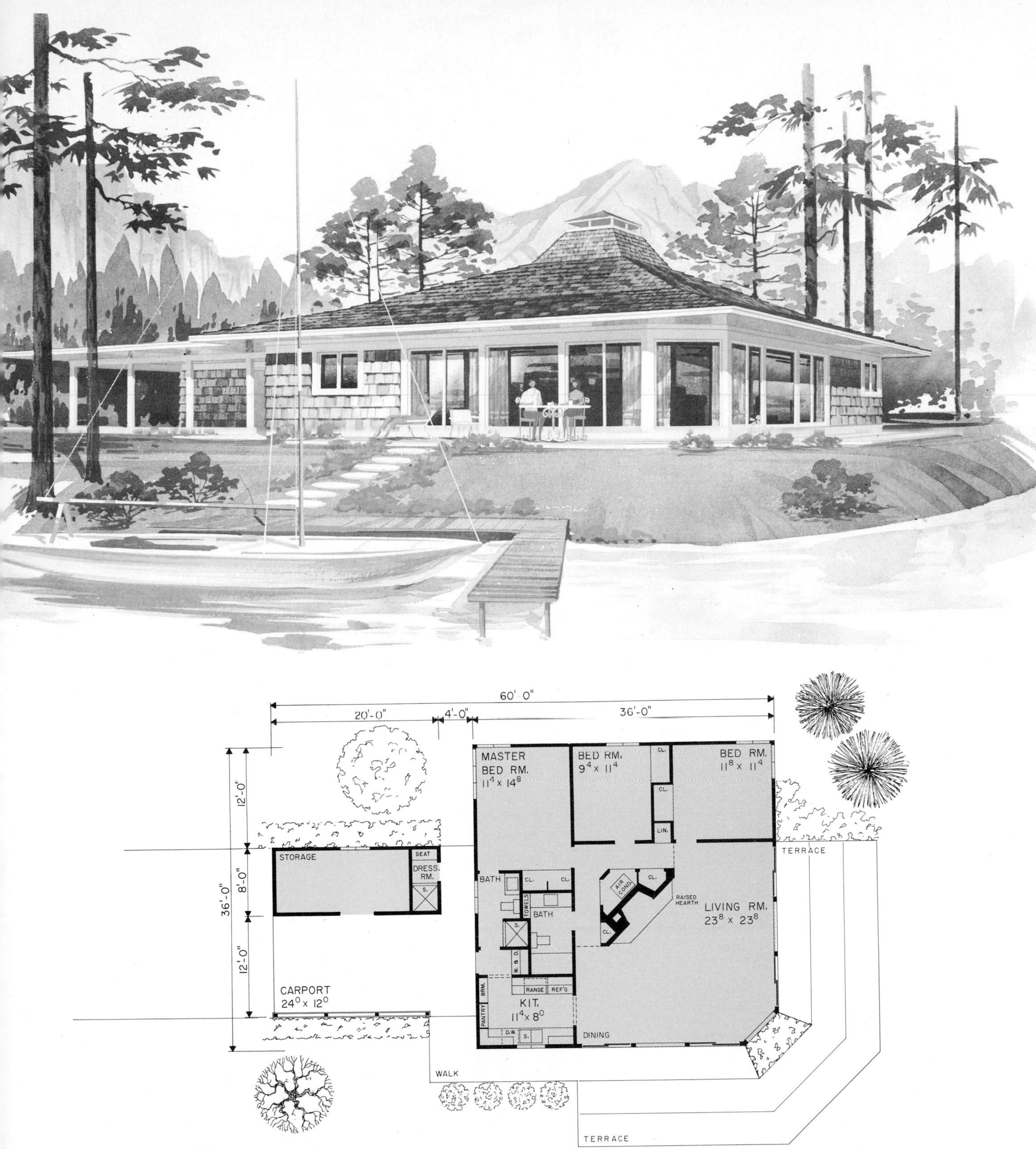

Design V42457 Square Footage: 1,288

● Leisure living will indeed be graciously experienced in this hip-roofed second home. Except for the clipped corner, it is a perfect square measuring 36 x 36 feet. The 23 foot square living room enjoys a great view of the surrounding environment by virtue of the expanses of glass. The wide overhanging roof affords protection from the sun. The "open planning" adds to the spaciousness of the interior. The focal point is the raised hearth fireplace. The three bedrooms are serviced by two full baths which are also accessible to other areas. The kitchen, looking out upon the water, will be a delight to work in. Observe the carport, the big bulk storage room and the dressing room with its stall shower. This design has great planning for a leisure-time second home.

Design V41486

Square Footage: 480

● You'll be anxious to start building this delightful little vacation home. Whether you do it yourself, or engage professional help, you will not have to wait long for its completion.

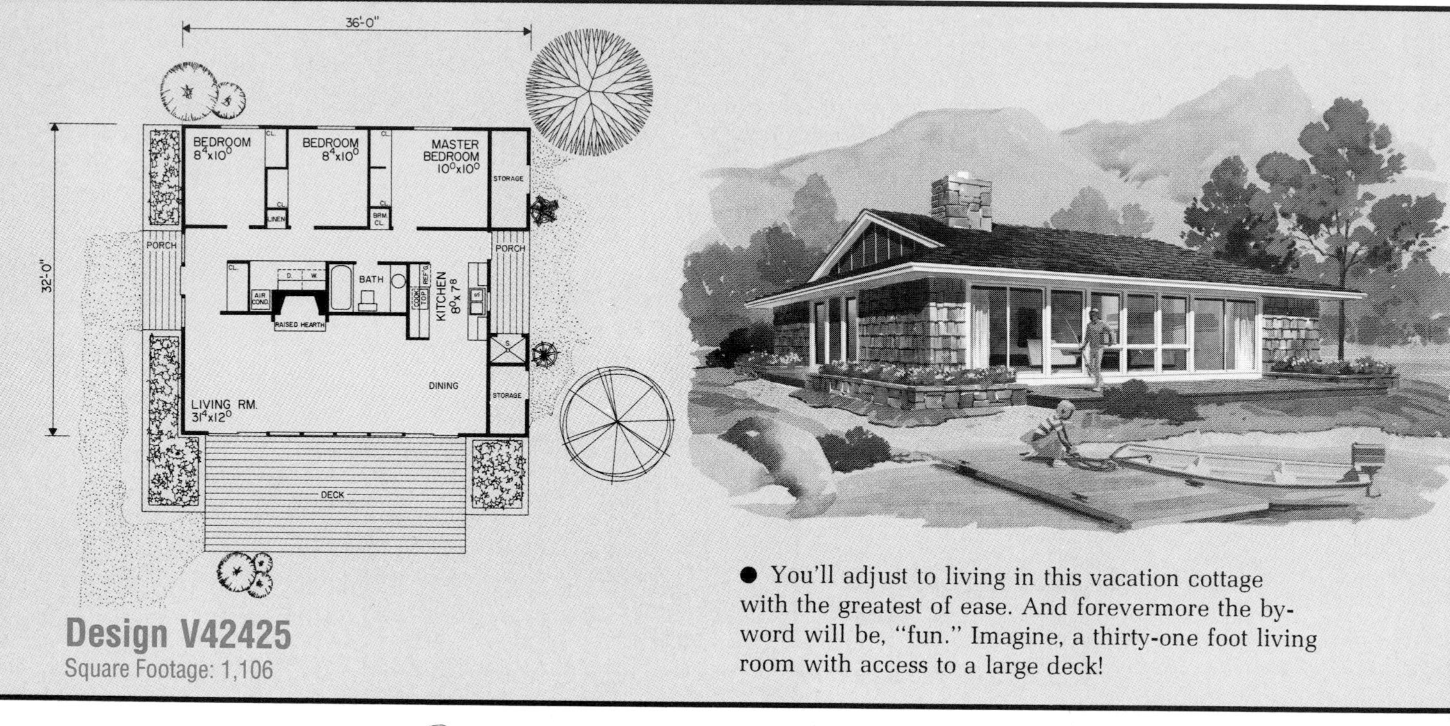

● You'll adjust to living in this vacation cottage with the greatest of ease. And forevermore the by-word will be, "fun." Imagine, a thirty-one foot living room with access to a large deck!

Design V42425

Square Footage: 1,106

Design V41495

Square Footage: 800

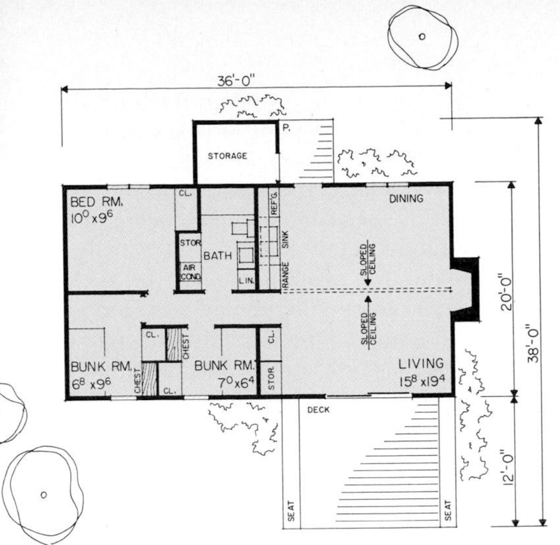

● The kids won't be able to move into this vacation retreat soon enough. Two bunk rooms plus another bedroom for Mom and Dad. Open-planned living area. A real leisure-time home.

Design V41488

Square Footage: 720

● A second home with the informal living message readily apparent both inside and out. The zoning of this home is indeed most interesting – and practical, too. Study the plan carefully.

Design V41462

Square Footage: 1,176

Design V42423

Square Footage: 864

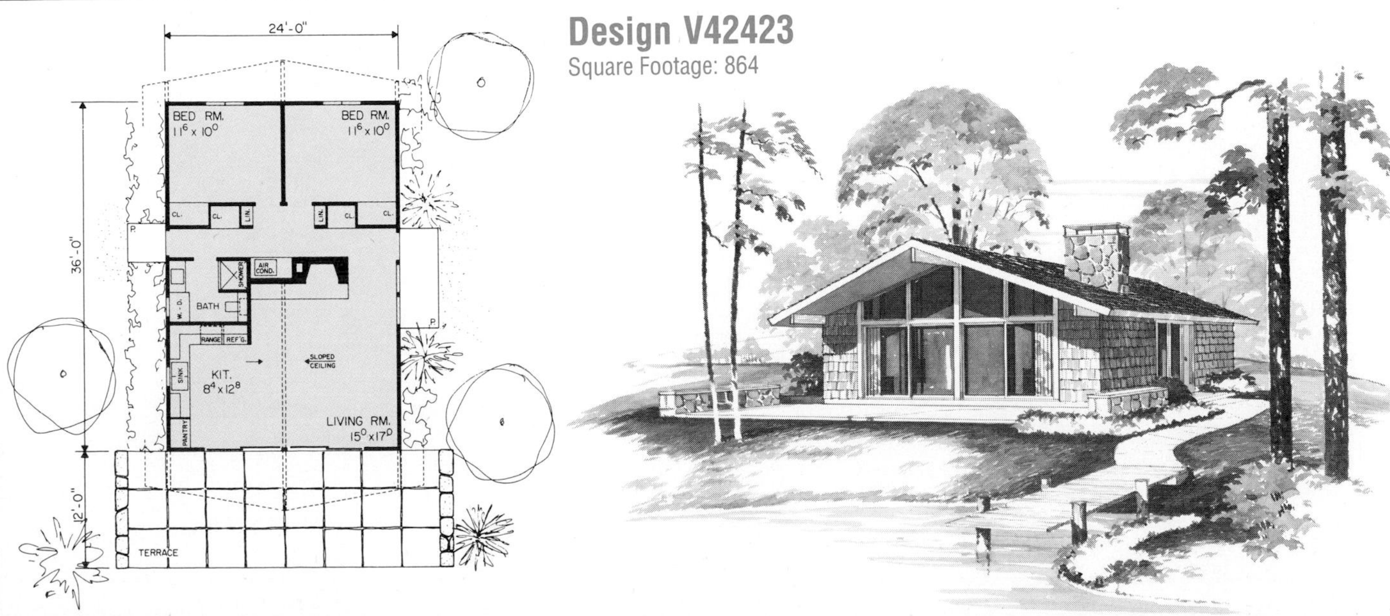

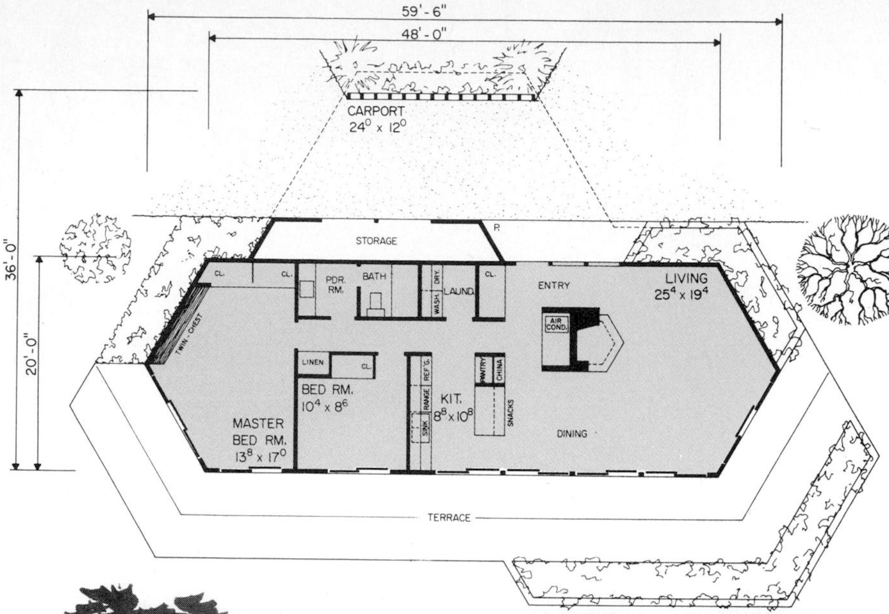

59'-6"
48'-0"
CARPORT
24^0 x 12^0
STORAGE
CL.
CL.
PDR. RM.
BATH
DRY
WASH
LAUND.
CL.
ENTRY
LIVING
25^4 x 19^4
AIR COND.
TWIN CHEST
LINEN
CL.
BED RM.
10^4 x 8^6
REF'G.
RANGE
SINK
KIT.
8^8 x 10^8
PANTRY
CHINA
SNACKS
DINING
MASTER BED RM.
13^8 x 17^0
36'-0"
20'-0"
TERRACE

● Your setting for this refreshing six-sided home may differ tremendously from the picture below. But, whatever the character of the surroundings, the flair of distinction and the degree of livability will not change. This is truly a home away from home. As you welcome the new living patterns, you also will embrace the delightful change of pace. There are eight sets of sliding glass doors which facilitate passage in-and-out-of-doors.

Design V42421

Square Footage: 1,075

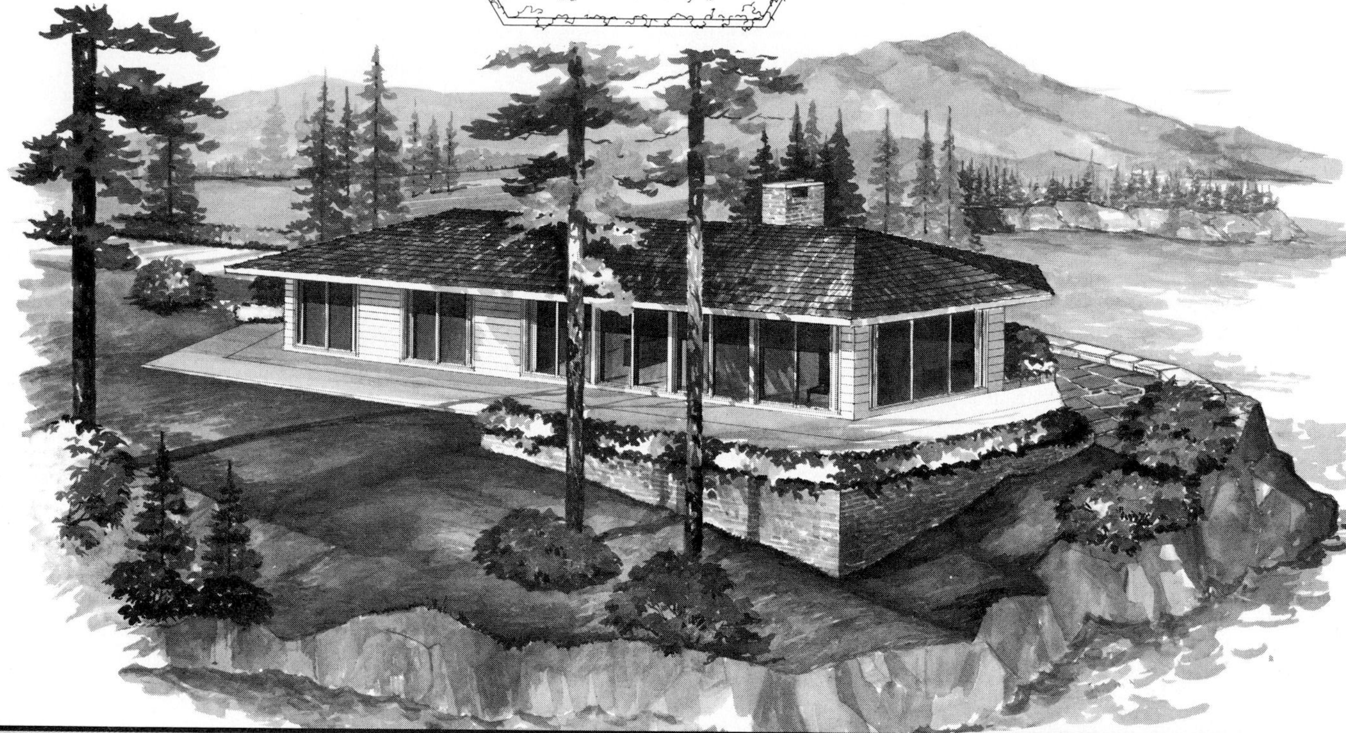

Design V41458 Square Footage: 576

Design V41409

Square Footage: 1,120

● This flat-roofed, T-shaped leisure-time home proves the point that good zoning is good sense in any plan. It is interesting to note the practical result of two complete squares functioning together to provide convenient vacation living. The three bedroom, two full bath sleeping wing will enjoy its privacy from the spacious, open-planned, living area. The storage potential both inside and out is outstanding. Observe the built-in units. The raised hearth fireplace will be a favorite feature. The L-shaped deck will be a popular spot for young and old alike.

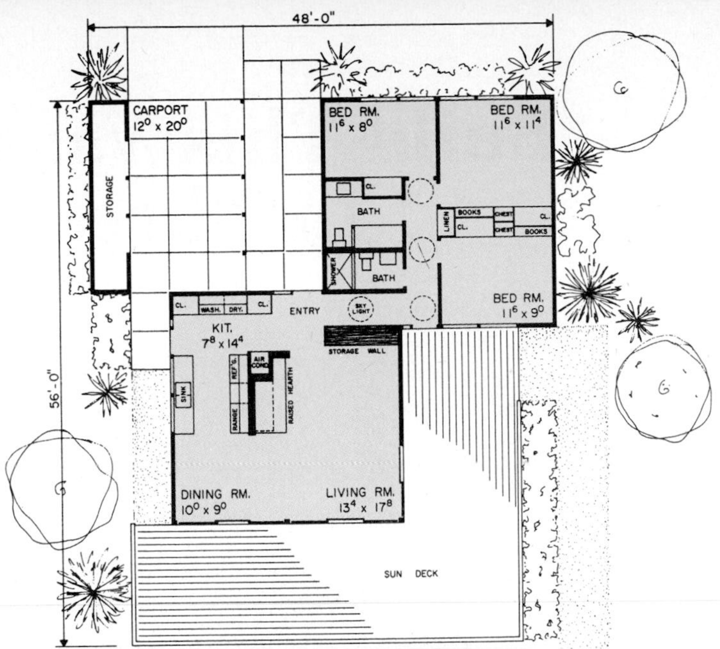

Design V41435

Square Footage: 864

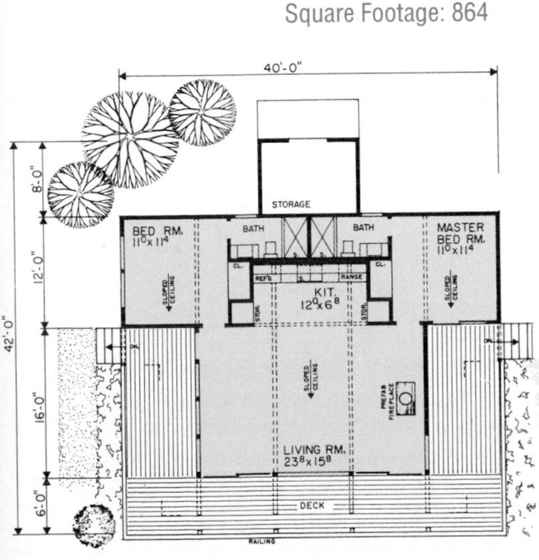

Build This Vacation Home In Three Stages

Design V41425 Basic Unit: 576 square feet; Expanded Unit: 1,152 square feet

● Here is a vacation home that can be easily built in three stages. This procedure will stretch your building budget and enable you to continue as your finances permit. Blueprints show details for the construction of the basic unit first. This features the kitchen, bath, bedroom and living room. The second stage can be either the addition of the two extra bedrooms, or the screened porch. Each addition is a modular 12 x 24 foot unit. The ceilings are sloping thus contributing to the feeling of spaciousness. The finished house has excellent storage facilities. If desired, the screened porch could be modified to be built as a family room addition. Such a move would permit year 'round use. Note the perfectly rectangular shape of this home which will result in economical construction costs.

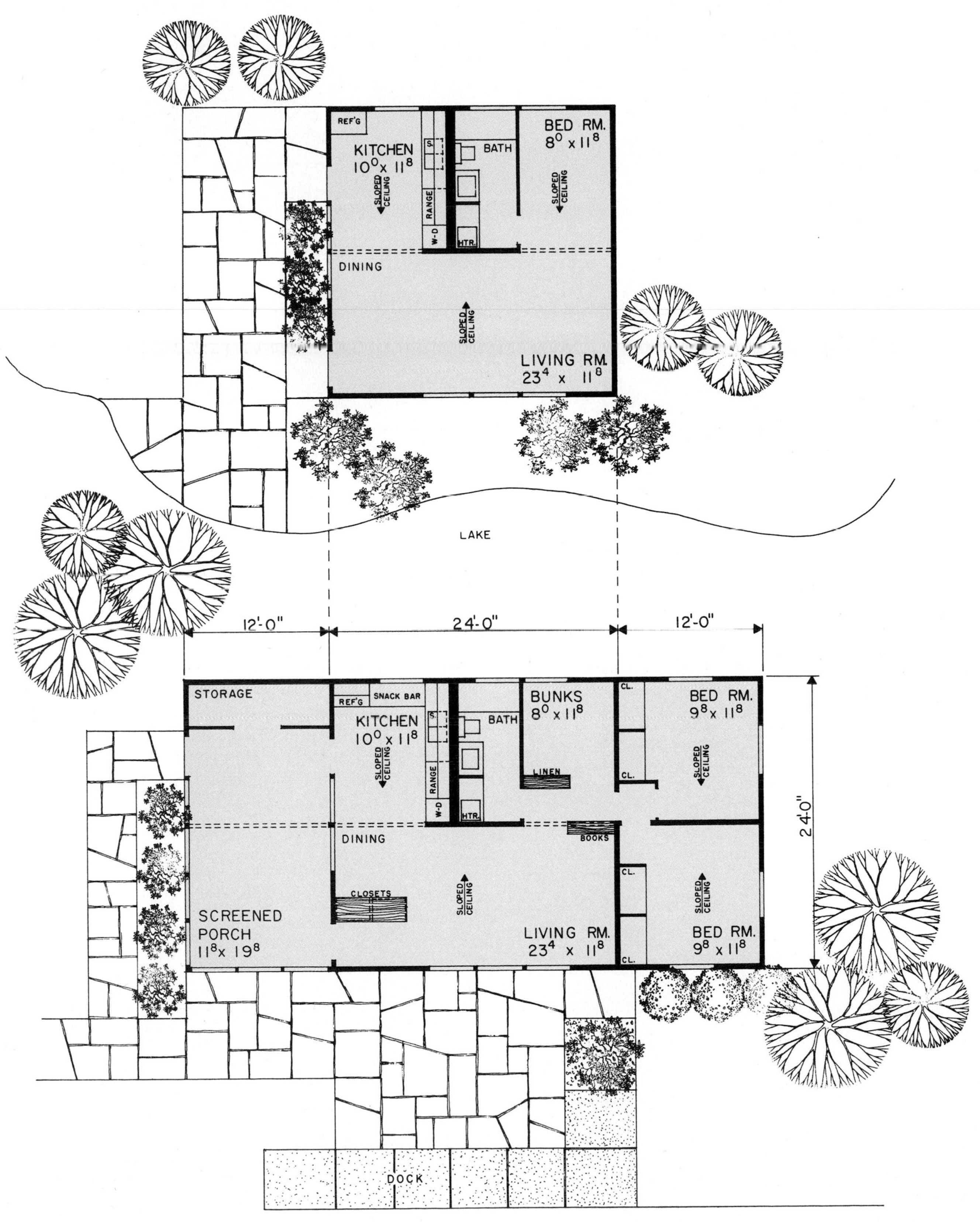

REF'G
KITCHEN
10⁰ x 11⁸
SLOPED CEILING
S.
RANGE
W-D
BATH
HTR.
BED RM.
8⁰ x 11⁸
SLOPED CEILING
DINING
SLOPED CEILING
LIVING RM.
23⁴ x 11⁸
LAKE
12'-0"
24'-0"
12'-0"
STORAGE
REF'G
SNACK BAR
KITCHEN
10⁰ x 11⁸
SLOPED CEILING
RANGE
W-D
BATH
HTR.
BUNKS
8⁰ x 11⁸
LINEN
CL.
BED RM.
9⁸ x 11⁸
CL.
SLOPED CEILING
24'-0"
DINING
BOOKS
CLOSETS
SLOPED CEILING
CL.
SLOPED CEILING
SCREENED
PORCH
11⁸ x 19⁸
LIVING RM.
23⁴ x 11⁸
CL.
BED RM.
9⁸ x 11⁸
DOCK
LAKE

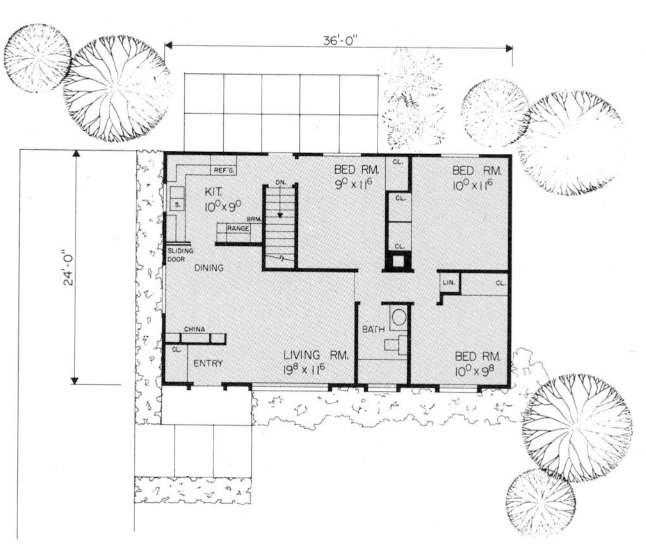

Design V42167

Square Footage: 864

● This 36' x 24' contemporary rectangle will be economical to build whether you construct the basement design at left, V42167, or the non-basement version below, V42168.

Design V42168

Square Footage: 864

● This non-basement design features a storage room and a laundry area with cupboards above the washer and dryer. Notice the space in the kitchen for eating.

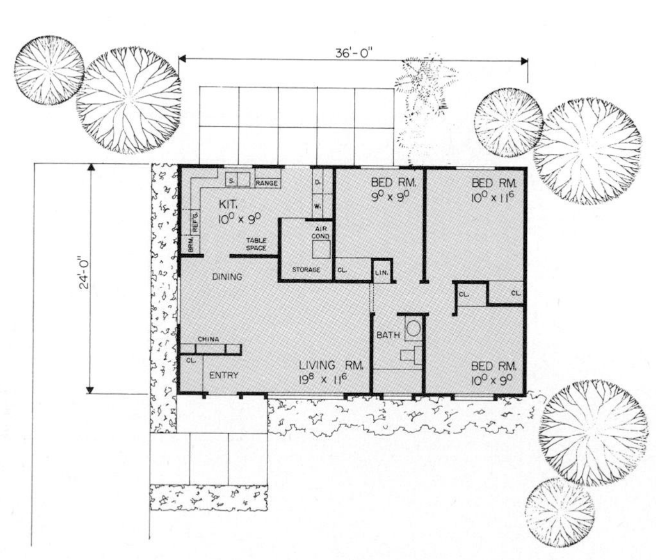

TWO-STORY VACATION HOMES . . . *are a*

rand choice for spacious vacation living. They provide adequate and private sleeping arrangements and often a second-story lounge for quiet imes. It is also not unusual to find balconies, sloped ceilings, and open stairwell designs.

Design V42887 First Floor: 1,338 square feet; Second Floor: 661 square feet; Total: 1,999 square feet

● This attractive, contemporary 1½-story will be the envy of many. First, examine the efficient kitchen. Not only does it offer a snack bar for those quick meals but also a large dining room. Notice the adjacent dining porch. The laundry and garage access are also adjacent to the kitchen. An exciting feature is the gathering room with fireplace. The first floor also offers a study with a wet bar and sliding glass doors that open to a private porch. This will make those quiet times cherishable. Adjacent to the study is a full bath followed by a bedroom. Upstairs a large master bedroom suite occupies the entire floor. It features a bath with an oversized tub and shower, a large walk-in closet with built-ins and an open lounge with fireplace. Both the lounge and master bedroom, along with the gathering room, have sloped ceilings. Develop the lower level for additional space.

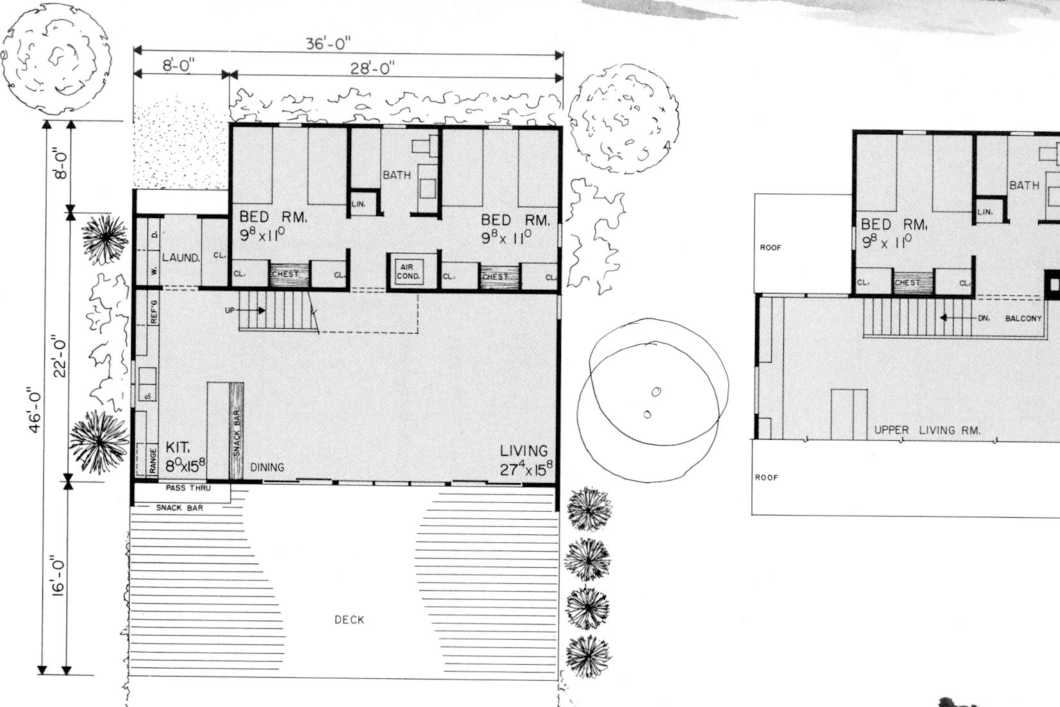

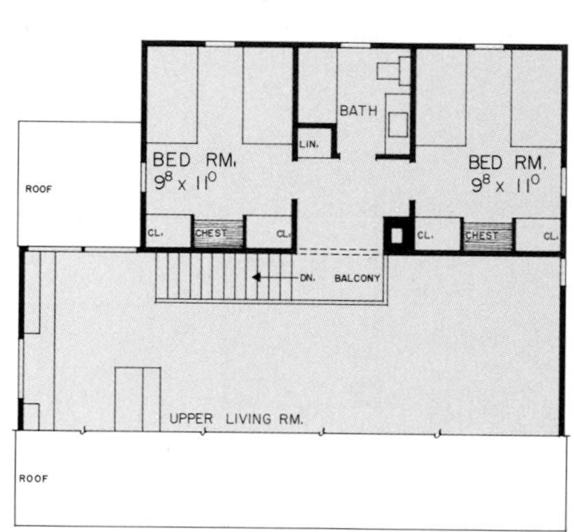

Design V42419

First Floor: 1,018 square feet
Second Floor: 392 square feet
Total: 1,410 square feet

● Dramatic appeal, are the words which aptly describe this two-story family haven. The architectural detailing which encloses a spacious interior is, indeed, refreshing. Of unusual interest are such features as the roof areas, the window treatment and the large wood deck. The sleeping potential is exceptional and will be restricted only by the number of bunk beds you decide to place in each of the four bedrooms. Observe closets.

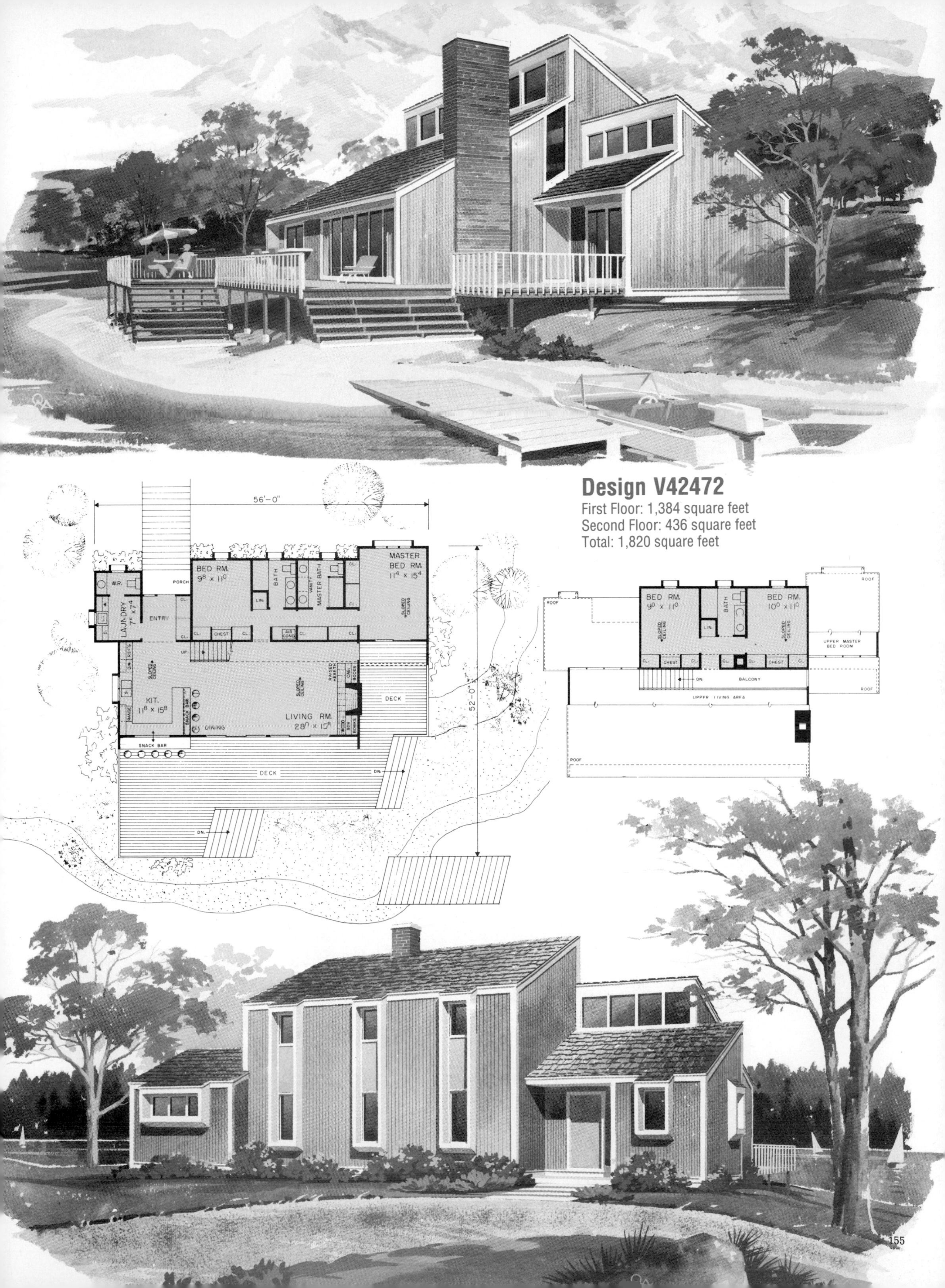

Design V42472

First Floor: 1,384 square feet
Second Floor: 436 square feet
Total: 1,820 square feet

Design V41450 First Floor: 1,008 square feet; Second Floor: 476 square feet; Total: 1,484 square feet

● What leisure-time fun you, your family and friends will experience in this appealing and wonderfully planned design. And little wonder, for all the elements are present to guarantee vacation living patterns. Four good-sized bedrooms solve the problem of accommodating overnight weekend guests. A full bath on each floor is an important feature. In addition, there is a stall shower handy to the side entrance - just the right location to cater to the requirements of swimmers. The sweeping outdoor deck will be a favorite gathering spot. The living room is a full 27 feet long. It will be a great area to accommodate a crowd. Additional space on the screened-in porch.

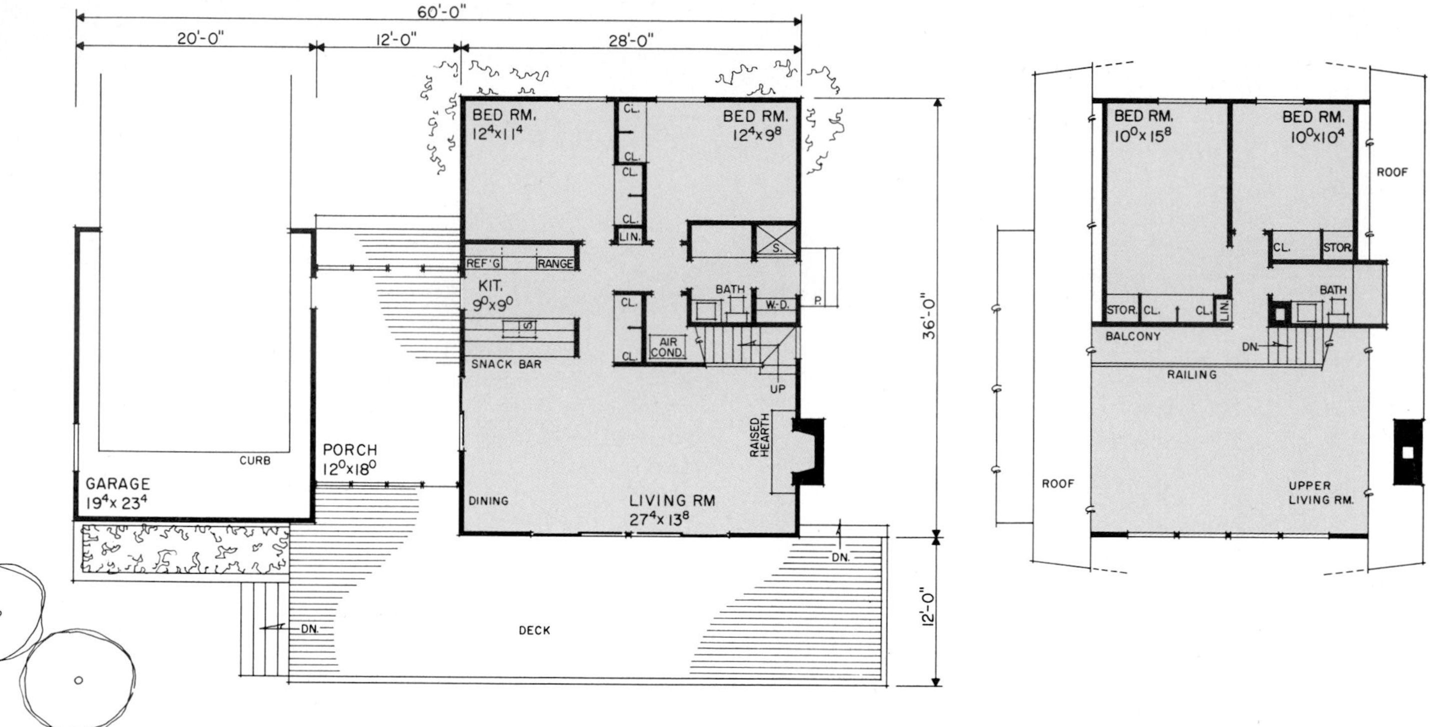

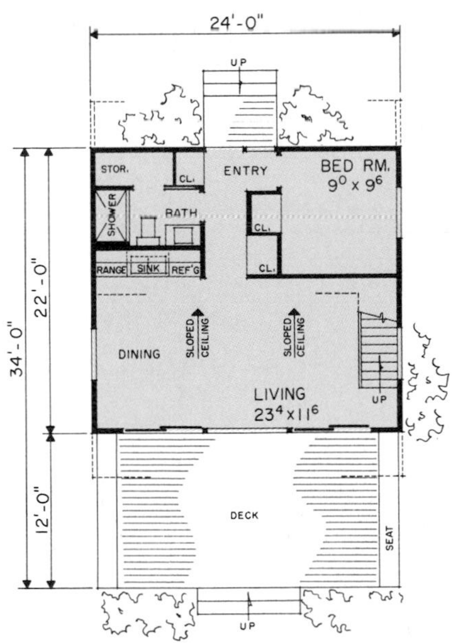

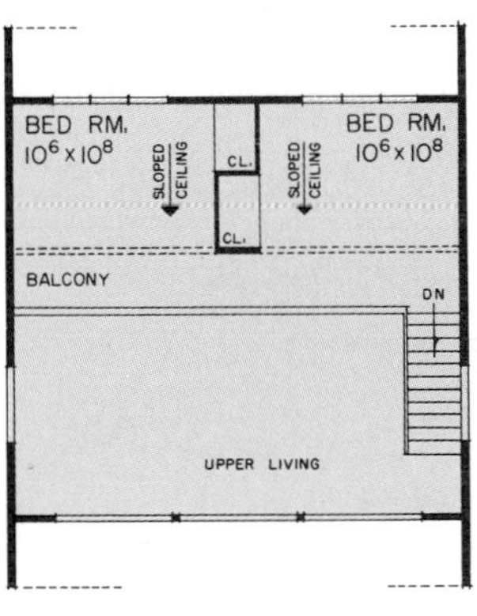

Design V41464 First Floor: 528 square feet; Second Floor: 272 square feet; Total: 1,800 square feet

● A world of care will pass you by as you and your family enjoy all that this distinctive design and its setting have to offer. The economically built floor plan offers an abundance of vacation living potential. There are three bedrooms, fine storage facilities and sloped ceilings. There is a strip kitchen, a full bath, an appealing balcony, a generous living area and an outdoor deck. The use of glass, as in so many vacation homes, is most interesting. While it carries an impressive design impact it is also practical. Study its use and how your family will function during their vacation times. Any location will be a perfect backdrop for this two-story vacation design.

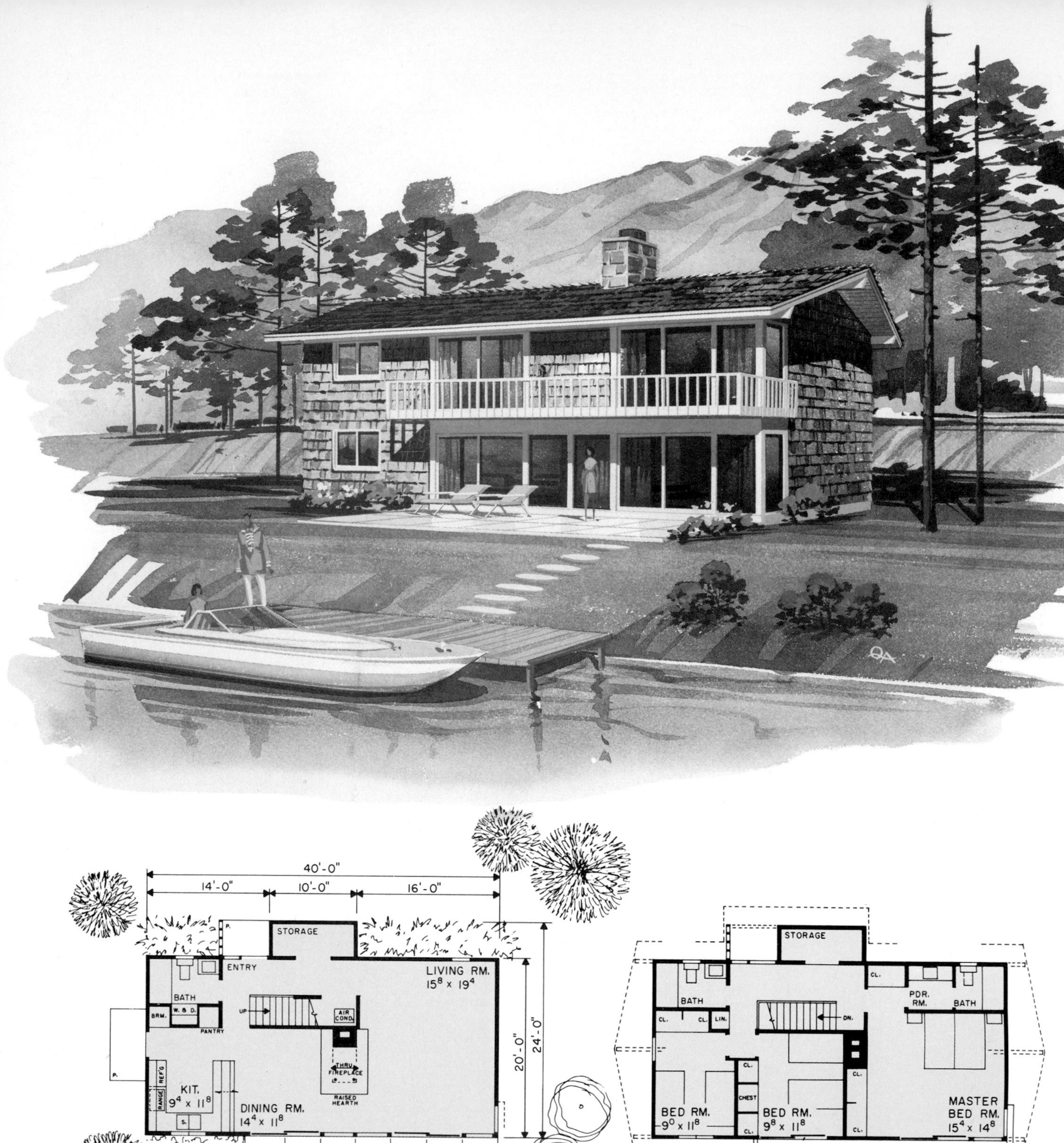

Design V42437

First Floor: 840 square feet
Second Floor: 840 square feet
Total: 1,680 square feet

● Your living patterns as pursued in this two-story second home will leave nothing to be desired. This 20 x 40 foot rectangle delivers all the basic livability features you would demand of your year 'round domicile. As traditional as your family's living patterns will be, they will be experienced in an aura of comfort and informality. You will be constantly aware of your chosen vacation home environment. Should you have a view to be preserved, proper orientation will assure the fullest enjoyment from all major rooms in the house. Imagine the view from each of the bedrooms, the kitchen, the dining and living room. There are three baths and plenty of storage facilities.

Design V42422 First Floor: 1,056 square feet; Second Floor: 1,056 square feet; Total: 2,112 square feet

● The multi-family residence does not have to be restricted to the year 'round suburban living environment. If this type of housing is sound in the city, it may be particularly so in vacationland. This design offers plenty of space for two families. The soundproof wall assures the utmost in privacy from noise of the adjoining neighbor. Each unit offers three bedrooms, 1½ baths, a huge living area, an efficient kitchen and fine storage facilities. Sliding glass doors are features of two of the upstairs bedrooms. They lead to the balcony which looks down to the lower terrace. Development of a two family outdoor living area will be lots of fun for the two families to partake.

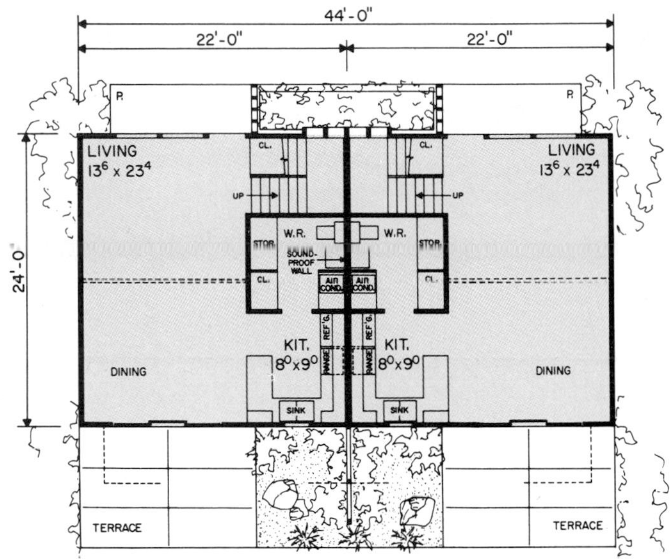

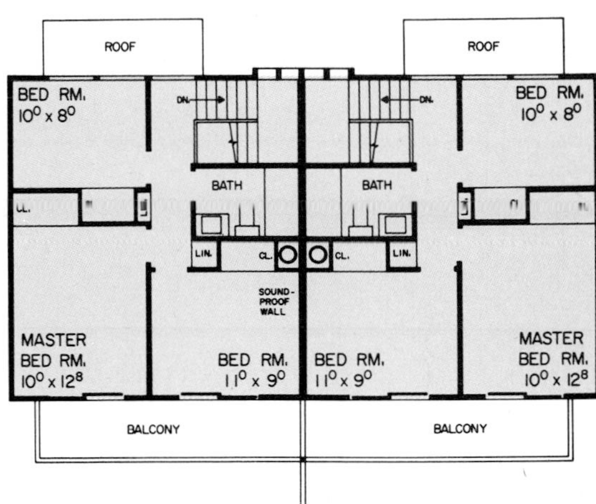

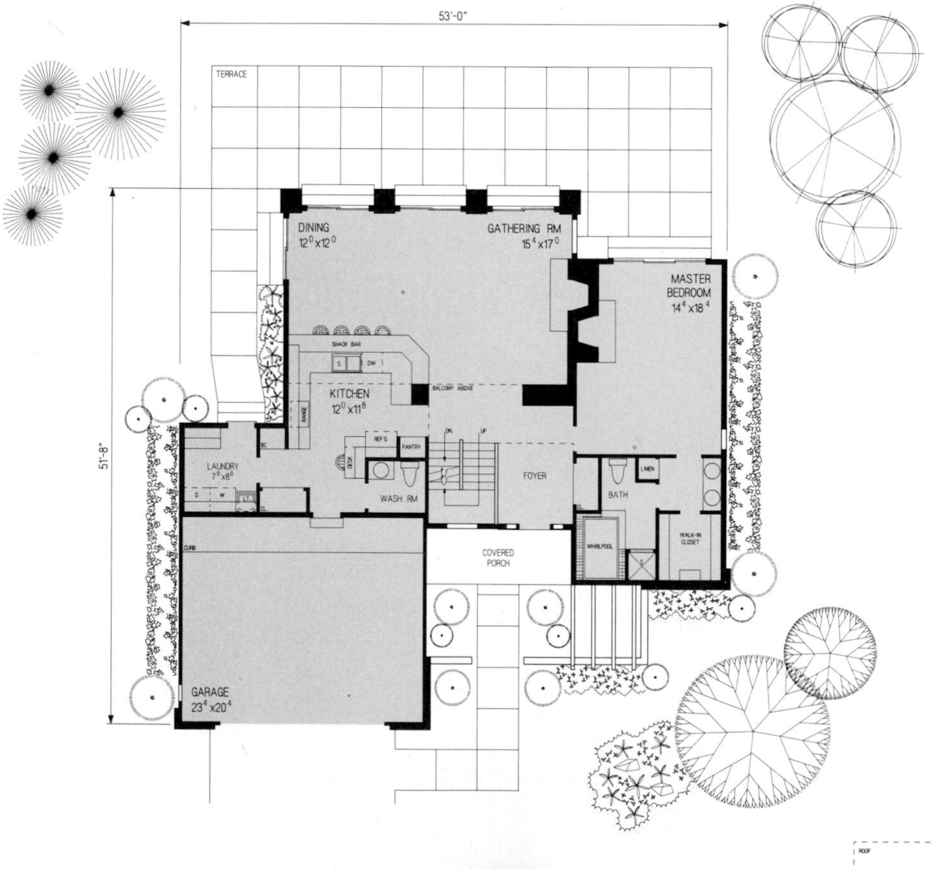

Design V42490

First Floor: 1,414 square feet
Second Floor: 620 square feet
Total: 2,034 square feet

● Split-bedroom planning makes the most of this contemporary plan. The master suite pampers with a lavish bath and a fireplace. The living areas are open and have easy access to the rear terrace.

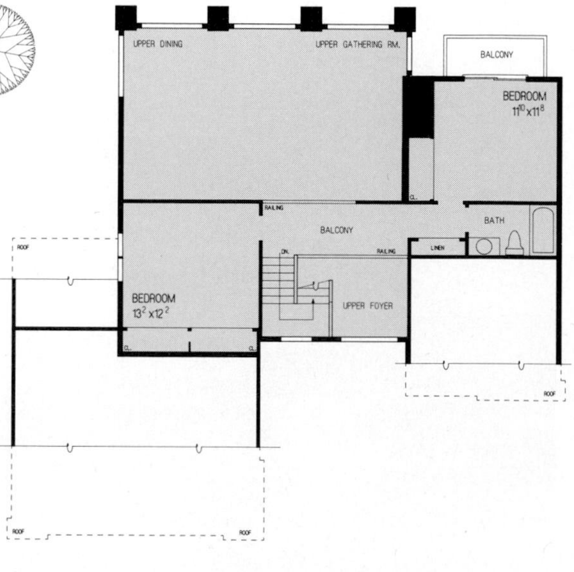

CUSTOMIZABLE

Custom Alterations? See page 251 for customizing this plan to your specifications.

Design V42491

First Floor: 1,060 square feet
Second Floor: 580 square feet
Total: 1,640 square feet

● This modest-looking plan surprises everyone with its wealth of amenities inside. Look for a U-shaped kitchen with snack bar, morning room, sunken gathering room (note fireplace with wood box), and abundant built-ins. The master suite on the second floor is a true eye-catcher.

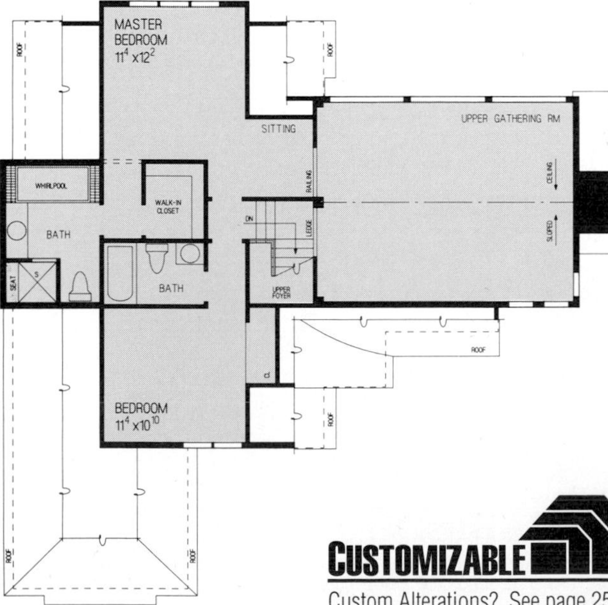

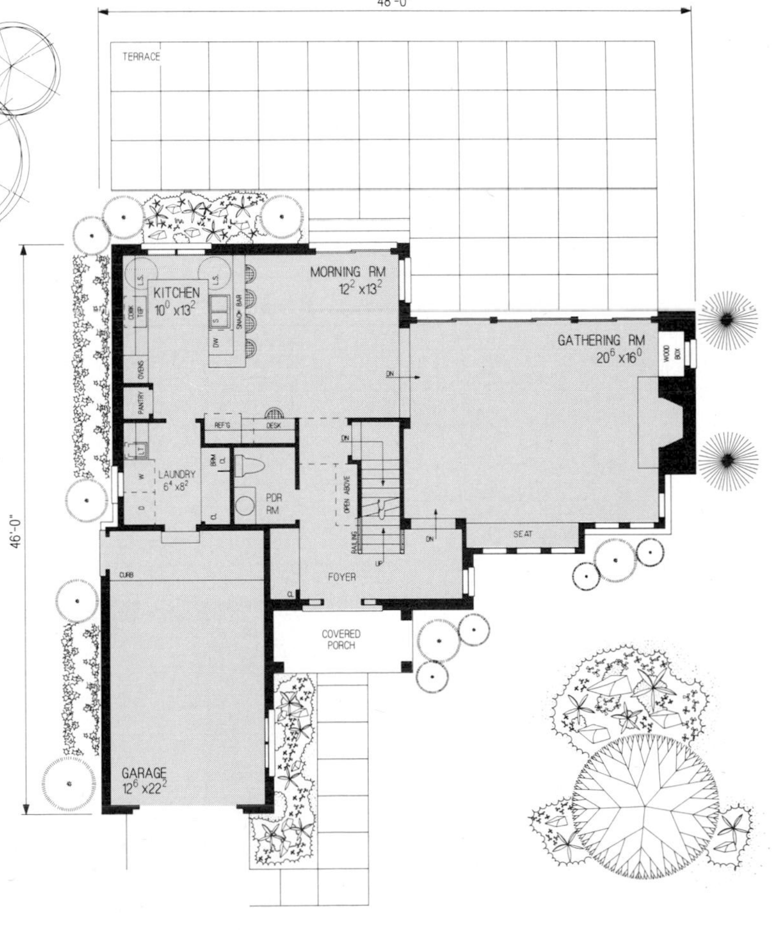

CUSTOMIZABLE

Custom Alterations? See page 251 for customizing this plan to your specifications.

Design V41492

First Floor: 608 square feet
Second Floor: 120 square feet
Total: 728 square feet

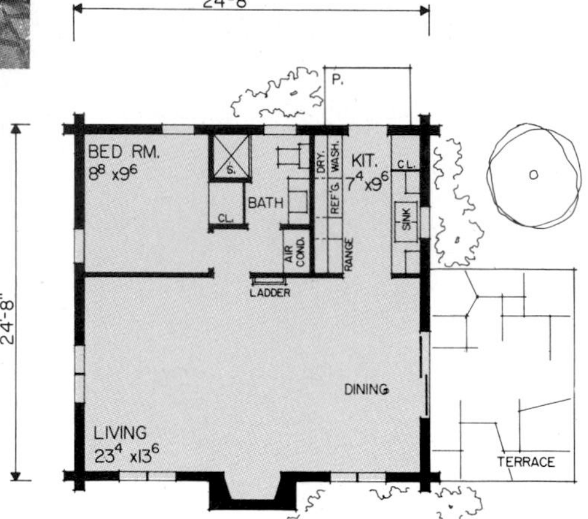

● It will not matter one bit where this log cabin is built, for there will be many paths beaten to its doors. The massive stone chimney seems to foretell of the warm hospitality awaiting inside. The big living area is dominated, as well it should be, by the centered fireplace.

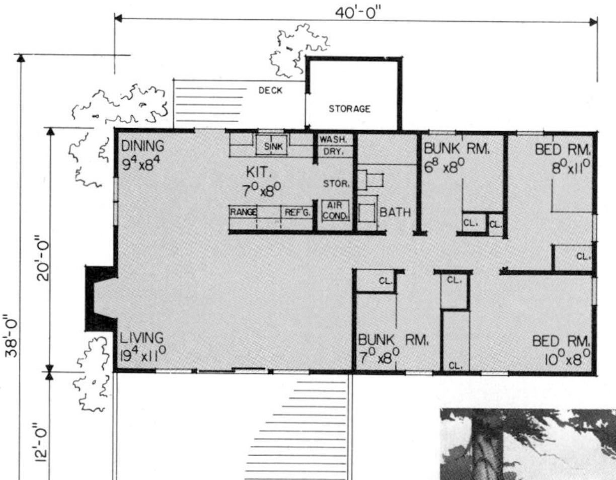

● The rustic charm of this 40' x 20' rectangle will be hard to beat. Its appeal is all the more enticing when all that livability is the result of such economy of construction. In addition to the two bedrooms, there are two bunk rooms. Then, there is the big living/dining area with fireplace.

Design V41489

Square Footage: 800

Design V41483

First Floor: 816 square feet
Second Floor: 642 square feet
Total: 1,458 square feet

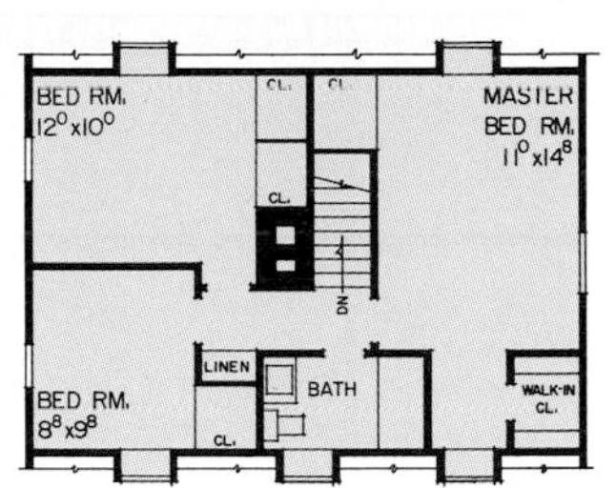

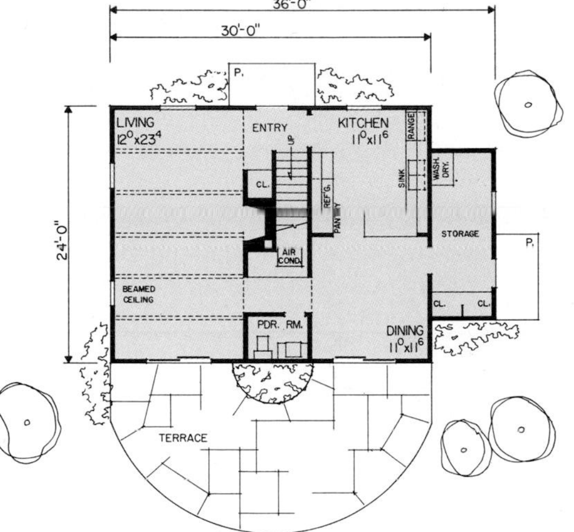

● Take the charm of early America to the lakeshore with you. The graciousness of this little gambrel-roofed vacation home will be with you always. In fact, it will improve with age. The narrow, horizontal siding, the wide corner boards, the projecting dormers, the muntined windows and the center chimney create an aura of authenticity. Observe the outstanding livability.

Design V41484

First Floor: 840 square feet
Second Floor: 684 square feet
Total: 1,524 square feet

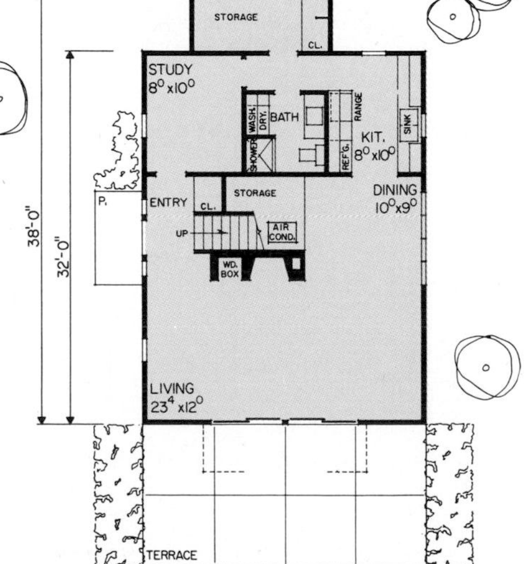

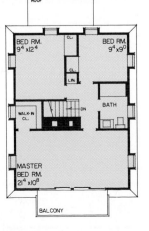

● Your French Mansard vacation cottage will be the talk of the area. And you'll surely love all the comments that you receive on the unique exterior. You'll be proud of the design distinction that will be yours. But, aside from the exterior appeal of this home, there is plenty in the way of floor plan livability to recommend it for high honors. Study the features.

Design V41496

First Floor: 768 square feet
Second Floor: 288 square feet
Total: 1,056 square feet

● If your vacation home desires include the wish for something distinctive in the way of exterior design, you'll find this unique home a tempting choice. The overhanging shed roof, the interesting glass areas and the vertical siding help create an attractive facade. Inside, the living area is big and spacious. Each floor features a good sized bedroom with a full bath nearby. The ceiling is sloped and has exposed beams.

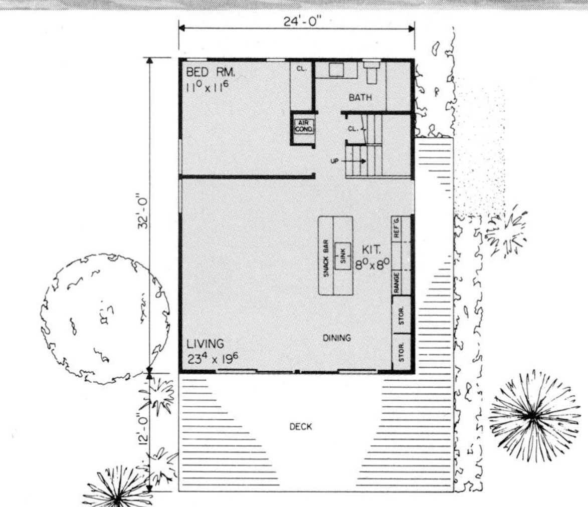

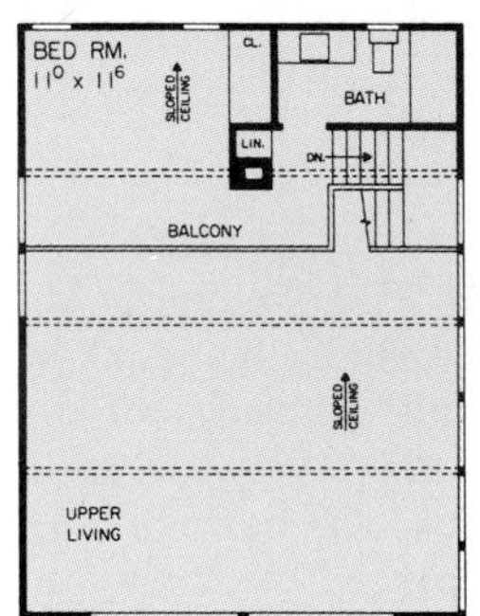

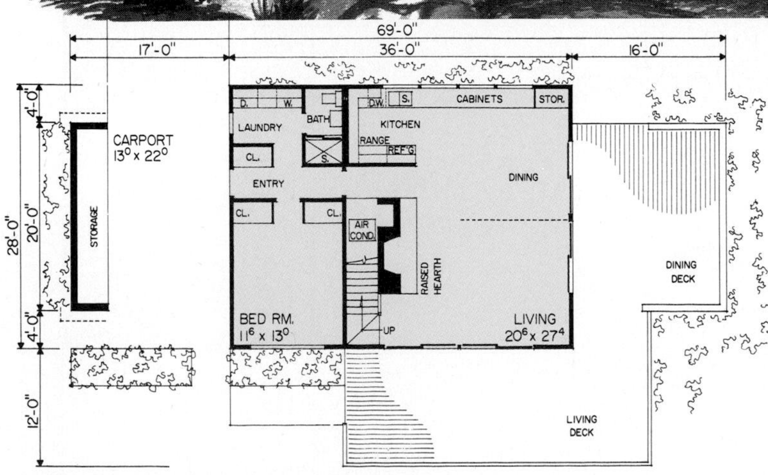

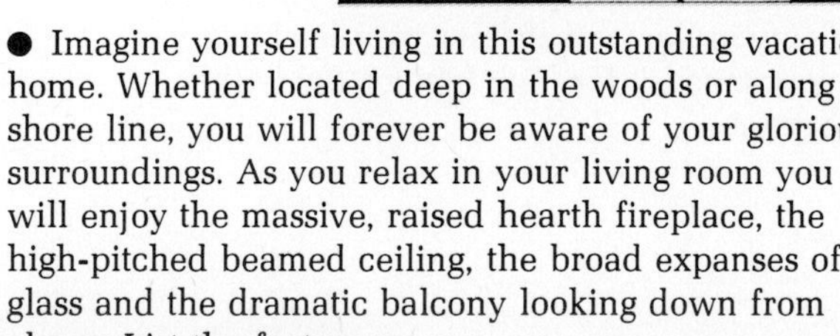

● Imagine yourself living in this outstanding vacation home. Whether located deep in the woods or along the shore line, you will forever be aware of your glorious surroundings. As you relax in your living room you will enjoy the massive, raised hearth fireplace, the high-pitched beamed ceiling, the broad expanses of glass and the dramatic balcony looking down from above. List the features.

Design V41427

First Floor: 1,008 square feet
Second Floor: 688 square feet; Total: 1,696 square feet

MULTI-LEVEL VACATION HOMES . . . *are*

the perfect answer for sloping or hillside lots. And many levels provide a host of living patterns well adapted to vacation lifestyles, making these homes not only dramatic in their appeal but practical to develop. Decks, balconies, and terraces all function well in the multi-level design.

Design V42485 Main Level: 1,108 square feet
Lower Level: 983 square feet; Total: 2,091 square feet

● This hillside vacation home gives the appearance of being a one-story from the road. However, since it is built off the edge of a slope, the rear exterior is a full two-story structure. Notice the projecting deck and how it shelters the terrace. Each of the generous glass areas is protected from the summer sun by the overhangs and the extended walls. The clerestory windows of the front exterior provide natural light to the center of the plan.

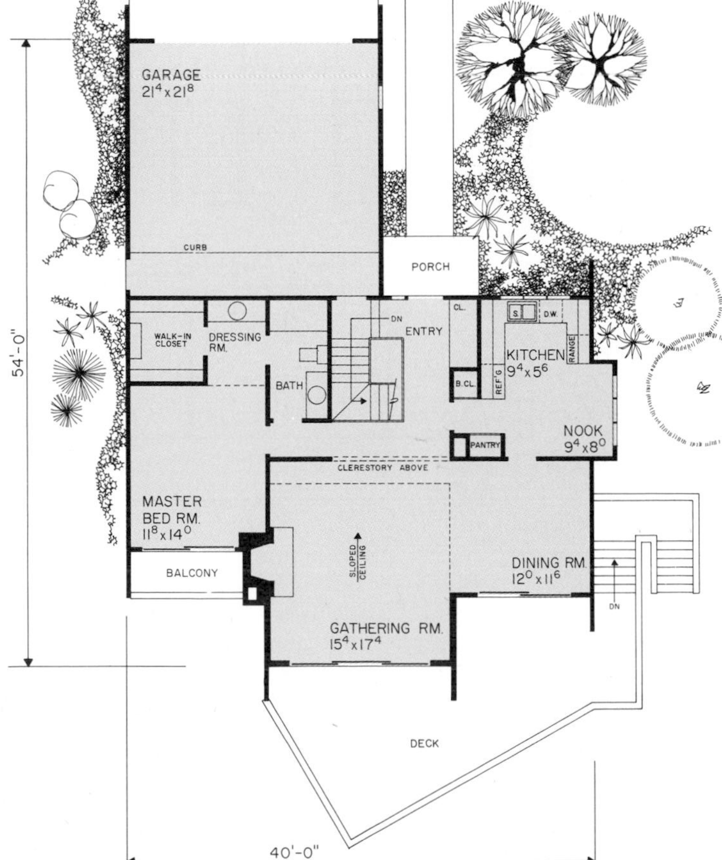

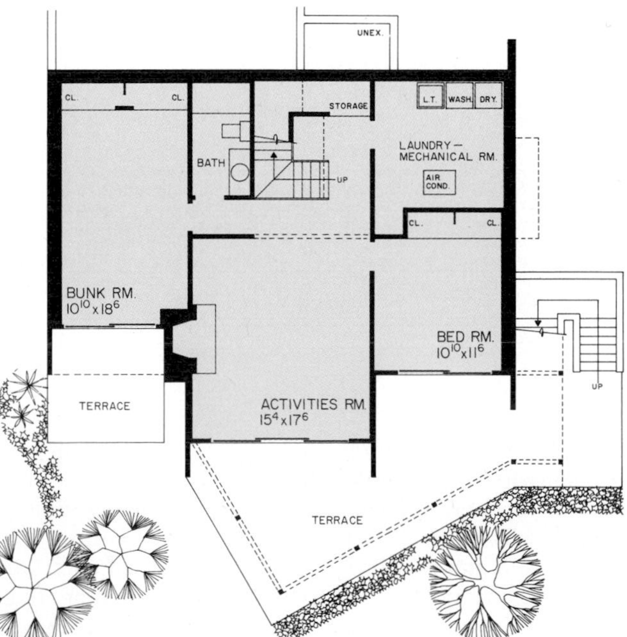

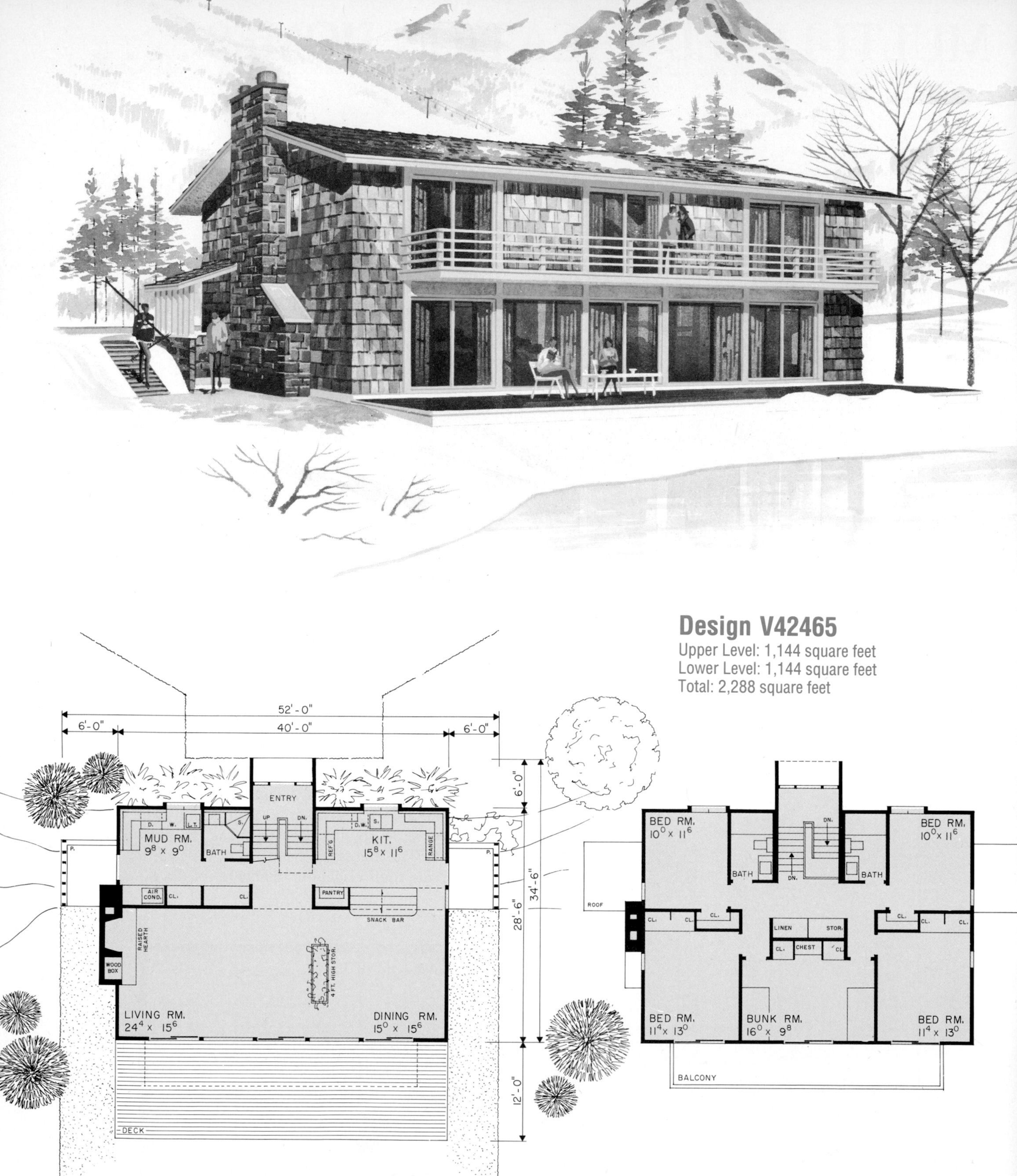

Design V42465

Upper Level: 1,144 square feet
Lower Level: 1,144 square feet
Total: 2,288 square feet

● Here is a ski or hunting lodge which will cater successfully to a crowd. Or, here is a summer home which will be ideal for your own family and an occasional weekend guest. Whatever its purpose, this bi-level design will serve admirably. And little wonder. There is plenty of space as illustrated by the 39 foot living-dining area, the 15 foot kitchen, the three full baths, the four sizable bedrooms and the large bunk room. In addition, there is the mud room. The features do not end there. The list continues and includes the raised hearth fireplace, snack bar, planter/storage unit, an abundance of closets, sliding glass doors and a wonderful balcony. Note the two covered side entrances at each end of the house. A great convenience.

Design V42438

Upper Level: 977 square feet
Lower Level: 987 square feet
Total: 1,964 square feet

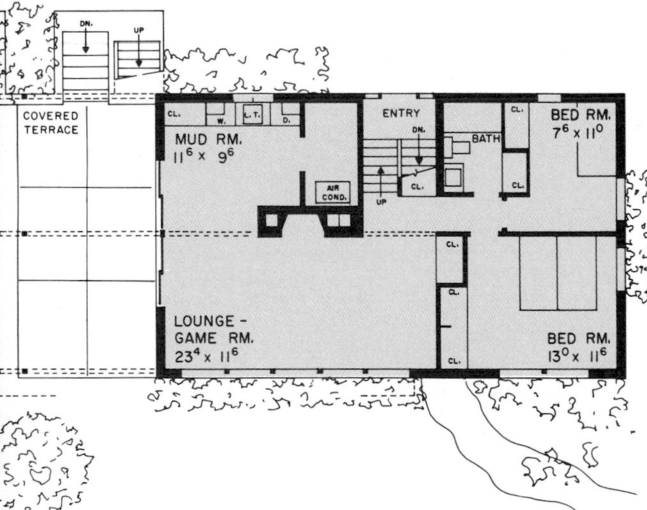

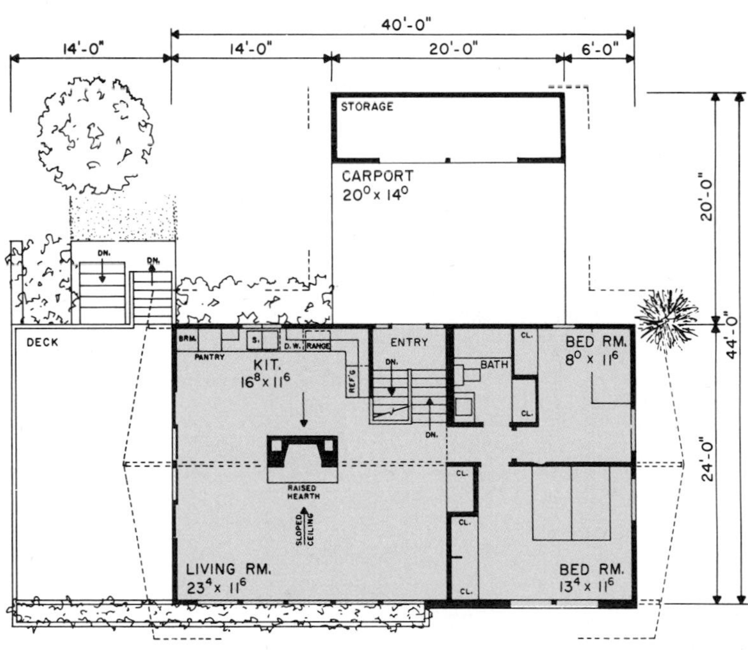

● A great bi-level that could easily be adapted to either a flat or sloping site. As you walk into the main entry beneath the carport, you will either go up a short stairway to the upper main level or down a few stairs to the lower recreation level. In addition to the spacious living areas each level features two bedrooms, a full bath, a fireplace, two sets of sliding glass doors and good storage potential. The kitchen of the upper level is efficient and has plenty of space for eating. Directly below is the mud room complete with laundry equipment. The two large outdoor living areas, the deck and terrace, will be favorite spots to soak up the surroundings. Note the sloping ceilings of the living area and kitchen and the bulk storage unit. The lounge-game room will be in constant use.

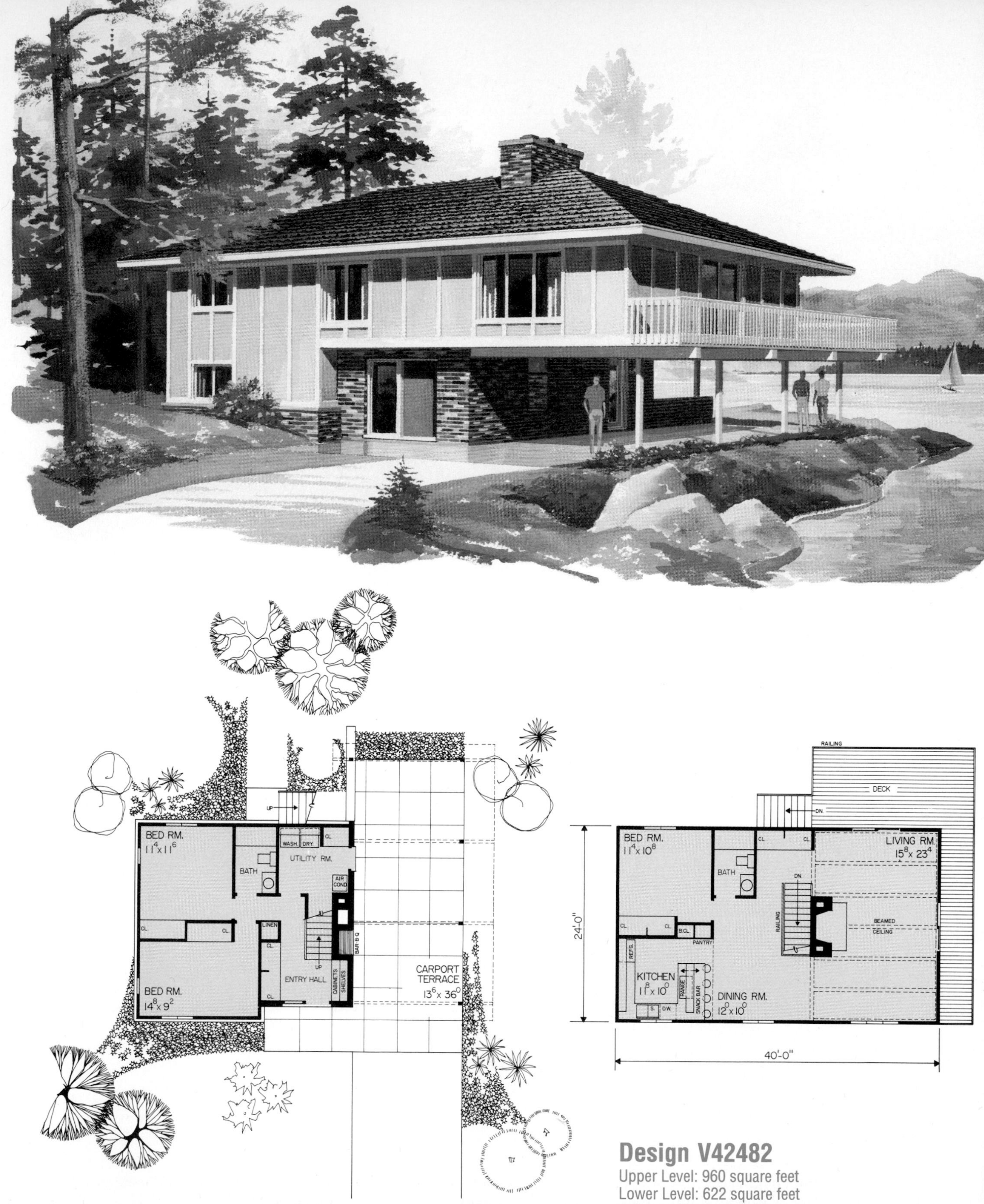

Design V42482

Upper Level: 960 square feet
Lower Level: 622 square feet
Total: 1,582 square feet

● This home offers its occupants a sunny deck which is accessible from two sets of sliding glass doors in the beamed ceilinged living room. The dining room plus an informal snack bar are available for eating. Three bedrooms and two full baths to serve the family for sleeping arrangements. The deck acts as a cover for the carport/terrace. A great area when hiding away from the weather is necessary.

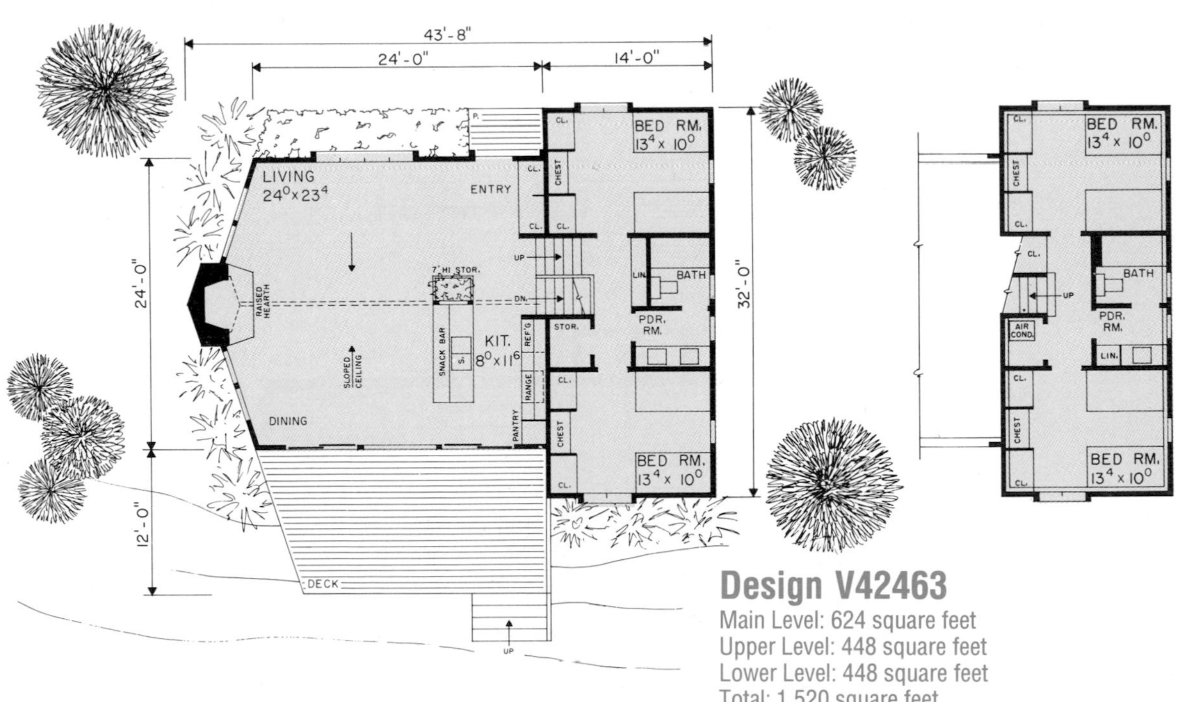

Design V42463

Main Level: 624 square feet
Upper Level: 448 square feet
Lower Level: 448 square feet
Total: 1,520 square feet

● If you like split-level living there is no reason why your second home can't provide you with those living patterns. If you haven't ever lived in a split-level home, here is your opportunity to do so. The one-story portion of this plan houses the living areas. The two-story section comprises the sleeping zones. Open planning results in a gloriously spacious living, dining and kitchen area. The raised hearth fireplace is strategically located and will be enjoyed from the main living area and even the kitchen. Each of the two sleeping levels features two very good sized bedrooms, a compartmented bath and excellent storage facilities. The use of double bunks will really enable you to entertain a crowd on those glorious holiday weekends. Note built-in chests.

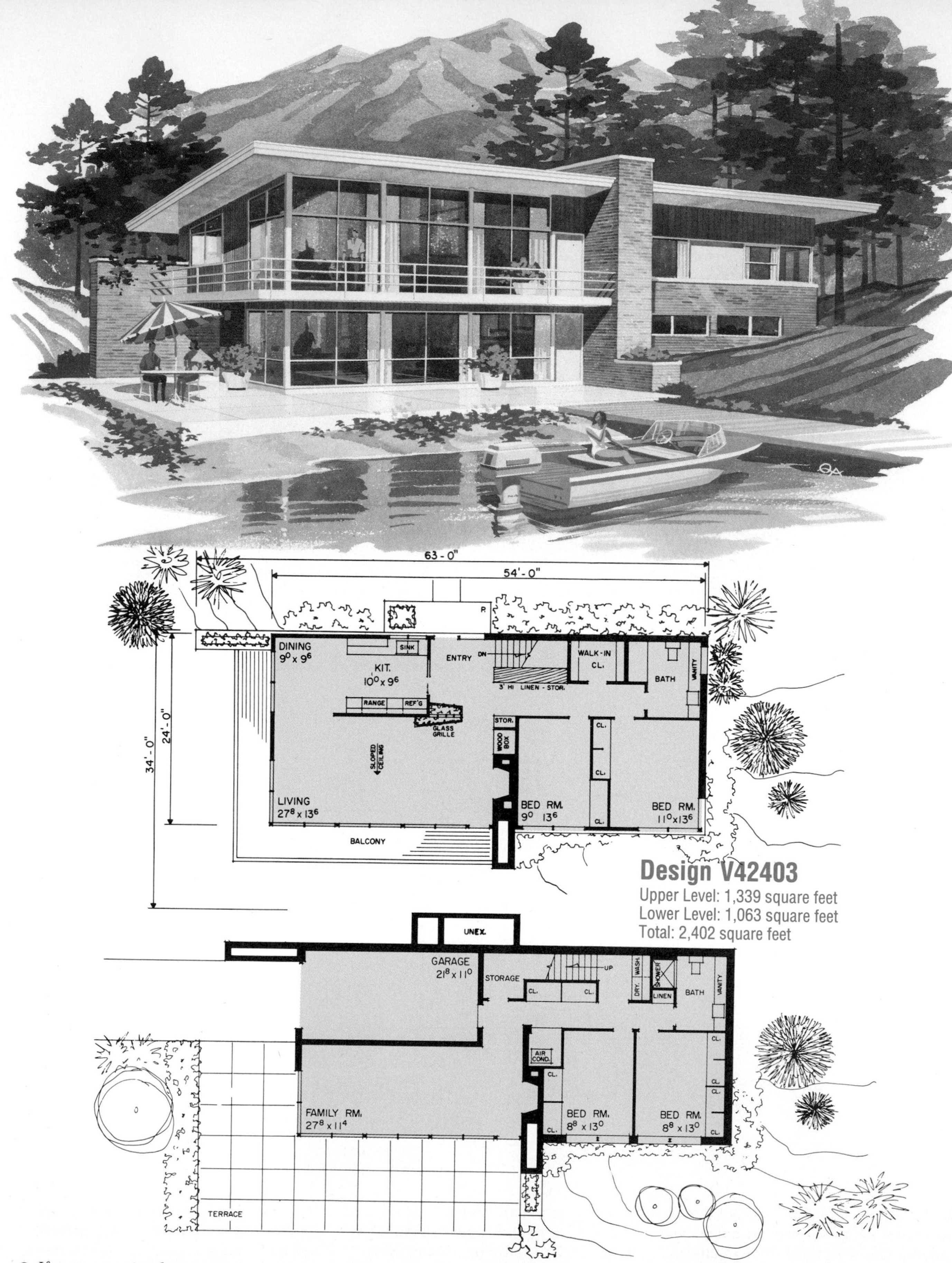

Design V42403

Upper Level: 1,339 square feet
Lower Level: 1,063 square feet
Total: 2,402 square feet

● If your vacation home site has a view, be sure your choice of design provides you and your family with the opportunity to enjoy it to the fullest extent possible. Projecting from a sloping site this bi-level haven permits a great view from each level. The shed type roof results in sloped ceilings for the living room. Together with all that glass, the fireplace and the outdoor balcony will be everyone's favorite spot. Don't miss the four bedrooms.

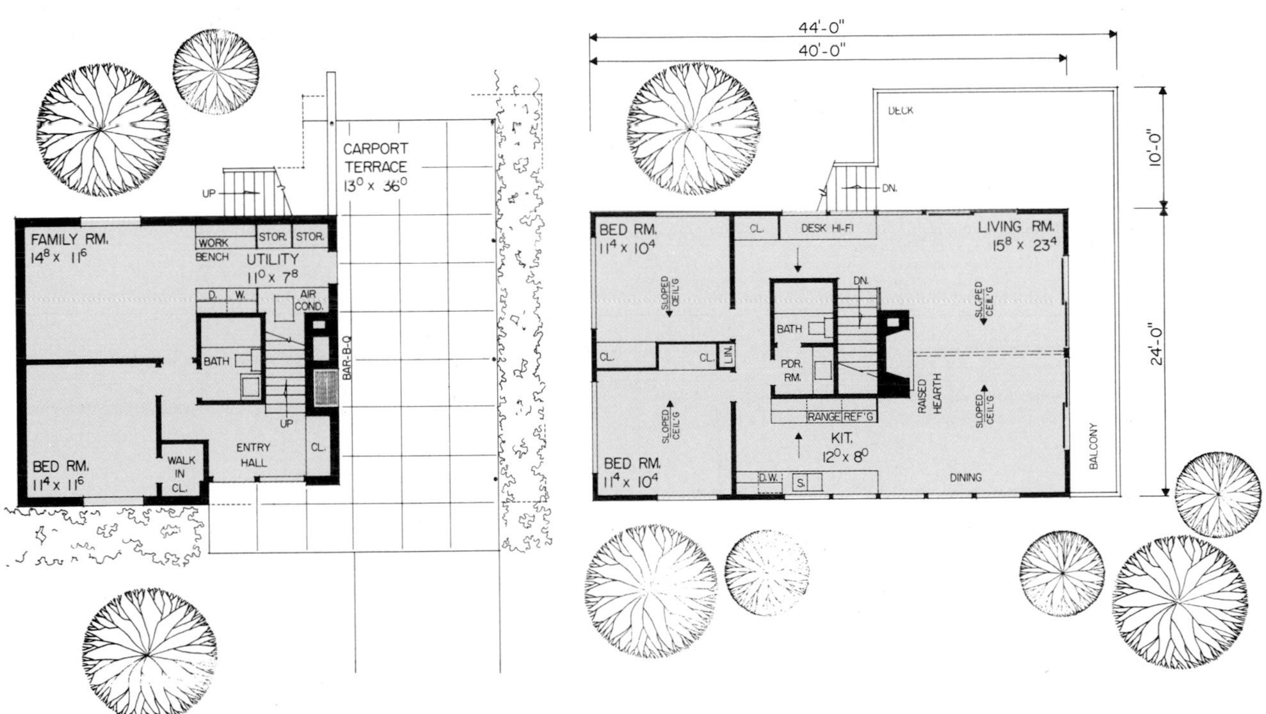

Design V41445

Upper Level: 960 square feet
Lower Level: 628 square feet
Total: 1,588 square feet

● Why not give two-level living a try and make your leisure-time home something delightfully different? If there is plenty of countryside or water around, you'll love viewing it from the upper level. And the best seat in the house will not be inside at all, but one on the balcony or deck. While the upper level is a complete living unit with its two bedrooms, bath, kitchen and spacious living area; the lower level with its one bedroom, bath, utility room (make it a kitchen) and family room could be a complete living unit itself. However called upon to function, this design has plenty of flexible space. Don't miss the fireplace on the upper level.

Design V42455

Upper Level: 864 square feet
Lower Level: 864 square feet
Total: 1,728 square feet

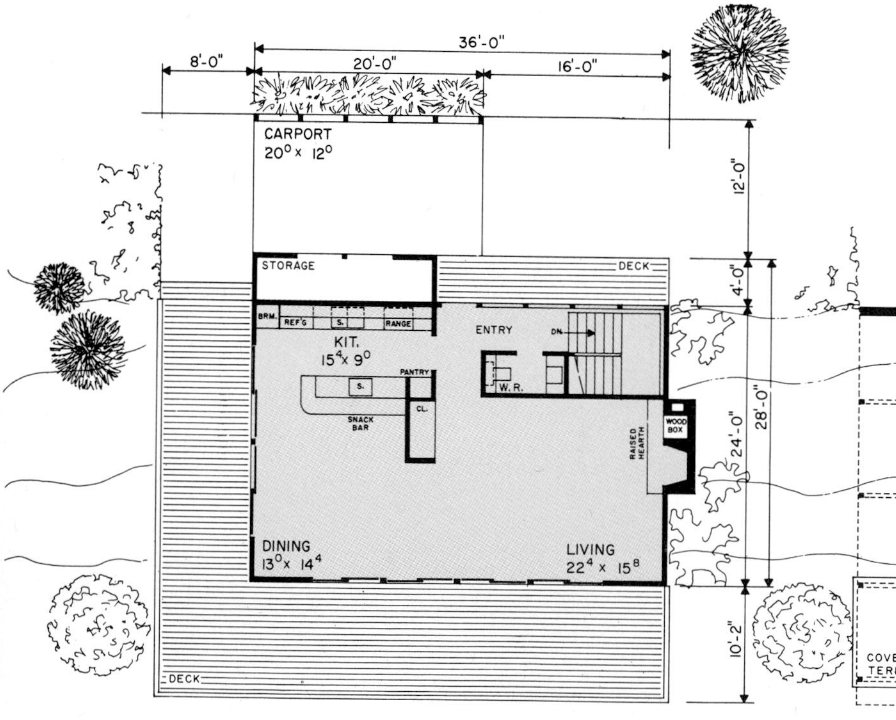

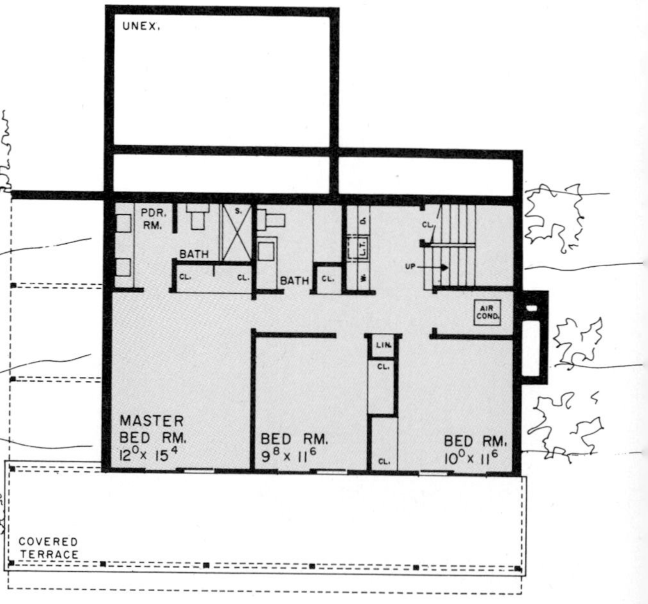

8'-0" 36'-0" 20'-0" 16'-0"

CARPORT $20^0 \times 12^0$

12'-0" 4'-0" 24'-0" 28'-0" 10'-2"

STORAGE DECK BRM. REF'G S. RANGE ENTRY DN. KIT. $15^4 \times 9^0$ PANTRY S. SNACK BAR CL. W.R. RAISED HEARTH WOOD BOX

DINING $13^0 \times 14^4$ LIVING $22^4 \times 15^8$ DECK

UNEX. PDR. RM. S. BATH CL. CL. BATH CL. CL. UP AIR COND. LIN. CL.

MASTER BED RM. $12^0 \times 15^4$ BED RM. $9^8 \times 11^6$ CL. BED RM. $10^0 \times 11^6$

COVERED TERRACE

● What delightful vacation living experiences will be in store for the owners and guests of this great second home. Designed for a sloping site, the lakeside elevation has both the upper and lower levels completely exposed for the fullest enjoyment of indoor-outdoor living patterns. The wooden deck, which runs the full length of two sides of the house, is but a step from the upper level living areas. The covered terrace is readily accessible from the lower level bedrooms. The carport with its bulk storage room is located on the same grade as the upper level. The wonderful living-dining area is 35 feet in length. It features sliding glass doors and a strategically placed raised hearth fireplace. Don't miss the snack bar, the wash room, the two full baths and the powder room.

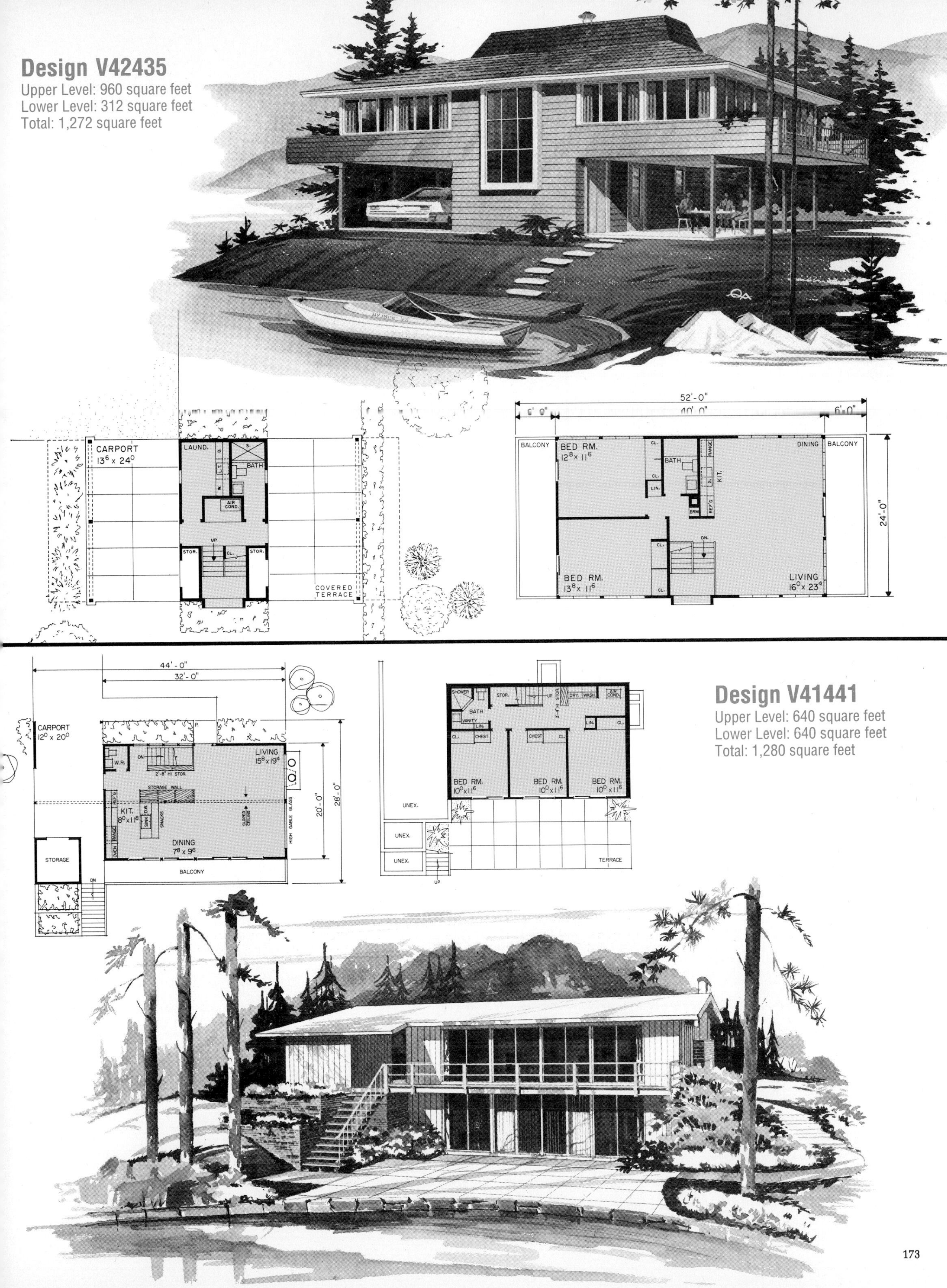
Design V42435
Upper Level: 960 square feet
Lower Level: 312 square feet
Total: 1,272 square feet
CARPORT 13⁶ x 24⁰
LAUND.
BATH
AIR COND.
UP
STOR.
CL.
STOR.
COVERED TERRACE
52'-0"
6'-0"
40'-0"
6'-0"
BALCONY
BED RM. 12⁸ x 11⁶
CL.
BATH
RANGE
DINING
BALCONY
KIT.
LIN.
REF'G
BRM
24'-0"
DN.
BED RM. 13⁸ x 11⁶
LIVING 16⁰ x 23⁴
44'-0"
32'-0"
CARPORT 12⁰ x 20⁰
W.R.
DN
2'-8" HI STOR.
LIVING 15⁸ x 19⁴
STORAGE WALL
KIT. 8⁰ x 11⁸
SNACKS
SLOPED CEILING
HIGH GABLE GLASS
20'-0"
28'-0"
DINING 7⁸ x 9⁶
STORAGE
BALCONY
SHOWER
STOR.
UP
DRY.
WASH.
AIR COND.
BATH
VANITY
LIN.
CHEST
CL.
BED RM. 10⁰ x 11⁶
BED RM. 10⁰ x 11⁶
BED RM. 10⁰ x 11⁶
UNEX.
UNEX.
UNEX.
TERRACE
UP
Design V41441
Upper Level: 640 square feet
Lower Level: 640 square feet
Total: 1,280 square feet

Design V41465

First Floor: 784 square feet
Second Floor: 434 square feet
Total: 1,218 square feet

● Can you imagine the mounting excitement as your family arrives for the weekend at this distinctive cottage? The joy will be overwhelming as the atmosphere becomes alive with the anticipation of fun. A quick look at this exterior reveals how delightfully different in character it is. A study of the floor plan reveals facilities for joyful living patterns. There are three bedrooms, two full baths, a U-shaped kitchen and a spacious living-dining area. Observe the balcony looking down into the living room. Sliding glass doors permit the living area to function with the deck.

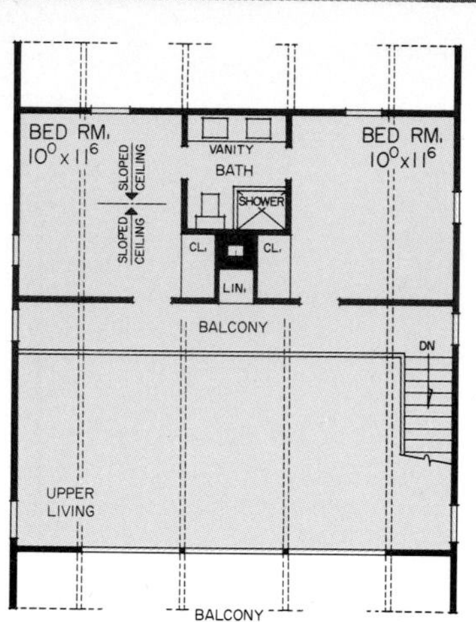

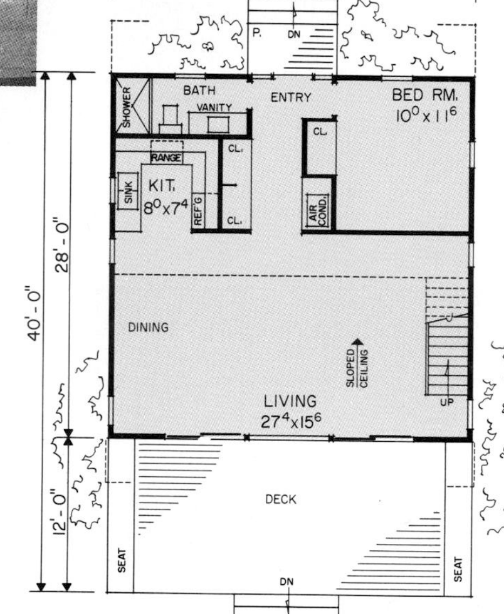

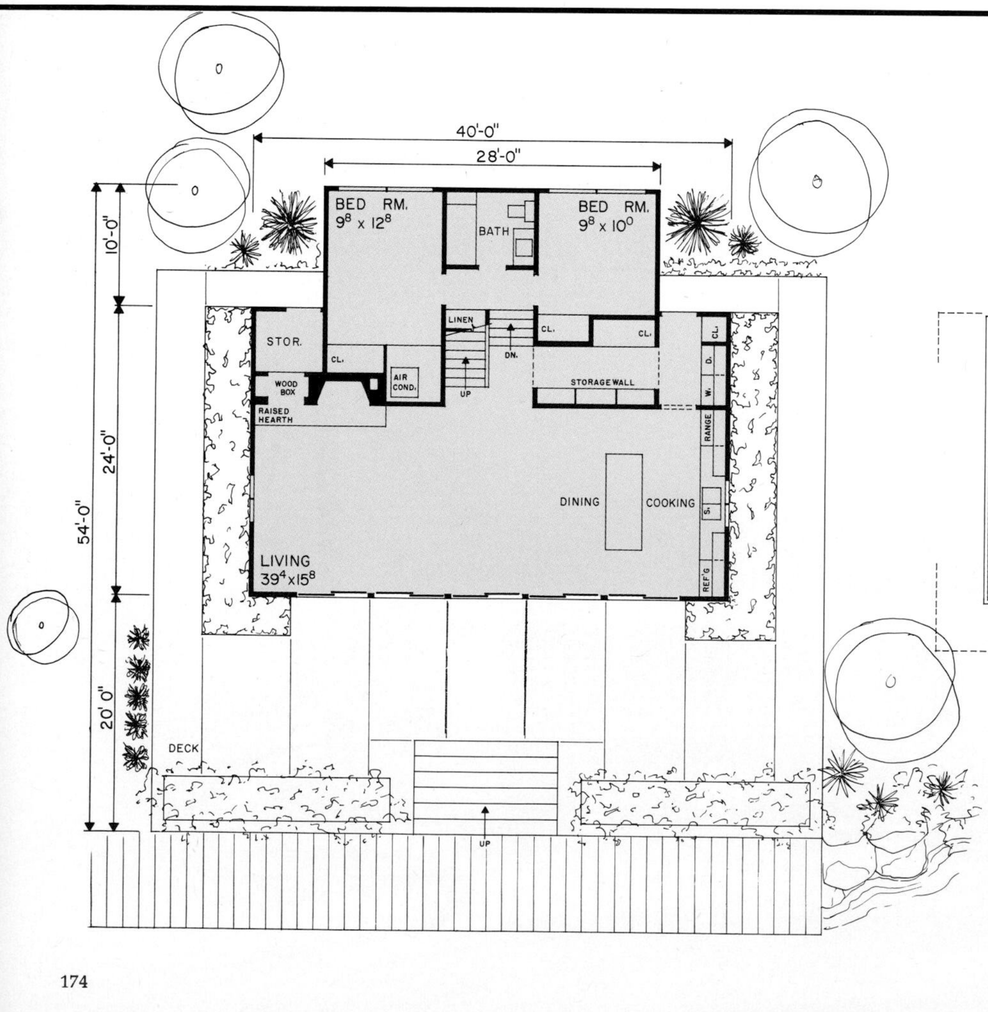

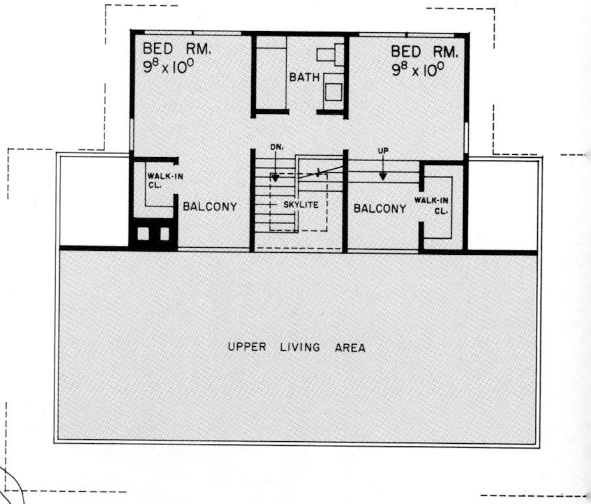

Design V42414

Main Level: 870 square feet
Upper Level: 474 square feet
Lower Level: 334 square feet
Total: 1,678 square feet

Design V41437

Upper Level: 592 square feet
Lower Level: 592 square feet
Total: 1,184 square feet

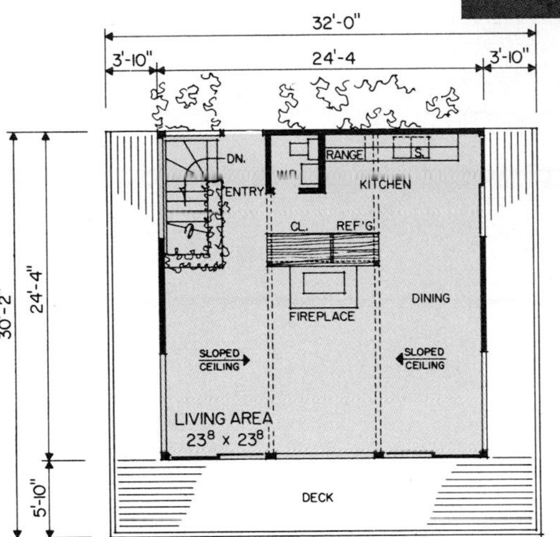

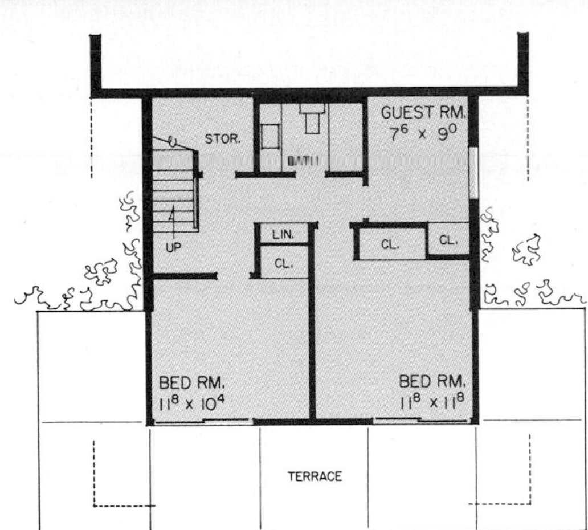

● A compact leisure-time home with plenty of livability and a refreshing exterior. Whether overlooking the lake shore, or perched deep in the woods, the view of the surrounding outdoors will be enjoyed to the fullest. The expanses of glass will permit those inside to be delightfully conscious of nature's beauty. The deck, which envelops the cottage on three sides, will become the favorite spot to enjoy outdoor relaxation.

● Do you think you might like your vacation home to have a light touch of the Oriental flavor? The character of the peaked, wide overhanging roof, to be sure, is refreshing. Completing the setting is the deck and raised planters. The focal point of the interior is the 39 foot living area. The in-line kitchen is at one end with open planning to make available all the dining space the occasion may demand. The wall of windows and the high ceiling further enhances the feeling of spaciousness. From the second floor balcony you can look down into the living area.

Design V42470 Upper Level: 1,226 square feet; Lower Level: 805 square feet; Total: 2,031 square feet

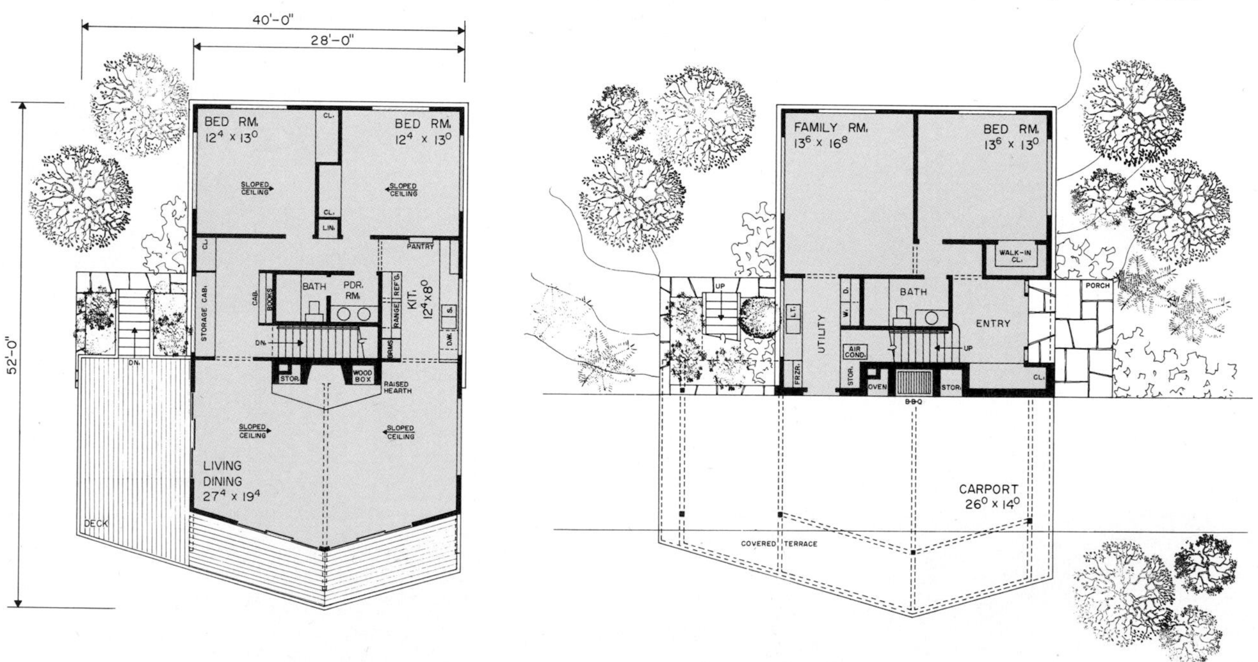

● You will enter this vacation home on the lower level. Here, the main entry routes traffic to the family room and extra bedroom. A full bath is centrally located. Then, up a full flight of stairs to the main living level. There is a feeling of great spaciousness with all those windows and the sloped ceiling throughout. The focal point of the 27 foot living area will be the raised hearth fireplace. It is centrally located and has a storage unit and wood box. Traffic will flow easily to and from the outdoor deck as a result of the three sets of sliding glass doors. The efficient kitchen and good storage facilities will help assure convenient living. On the lower level, below the deck and living area, there is excellent outdoor living potential. This area, may also double as shelter for the car or boat. Don't overlook the outdoor cooking facilities, oven and barbecue, plus storage unit in the sheltered area.

Design V41457 Upper Level: 640 square feet; Lower Level: 640 square feet; Total: 1,280 square feet

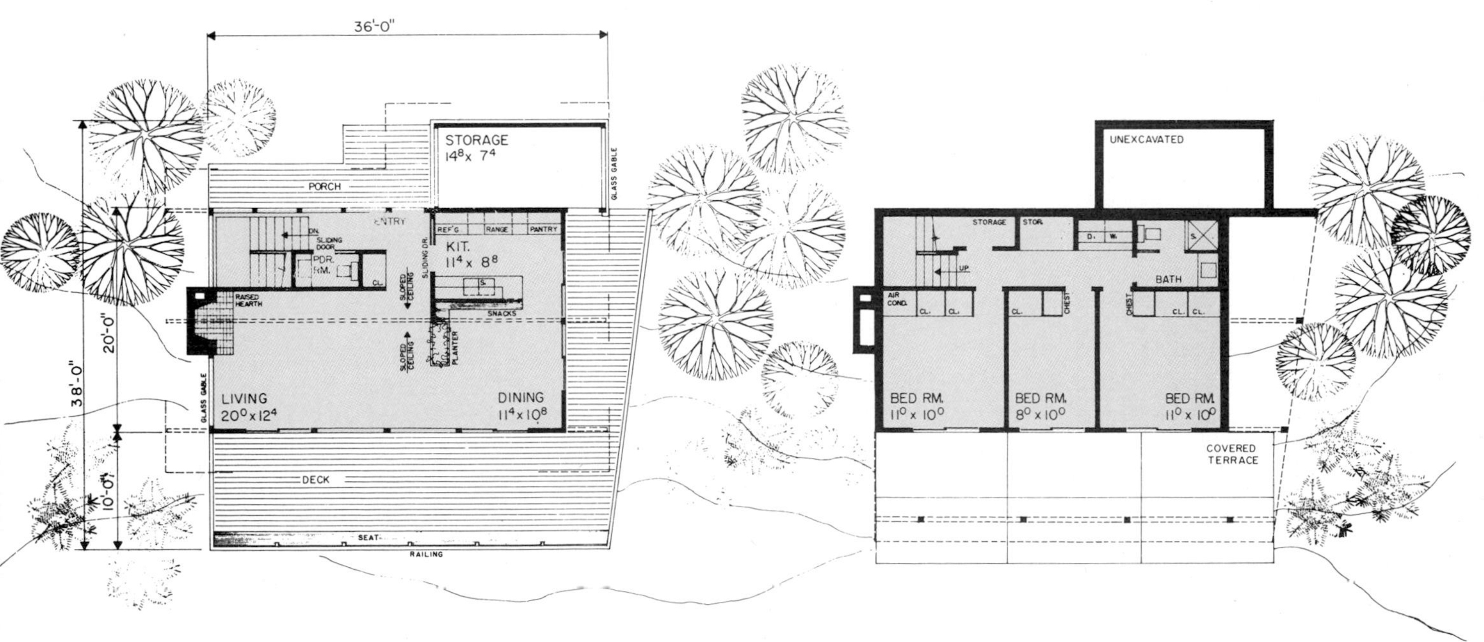

● This hillside vacation home seems to just grow right out of its sloping site. The street view of this design appears to be a one-story. It, therefore, is putting its site to the best possible use. As a result of being able to expose the lower level, the total livable floor area of the house is doubled. This is truly the most practical and economical manner by which to increase livability so dramatically. The upper level is the living level. This is just where you want to be during the day when there is a delightful view to be enjoyed from a high vantage point. For outdoor living there is the big deck which wraps around one side of the house with the covered terrace below sheltered from the weather. Dressing rooms are easily accessible when swimming is the primary activity.

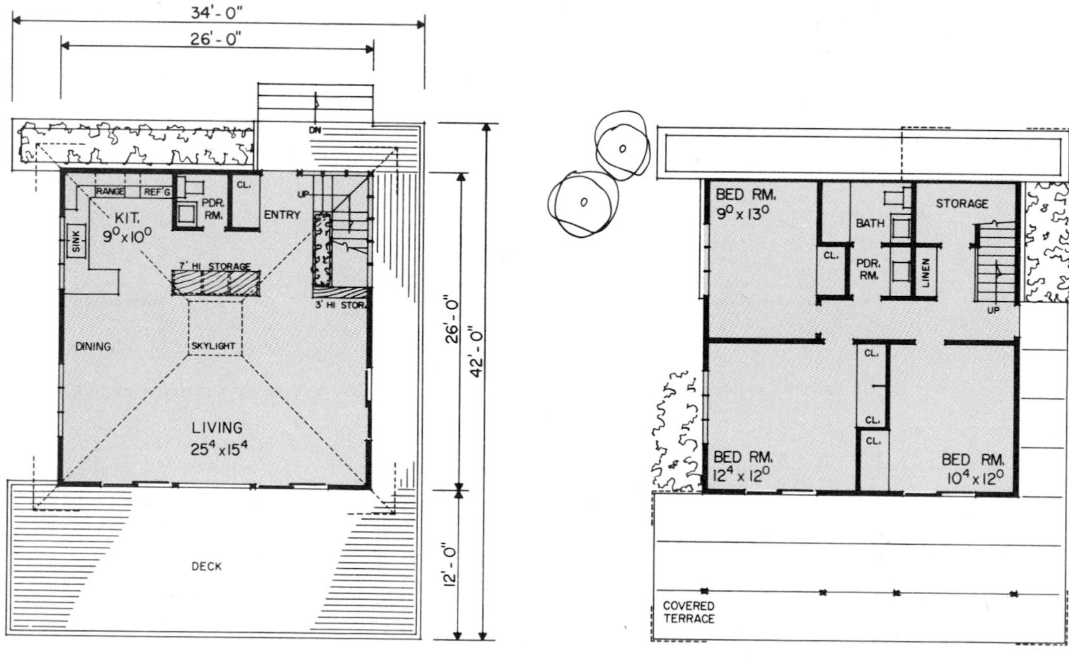

Design V41468 Upper Level: 676 square feet; Lower Level: 676 square feet; Total: 1,352 square feet

● Vacation living patterns, because of the very nature of things, are different than the everyday living of the city or suburban America. However, they can be made to be even more delightfully so, when called upon to function in harmony with such a distinctive two-level design as this. The upper level is the pleasantly open and spacious living level. The ceilings are sloped and converge at the skylight. Outside the glass sliding doors is the large deck which looks down onto the surrounding countryside. The lower level is the sleeping level with three bedrooms and a full bath. The covered terrace is just outside two of the bedrooms through sliding glass doors.

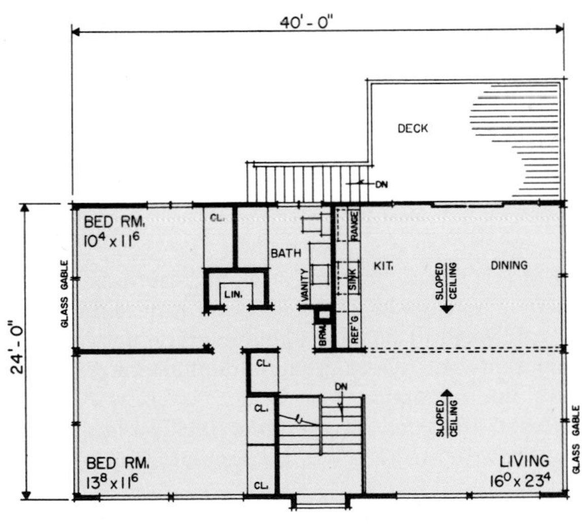

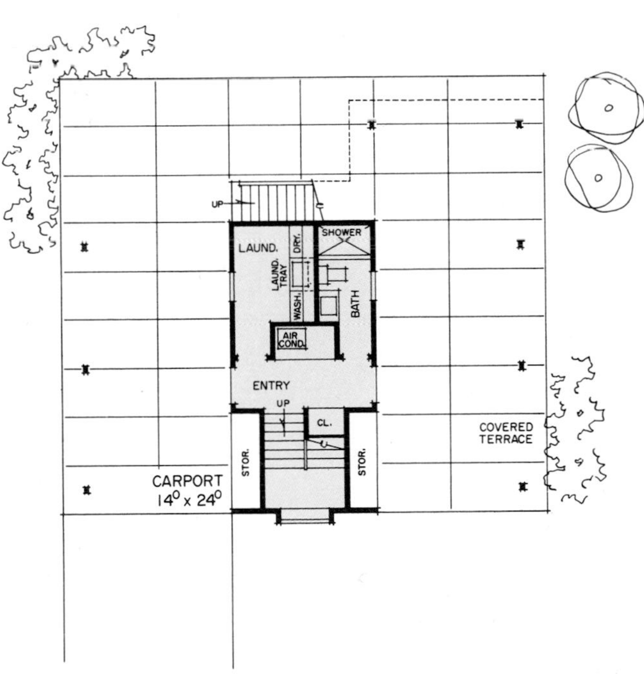

Design V41466 Upper Level: 960 square feet; Lower Level: 288 square feet; Total: 1,248 square feet

● A second home to satisfy your desires for something different both in the way of design and living patterns. This T-shaped home is surely dramatic and unique in its exterior styling and shape. Its pleasing proportion and contemporary styling will be a credit to your good taste while satisfying your quest for distinction. Entering the lower level from either the covered terrace or the carport, you go right upstairs to the spacious living area. The large projecting box bay window provides a dramatic backdrop. Two glass walls, the glass gabled end and the sloped ceilings, help create a most cheerful atmosphere and allow an unrestricted view of the outdoors.

Design V41498 Main Level: 768 square feet; Upper Level: 546 square feet; Lower Level: 768 square feet; Total: 2,082 square feet

● If it is space you need in your leisure living home, you should give a lot of thought to this multi-level design. It has just about everything to assure a pleasant visit. There are abundant sleeping facilities, fine recreational areas, 2½ baths, an excellent kitchen and good storage potential. The large deck and covered terrace will be popular spots.

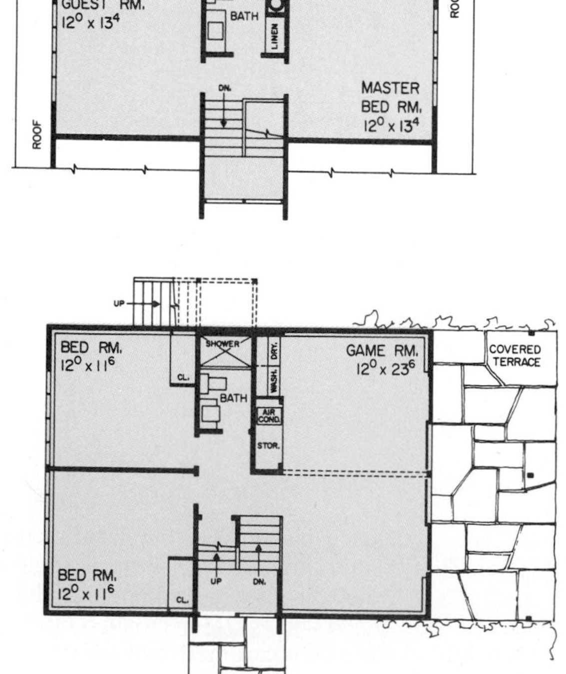

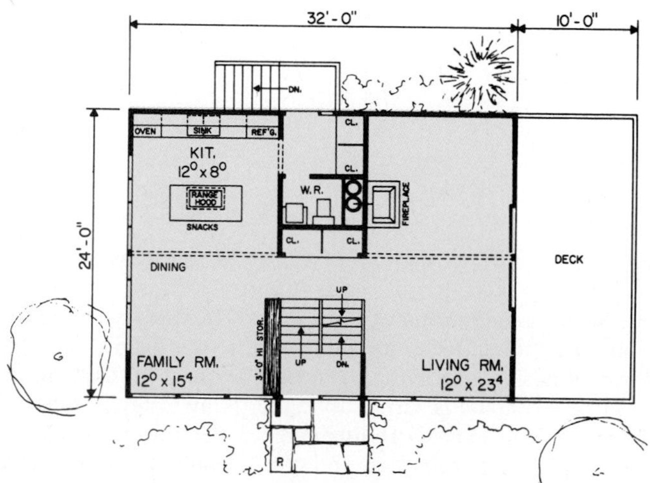

● Finding sleeping space for the weekend gang that often shows up at the cottage, is frequently a major problem. Further, having adequate bath facilities presents an additional problem much of the time. This two-level design does a magnificent job in alleviating these problems to provide trouble-free leisure living. In addition to the four bedrooms, there are two bunk rooms! Two full baths, each with a stall shower and built-in vanity, are convenient to the bedrooms. A third bath is located on the lower level adjacent to the family room. The kitchen area provides plenty of space for eating. Observe the two-way fireplace in the living room plus a fireplace in the family room.

Design V41434

Upper Level: 1,376 square feet
Lower Level: 576 square feet
Total: 1,952 square feet

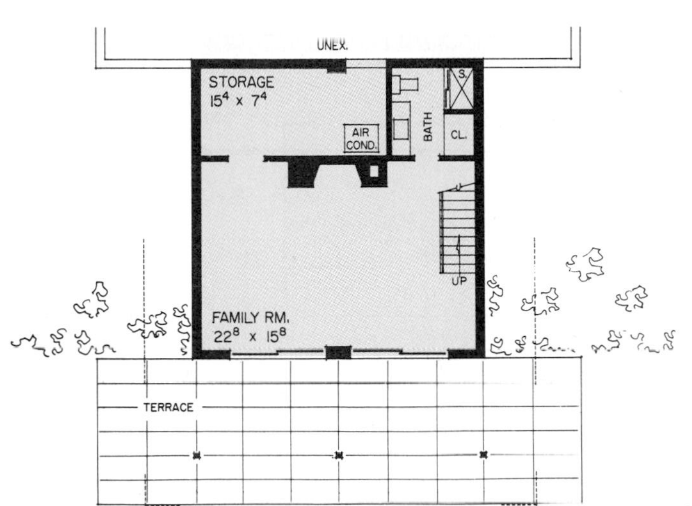

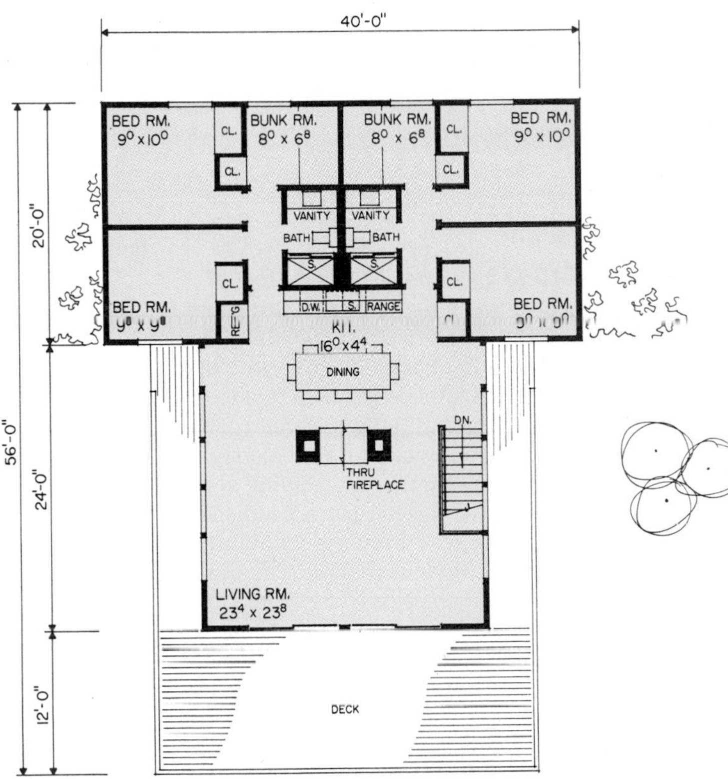

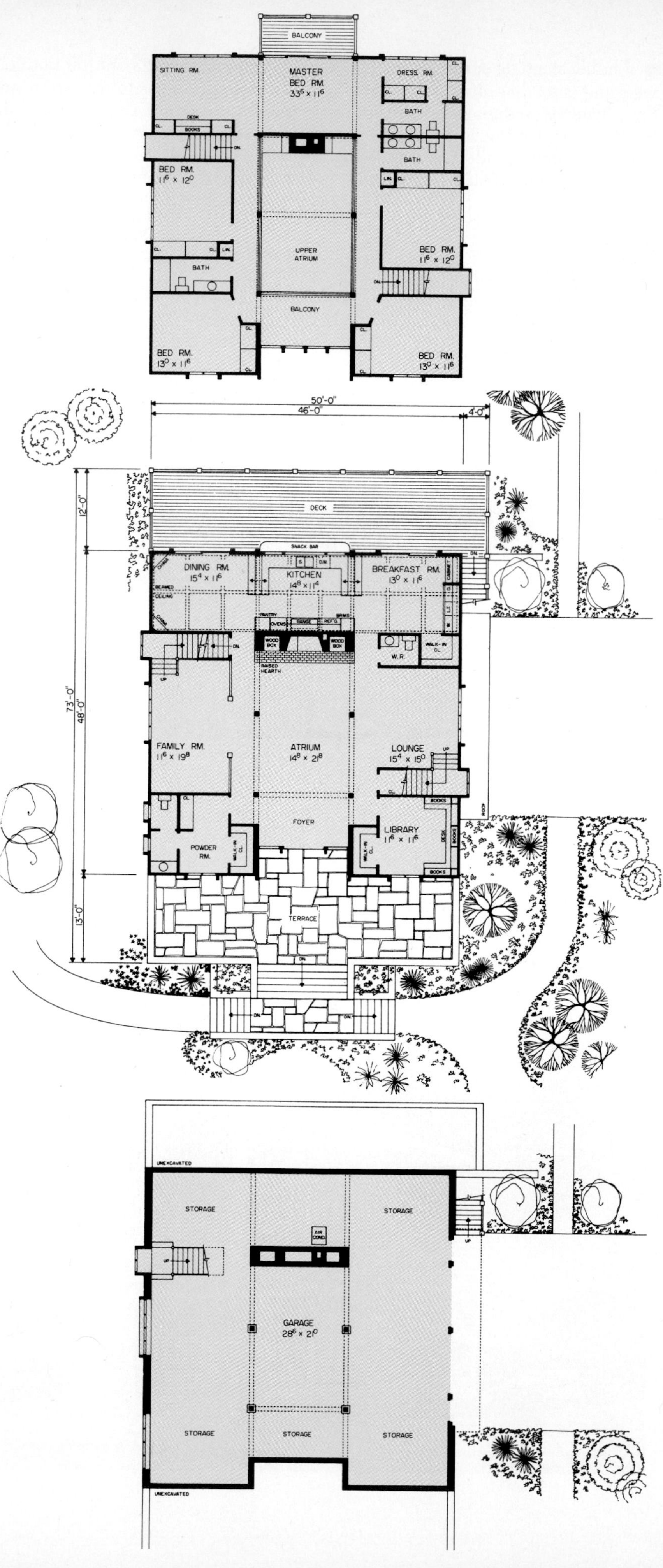

Design V42476

First Floor: 2,166 square feet
Second Floor: 1,886 square feet
Total: 4,052 square feet

● Here is over 4,000 square feet of second home livability all wrapped-up in a two-story structure which is charming in character. As for the livability, the interior features unsurpassed informal living potential. The five bedroom second floor balcony looks down into the huge living area. The massive raised hearth fireplace may be enjoyed from the family room as well as the lounge area. The dining room-kitchen-breakfast room area highlights a beamed ceiling. Note outdoor snack bar. Other features include the library, the 33 foot master bedroom, the excellent bath facilities, the two flights of stairs to the second floor and the big basement area where the garage is located.

Design V42169

Main Level: 2,381 square feet
Lower Level: 2,010 square feet
Total: 4,391 square feet

● Behold, the view! If, when looking toward the rear of your site, nature's scene is breathtaking or in any way inspiring, you may wish to maximize your enjoyment by orienting your living areas to the rear of your plan. In addition to greater enjoyment of the landscape, such floor planning will provide extra privacy from the street. The angular configuration can enhance the enjoyment of a particular scene, plus it adds appeal to the exterior of the design. A study of both levels reveals that the major living areas look out upon the rear yard. Further, the upper level rooms have direct access to the decks and balcony. The kitchen with its large window over the sink is not without its view. With five bedrooms, plus a library, a game, activities and hobby room, the active family will have an abundance of space to enjoy individualized pursuits. Can't you envision your family living in this house?

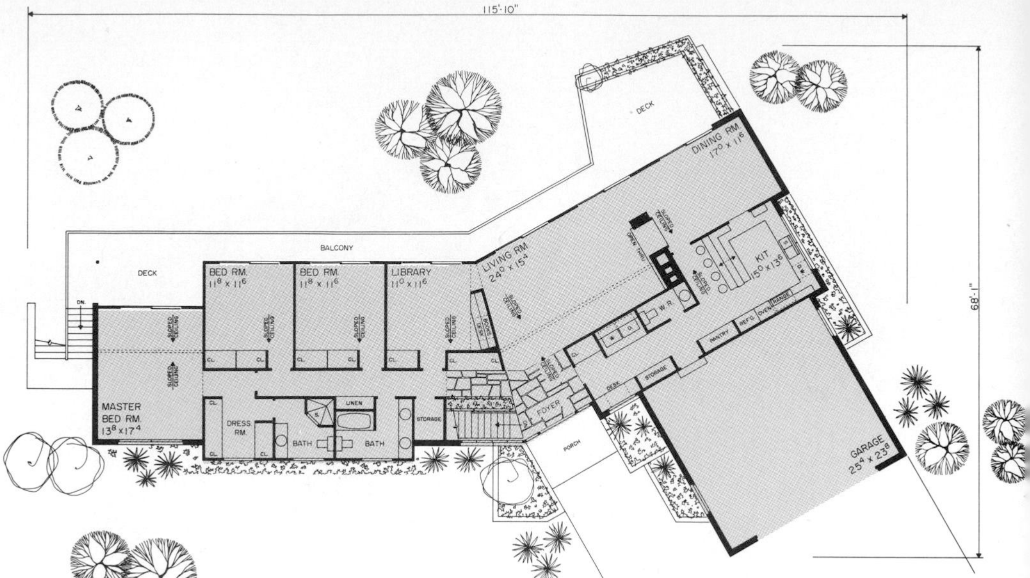

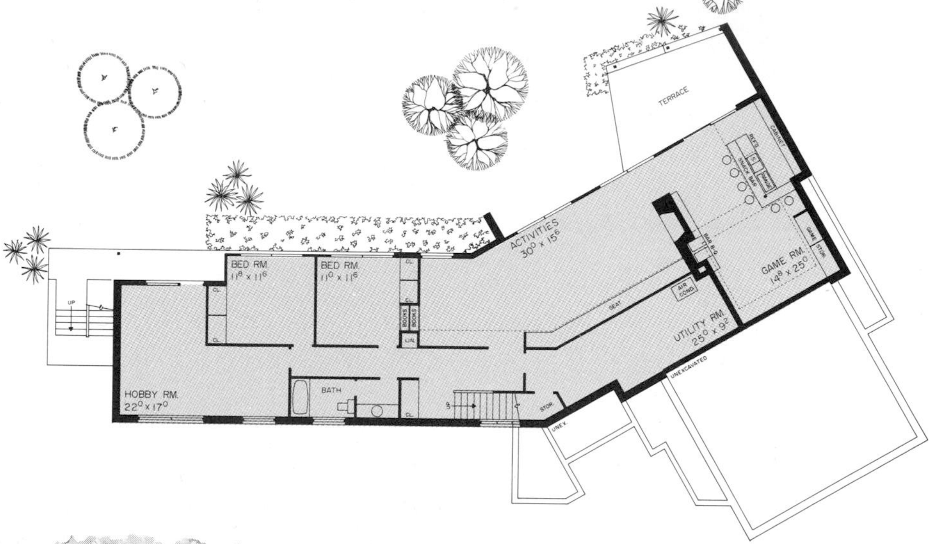

Design V41739 Main Level: 1,281 square feet; Sleeping Level: 857 square feet; Lower Level: 687 square feet; Total: 2,825 square feet

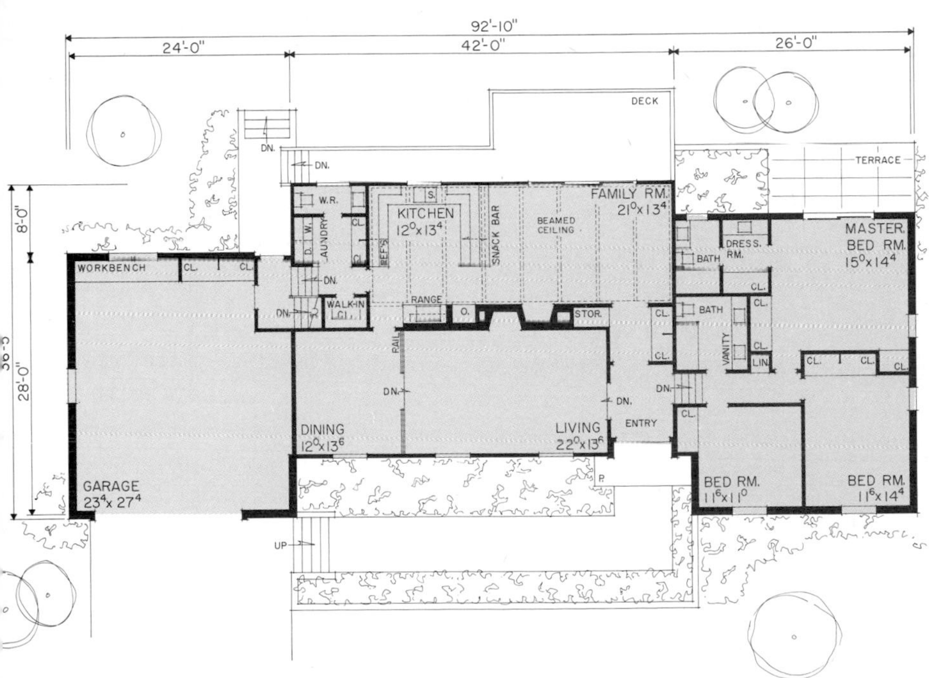

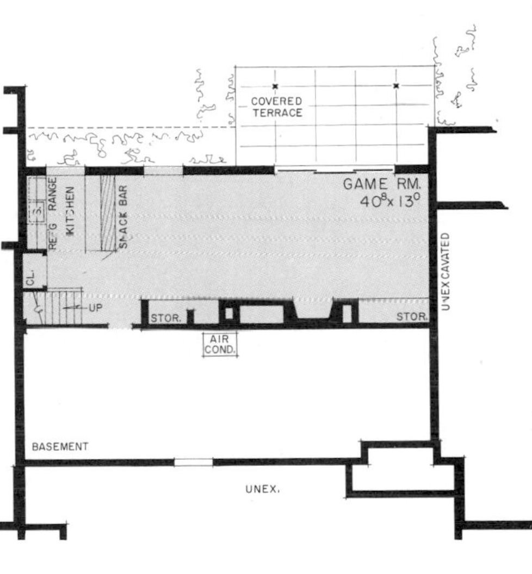

Design V42551

Main Level: 819 square feet; Upper Level: 818 square feet
Lower Level: 818 square feet; Total: 2,455 square feet

● This multi-level design is perfect for a family that enjoys lots of livability. Sloped ceilings highlight a spacious living room and study. A few steps down is an efficient kitchen with an adjacent dining room. The large family room will be a great asset. The upper level has two bedrooms and a master bedroom. The master bedroom has doors that open for a view of the living room below. A unique feature is the skylight above the planting area of the lower level.

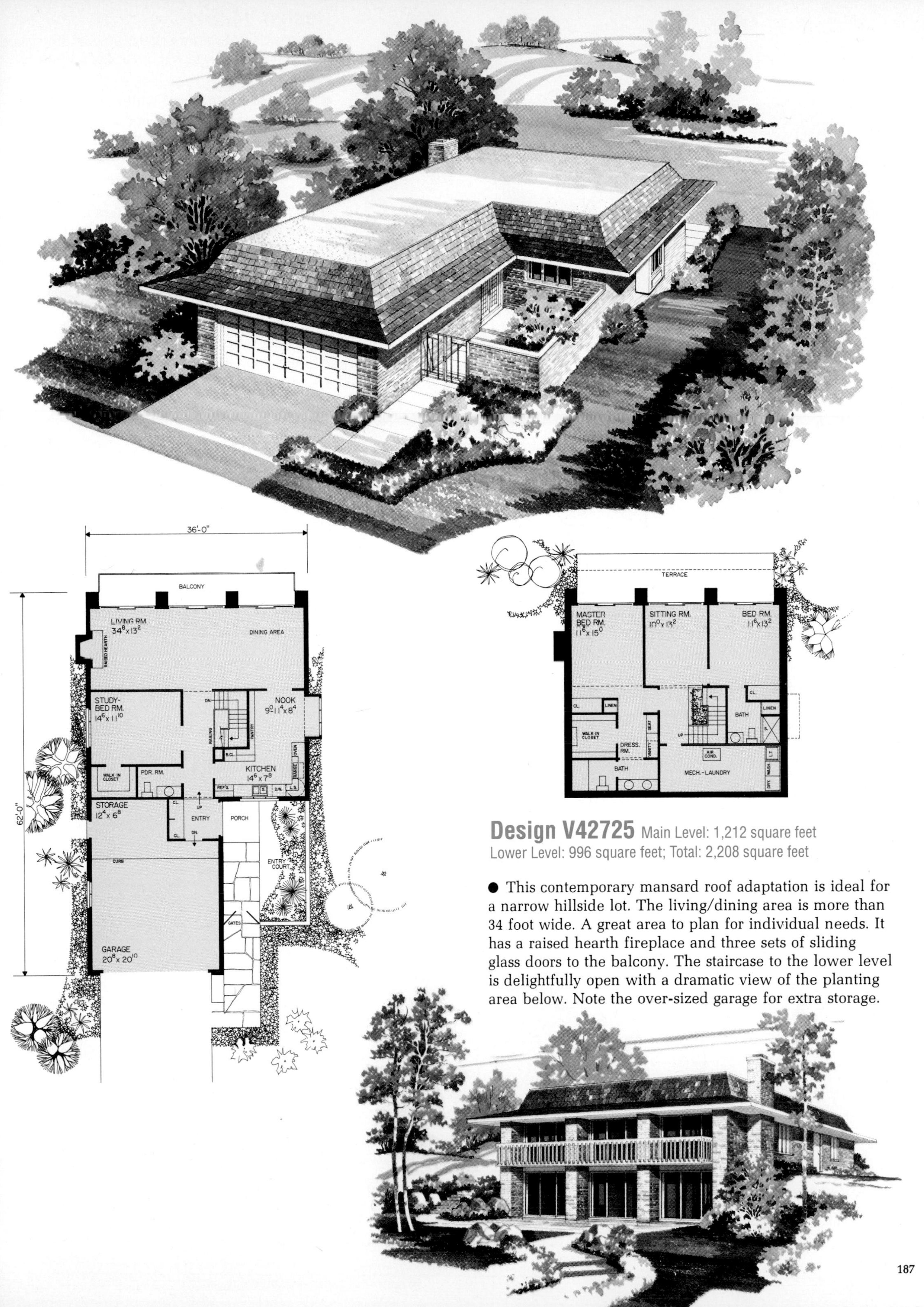

Design V42725 Main Level: 1,212 square feet Lower Level: 996 square feet; Total: 2,208 square feet

● This contemporary mansard roof adaptation is ideal for a narrow hillside lot. The living/dining area is more than 34 foot wide. A great area to plan for individual needs. It has a raised hearth fireplace and three sets of sliding glass doors to the balcony. The staircase to the lower level is delightfully open with a dramatic view of the planting area below. Note the over-sized garage for extra storage.

Design V42841

Main Level: 1,044 square feet; Upper Level: 851 square f
Lower Level: 753 square feet; Total: 2,648 square feet

D

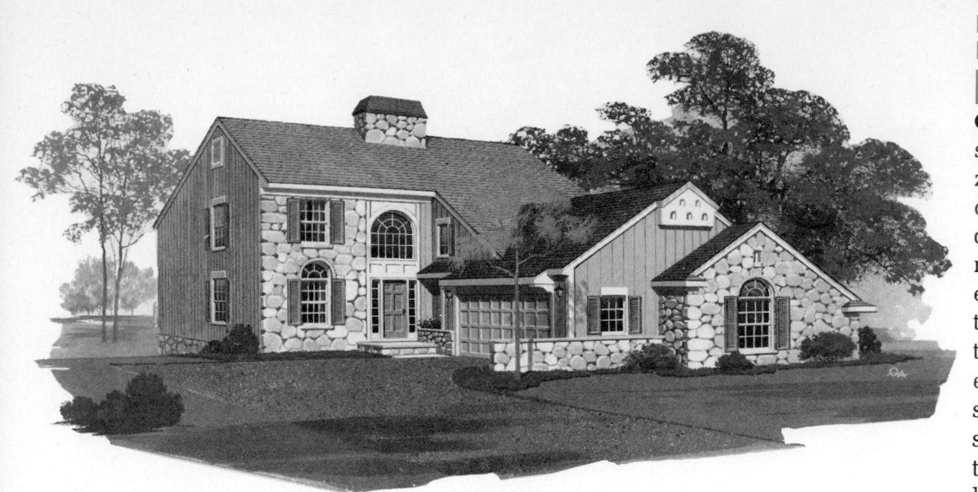

● This spacious tri-level with traditional stone exterior offers excellent comfort and zoning for the modern family. The rear opens to balconies and a deck that creates a covered patio below. A main floor gathering room is continued above with an upper gathering room. The lower level offers an activities room with raised hearth, in addition to an optional bunk room with bath. A modern kitchen on main level features a handy snack bar, in addition to a dining room. A study on main level could become an optional bedroom. The master bedroom is located on the upper level, along with a rectangular bunk room with its own balcony.

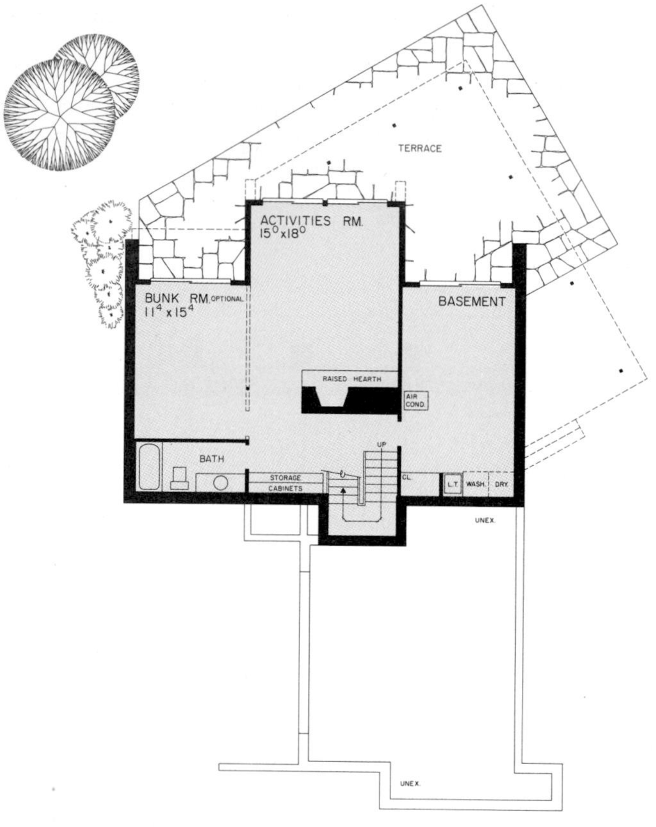

TERRACE
ACTIVITIES RM.
15⁰ x18⁰
BUNK RM. OPTIONAL
11⁴ x 15⁴
BASEMENT
RAISED HEARTH
AIR COND.
BATH
STORAGE CABINETS
UP
CL.
L.T.
WASH.
DRY.
UNEX.
UNEX.

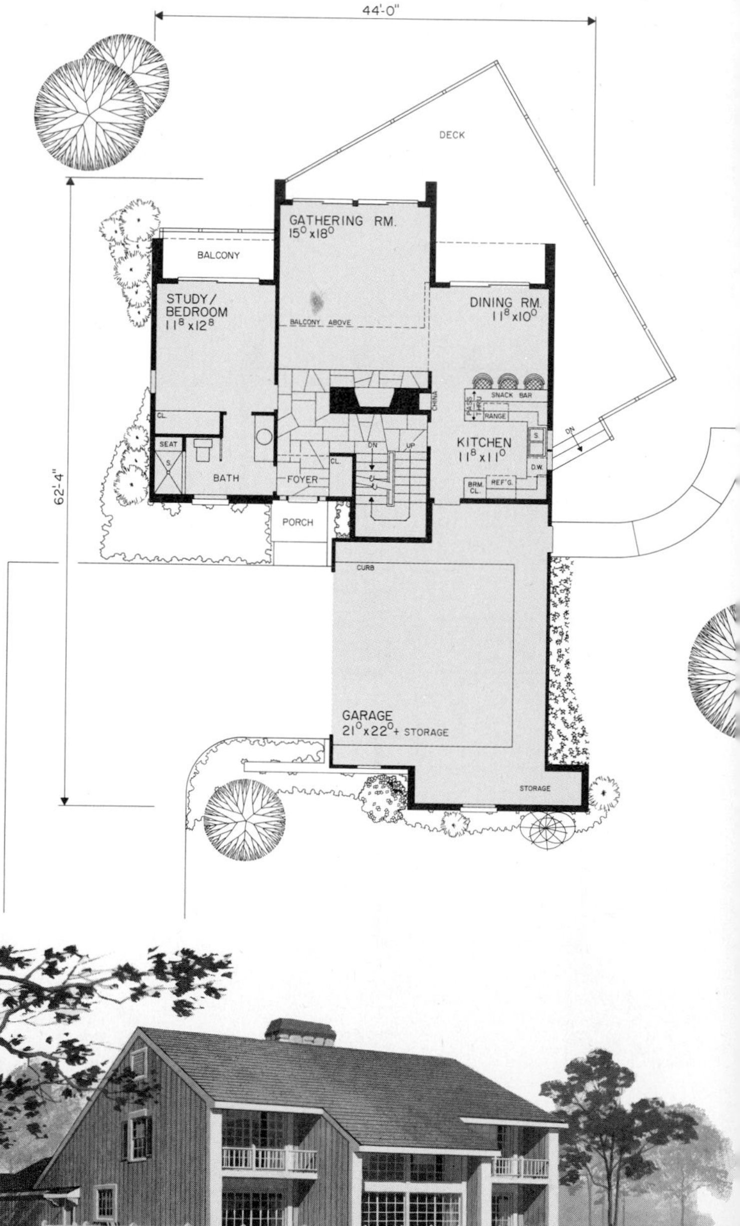

44'-0"
DECK
GATHERING RM.
15⁰ x18⁰
BALCONY
STUDY/ BEDROOM
11⁸ x12⁸
BALCONY ABOVE
DINING RM.
11⁸ x10⁰
SNACK BAR
RANGE
CHINA
KITCHEN
11⁸ x11⁰
CL.
SEAT
BATH
CL.
FOYER
DN
UP
DN
BRM CL.
REF'G.
D.W.
PORCH
62'-4"
CURB
GARAGE
21⁰x22⁰ + STORAGE
STORAGE

BALCONY
UPPER GATHERING RM.
BALCONY
BEDROOM
11⁸ x12⁸
BUNK RM.
11⁸ x18⁸
RAILING
LOUNGE
15⁰ x6⁰
LINEN
CL.
RAILING
DN
RAILING
BATH
UPPER FOYER
CL.
CL.
SEAT

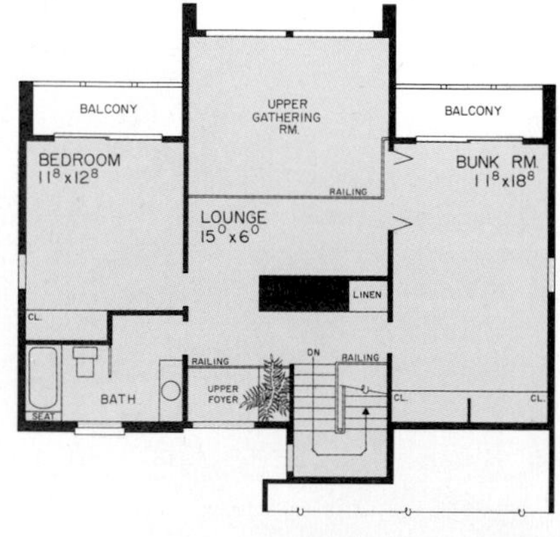

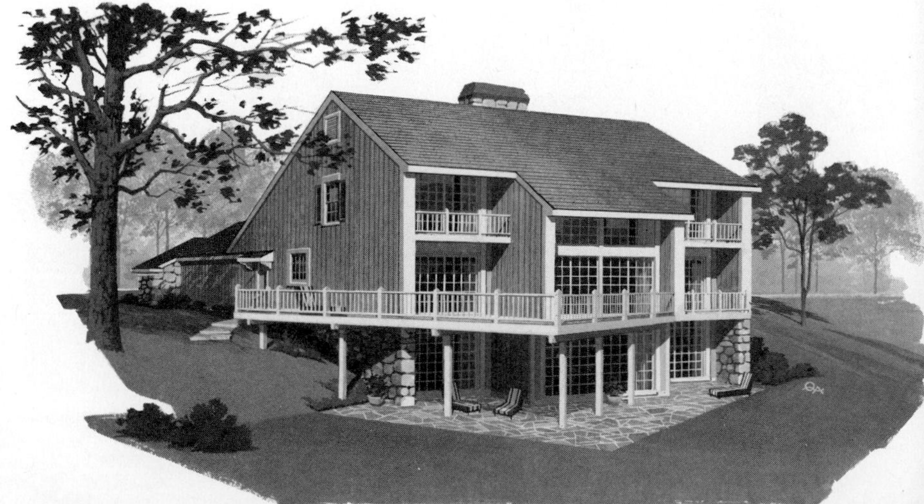

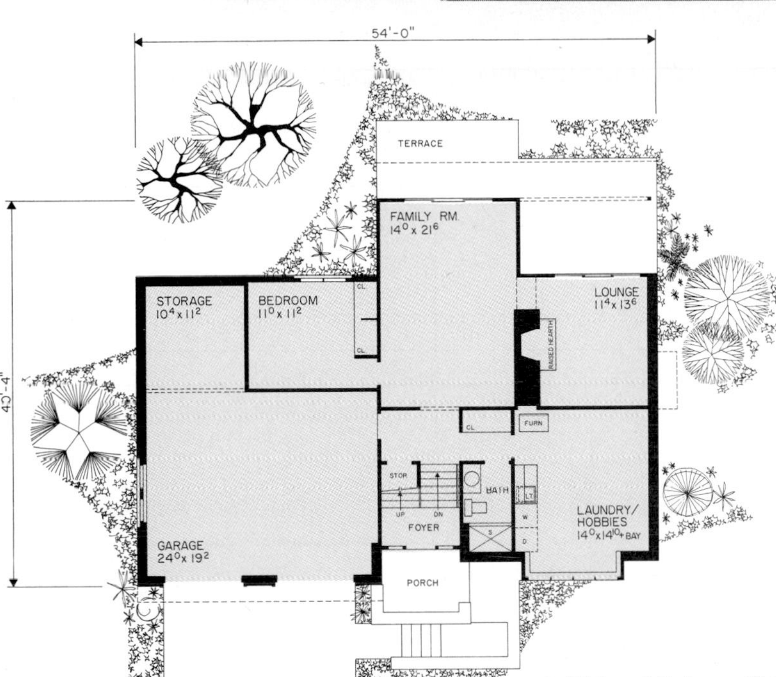

Design V42843

Upper Level: 1,861 square feet
Lower Level: 1,181 square feet
Total: 3,042 square feet

L

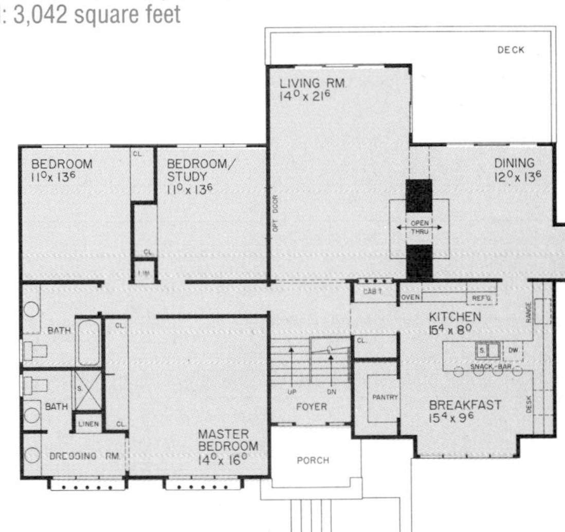

● Bi-level living will be enjoyed to its fullest in this Spanish styled design. There is a lot of room for the various family activities. Informal living will take place on the lower level in the family room and lounge. The formal living and dining rooms, sharing a thru-fireplace, are located on the upper level.

Design V42546

Main Level: 1,143 square feet; Upper Level: 746 square feet
Lower Level: 1,143 square feet; Total: 3,031 square feet

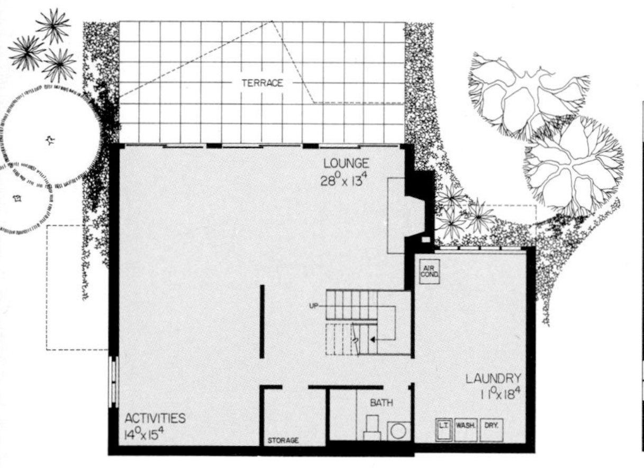

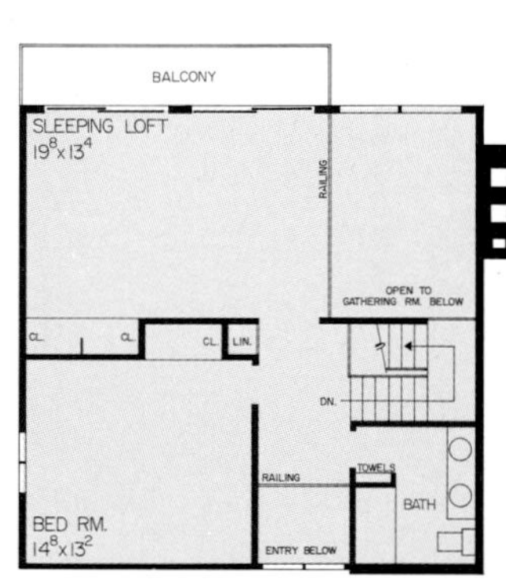

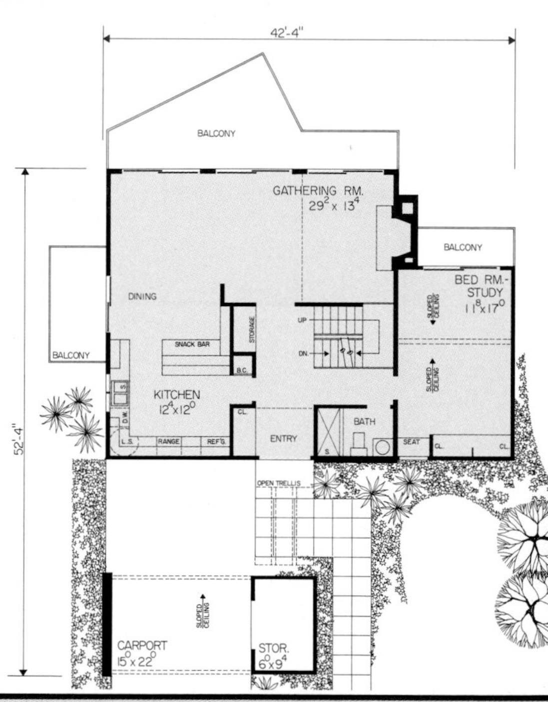

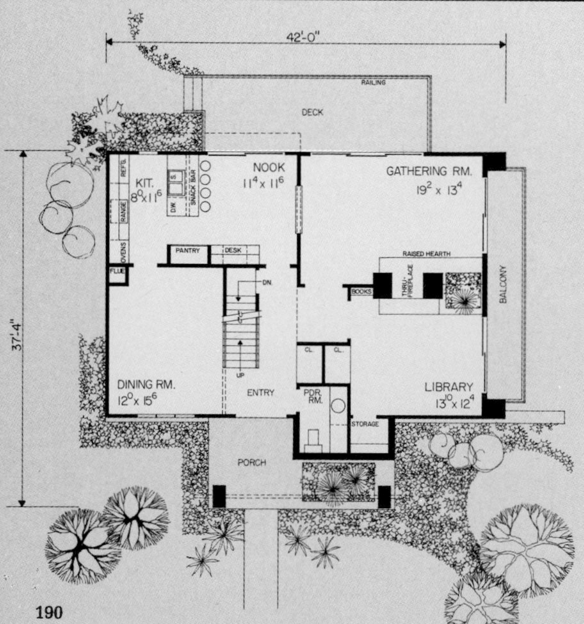

Design V42770

Main Level: 1,182 square feet
Upper Level: 998 square feet
Total: 2,180 square feet

● If you are looking for a home with loads of livability, then consider these two-story contemporary homes which have an exposed lower level.

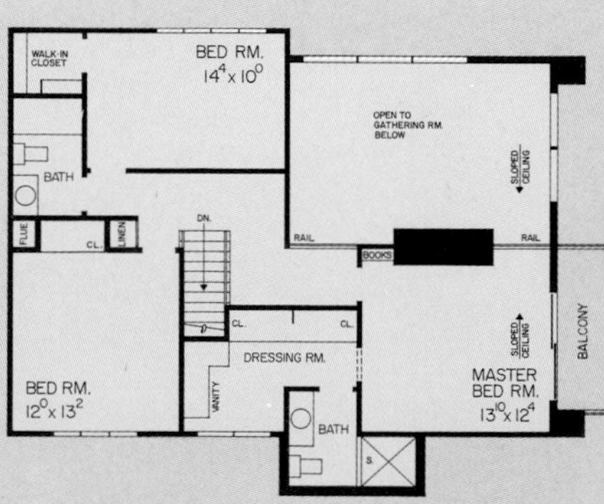

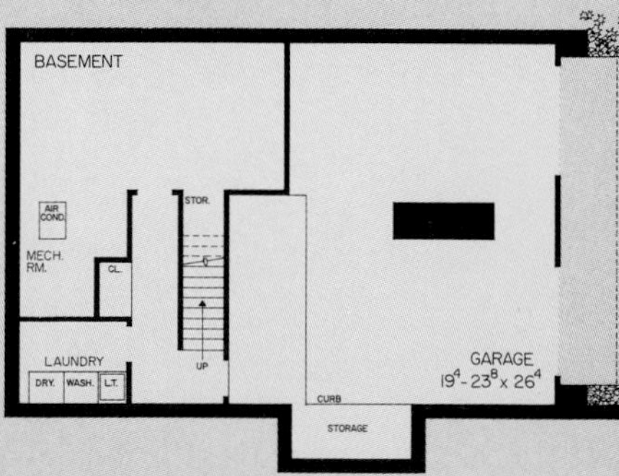

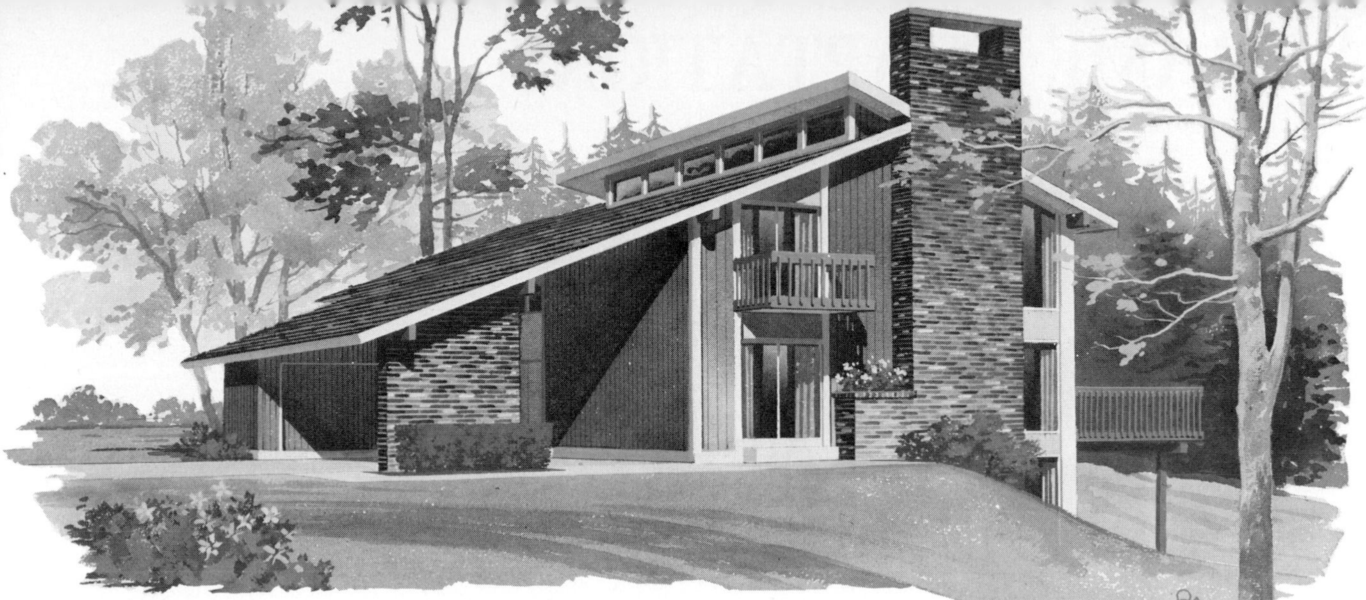

Design V42548 Main Level: 1,109 square feet; Upper Level: 739 square feet
Lower Level: 869 square feet; Total: 2,717 square feet

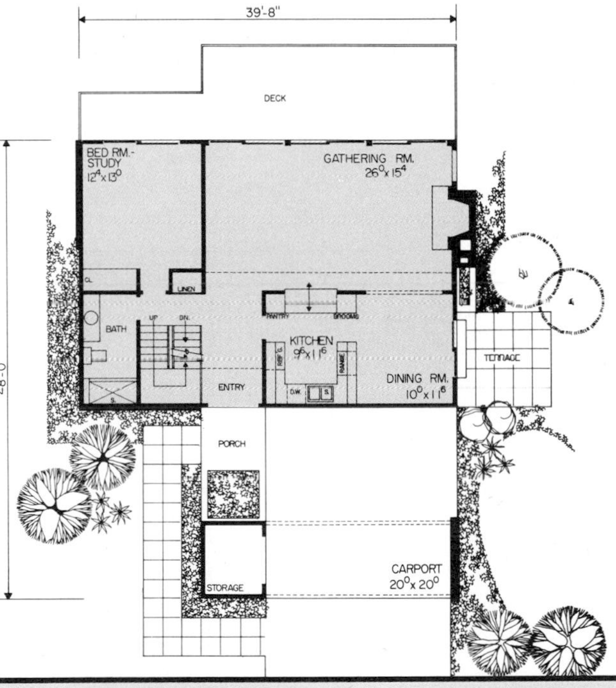

39'-8"
DECK
BED RM.-STUDY
12^4 x 13^0
GATHERING RM.
26^0 x 15^4
CL.
LINEN
BATH
UP
DN.
PANTRY
KITCHEN
9^6 x 11^6
ENTRY
DINING RM.
10^0 x 11^6
TERRACE
48'-0"
PORCH
STORAGE
CARPORT
20^0 x 20^0

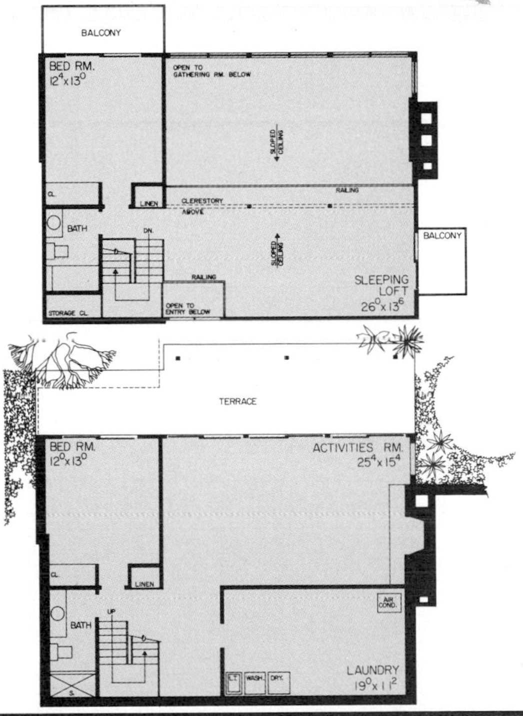

BALCONY
BED RM.
12^4 x 13^0
OPEN TO GATHERING RM. BELOW
SLOPED CEILING
CL.
LINEN
CLERESTORY ABOVE
RAILING
BATH
DN.
BALCONY
SLOPED CEILING
RAILING
STORAGE CL.
OPEN TO ENTRY BELOW
SLEEPING LOFT
26^0 x 13^6
TERRACE
BED RM.
12^0 x 13^0
ACTIVITIES RM.
25^4 x 15^4
CL.
LINEN
UP
BATH
AIR COND.
WASH
DRY
LAUNDRY
19^0 x 11^2

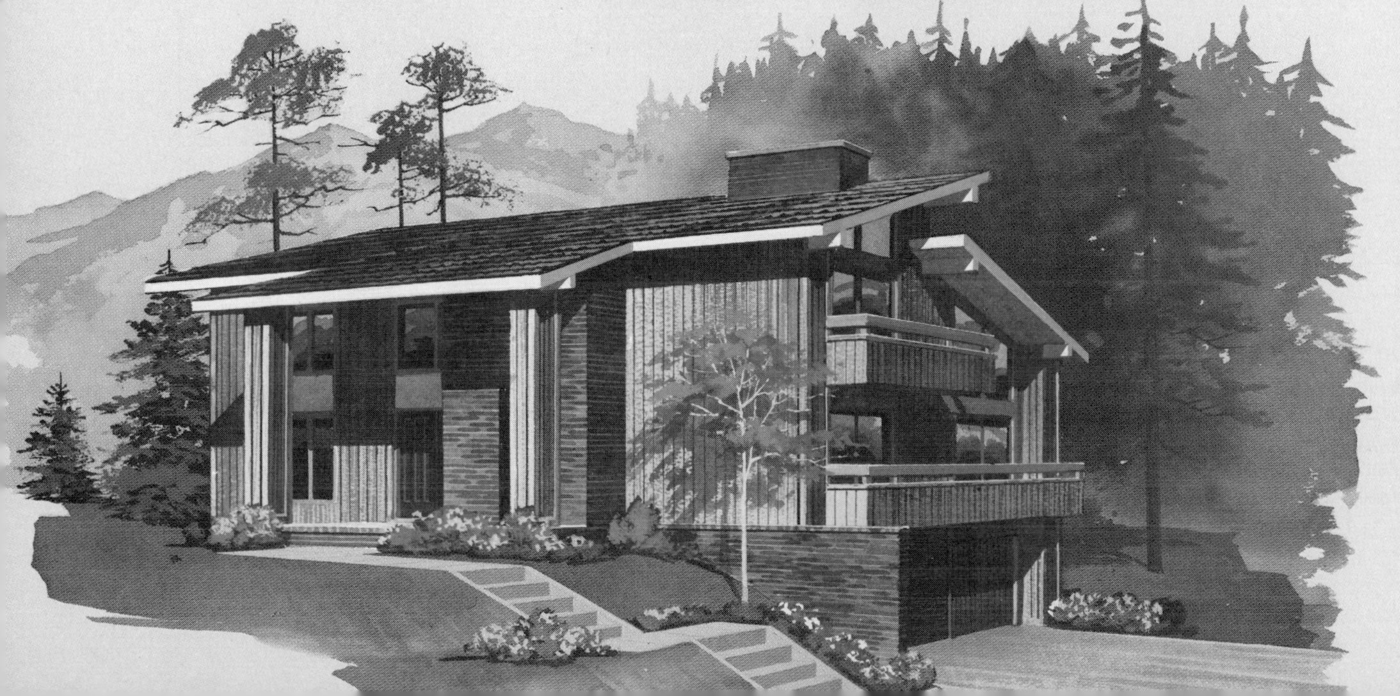

A-FRAME ADAPTATIONS . . . *are designed for use as seasonal homes and are at their best when enjoyed in mild weather. The soaring roof lines, expanse of glass, decks and balconies, and uniqueness of their construction all add up to an unmatched measure of distinction. Look for second-story lofts for added sleeping room.*

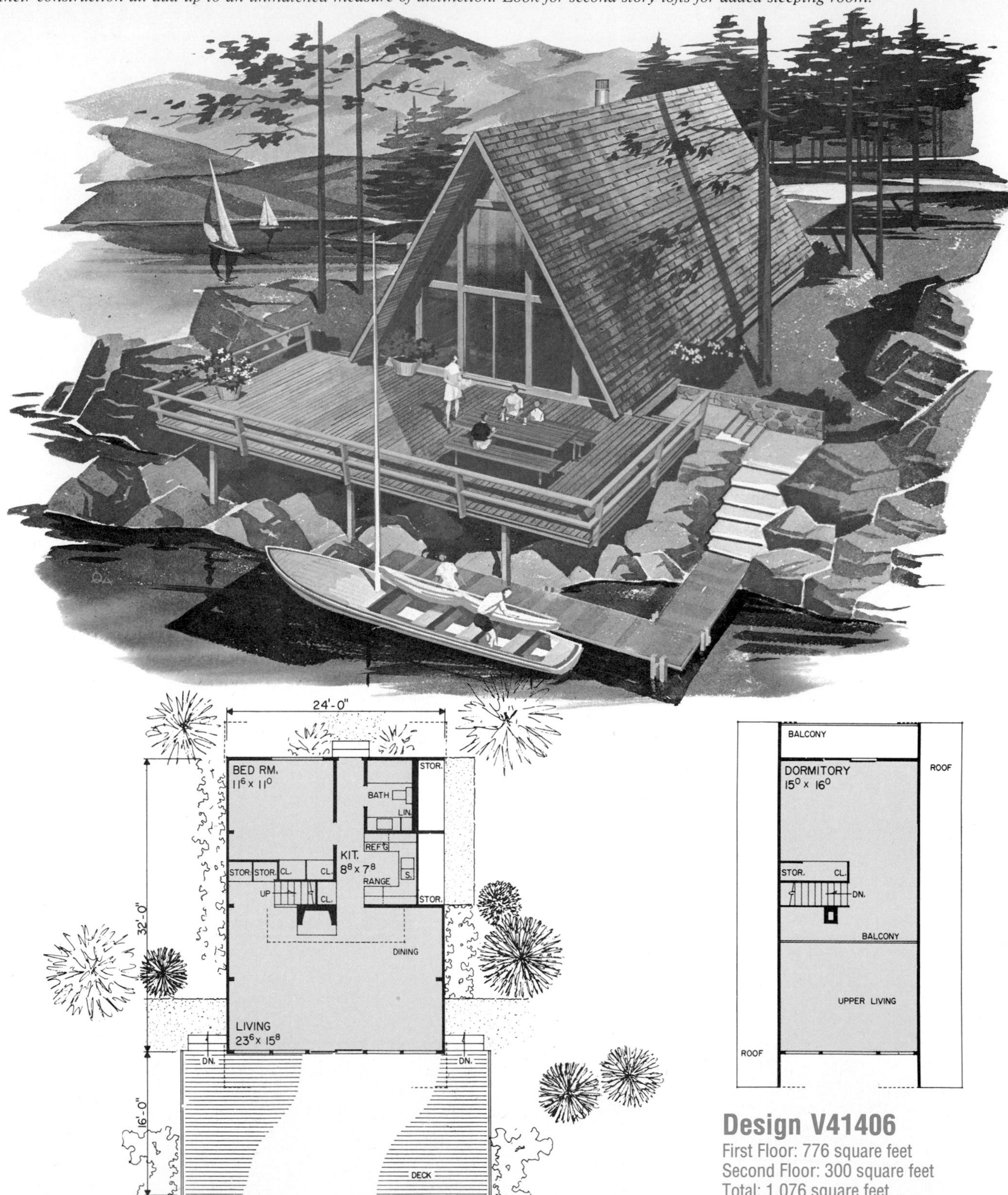

Design V41406

First Floor: 776 square feet
Second Floor: 300 square feet
Total: 1,076 square feet

● A spacious 23-foot by 15-foot living room is really something to talk about. And when it has a high, vaulted ceiling and a complete wall of windows it is even more noteworthy. Because of the wonderful glass area, the livability of the living room seems to spill right out onto the huge wood deck. In addition to the bedroom downstairs, there is the sizable dormitory upstairs for sleeping quite a crew. Sliding glass doors open onto the outdoor balcony from the dormitory. Don't miss the fireplace, the efficient kitchen and the numerous storage facilities. The outside storage units are accessible from just below the roof line and are great for all the recreational equipment. Don't be without the exceptional wood deck. It will make a vital contribution to your outdoor vacation enjoyment.

Design V42431 First Floor: 1,057 square feet; Second Floor: 406 square feet; Total: 1,463 square feet

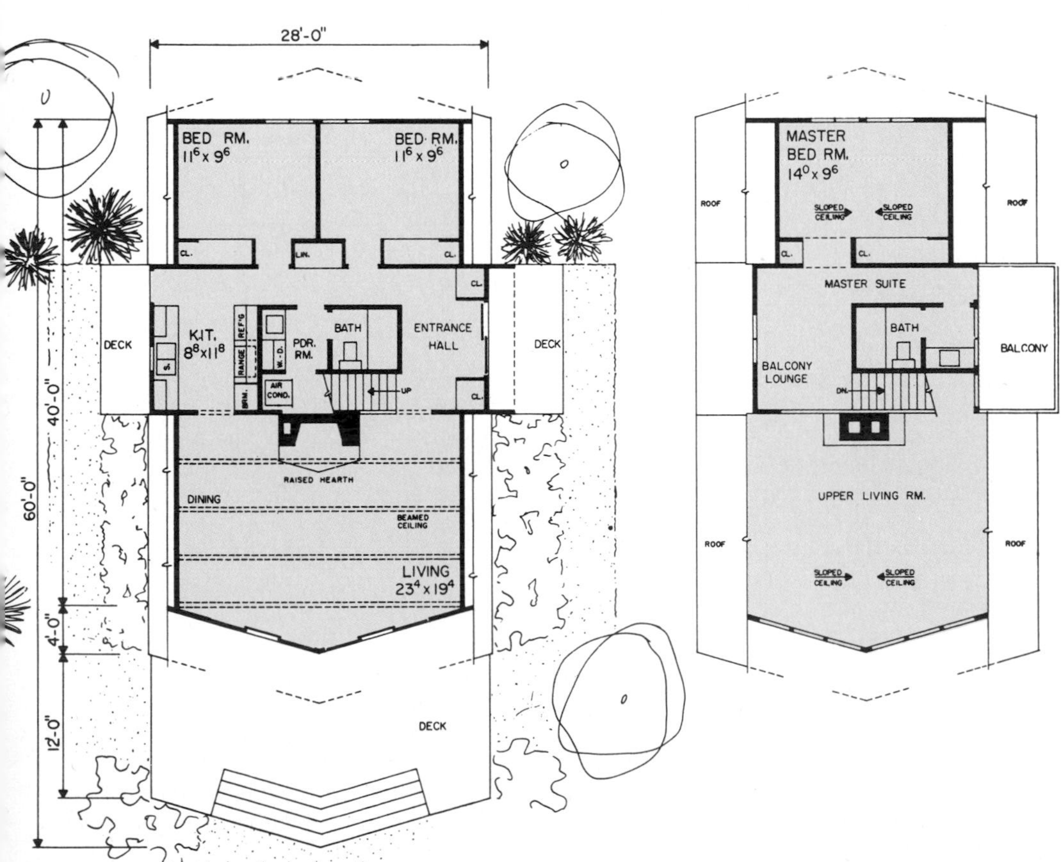

● A favorite everywhere – the A-frame vacation home. Its popularity is easily discernible at first glance. The stately appearance is enhanced by the soaring roof lines and the dramatic glass areas. Inside, the breathtaking beauty of outstanding architectural detailing also is apparent. The high ceiling of the living room slopes and has exposed beams. The second floor master suite is a great feature. Observe the raised-hearth fireplace and the outdoor balcony. This outdoor spot certainly will be a quiet perch for sunbathing on a warm afternoon.

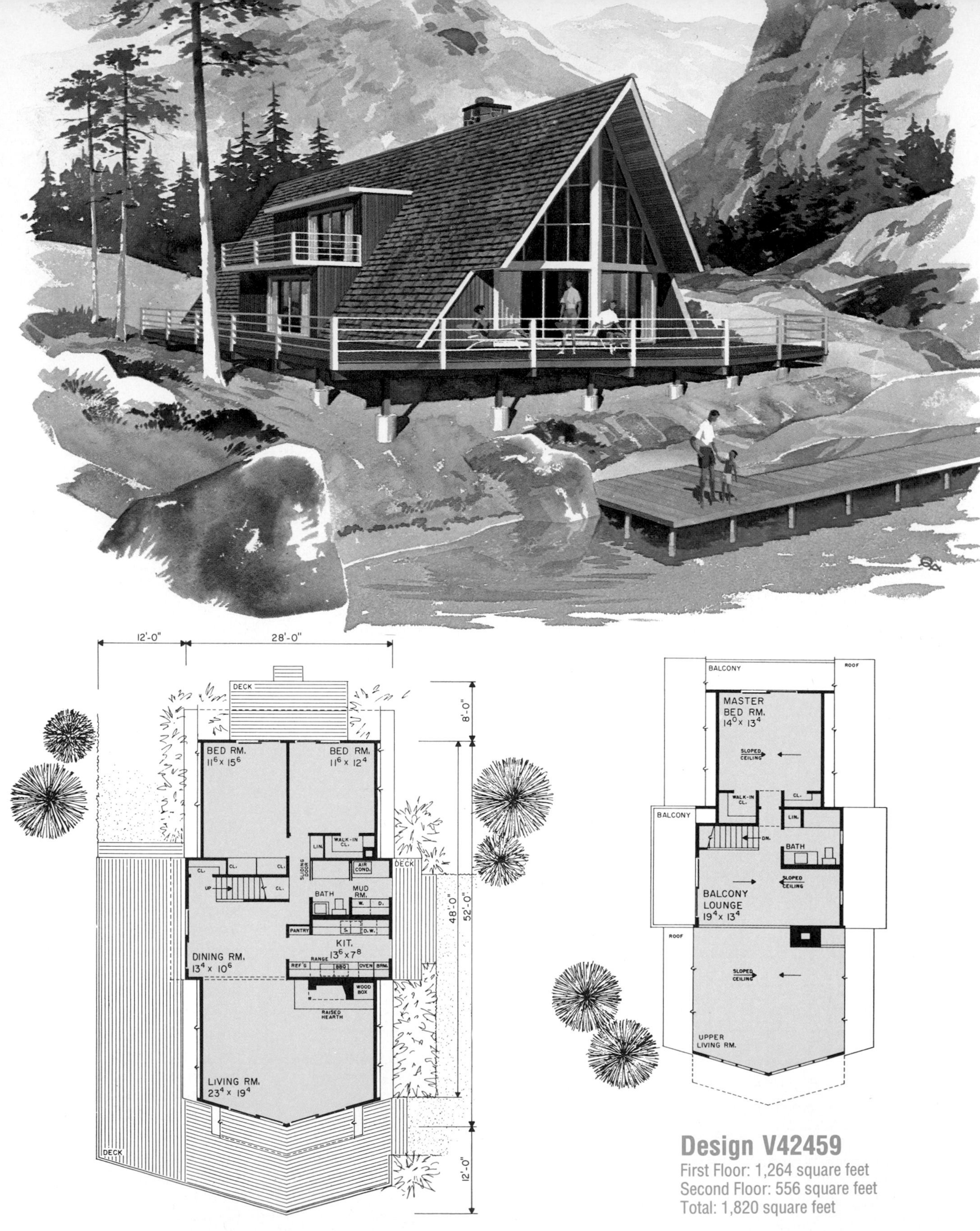

Design V42459

First Floor: 1,264 square feet
Second Floor: 556 square feet
Total: 1,820 square feet

● Dramatic, indeed! The soaring roof projects and heightens the appeal of the slanted glass gable end. The expanse of the roof is broken to provide access to the side deck from the dining room. Above is the balcony of the second floor lounge. This room with its high sloping ceiling looks down into the spacious first floor living room. The master bedroom also has an outdoor balcony. Back downstairs there are loads of features. They include two large bedrooms, a big dining room and a huge living room. Particularly noteworthy is the direct accessibility of the kitchen and mud room/bath from the outdoors. These are truly convenient traffic patterns for the active family. The raised hearth fireplace commands its full share of attention as it rises toward the sloping ceiling.

Design V41476 Main Level: 1,225 square feet; Upper Level: 560 square feet; Lower Level: 905 square feet; Total: 2,690 square feet

● This colorful A-frame will adapt to its surroundings in a most dramatic manner. The large glass areas and the outdoor decks will permit the fullest enjoyment of the outdoors. The lounges of the lower level and the upper level function with outdoor living areas and will be favorite gathering spots. From the upper level lounge you will look down into the cozy living room. The family dining room will enjoy its own view. It is but a step from the huge deck. There are three bedrooms, 2½ baths and plenty of recreation and storage space.

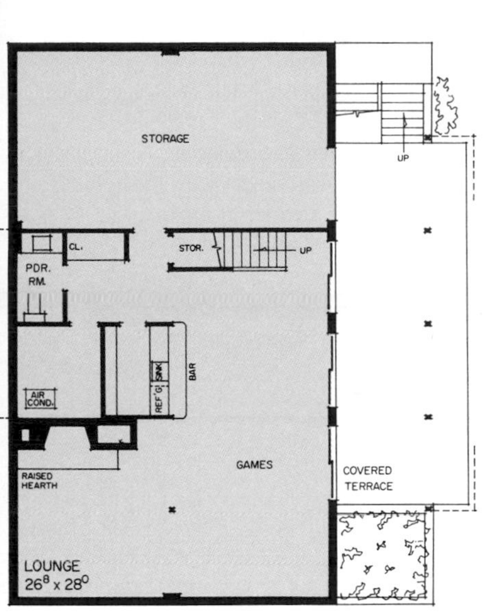

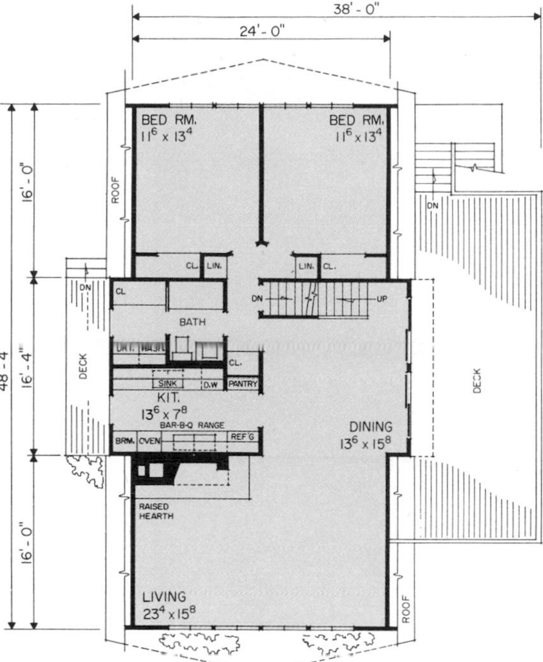

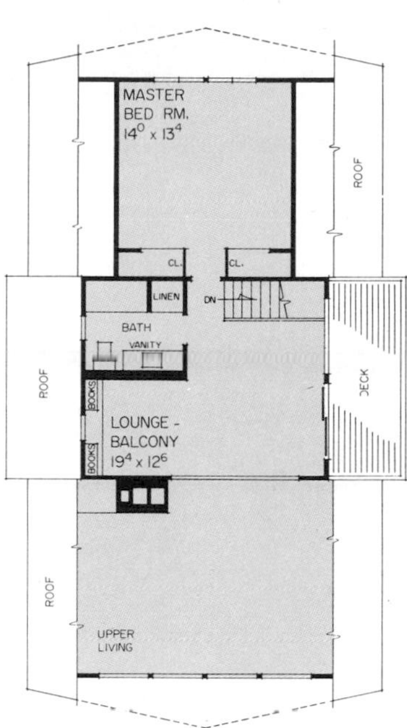

● Perhaps more than any other design in recent years the A-frame has captured the imagination of the prospective vacation home builder. There is a gala air about its shape that fosters a holiday spirit whether the house be a summer retreat or a structure for year 'round living. This particular A-frame offers a lot of living for there are five bedrooms, two baths, an efficient kitchen, a family-dining area and outstanding storage. As in most designs of this type, the living room with its great height and large glass area is extremely dramatic at first sight.

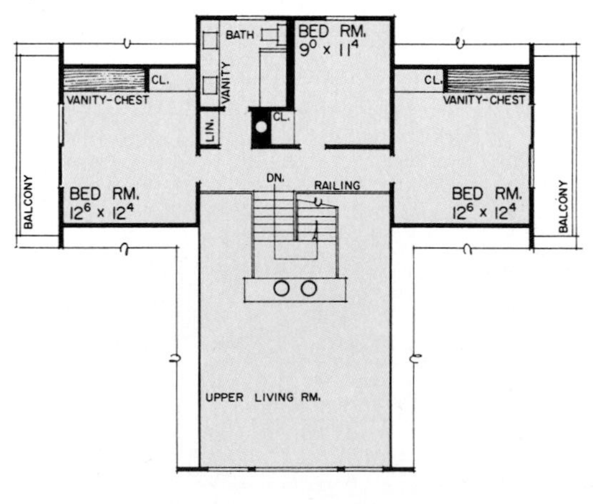

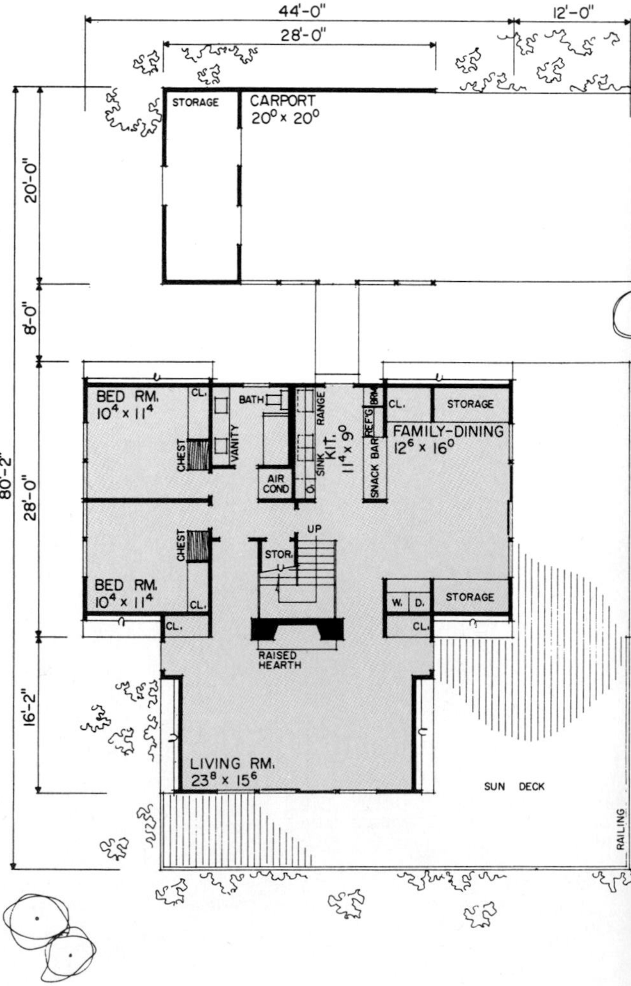

Design V41432 First Floor: 1,512 square feet; Second Floor: 678 square feet; Total: 2,190 square feet

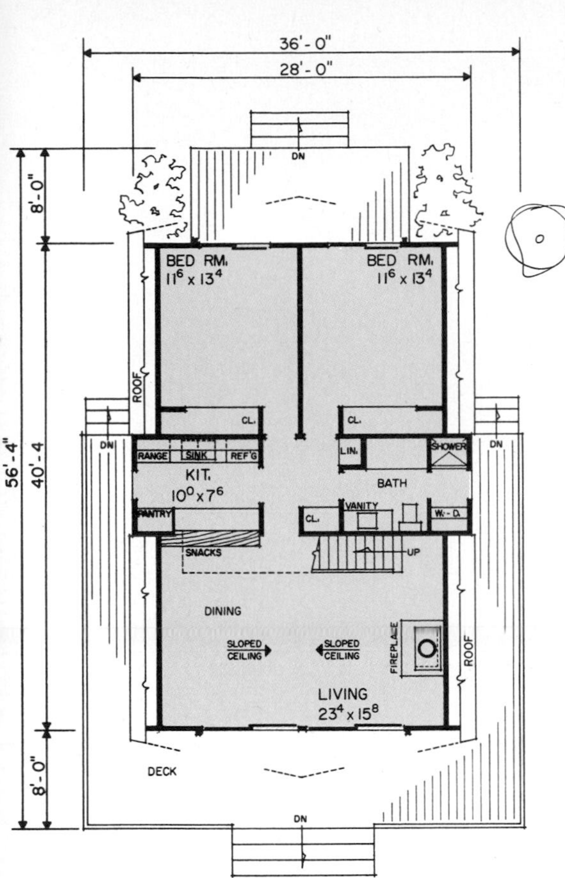

Design V41470

First Floor: 1,000 square feet; Second Floor: 482 square feet
Loft: 243 square feet; Total: 1,725 square feet

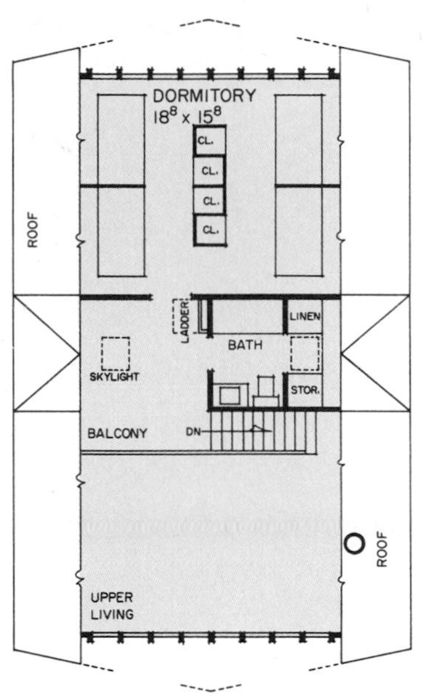

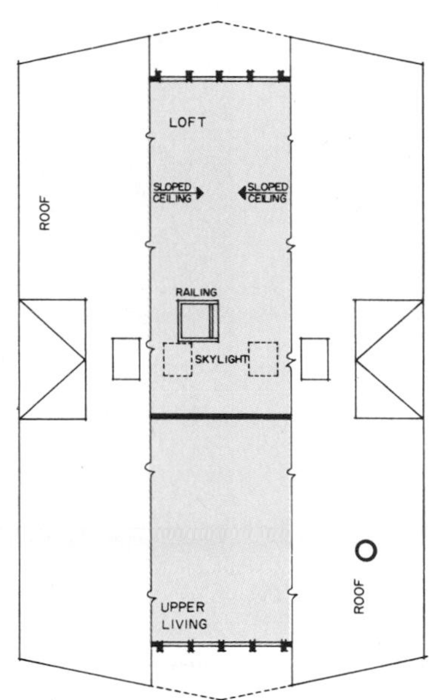

● Three-level, A-frame living can be dramatic and, also, offer your family living patterns that will be a lot of fun all throughout the year. The ceiling of the living room soars upward to an apex of approximately twenty-four feet. Both the second floor and the upper level loft can look down into the living room below. The wall of glass permits a fine view of the outdoors from each of these levels. With all those sleeping facilities even the largest of families will have space left over for a few extra friends. Note two baths, efficient kitchen, snack bar and deck which are available to serve your everyday needs. A home to be enjoyed no matter what the occasion.

Design V42467 First Floor: 720 square feet; Second Floor: 483 square feet; Total: 1,203 square feet

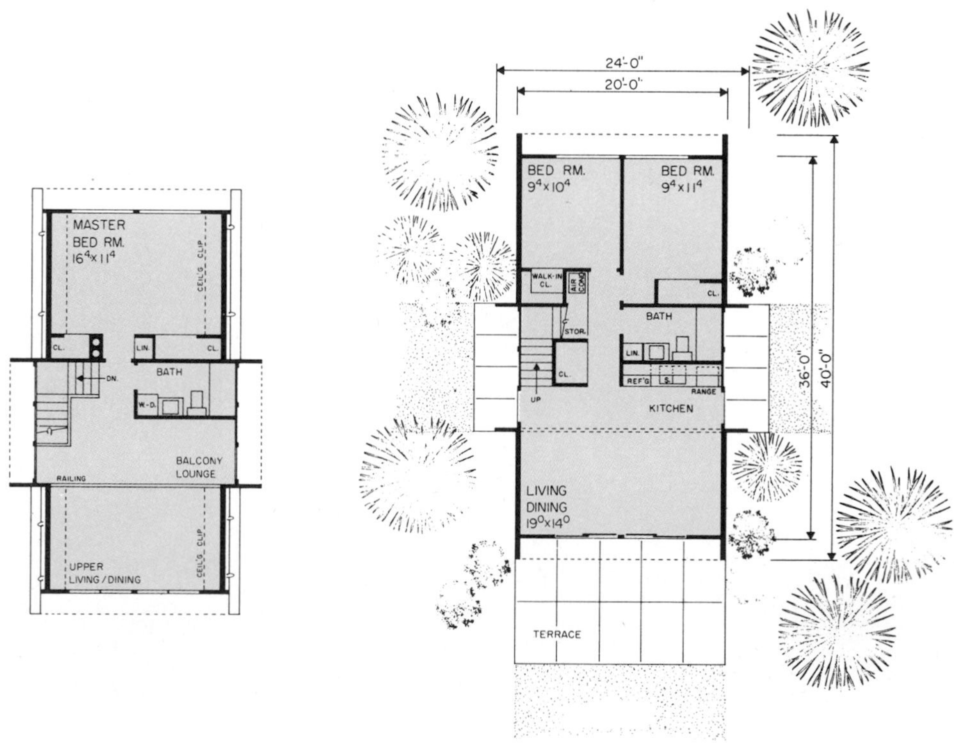

● Here is another dramatic variation of the popular A-frame. The roof modifications result in a structure that is somewhat similar to the configuration of the mansard roof. The utilization of the form with those large glass areas produces a blending of traditional and contemporary design features. The more nearly vertical side walls of this type of a design results in a greater amount of space inside than offered by the usual A-frame. Observe the great amount of livability in this plan. In addition to the two downstairs bedrooms, there is an upstairs master bedroom. Also there is a second full bath and a balcony lounge overlooking the living room. When needed, the lounge area could accommodate a couple of cots for weekend vacationers. Count the storage facilities.

Design V42469 First Floor: 720 square feet; Second Floor: 483 square feet; Total: 1,203 square feet

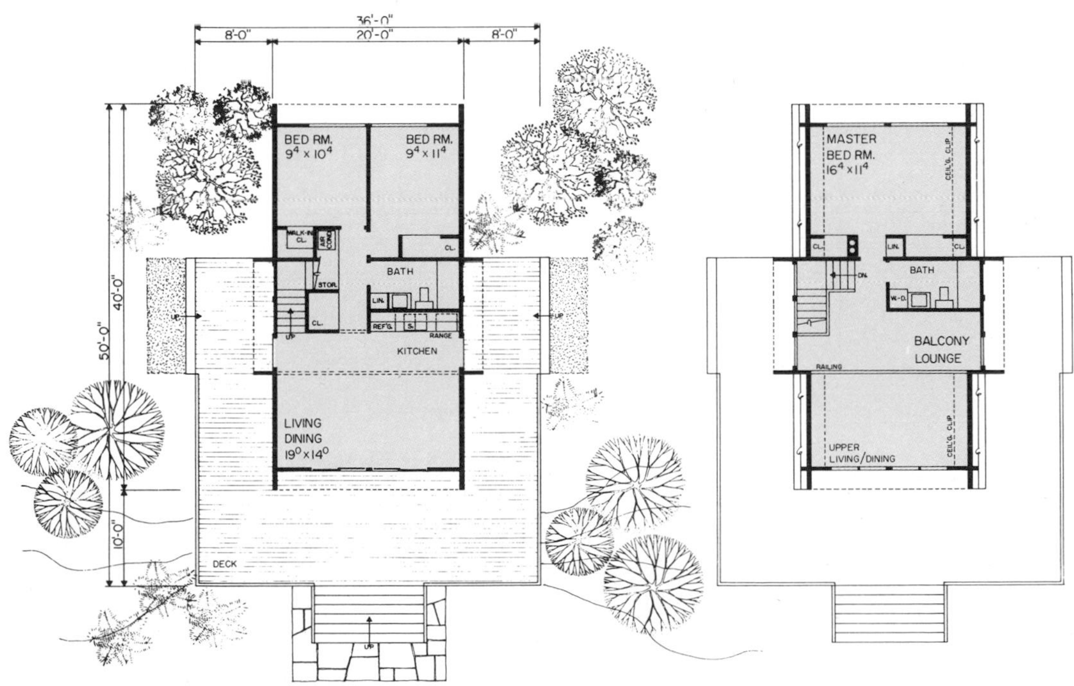

● If yours is a hankering for a truly distinctive second home of modest size with excellent livability and tailored for the moderate building budget, this pleasingly proportioned design may just satisfy your specifications. This 20' x 40' rectangle certainly has its own flair of individuality. Its raised deck and railing add that extra measure of appeal. The projecting roof and side-walls create a protective recess for the dramatic wall of glass. Such an expanse of glass provides the living-dining area with an abundance of natural light and helps assure a fine awareness of the outdoors. The kitchen is compact and efficient. While there are two bedrooms and full bath downstairs the master bedroom and bath occupy the upper level. The balcony provides extra lounge space.

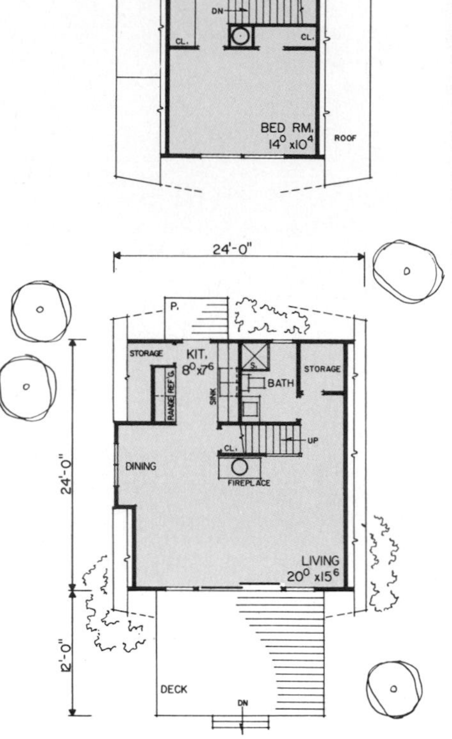

Design V41490

First Floor: 576 square feet; Second Floor: 362 square feet; Total: 938 square feet

● Wherever situated – in the northern woods, or on the southern coast, these enchanting A-frames will function as perfect retreats. Whether called upon to serve as hunting lodges, ski lodges or summer havens, they will perform admirably. The size of the first floor of each design is identical. However, the layouts are quite different. Which do you prefer Design V41490, above, with a two bedroom second floor or Design V41491, below, with a loft on the second floor?

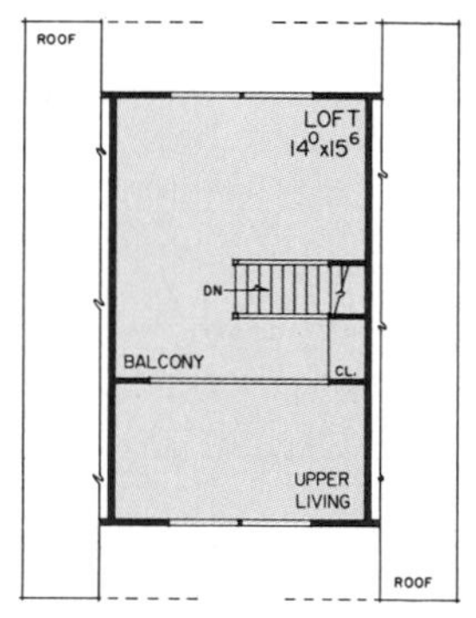

Design V41491

First Floor: 576 square feet; Second Floor: 234 square feet; Total: 810 square feet

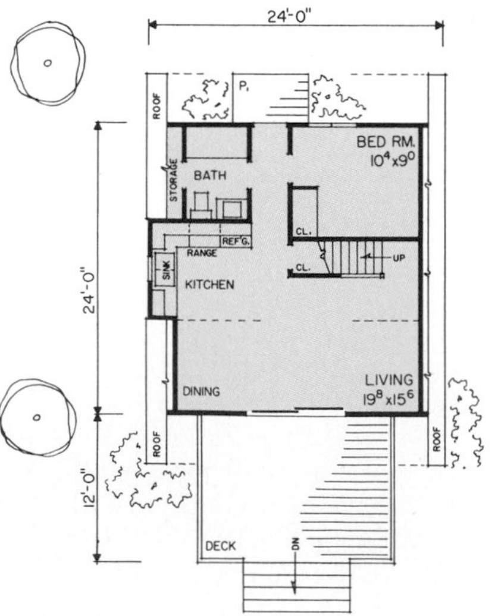

Design V41494 First Floor: 768 square feet; Second Floor: 235 square feet; Total: 1,003 square feet

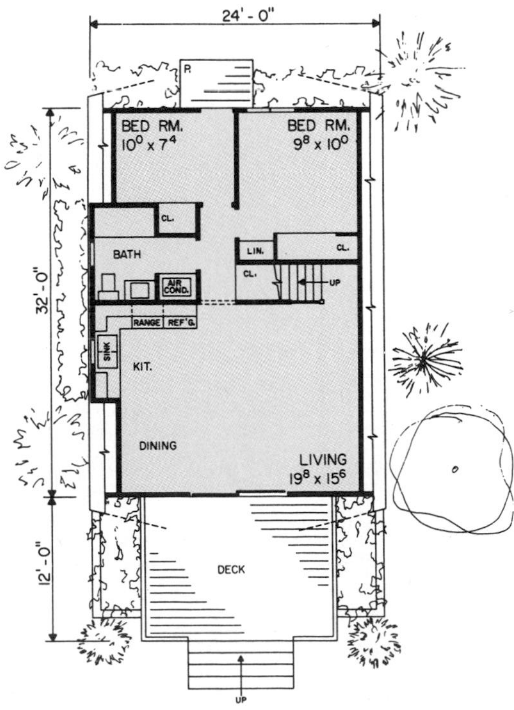

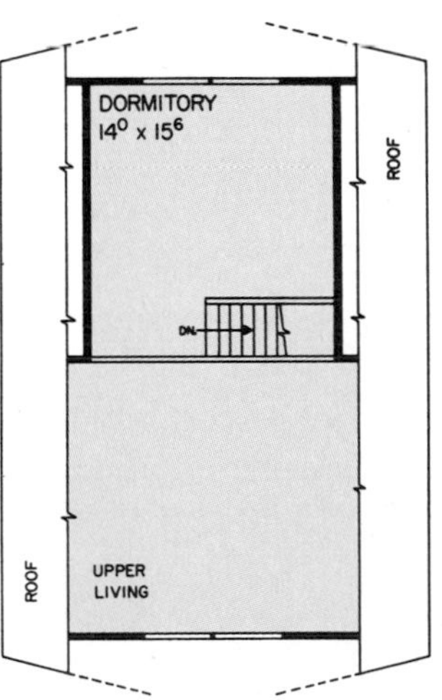

● When you walk out upon your dock with this newly completed A-frame in the background, you will have set the stage for a whole new pattern of living. This efficient second home highlights two bedrooms on the first floor and a dormitory on the second. The high ceiling of the living room is dramatic, indeed.

Design V41415

First Floor: 504 square feet
Second Floor: 160 square feet
Total: 664 square feet

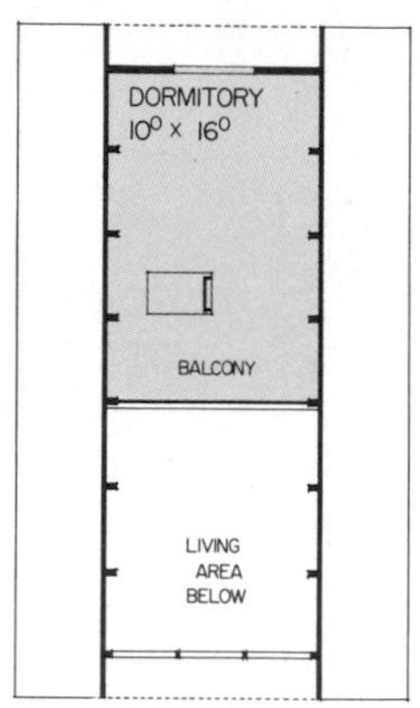

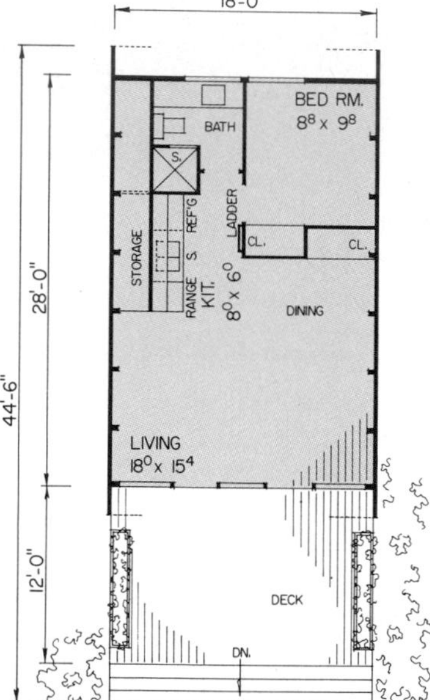

● These charming, low-cost A-frames will be hard to beat for carefree, informal living. The lakeside exteriors of these vacation homes feature delightfully vertical expanses of glass, thus affording unrestricted views of the outdoors. The large wood decks function with the living areas. Access to the second floor of each plan is by way of the ladder.

Design V41416

First Floor: 360 square feet
Second Floor: 80 square feet
Total: 440 square feet

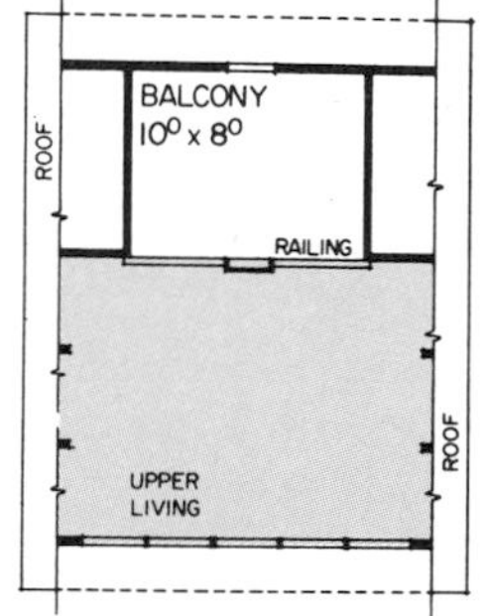

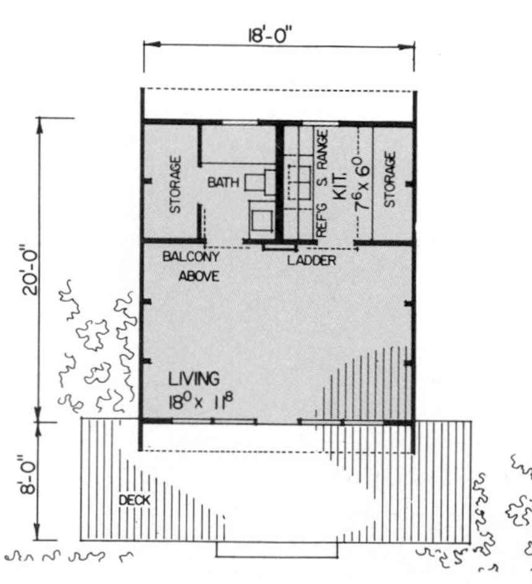

Design V41448

First Floor: 776 square feet
Second Floor: 300 square feet
Total: 1,076 square feet

● Here are three dramatic A-frames designed to fit varying budgets and family living requirements. Compare the size of Design V41416 at left with that of V41448. While the difference in livability features is great, so is the difference in construction costs. However, the significance each design represents to the family's basic life style is similar. The proud owners of either home will enjoy all the benefits and experiences that come from leisure-time, second-home living. Study the interior of V41415. It, too, has much to offer the fun-oriented family during those special moments.

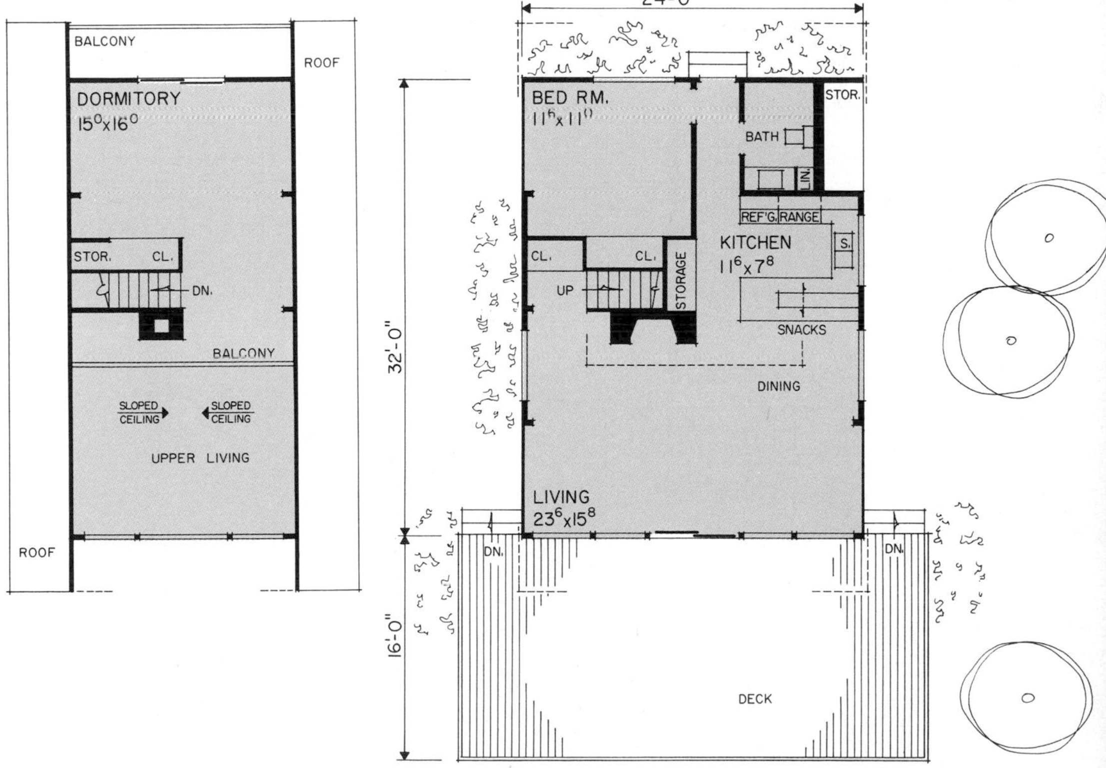

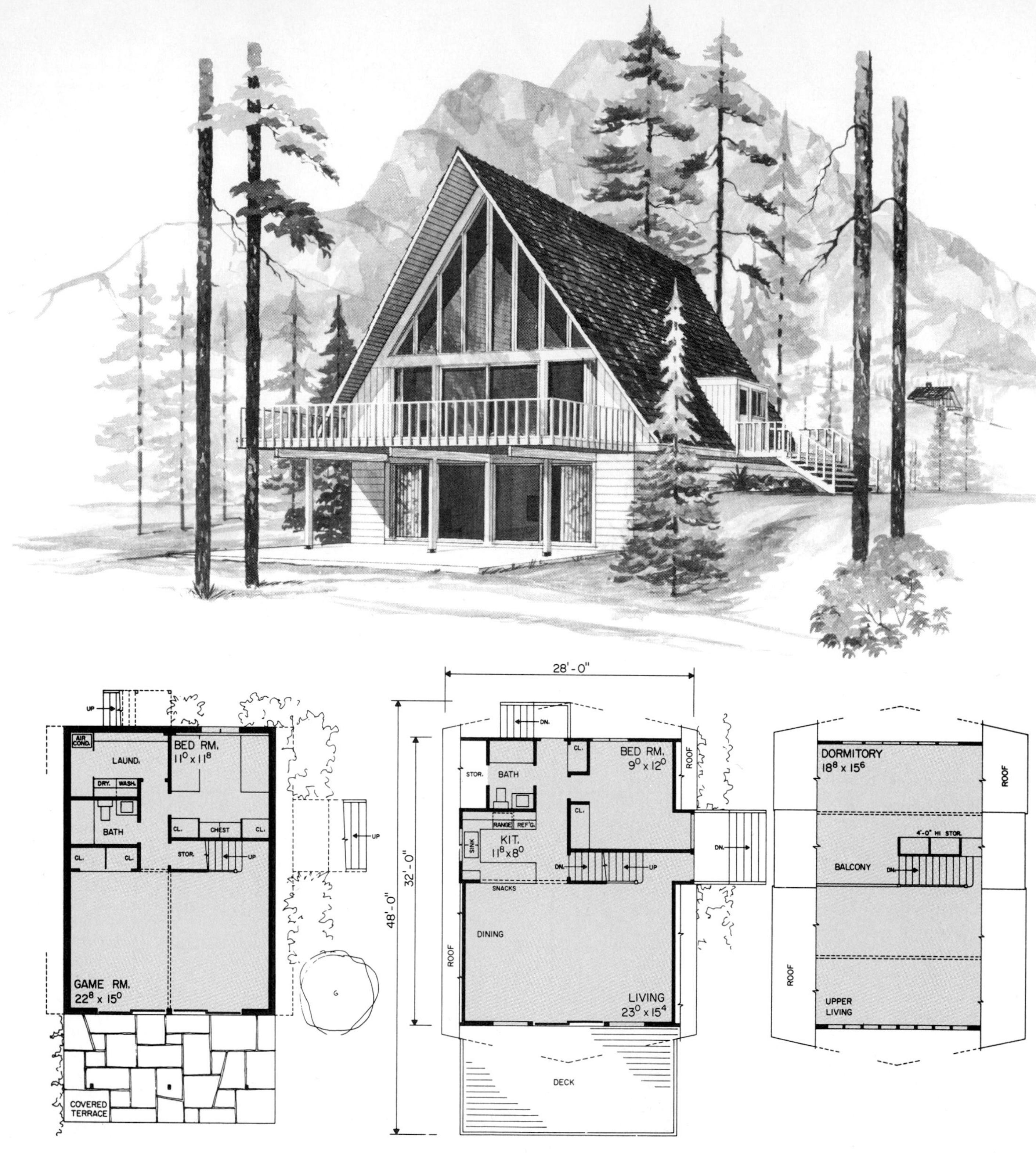

Design V41499 Main Level: 896 square feet; Upper Level: 298 square feet; Lower Level: 896 square feet; Total: 2,090 square feet

● Three level living results in family living patterns which will foster a delightful feeling of informality. Upon arrival at this charming second home, each family member will enthusiastically welcome the change in environment - both indoors and out. Whether looking down into the living room from the dormitory balcony, or walking through the sliding doors onto the huge deck, or participating in some family activity in the game room, everyone will count the hours spent here as relaxing ones. Study the plan carefully. Note the sleeping facilities on each of the three levels. Two bedrooms and a dormitory in all to sleep the family and friends comfortably. There are two full baths, a separate laundry room and plenty of storage. Don't miss the efficient U-shaped kitchen.

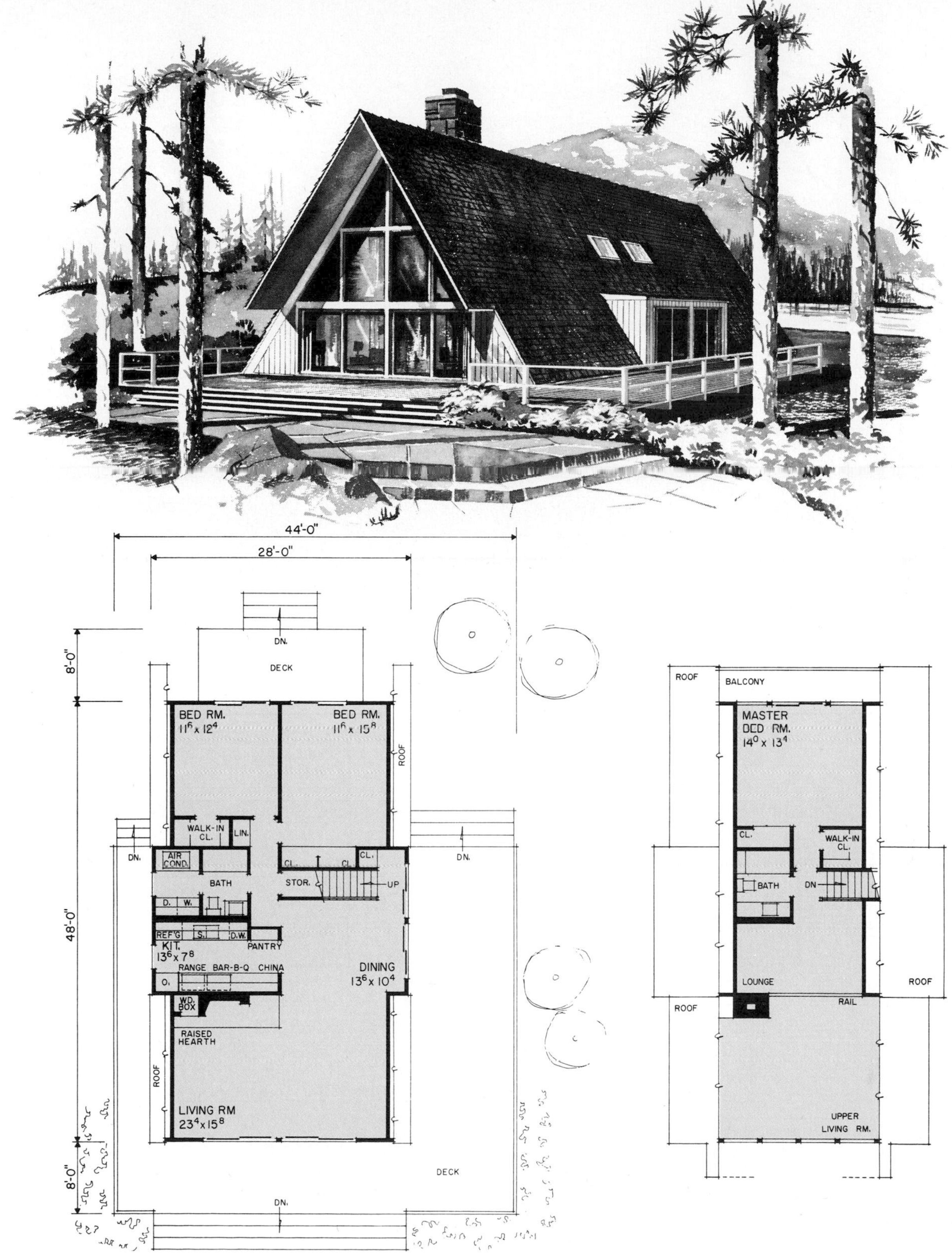

Design V41451 First Floor: 1,224 square feet; Second Floor: 464 square feet; Total: 1,688 square feet

● This dramatic A-frame will surely command its share of attention wherever located. Its soaring roof and large glass areas put this design in a class all of its own. Raised wood decks on all sides provide delightful outdoor living areas. In addition, there is a balcony outside the second floor master bedroom. The living room will be the focal point of the interior. It will be wonderfully spacious with all that glass and the high roof. The attractive raised hearth fireplace will be a favorite feature. Another favored highlight will be the lounge area of the second floor where it is possible to look down into the living room. The work center has all the conveniences of home. Note the barbecue unit, pantry and china cabinet which are sure to help provide ease of living.

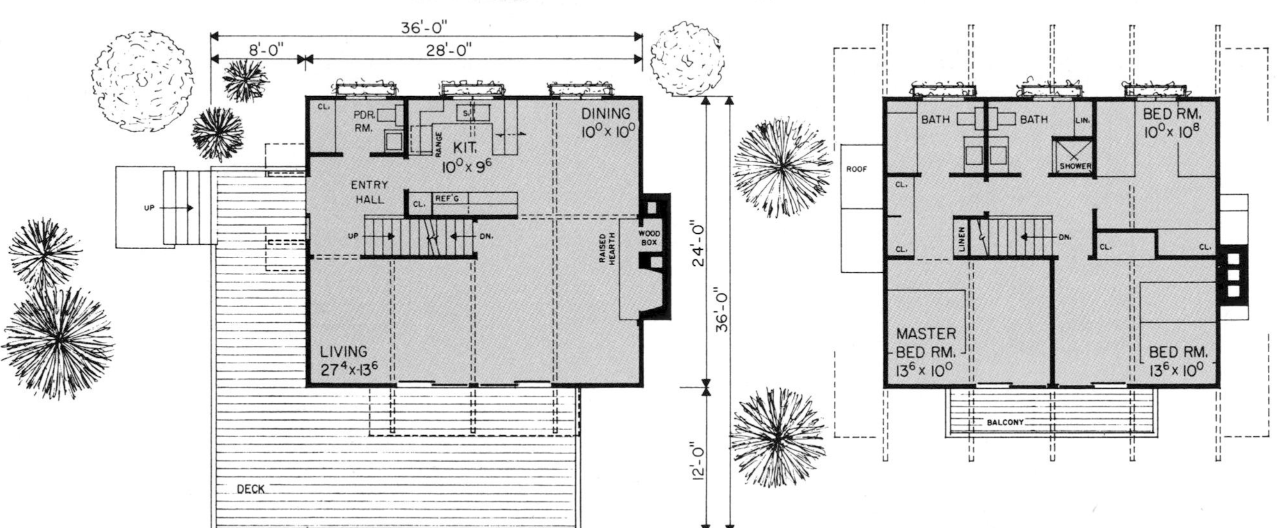

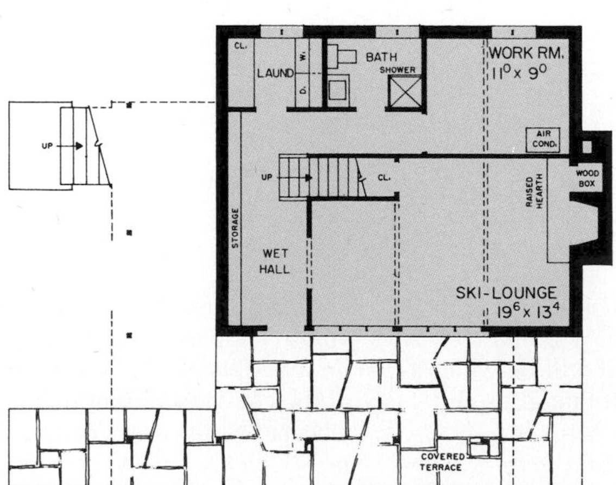

Design V42429 Main Level: 672 square feet; Upper Level: 672 square feet; Lower Level: 672 square feet Total: 2,016 square feet

● A ski lodge with a Swiss chalet character. If you are a skier, you know that all the fun is not restricted to schussing the slopes. A great portion of the pleasure is found in the living accommodations and the pursuant merriment fostered by good fellowship. As for the specific features which will surely contribute to everyone's off-the-slopes fun consider: the outdoor deck, balcony and covered terrace; the ski lounge; the two fireplaces; and the huge L-shaped living and dining room area. The three bedrooms are of good size and with bunk beds will sleep quite a crew. Note the wet hall for skis, the all important work room and the laundry.

CHALET CHARM . . .

has an image all its own. While it seems to conjure pictures of the rolling Swiss countryside, it has long been a favorite style of many in this country. Whether called upon to function as the family's haven for summer or winter fun, the chalet form will serve its occupants admirably. Balconies overlooking outdoor decks below enhance the indoor-outdoor livability that these designs offer.

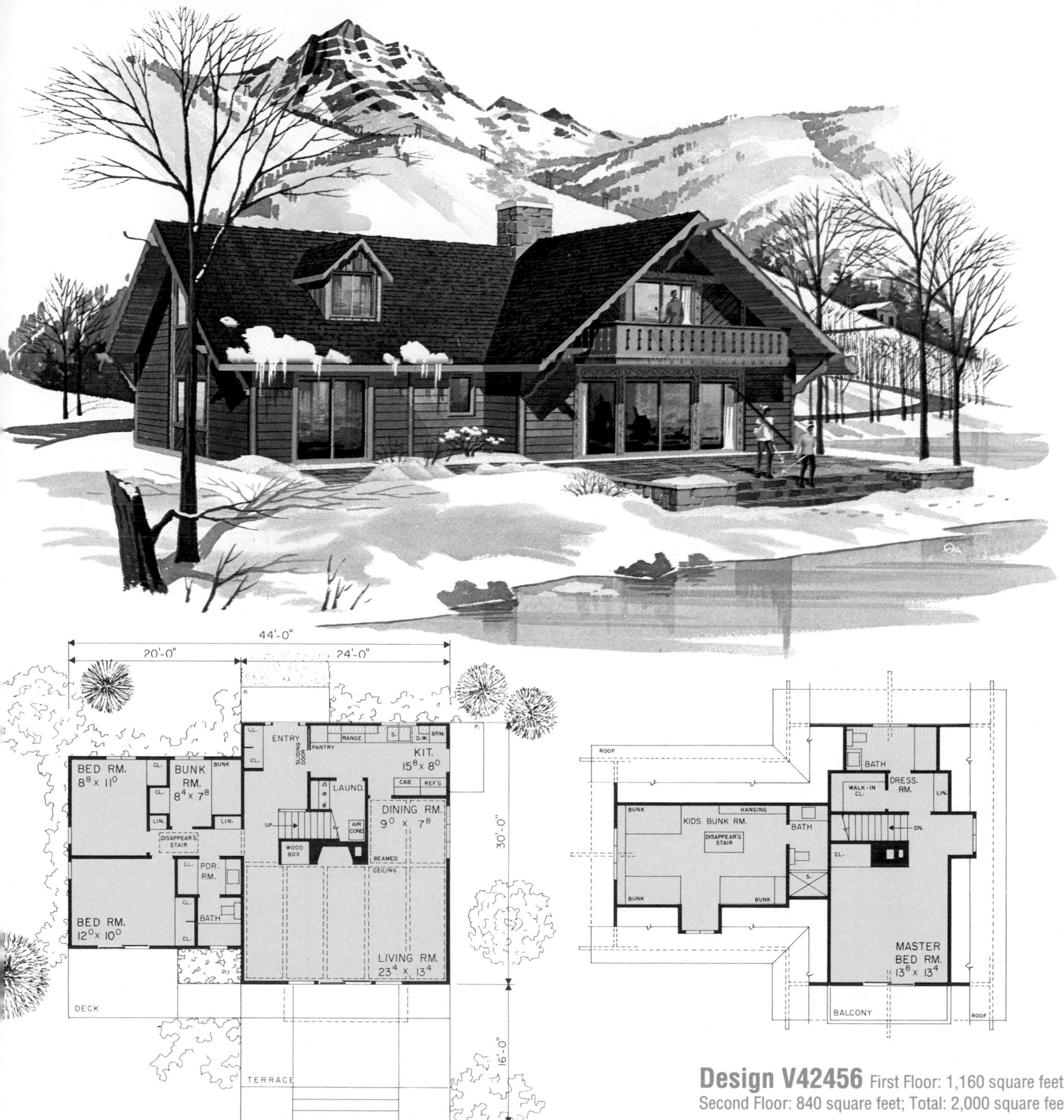

Design V42456 First Floor: 1,160 square feet
Second Floor: 840 square feet; Total: 2,000 square feet

● Here's how your Swiss chalet adaptation may look in the winter. Certainly an appealing design whatever the season. A delightful haven for skiers, fishermen and hunters alike. As for sleeping facilities, you'll really be able to pack 'em in. The first floor has two bedrooms plus a room which will take a double bunk. Across the hall is the compartment bath. A disappearing stair unit leads to the children's bunk room. The placement of single bunks or cots will permit the sleeping of three or four more. A bath with stall shower is nearby. The master bedroom suite is complete with walk-in closet, dressing room and private bath and opens onto the balcony. There is plenty of space in the L-shaped living-dining area with wood box and fireplace to accommodate the whole gang.

● It will not make any difference where you locate this chalet-type second home. The atmosphere it creates will be one for true leisure living. To guarantee sheer enjoyment you wouldn't even have to be situated close to the water. And little wonder with such an array of features as: the big deck, the fine porch and the two balconies. For complete livability there are four bedrooms, two full baths, an outstanding U-shaped kitchen, a large living area with a raised hearth fireplace and a super-abundance of closet and storage facilities. Of particular interest is the direct access from outdoors to the first floor bath with its stall shower.

Design V42412

First Floor: 1,120 square feet
Second Floor: 664 square feet
Total: 1,784 square feet

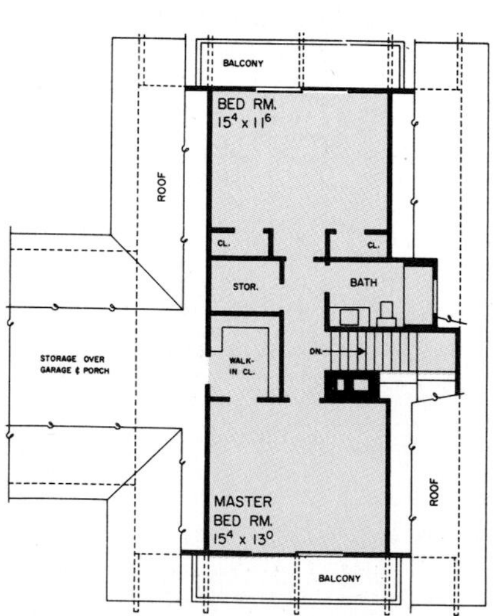

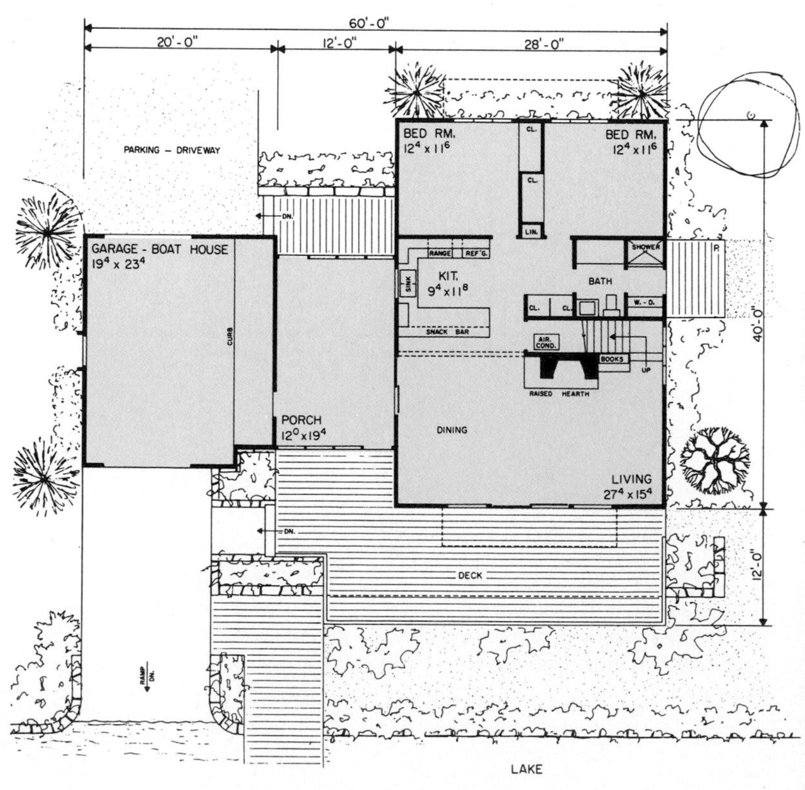

Design V42430 First Floor: 1,238 square feet; Second Floor: 648 square feet; Total: 1,886 square feet

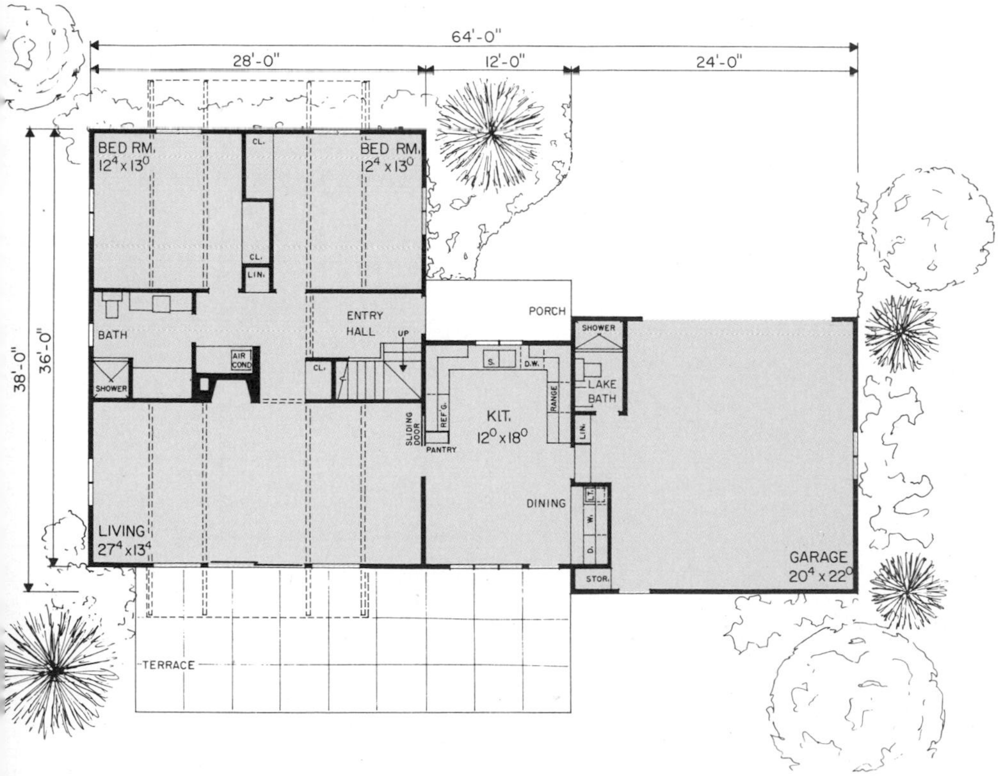

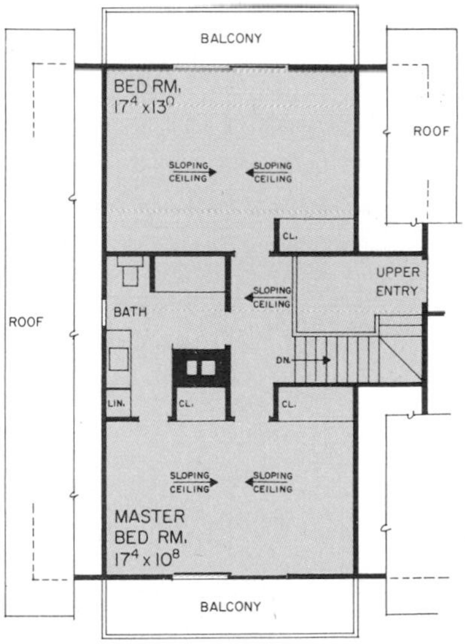

● Another Swiss chalet adaptation which will serve its occupants admirably during the four seasons of the year. The sun-drenched balcony and the terrace will be enjoyed as much by the skiers in the winter as by the swimmers in the summer. All the various areas are equally outstanding. For sleeping, there are four big bedrooms. They are supported by two full baths – one has both tub and stall shower. For relaxation, there is the big living room. It has a fireplace and a large glass area to preserve the view. For eating, there is the U-shaped kitchen and its adjacent dining area. Don't miss beamed ceilings of first floor, nor sloping ceilings of second floor. Note the positioning of the lake bath adjacent to the kitchen entrance. Truly a strategic and convenient location.

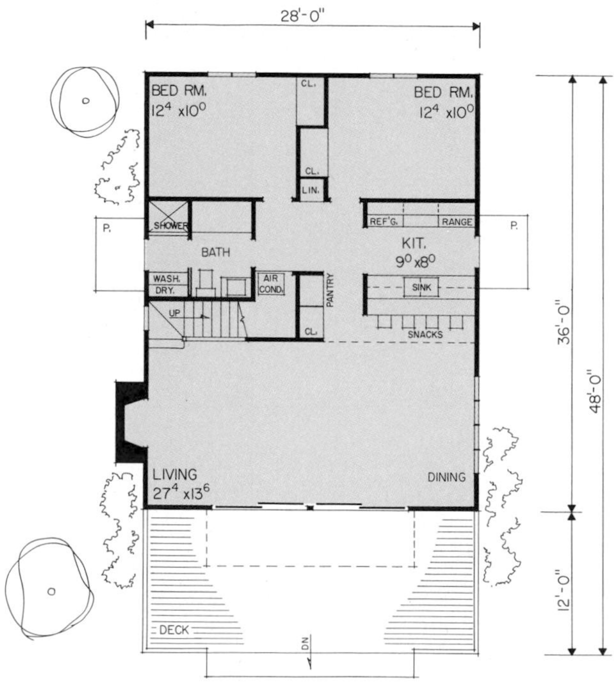

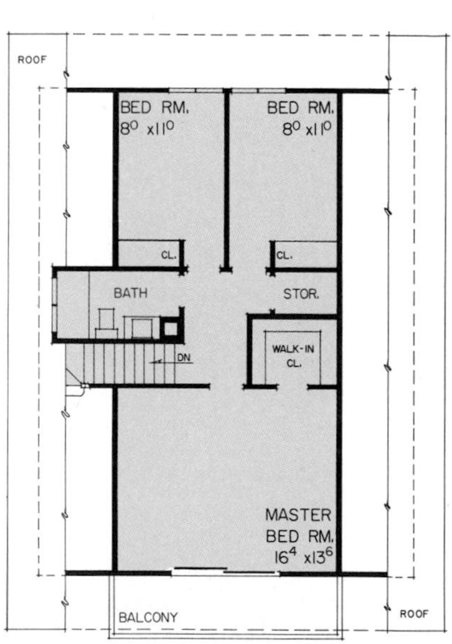

Design V41482 First Floor: 1,008 square feet; Second Floor: 637 square feet; Total: 1,645 square feet

● Here's a chalet right from the pages of the travel folders. Whether the setting reflects the majestic beauty of a winter scene, or the tranquil splendor of a summer landscape, this design will serve its occupants well. In addition to the big bedrooms on the first floor, there are three more upstairs. The large master bedroom has a balcony which looks down into the lower wood deck. There are two full baths. The first floor bath is directly accessible from the outdoors. Note snack bar and pantry of the kitchen. Laundry area is adjacent to side door.

Design V41473 First Floor: 672 square feet; Second Floor: 234 square feet; Total: 906 square feet

● You won't find many leisure-time designs with more charm than this compact, efficient and low cost home. The moderately pitched, wide-overhanging roof and the strikingly simple glass areas result in a very positive and pleasing identity. Three pairs of sliding glass doors open from the wood deck into the cheerfully lighted living area with its high sloping ceiling. A corner of this generous living area will be more than adequate for the preparation of meals. Across the room is the appealing prefabricated fireplace. Note storage units.

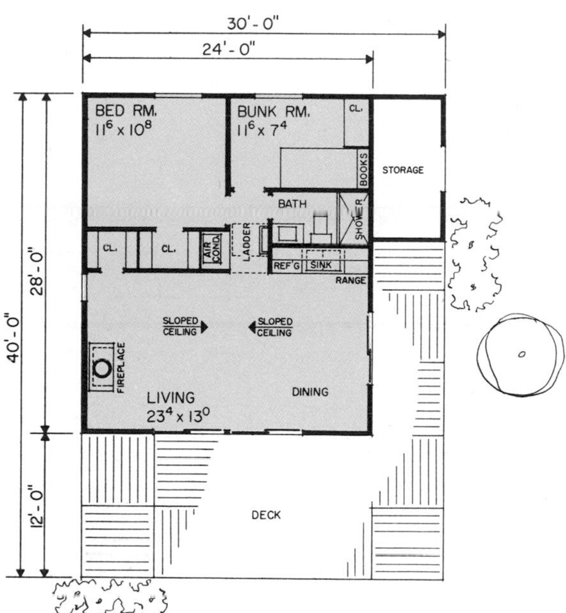

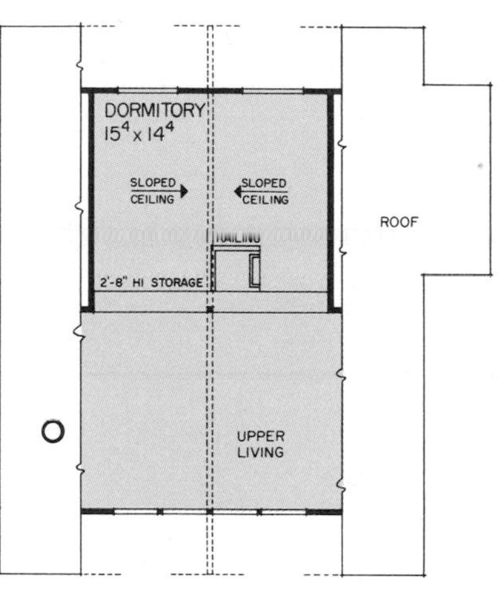

● Here is the epitome of private ski lodges. Or, if you live in an area where there is no snow, this will be a great chalet for just plain enjoying the surrounding green countryside. Whatever the environment, this retreat will serve its occupants to perfection. And little wonder. There are three levels of livability. There is plenty of space - from the lower level lounge, to the 35 foot living room, to the upper level dormitory. Note the two fireplaces, the fine kitchen, the excellent bath facilities and the outdoor decks and balconies.

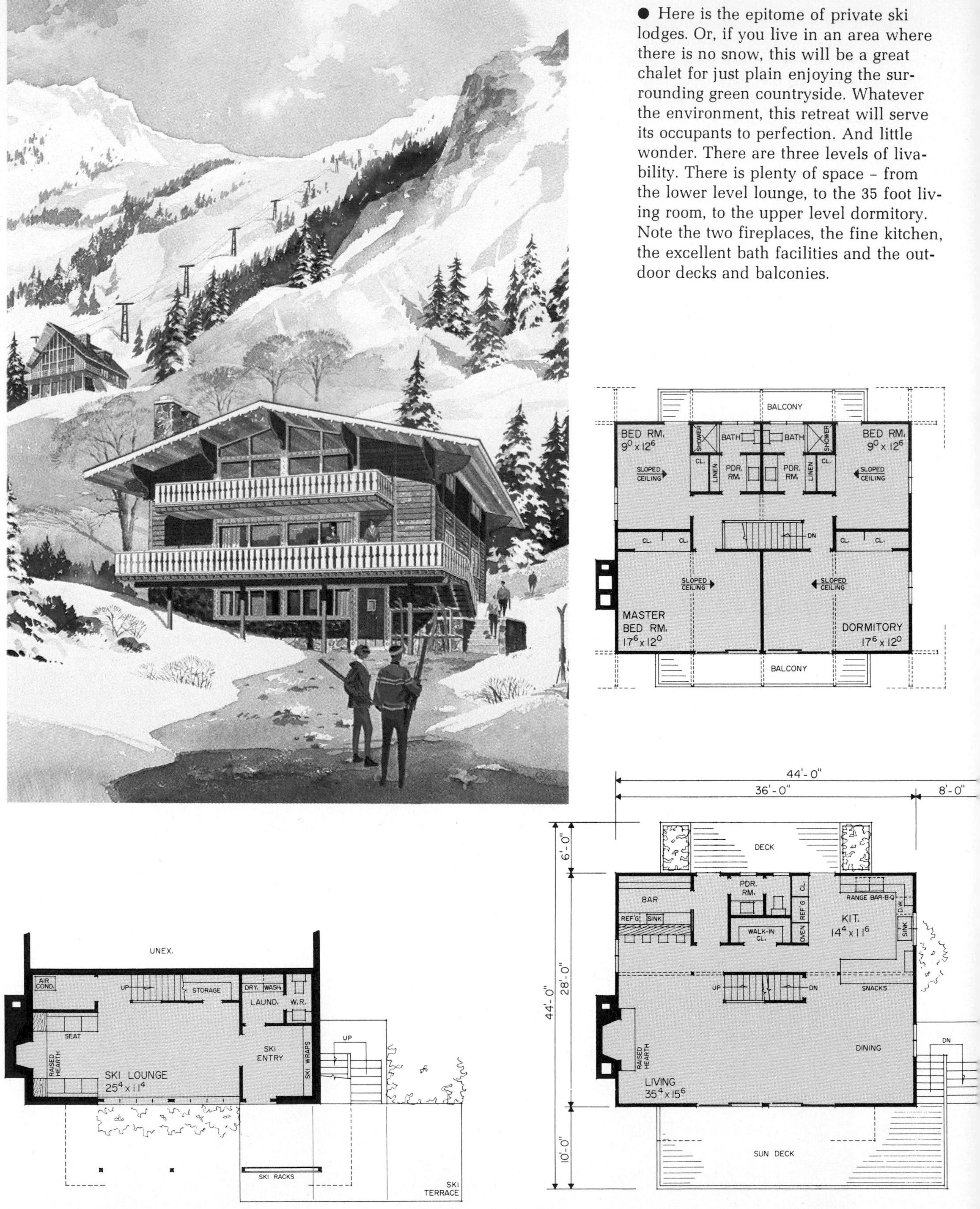

Design V41474 Main Level: 1,008 square feet; Upper Level: 1,008 square feet; Lower Level: 594 square feet; Total: 2,610 square feet

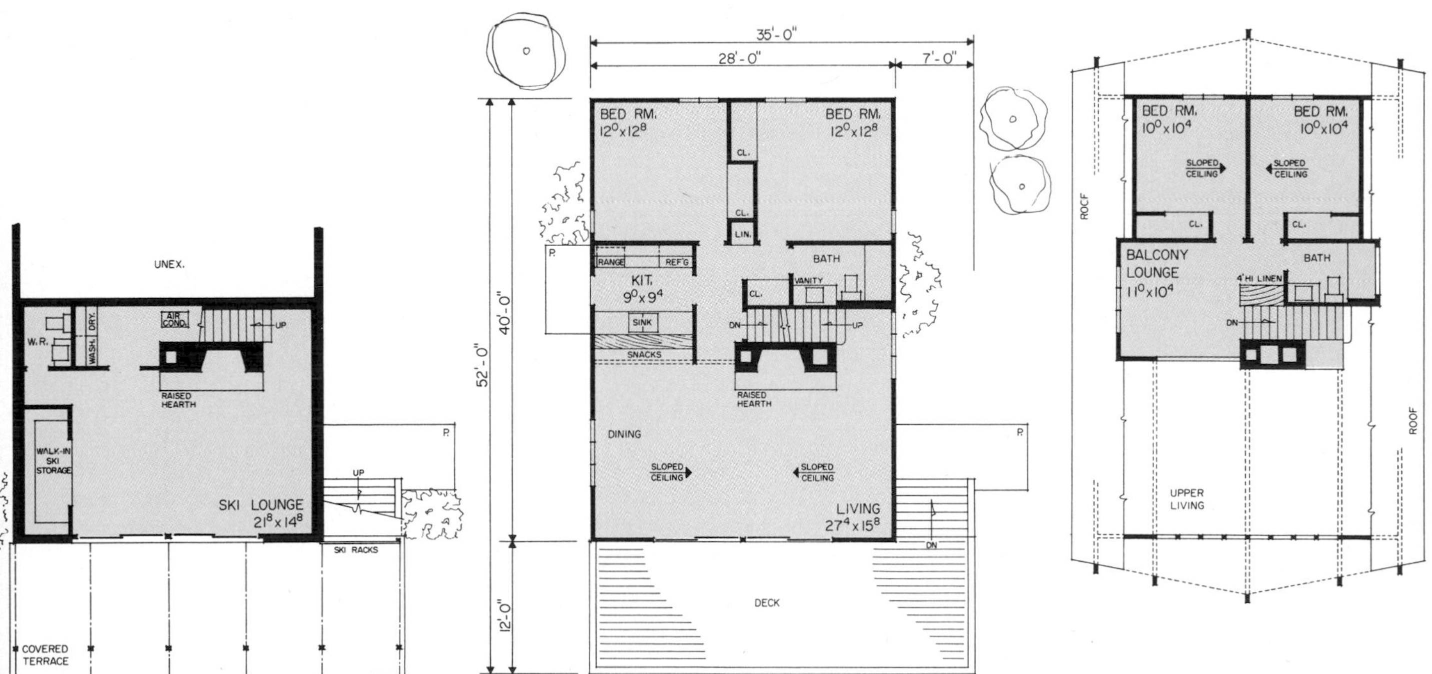

Design V41475 Main Level: 1,120 square feet; Upper Level: 522 square feet; Lower Level: 616 square feet; Total: 2,258 square feet

● Skiers take notice! This vacation home tells an exciting story of activity - and people. Whether you build this design to function as your ski lodge, or to serve your family and friends during the summer months, it will perform ideally. It would take little imagination to envision this second home overlooking your lakeshore site with the grown-ups sunning themselves on the deck while the children play on the terrace. Whatever the season or the location, visualize how your family will enjoy the many hours spent in this delightful chalet adaptation.

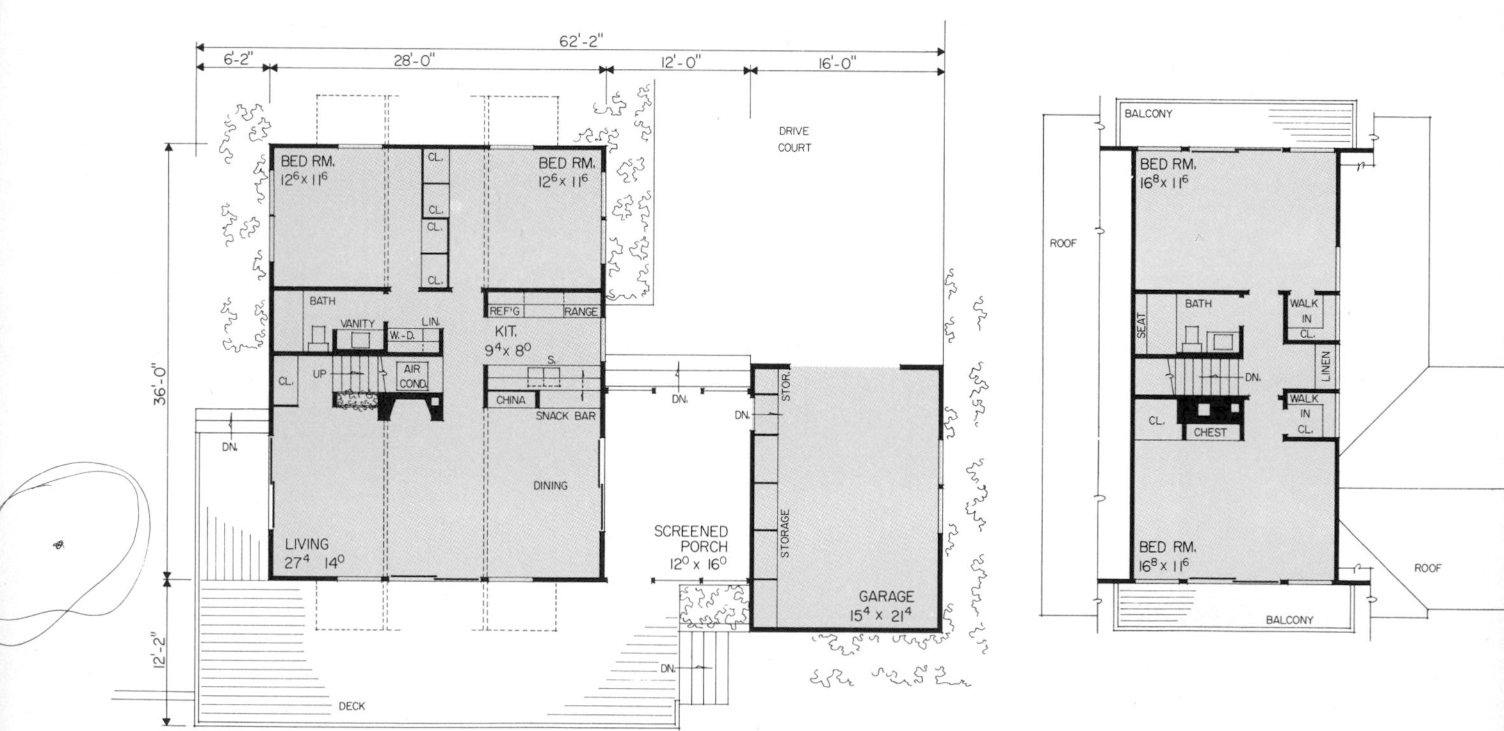

Design V41422 First Floor: 1,008 square feet; Second Floor: 624 square feet; Total: 1,632 square feet

● The chalet influence takes over on this design. If you have a big family, the four bedrooms of this vacation home will force you to take the second look. Notice the balcony off of each bedroom on the second floor and the fact that each bedroom has a walk-in closet. The first floor highlights many features highly desirable in the year-round home. Among these are the open-stairway with planter, the fire-place, the china cabinet and snack bar, the bathroom vanity and the efficient kitchen which will be free of unneces-sary thru traffic. Outdoor living will be enjoyed on the two outdoor balconies, the deck and even the screened-in porch between house and garage.

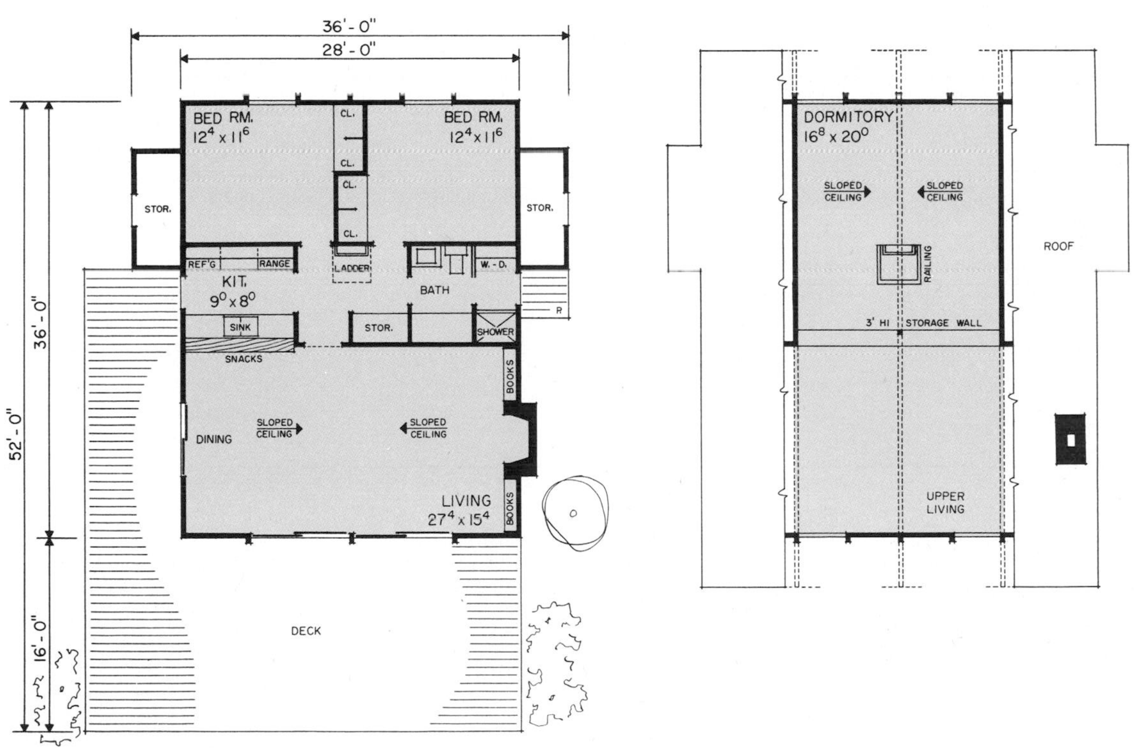

Design V41472 First Floor: 1,008 square feet; Second Floor: 546 square feet; Total: 1,554 square feet

● Wherever perched, this smart leisure-time home will surely make your visits memorable ones. The large living area with its sloped ceiling, dramatic expanses of glass and attractive fireplace will certainly offer the proper atmosphere for quiet relaxation. Keeping house will be no chore for the weekend homemaker. The kitchen is compact and efficient. There is plenty of storage space for all the necessary recreational equipment. There is a full bath and even a stall shower accessible from the outside for use by the swimmers. A ladder leads to the second floor sloped ceiling dormitory which overlooks the living/dining area. Ideal for the younger generation.

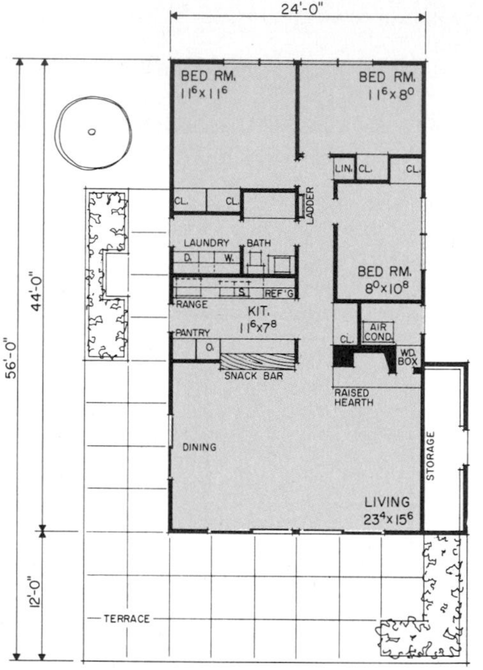

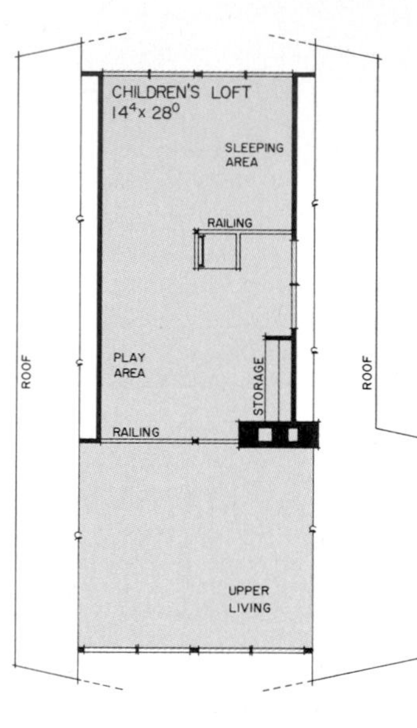

Design V41459

First Floor: 1,056 square feet
Second Floor: 400 square feet
Total: 1,456 square feet

● There is a heap of vacation living awaiting the gang that descends upon this smart looking chalet adaptation. If you have a narrow site, this design will be of extra interest to you. Should one of your requirements be an abundance of sleeping facilities, you'd hardly do better in such an economically built design. There are three bedrooms downstairs. A ladder leads to the second floor loft. The children will love the idea of sleeping here. In addition, there is a play area which looks down into the first floor living room. A great vacation home.

Design V42427

First Floor: 784 square feet
Second Floor: 504 square feet
Total: 1,288 square feet

● If ever a design had "vacation home" written all over it, this one has! Perhaps the most carefree characteristic of all is the second floor balcony which looks down into the wood deck. This balcony provides the outdoor living facility for the big master bedroom. Also occupying the second floor is the three-bunk dormitory. The use of bunks would be a fine utilization of this space. Panels through the knee walls give access to an abundant storage area. Downstairs there is yet another bedroom, a full bath and a 27 foot living room.

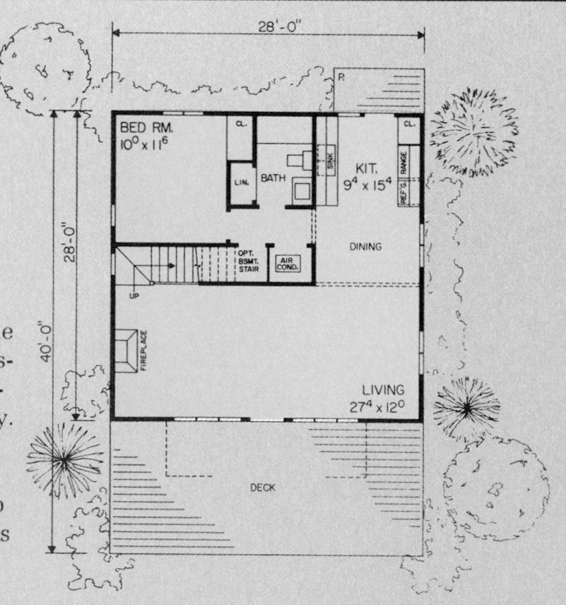

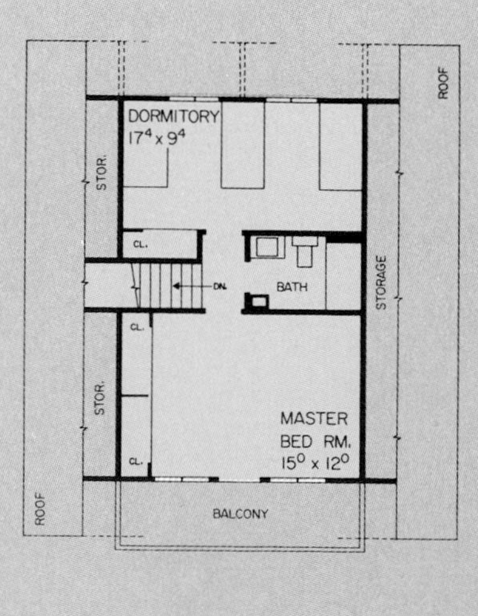

Design V41424

First Floor: 672 square feet
Second Floor: 256 square feet
Total: 928 square feet

● This chalet-type vacation home with its steep, overhanging roof, will catch the eye of even the most casual onlooker. It is designed to be completely livable whether the season be for swimming or skiing. The dormitory of the upper level will sleep many vacationers, while the two bedrooms of the first floor provide the more convenient and conventional sleeping facilities. The upper level overlooks the living and dining area with its beamed ceiling. The lower level provides everything that one would want for vacation living.

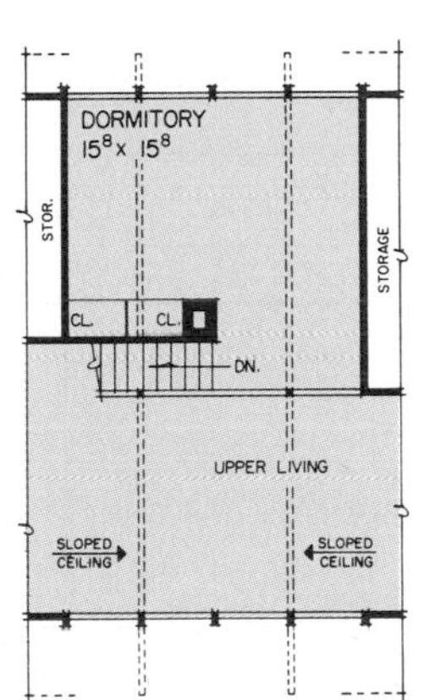

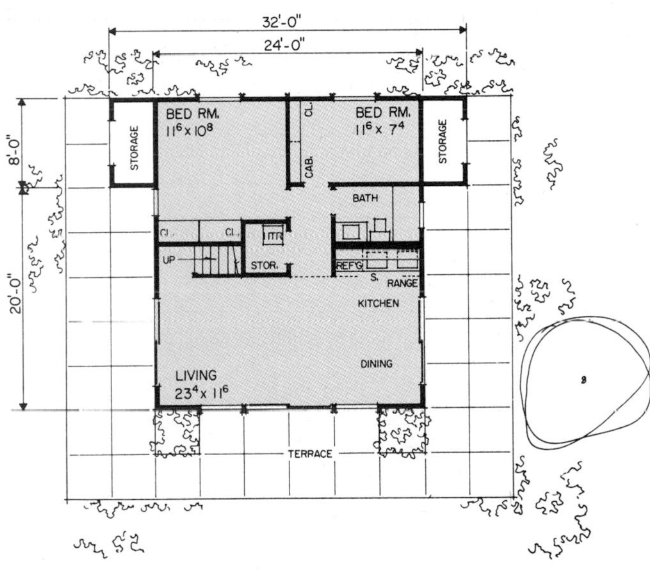

Design V42424

Square Footage: 1,456

● Here are three outstanding second homes which, in spite of their variation in size, have many things in common. Perhaps the most significant common denominator is the location of the living area and its unrestricted view of the outdoors. Each of the designs feature a glass gable end and sloping ceiling which assures the living zone of a bright and cheerful atmosphere. A study of the sizes and the livability of these designs is interesting. Regardless of the overall size of the interior, the open planning of the living areas results in plenty of space for your family and visitors to just sit around and talk.

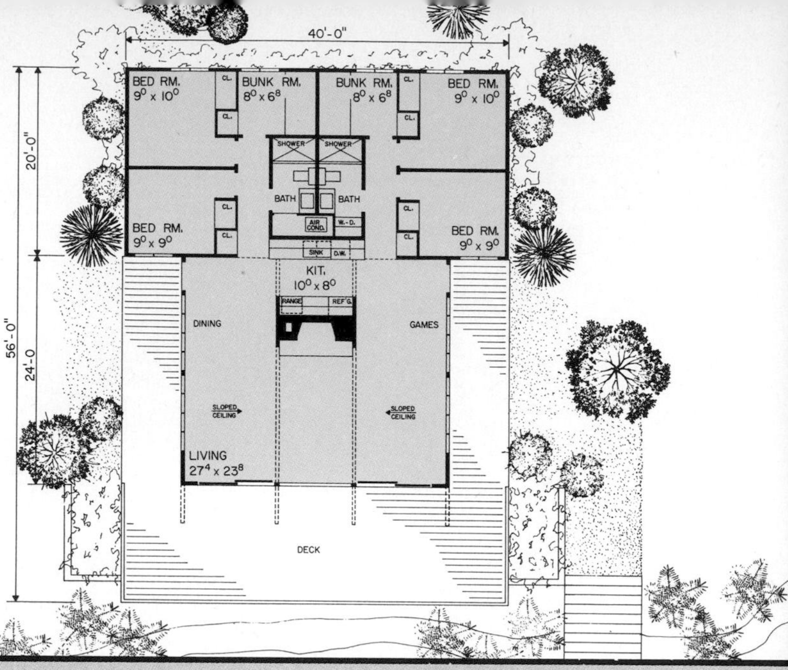

40'-0"
BED RM. 9⁰ x 11⁴
BUNKS 8⁴ x 8⁰
BUNKS 8⁴ x 8⁰
BED RM. 9⁰ x 11⁴
ENTRY
BATH
BATH
KIT. 7⁸ x 14⁰
GAMES
CHINA
SNACKS
FIREPLACE
SLOPED CEILING
SLOPED CEILING
DINING
LIVING 23⁶ x 19⁸
DECK
12'-0"
28'-2"
52'-2"
12'-0"

UNEX.
OVERHANG
STORAGE 23⁰ x 27⁸
TERRACE

Design V41410

Square Footage: 1,165

● Wherever perched, this cottage will offer interesting and distinctive living patterns. The sleeping zone will enjoy its full measure of privacy. The bunk rooms and the two larger bedrooms provide plenty of sleeping space. Note the two baths. The cheerful, spacious living area is bounded on three sides by an outdoor balcony. The large glass areas, the sloping ceilings and the exposed beams make this a delightful area. Below the living area is a huge area for boat storage.

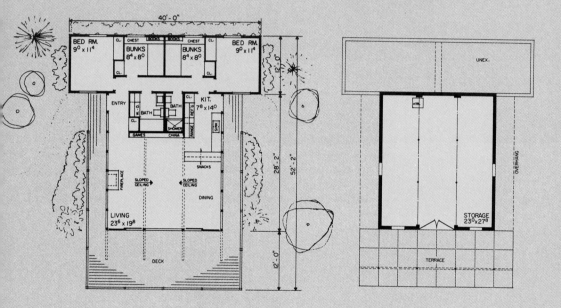

Design V42420

Upper Level: 768 square feet
Lower Level: 768 square feet
Total: 1,536 square feet

● Two-level living can be fun anytime. When it comes to two-level living at the lake, seashore or in the woods, the experience will be positively delightful. Whether indoor or outdoor, family living will have a great opportunity for expression. Note two huge living areas, four bedrooms and two baths.

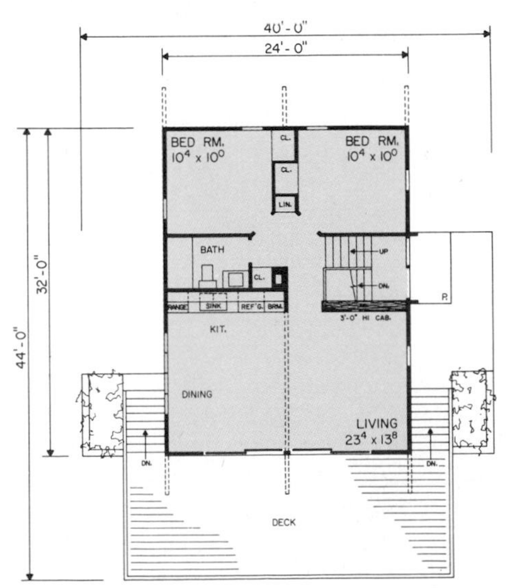

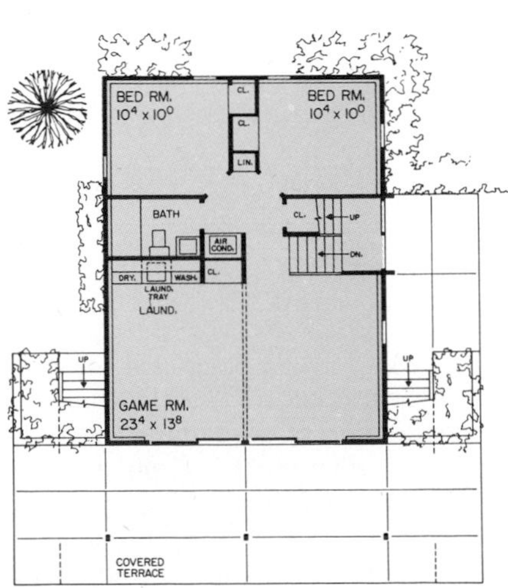

GEOMETRIC SHAPES . . .

offer interesting and exciting configurations for informal vacation-home living. In many cases, the room relationships and functions are quite unique. Be sure to note the varying living patterns these designs provide within a range of building budgets.

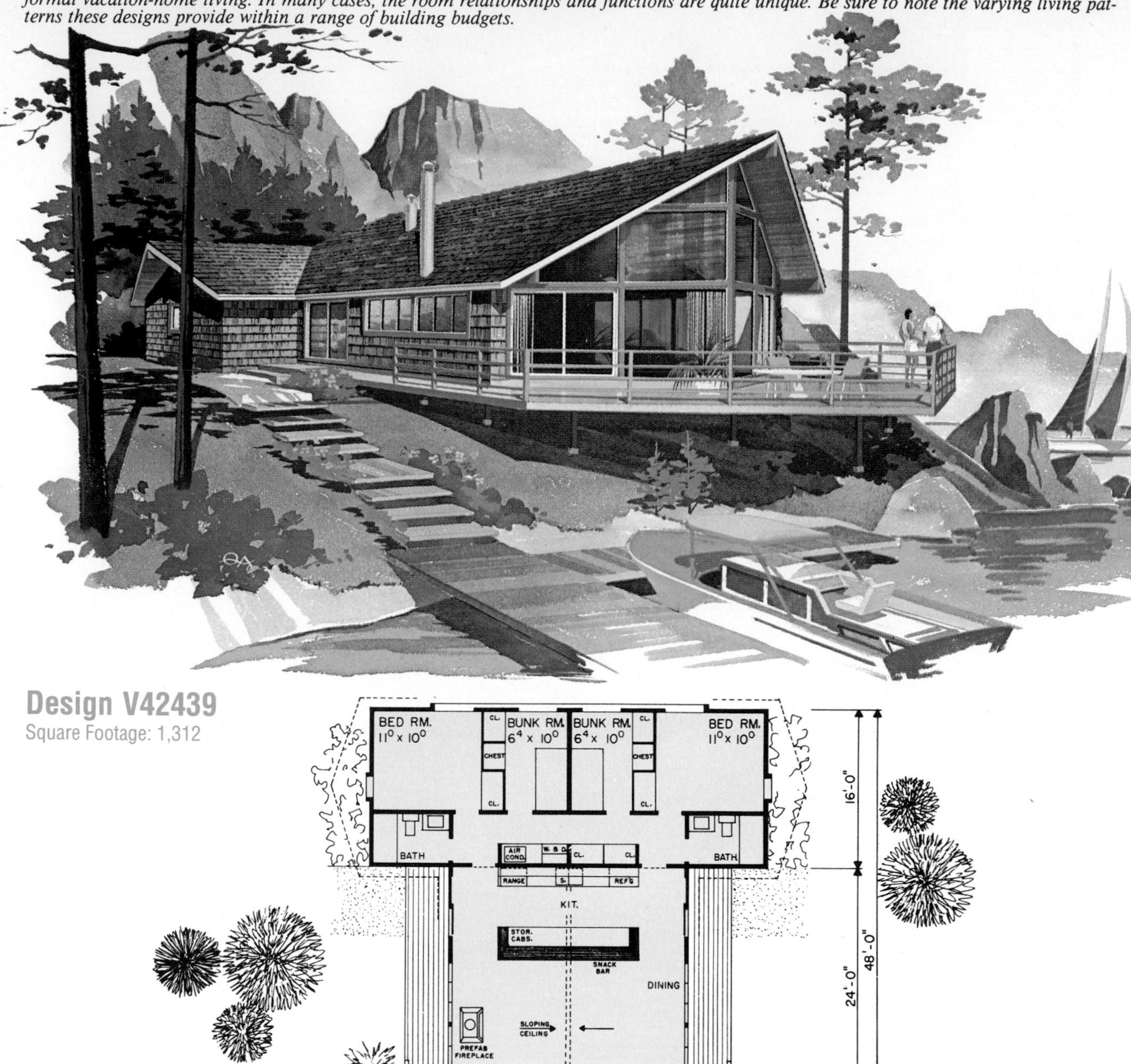

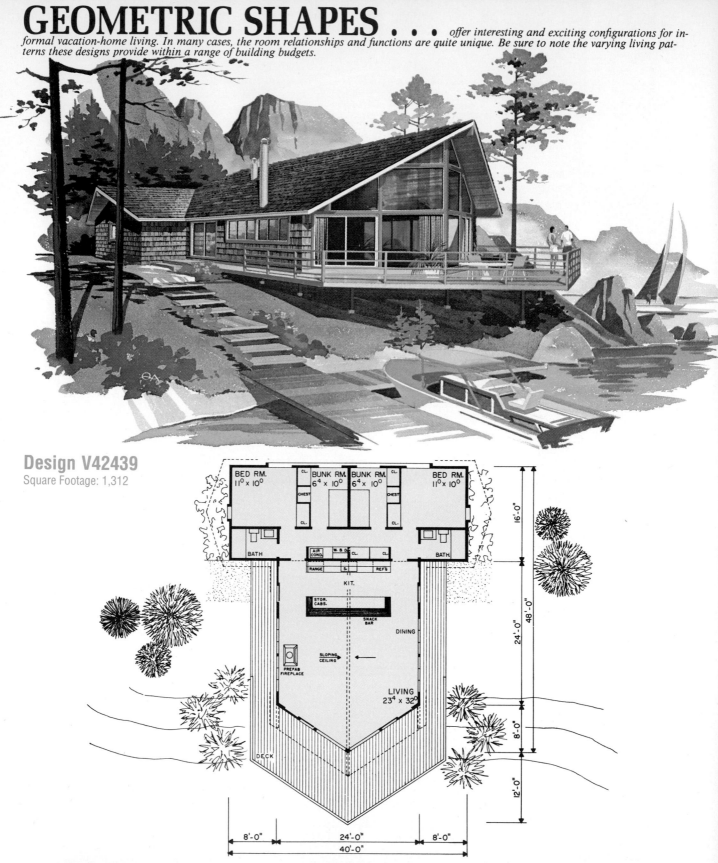

Design V42439

Square Footage: 1,312

● A wonderfully organized plan with an exterior that will surely command the attention of each and every passer-by. And what will catch the eye? Certainly the roof lines and the pointed glass gable end wall will be noticed immediately. The delightful deck will be quickly noticed, too. Inside a visitor will be thrilled by the spaciousness of the huge living room. The ceilings slope upward to the exposed ridge beam. A free-standing fireplace will make its contribution to a cheerful atmosphere. The kitchen is separated from the living area by a three-foot-high snack bar with cupboards below servicing the kitchen. What could improve upon the sleeping zone when it has two bedrooms, two bunk rooms, two full baths, two built-in chests and fine closet space?

Design V42418

Square Footage: 1,424

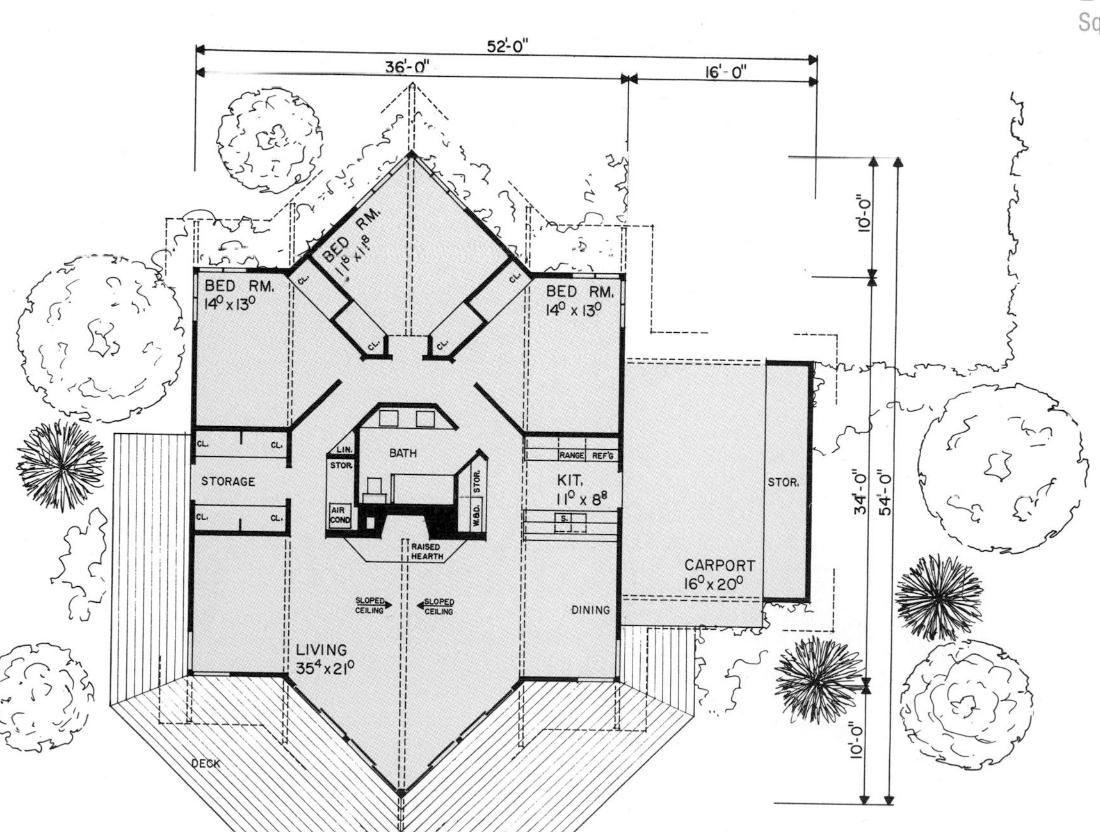

● You'll search a long time before locating a vacation home that is any more exciting than this fascinating angular retreat. Whatever its setting, it will surely command attention and also provide its happy owners with a lifetime of carefree living. The soaring roof lines, the cedar shakes, the appealing glass areas and the sloping, beamed ceilings are features.

Design V41431

Square Footage: 1,632

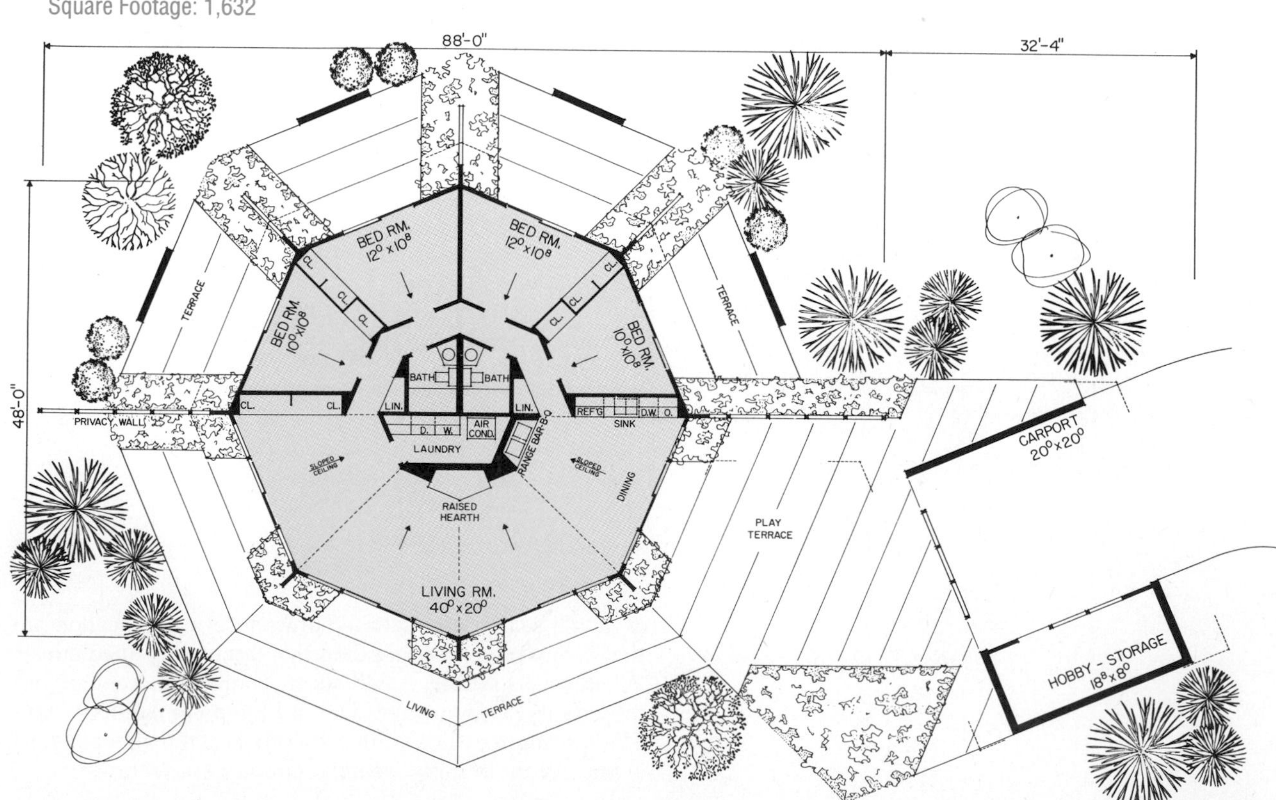

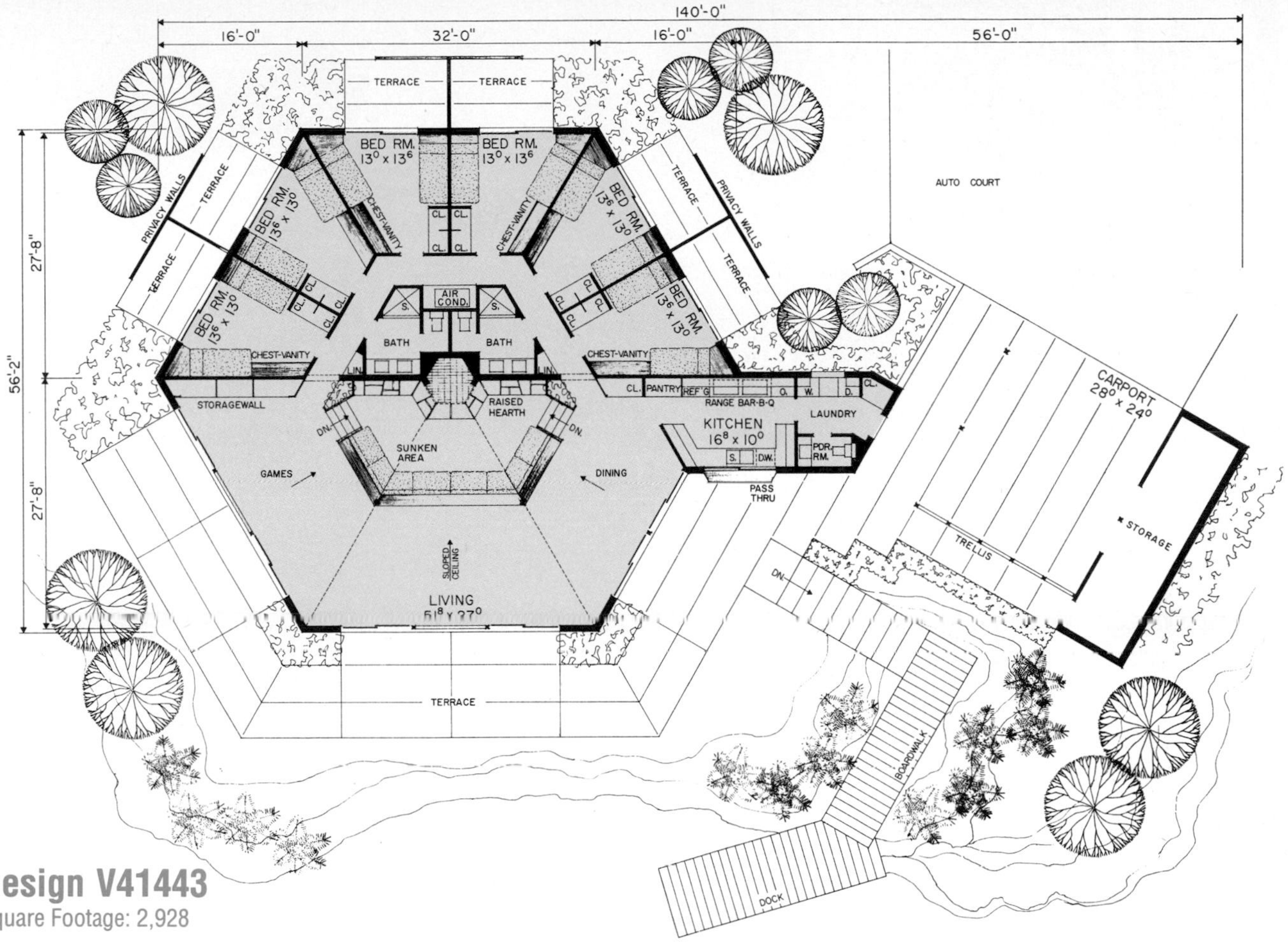

Design V41443

Square Footage: 2,928

● Is yours a big family? If so, you'll find the living and sleeping accommodations offered by this interesting hexagon exceptional, indeed. The spacious living area features plenty of glass and sliding doors which permit maximum enjoyment of the outdoors from within. A sunken area with built-in furniture in front of the raised hearth fireplace will be the favorite gathering spot. The sleeping area consists of six bedrooms. Built-in bunks would permit the sleeping of as many as 24 persons. Observe how each bedroom functions through sliding glass doors with its own outdoor terrace. Note the closet facilities and the built-in chest-vanity in each room. Two centrally located baths highlight twin lavatories and stall showers. Plumbing facilities are economically grouped.

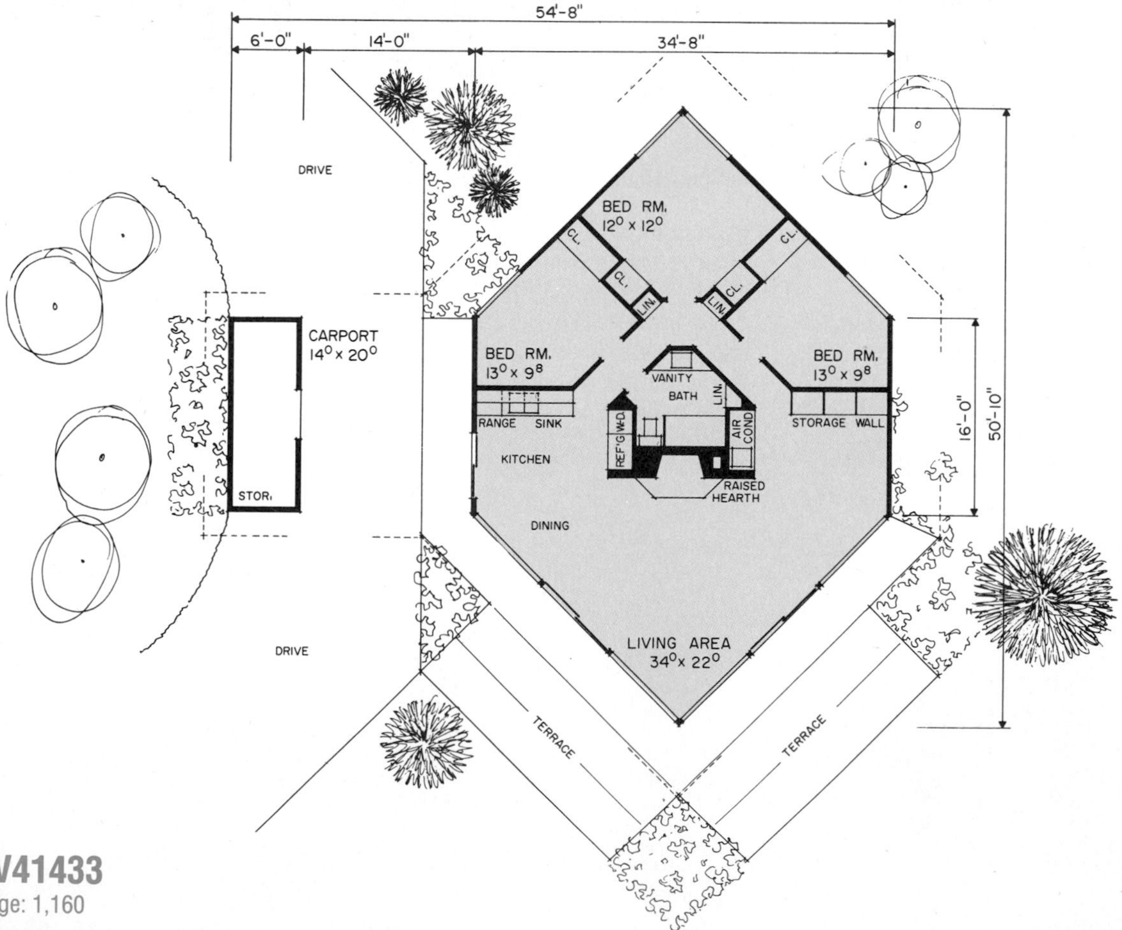

Design V41433

Square Footage: 1,160

● This hexagonal vacation, or leisure-time, home surely will prove to be a delightful haven away from the conventions of everyday living. Like a breath of fresh air, its uniqueness will make the hours spent in and around this second home memorable ones, indeed. The floor plan, in spite of its shape, reflects a wise and economical use of space. The spacious interior features a raised hearth fireplace, abundant storage facilities, a bathroom vanity and a combination washer-dryer space. Then, there is the attached carport and its bulk storage area for recreational and garden equipment. The wide, overhanging roof provides for protection from the rays of the hot summer sun. This will be a great house from which to enjoy the beauty of the countryside.

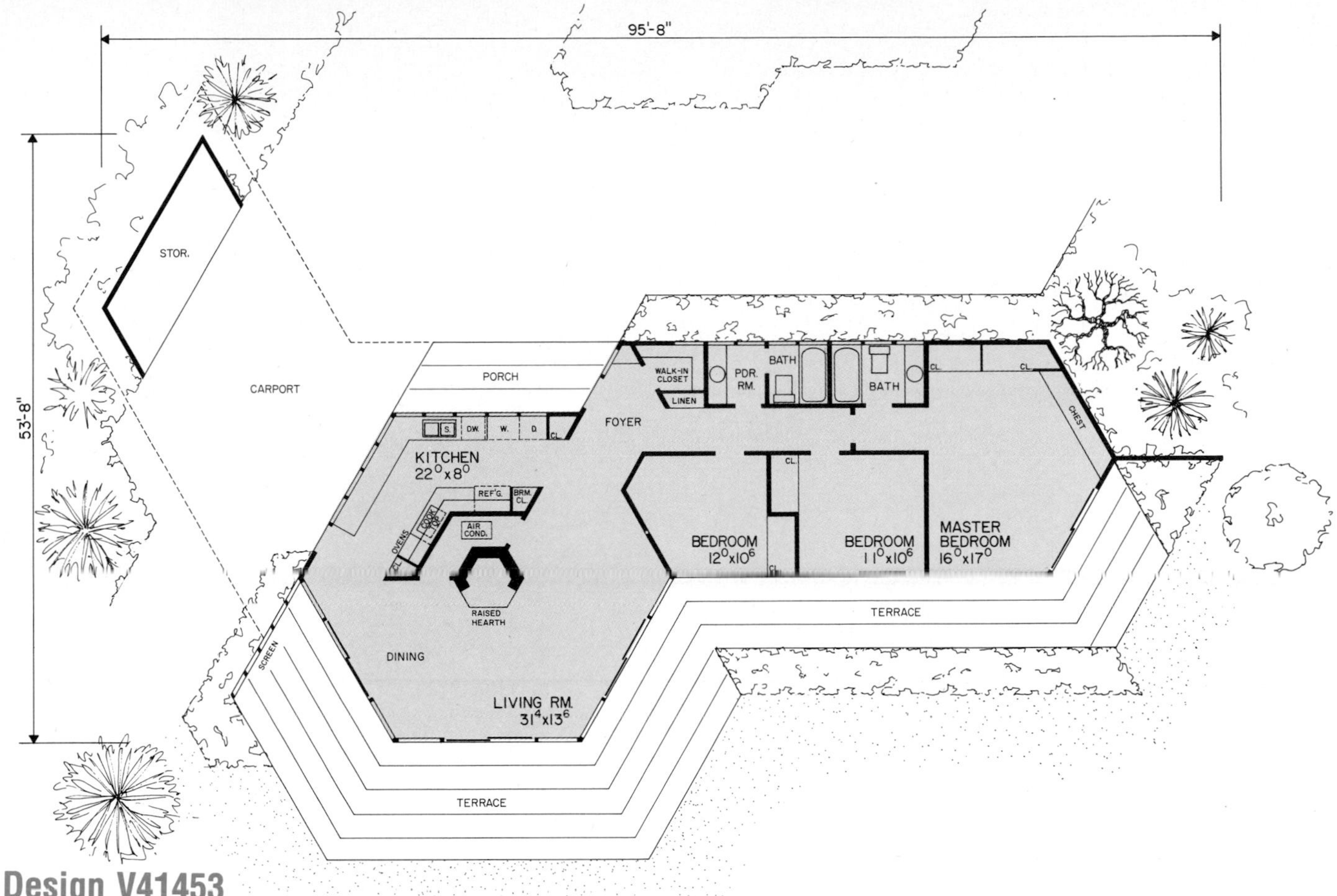

95'-8"

53'-8"

STOR.

CARPORT

PORCH

WALK-IN CLOSET

LINEN

PDR. RM.

BATH

BATH

CL.

CL.

FOYER

CHEST

KITCHEN
22⁰x8⁰

REF'G.

BRM. CL.

AIR COND.

OVENS

RAISED HEARTH

BEDROOM
12⁰x10⁶

BEDROOM
11⁰x10⁶

MASTER BEDROOM
16⁰x17⁰

TERRACE

SCREEN

DINING

LIVING RM.
31⁴x13⁶

TERRACE

Design V41453

Square Footage: 1,476

● An exciting design, unusual in character, yet fun to live in. This frame home with its vertical siding and large glass areas has as its dramatic focal point a hexagonal living area which gives way to interesting angles. The large living area features sliding glass doors through which traffic may pass to the terrace stretching across the entire length of the house. The wide overhanging roof projects over the terrace and results in a large covered area outside the sliding doors of the master bedroom. The sloping ceilings converge above the unique open fireplace with its copper hood. The drive approach and the angles of the covered front entrance make this an eye-catching design. Surely an extraordinary design for a new lease on living for summer or winter fun.

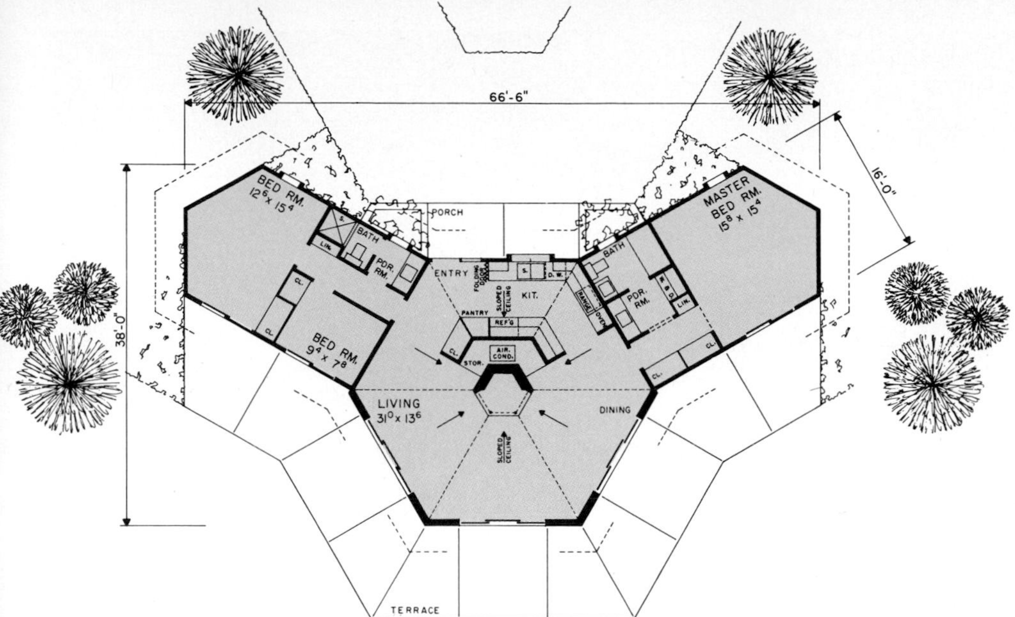

Design V42461

Square Footage: 1,400

● If you have the urge to make your vacation home one that has a distinctive flair of individuality, you should give consideration to the three designs illustrated here. Not only will you love the unique exterior appeal of your new home; but, also, the exceptional living patterns offered by the interior. The basic living area is a hexagon. To this space conscious geometric shape is added the sleeping wings with baths. The center of the living area has as its focal point a dramatic fireplace.

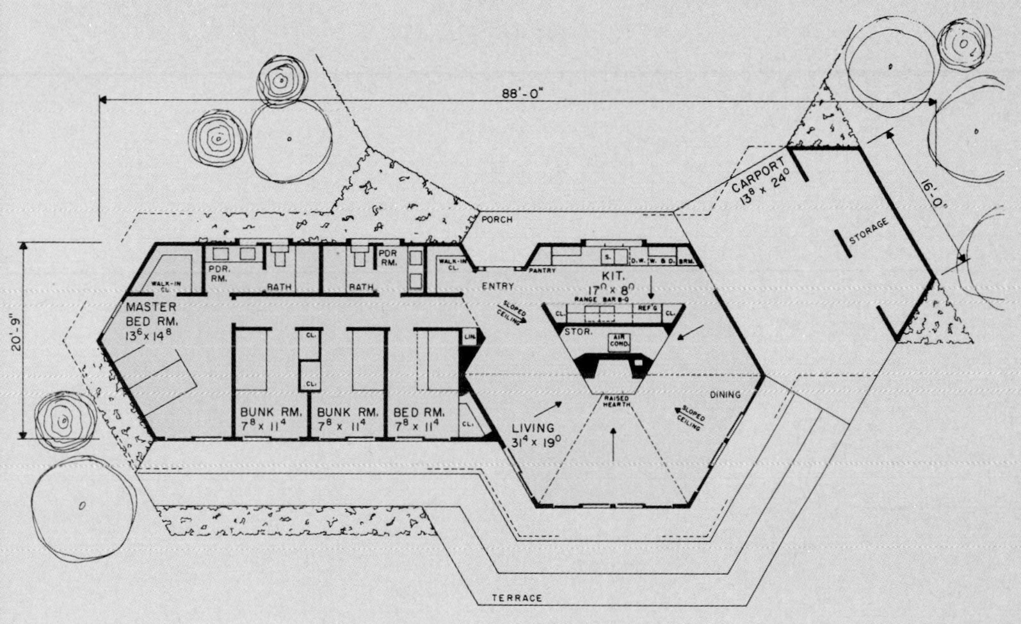

Design V42458

Square Footage: 1,406

● The six-sided living unit of each design is highlighted by sloping ceilings and an abundance of glass to assure a glorious feeling of spaciousness. The homemaker's center is efficient and will be a delight in which to prepare and serve meals. The design at left highlights a large master bedroom and three bunk rooms. The bath facilities are compartmented and feature twin lavatories. To service the family's storage needs there are two walk-in closets, utility unit and a bulk storage unit.

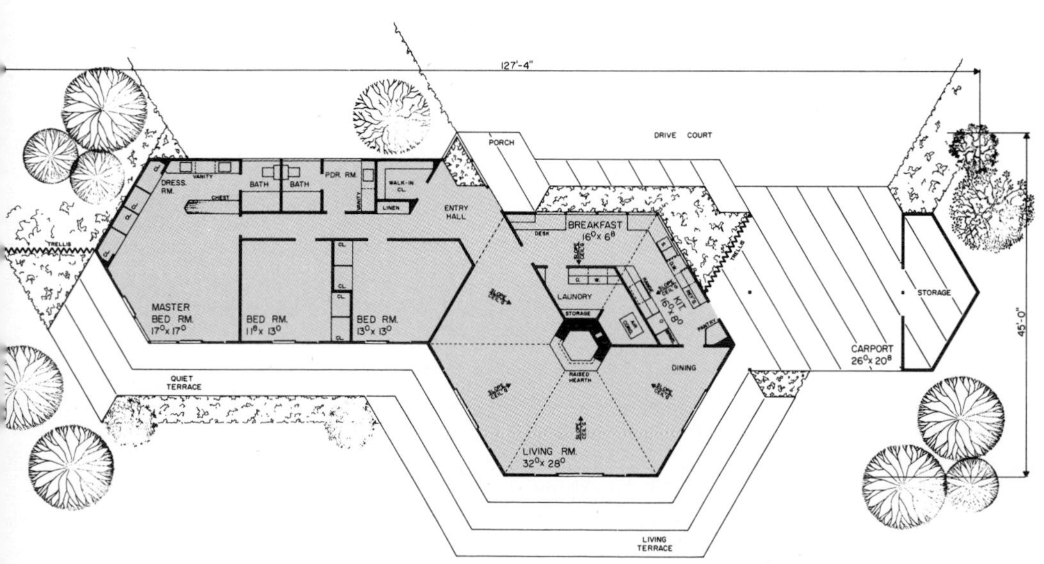

Design V42468

Square Footage: 2,140

● A major identifying characteristic of these three designs is the roof structure. The chimneys are an interesting design feature. Of significance are the indoor-outdoor relationships. Sliding glass doors put the sleeping and living areas but a step from the outdoor terraces. A comparison of sizes of these three designs is interesting. Which design satisfies your family's requirements best? Which best satisfies the budget?

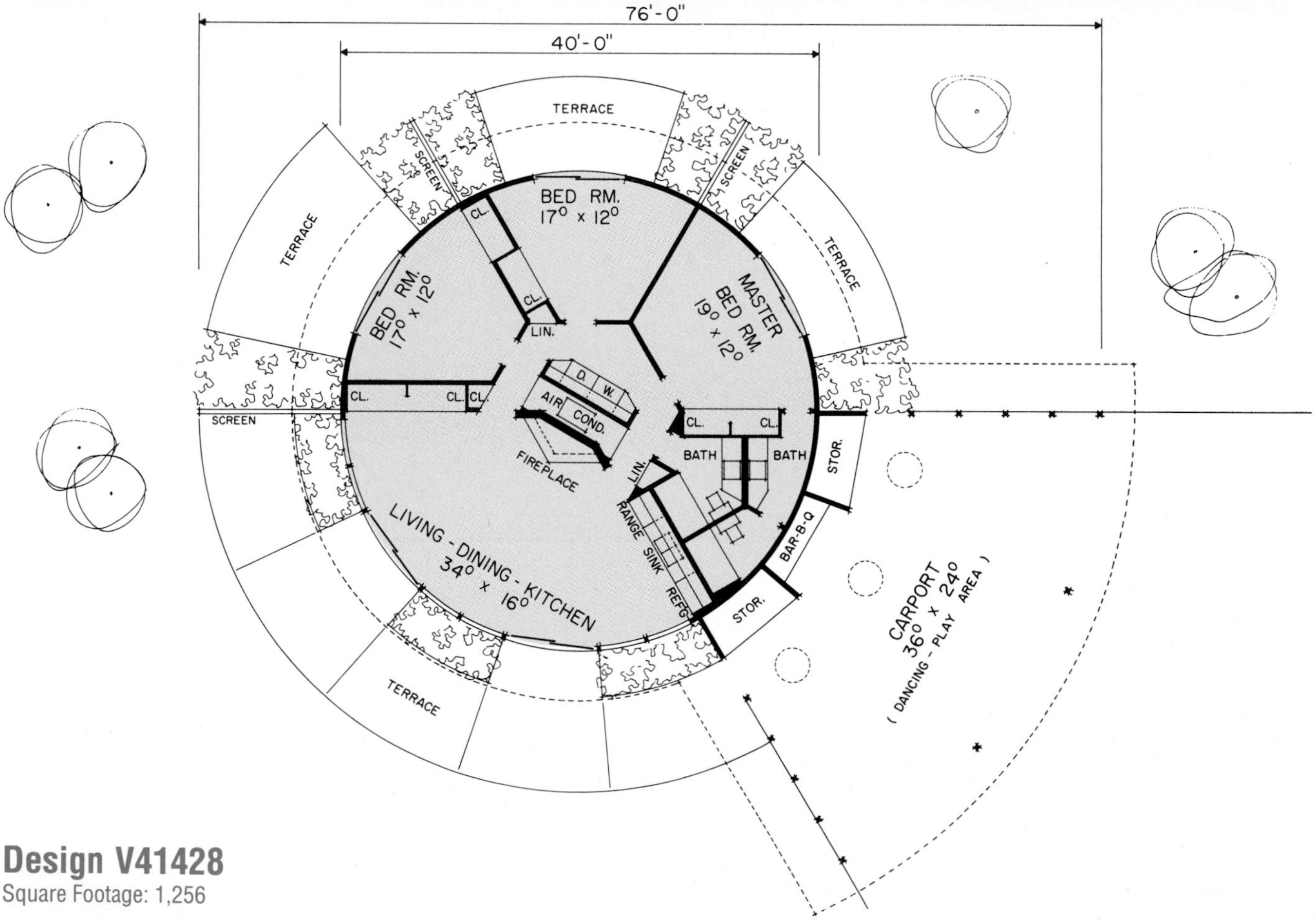

76'-0"
40'-0"
TERRACE
SCREEN
SCREEN
TERRACE
TERRACE
BED RM. $17^{0} \times 12^{0}$
BED RM. $17^{0} \times 12^{0}$
MASTER BED RM. $19^{0} \times 12^{0}$
CL.
CL.
LIN.
CL.
CL. CL.
D. W.
AIR COND.
FIREPLACE
CL.
CL.
BATH
BATH
STOR.
SCREEN
LIN.
RANGE
SINK
REFG.
BAR-B-Q
STOR.
LIVING - DINING - KITCHEN $34^{0} \times 16^{0}$
CARPORT $36^{0} \times 24^{0}$ (DANCING - PLAY AREA)
TERRACE

Design V41428

Square Footage: 1,256

● A round house is ideal for a light-hearted atmosphere, and what better spot for the light-in-heart than a vacation home? Terraces surround its circumference, accessible from each portion of the living and sleeping areas through sliding glass doors. The living area with its strip kitchen and dining space flares out from the dramatic fireplace. For economy, all the plumbing has been concentrated in one segment of the circle. The master bath and the second bath are located back-to-back. Note huge carport with barbecue and the privacy fences. This would be a great area for family outdoor activities when that never wanted inclement weather arrives.

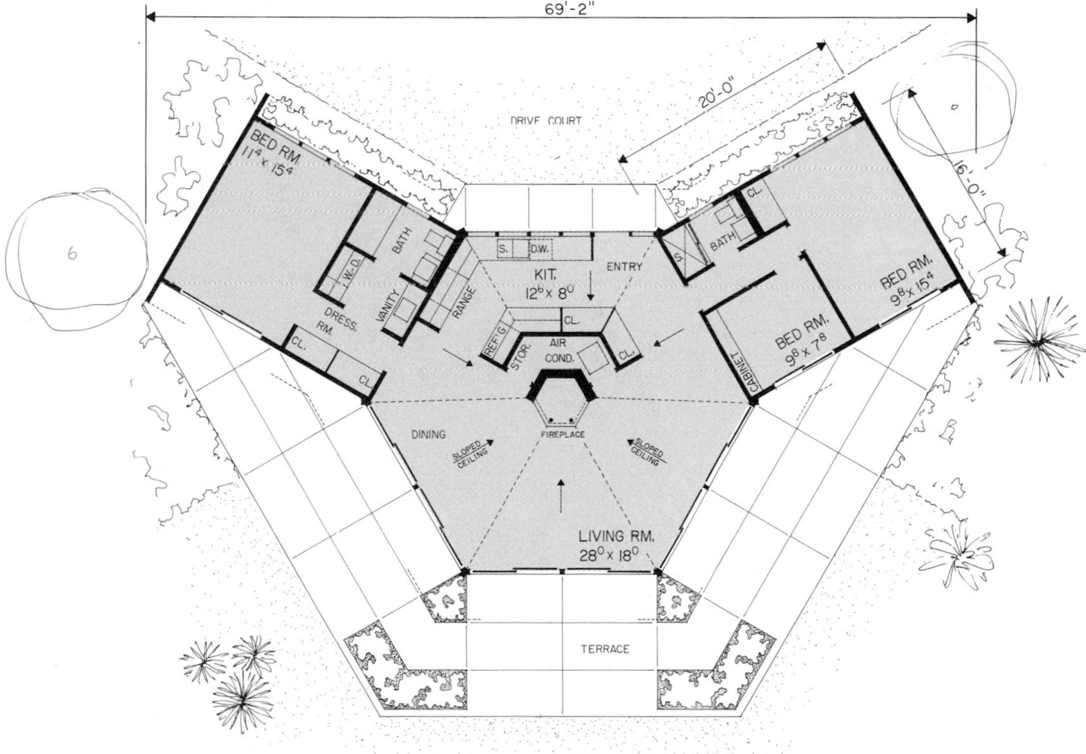

Design V41404

Square Footage: 1,336

● Here is an exciting design, unusual in character, yet fun to live in. This design with its frame exterior and large glass areas has as its dramatic focal point a hexagonal living area which gives way to interesting angles. The spacious living area features sliding glass doors through which traffic may pass to the terraces stretching across the entire length of the house. The wide overhanging roofs project over the terraces, thus providing partial protection from the weather. The sloping ceilings converge above the unique open fireplace. The sleeping areas are located in each wing from the hexagonal center. Three bedrooms in all to serve the family.

Design V41460 Upper Level: 1,035 square feet; Lower Level: 1,067 square feet; Total: 2,102 square feet

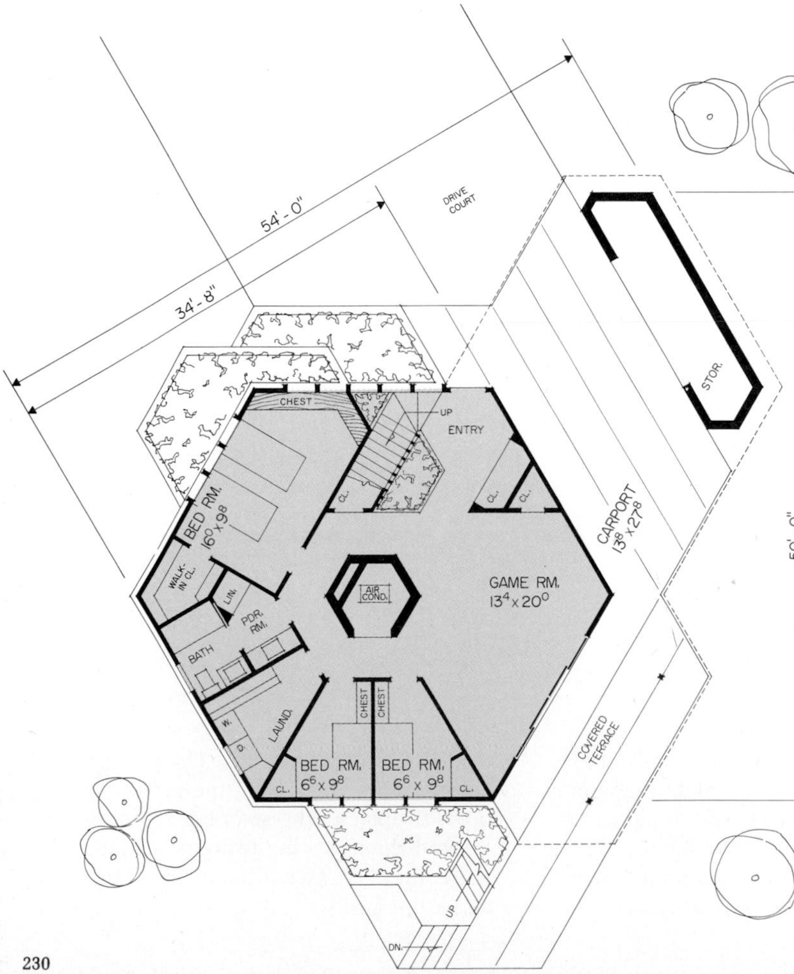

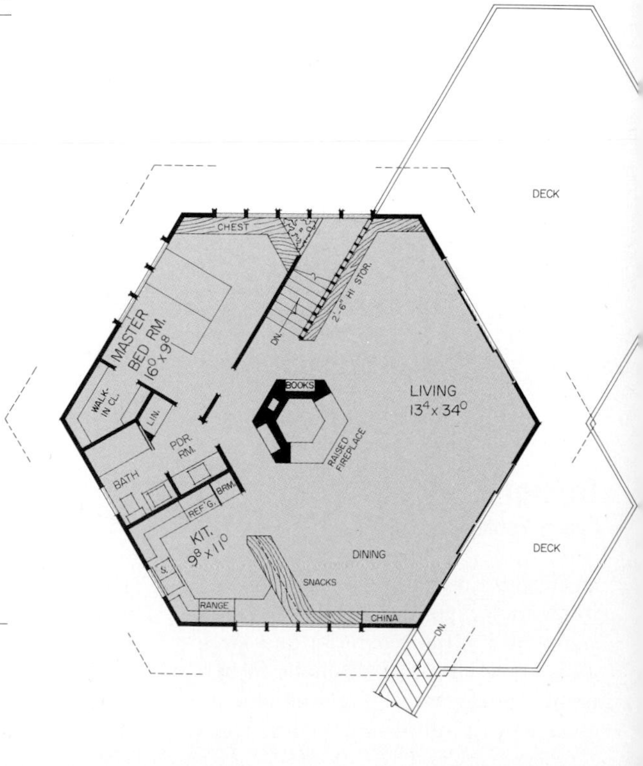

54'-0"
34'-8"
DRIVE COURT
STOR.
CHEST
UP
ENTRY
CL.
CL.
CL.
BED RM. $16^0 \times 9^8$
WALK-IN CL.
LIN.
PDR. RM.
AIR COND.
GAME RM. $13^4 \times 20^0$
CARPORT $13^8 \times 27^8$
BATH
W.
D.
LAUND.
CHEST
CHEST
BED RM. $6^6 \times 9^8$
BED RM. $6^6 \times 9^8$
CL.
CL.
COVERED TERRACE
50'-0"
UP
DN.

DECK
CHEST
DN.
2'-6" HI STOR.
MASTER BED RM. $16^0 \times 9^8$
WALK-IN CL.
LIN.
PDR. RM.
BOOKS
RAISED FIREPLACE
LIVING $13^4 \times 34^0$
BATH
BRM.
REF'G.
KIT. $9^8 \times 11^0$
DINING
SNACKS
RANGE
CHINA
DECK
DN.

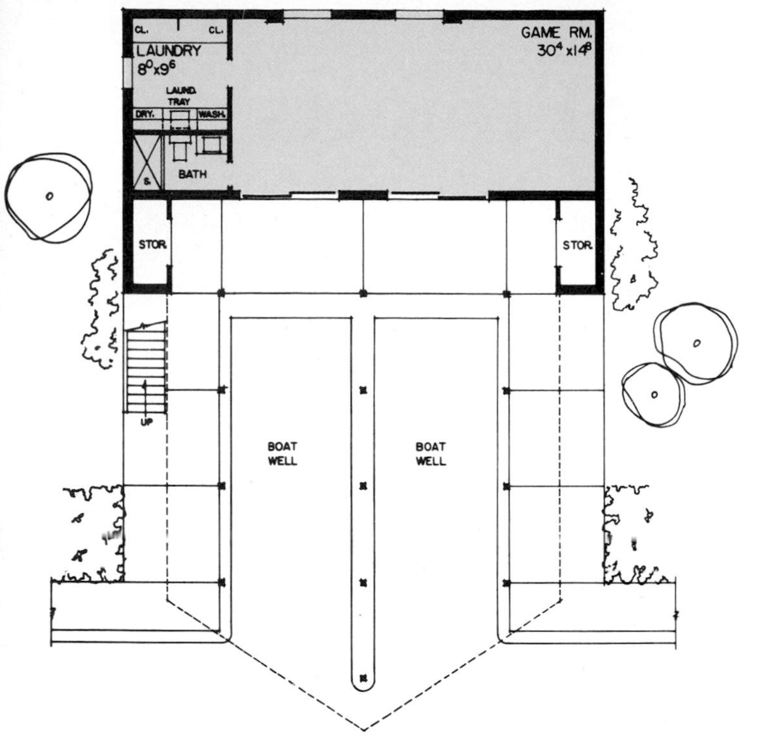

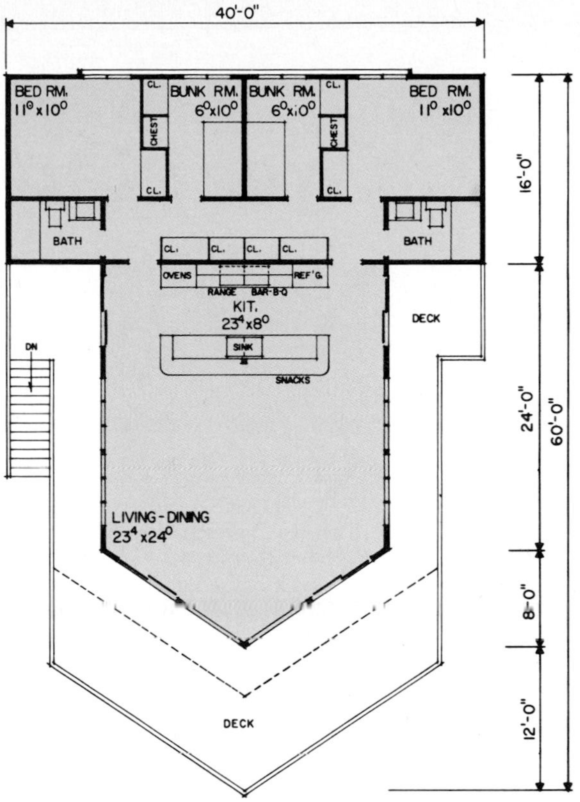

Design V41480 Upper Level: 1,312 square feet; Lower Level: 640 square feet; Total: 1,952 square feet

Great Outdoor Projects

No house should go empty-landed for long. If you're searching for just the right structure to fill up those wide open spaces, we've got five solid choices to show you. Among other exciting plans, you'll find a get-away-from-it-all gazebo that's big enough for small gatherings; a storage shed that does a number on clutter but looks great doing it; a two-dormer studio garage with all the comforts of home and a nice old-timey feel; and a gorgeous little crafts cottage with one very bright touch: an attached sunroom.

Plan V4-G108 is a good, solid gazebo; larger than most, it's better suited to entertaining alfresco. **Plan V4-G106** is no ordinary garage. In fact, it's a model building: room for two cars below and a complete studio apartment on top.

OUTDOOR PROJECTS INDEX & PRICE SCHEDULE

DESIGN		PAGE	PRICE	ADD'L SETS
V4-G106	Studio Garage	234	$40.00	$10.00
V4-G107	Storage Shed	235	$30.00	$10.00
V4-G108	Gazebo	233	$20.00	$10.00
V4-G109	Craft Cottage	236	$30.00	$10.00
V4-G111	Workshop Garage	237	$40.00	$10.00

TO ORDER, CALL TOLL FREE 1-800-521-6797, OR SEE PAGE 253.

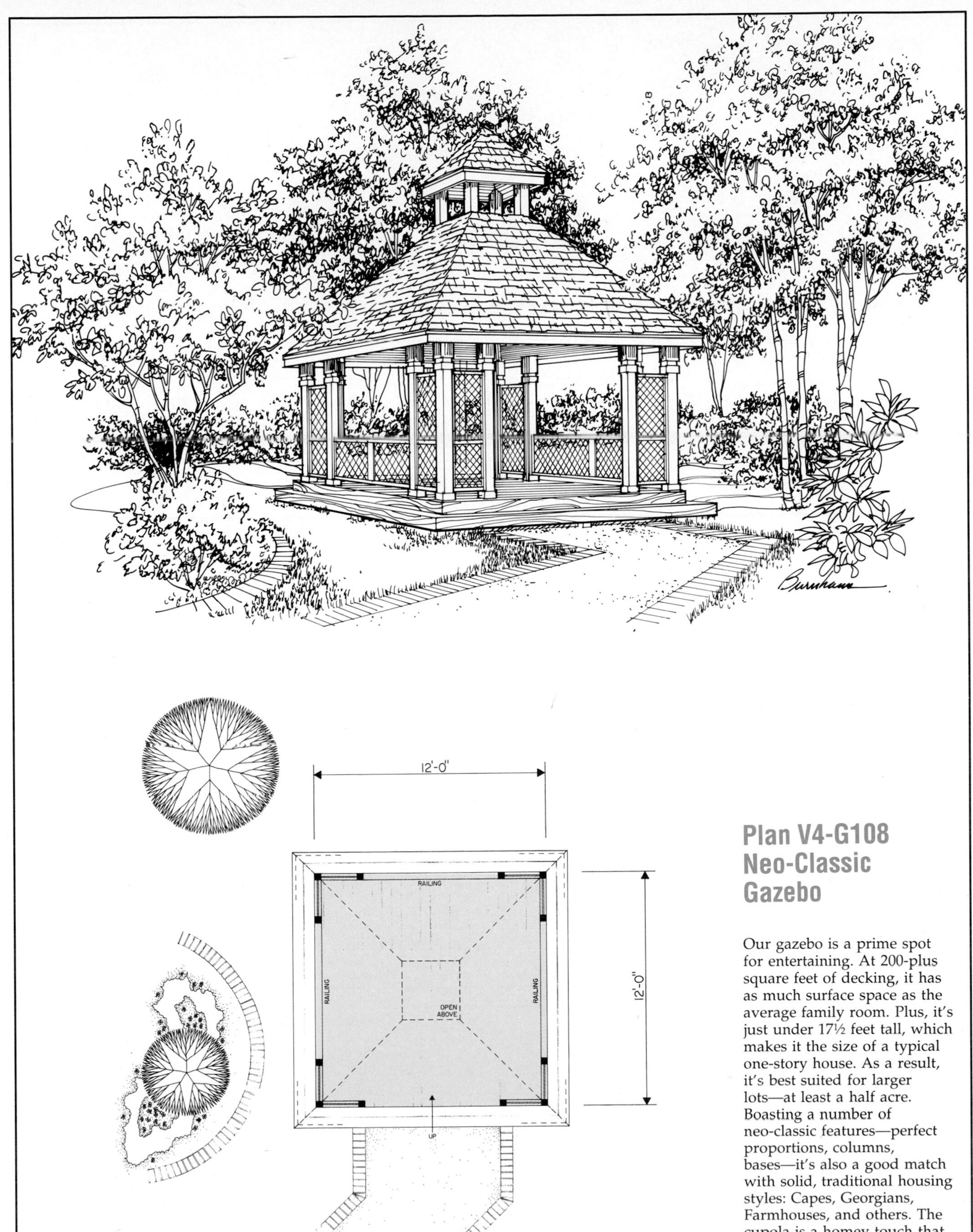

Plan V4-G108 Neo-Classic Gazebo

Our gazebo is a prime spot for entertaining. At 200-plus square feet of decking, it has as much surface space as the average family room. Plus, it's just under 17½ feet tall, which makes it the size of a typical one-story house. As a result, it's best suited for larger lots—at least a half acre. Boasting a number of neo-classic features—perfect proportions, columns, bases—it's also a good match with solid, traditional housing styles: Capes, Georgians, Farmhouses, and others. The cupola is a homey touch that lets light in to the decking below. Cedar or redwood are the building materials of choice.

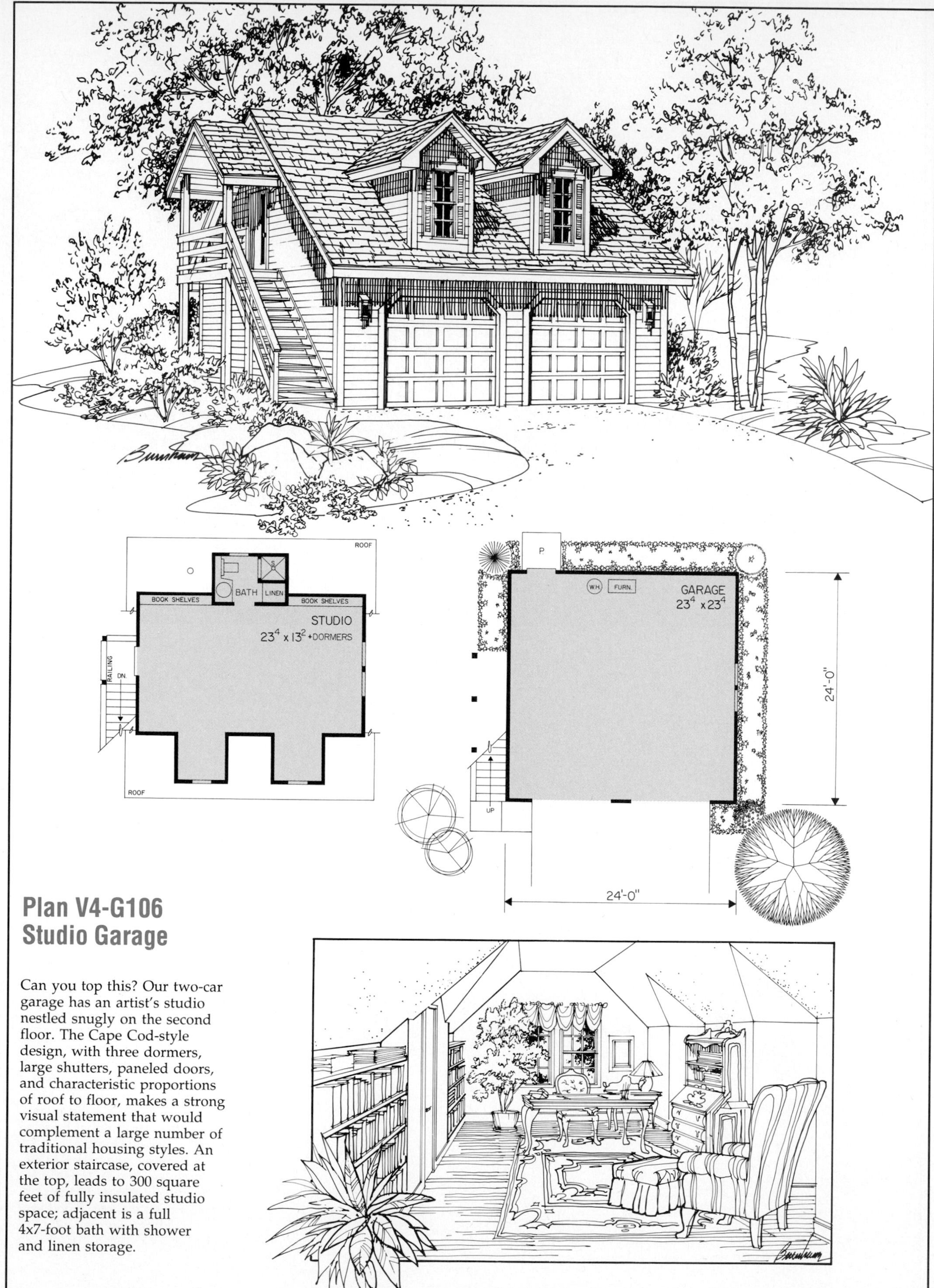

Plan V4-G106
Studio Garage

Can you top this? Our two-car garage has an artist's studio nestled snugly on the second floor. The Cape Cod-style design, with three dormers, large shutters, paneled doors, and characteristic proportions of roof to floor, makes a strong visual statement that would complement a large number of traditional housing styles. An exterior staircase, covered at the top, leads to 300 square feet of fully insulated studio space; adjacent is a full 4x7-foot bath with shower and linen storage.

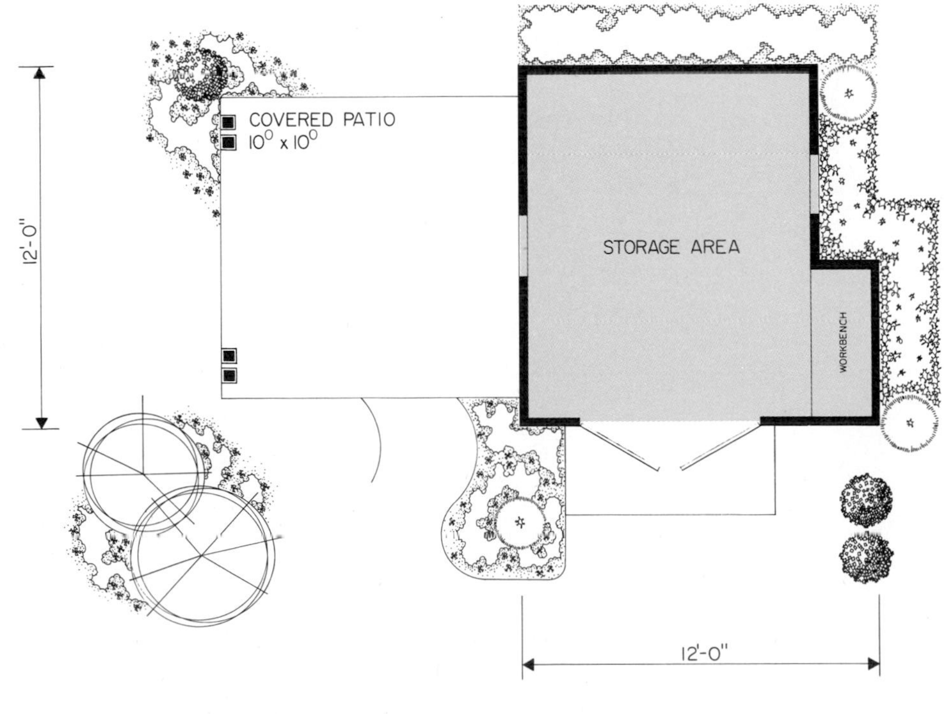

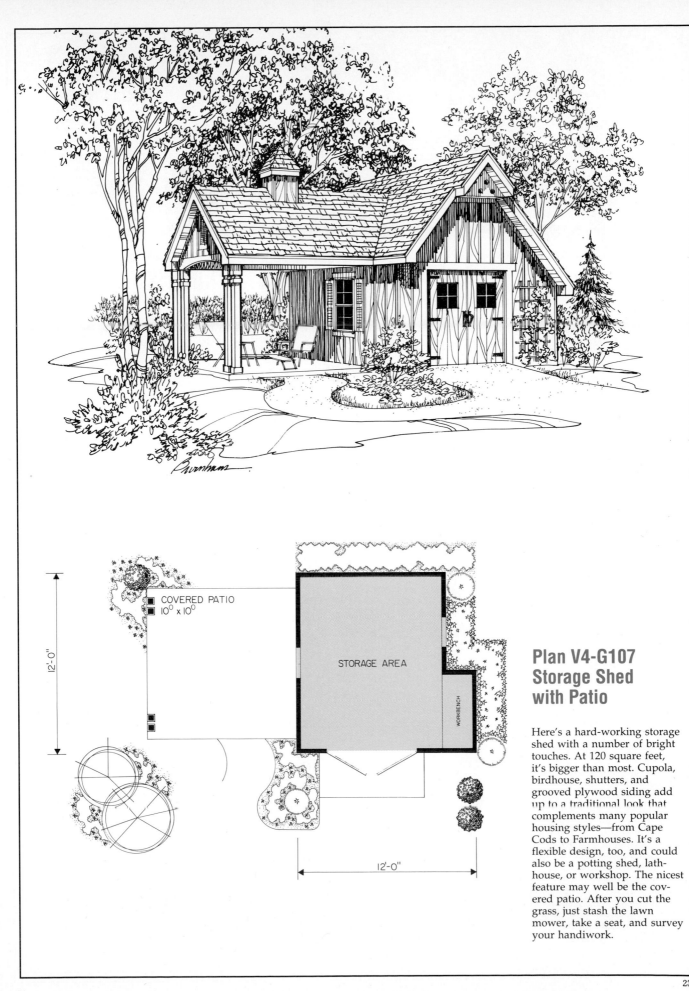

Plan V4-G107 Storage Shed with Patio

Here's a hard-working storage shed with a number of bright touches. At 120 square feet, it's bigger than most. Cupola, birdhouse, shutters, and grooved plywood siding add up to a traditional look that complements many popular housing styles—from Cape Cods to Farmhouses. It's a flexible design, too, and could also be a potting shed, lath-house, or workshop. The nicest feature may well be the covered patio. After you cut the grass, just stash the lawn mower, take a seat, and survey your handiwork.

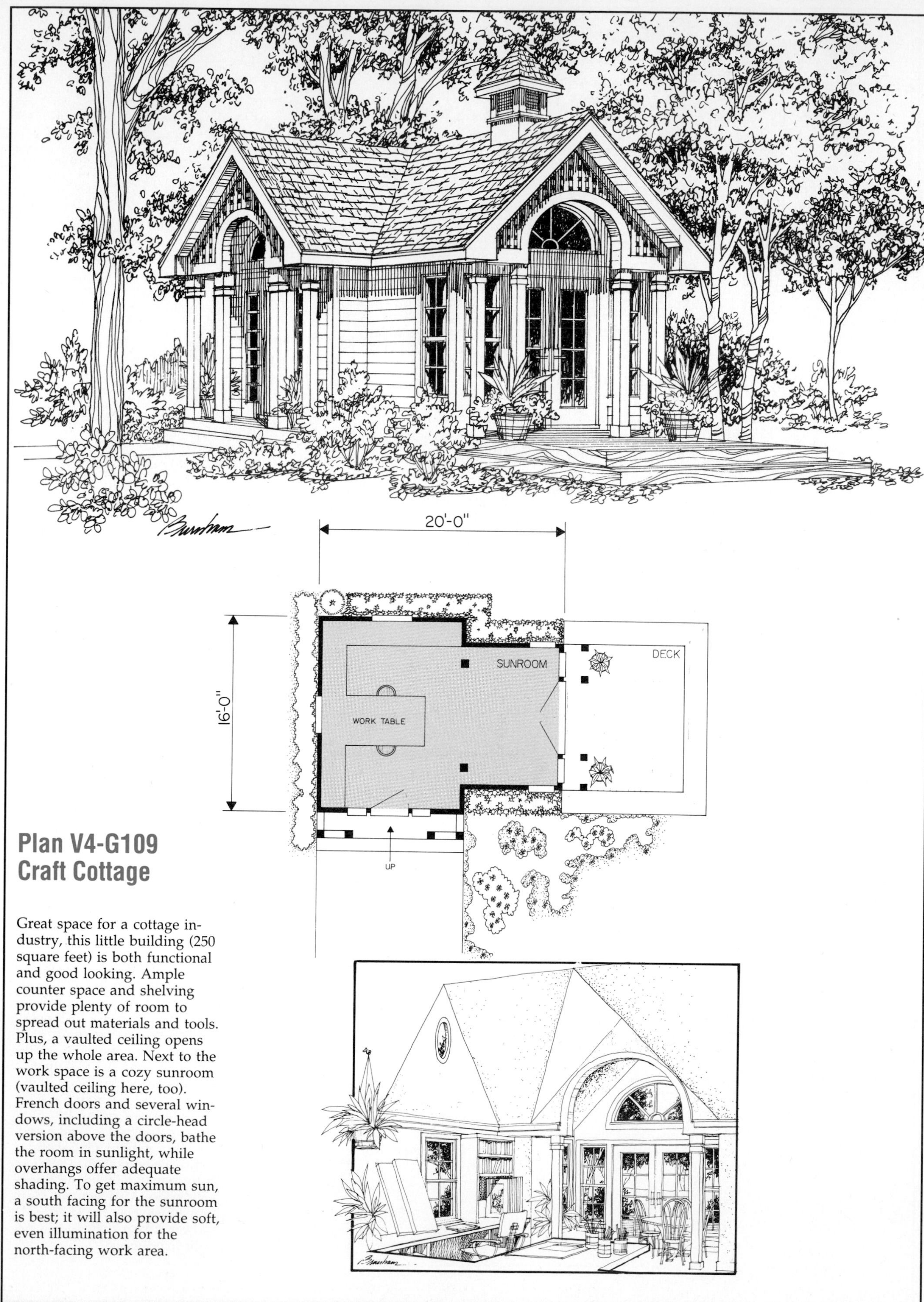

Plan V4-G109
Craft Cottage

Great space for a cottage industry, this little building (250 square feet) is both functional and good looking. Ample counter space and shelving provide plenty of room to spread out materials and tools. Plus, a vaulted ceiling opens up the whole area. Next to the work space is a cozy sunroom (vaulted ceiling here, too). French doors and several windows, including a circle-head version above the doors, bathe the room in sunlight, while overhangs offer adequate shading. To get maximum sun, a south facing for the sunroom is best; it will also provide soft, even illumination for the north-facing work area.

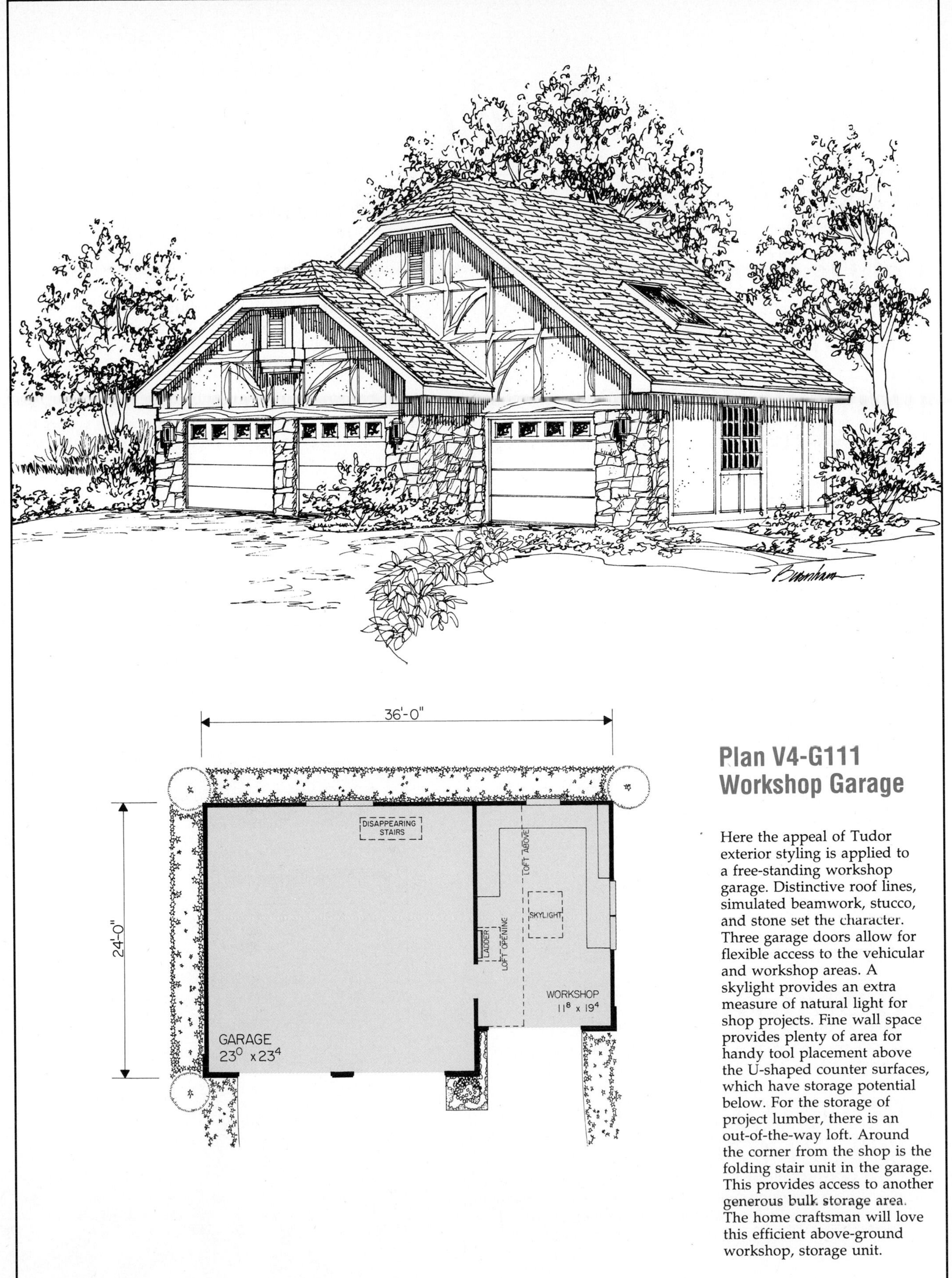

Plan V4-G111
Workshop Garage

Here the appeal of Tudor exterior styling is applied to a free-standing workshop garage. Distinctive roof lines, simulated beamwork, stucco, and stone set the character. Three garage doors allow for flexible access to the vehicular and workshop areas. A skylight provides an extra measure of natural light for shop projects. Fine wall space provides plenty of area for handy tool placement above the U-shaped counter surfaces, which have storage potential below. For the storage of project lumber, there is an out-of-the-way loft. Around the corner from the shop is the folding stair unit in the garage. This provides access to another generous bulk storage area. The home craftsman will love this efficient above-ground workshop, storage unit.

When You're Ready To Order . . .

Let Us Show You Our Home Blueprint Package.

Building a home? Planning a home? Our Blueprint Package contains nearly everything you need to get the job done right, whether you're working on your own or with help from an architect, designer, builder or subcontractors. Each Blueprint Package is the result of many hours of work by licensed architects or professional designers.

QUALITY

Hundreds of hours of painstaking effort have gone into the development of your blueprint set. Each home has been quality-checked by professionals to insure accuracy and buildability.

VALUE

Because we sell in volume, you can buy professional-quality blueprints at a fraction of their development cost. With our plans, your dream home design costs only a few hundred dollars, not the thousands of dollars that custom architects charge.

SERVICE

Once you've chosen your favorite home plan, you'll receive fast efficient service whether you choose to mail your order to us or call us toll free at 1-800-521-6797.

SATISFACTION

Our years of service to satisfied home plan buyers provide us the experience and knowledge that guarantee your satisfaction with our product and performance.

ORDER TOLL FREE 1-800-521-6797

After you've studied our Blueprint Package and Important Extras on the following pages, simply mail the accompanying order form on page 253 or call toll free on our Blueprint Hotline: 1-800-521-6797. We're ready and eager to serve you.

Each set of blueprints is an interrelated collection of floor plans, interior and exterior elevations, dimensions, cross-sections, diagrams and notations showing precisely how your house is to be constructed.

Here's what you get:

Frontal Sheet
This artist's sketch of the exterior of the house, done in realistic perspective, gives you an idea of how the house will look when built and landscaped. Large ink-line floor plans show all levels of the house and provide a quick overview of your new home's livability, as well as a handy reference for studying furniture placement.

Foundation Plan
Drawn to 1/4-inch scale, this sheet shows the complete foundation layout including support

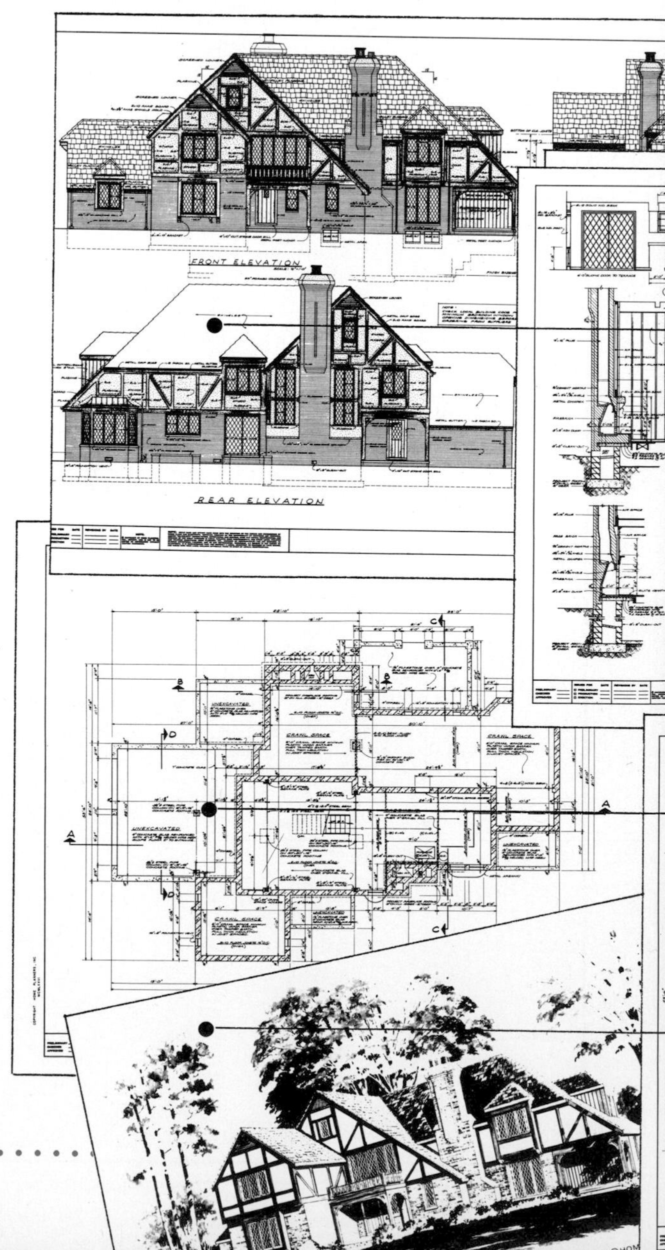

walls, excavated and unexcavated areas, if any, and foundation notes. If slab construction rather than basement, the plan shows footings and details for a monolithic slab. This page, or another in the set, also includes a sample plot plan for locating your house on a building site.

Detailed Floor Plans

Complete in 1/4-inch scale, these plans show the layout of each floor of the house. All rooms and interior spaces are carefully dimensioned and keys are provided for cross-section details given later in the plans. The positions of all electrical outlets and switches are clearly shown.

House Cross-Sections

Large scale views, normally drawn at 3/8 inch equals 1 foot, show sections or cut-aways of the foundation, interior walls, exterior walls, floors, stairways and roof details. Additional cross-sections are given to show important changes in floor, ceiling or roof heights or the relationship of one level to another. Extremely valuable for construction, these sections show exactly how the various parts of the house fit together.

Interior Elevations

These large-scale drawings show the design and placement of kitchen and bathroom cabinets, laundry areas, fireplaces, bookcases and other built-ins. Little "extras," such as mantelpiece and wainscoting drawings, plus moulding sections, provide details that give your home that custom touch.

Exterior Elevations

Drawings in 1/4-inch scale show the front, rear and sides of your house and give necessary notes on exterior materials and finishes. Particular attention is given to cornice detail, brick and stone accents or other finish items that make your home distinctive.

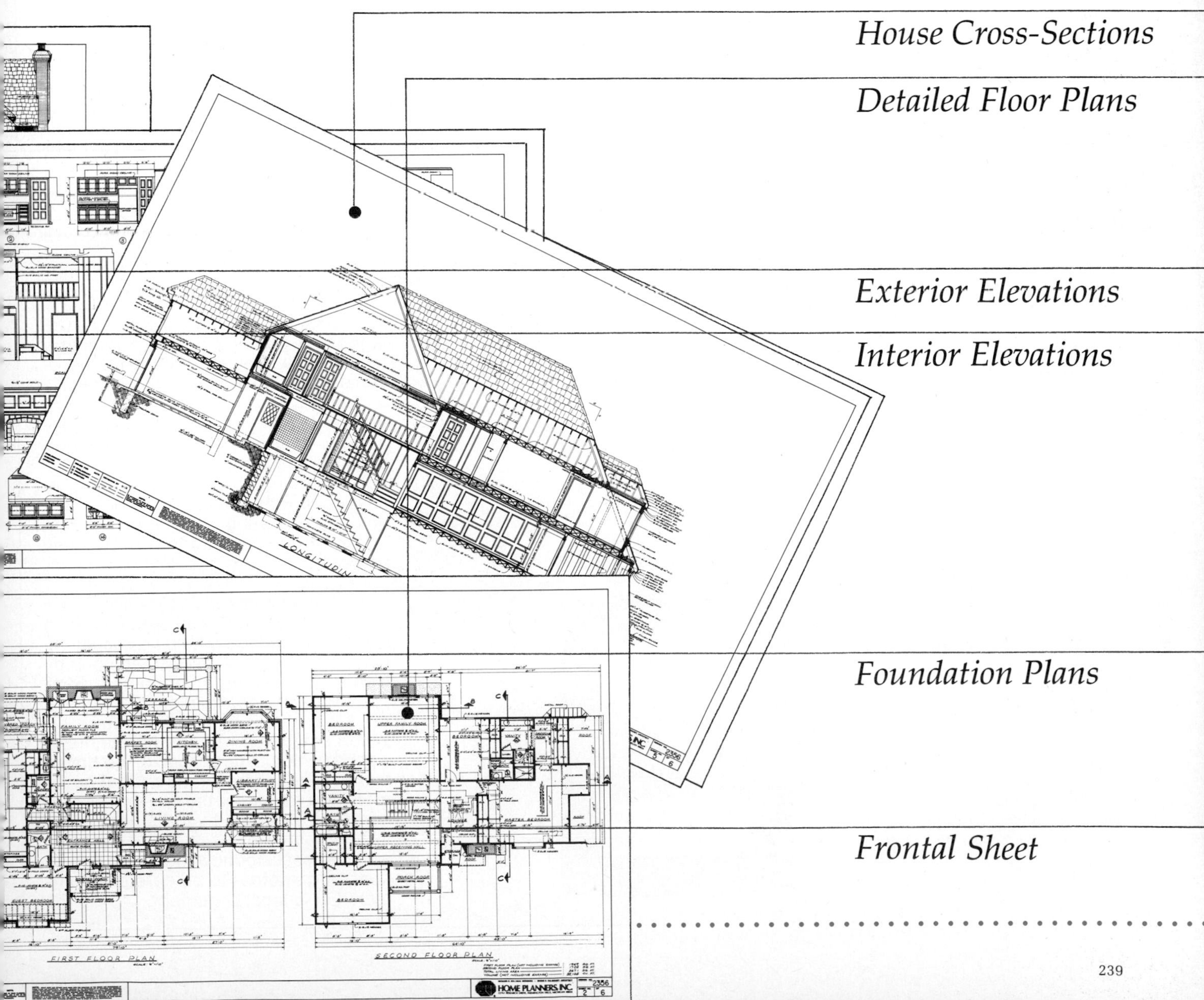

Important Extras To Do The Job Right!

Introducing six important planning and construction aids developed by our professionals to help you succeed in your home-building project.

To Order, Call Toll Free 1-800-521-6797

To add these important extras to your Blueprint Package, simply indicate your choices on the order form on page 253 or call us Toll Free 1-800-521-6797 and we'll tell you more about these exciting products.

Materials List

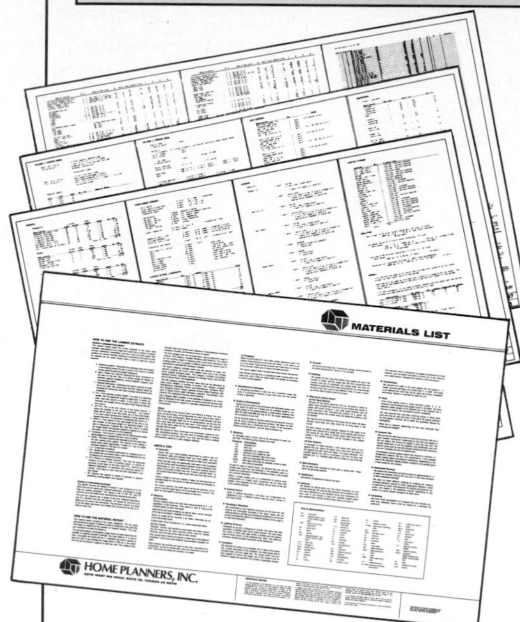

For many of the designs in our portfolio, we offer a customized materials take-off that is invaluable in planning and estimating the cost of your new home. This comprehensive list outlines the quantity, type and size of material needed to build your house (with the exception of mechanical system items). Included are:

- framing lumber
- roofing and sheet metal
- windows and doors
- exterior sheathing material and trim
- masonry, veneer and fireplace materials
- tile and flooring materials
- kitchen and bath cabinetry
- interior sheathing and trim
- rough and finish hardware
- many more items

(Note: Because of differing local codes, building methods, and availability of materials, our Materials Lists do not include mechanical materials. To obtain necessary take-offs and recommendations, consult heating, plumbing and electrical contractors. Materials Lists are not sold separately from the Blueprint Package.)

This handy list helps you or your builder cost out materials and serves as a ready reference sheet when you're compiling bids. It also provides a cross-check against the materials specified by your builder and helps coordinate the substitution of items you may need to meet local codes.

Specification Outline

This valuable 16-page document is critical to building your house correctly. Designed to be filled in by you or your builder, this booklet lists 166 stages or items crucial to the building process.

For the layman, it provides a comprehensive review of the construction process and helps in making the specific choices of materials, models and processes. For the builder, it serves as a guide to preparing a building quotation and forms the basis for the construction program.

Designed primarily as a reference for the homeowner, this Specification Outline can become a legally binding document. Once it is filled out and agreed upon by owner and builder, it becomes a complete Project Specification.

When combined with the blueprints, a signed contract and schedule, the Specification Outline becomes a legal document and record for the building of your home. Many home builders find it useful to order two of these outlines–one as a worksheet in formulating the specifications and another to be carefully completed as a legal document.

DETAIL SHEETS

If you want to know more about techniques—and deal more confidently with subcontractors—we offer these remarkably useful detail sheets. Each is an excellent tool that will enhance your understanding of these technical subjects.

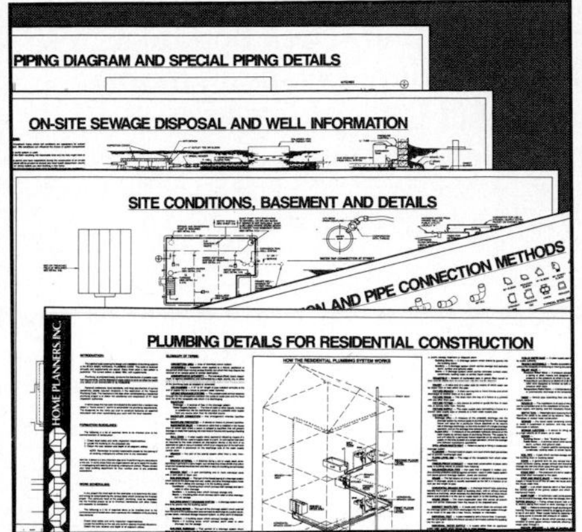

PLUMBING

The Blueprint Package includes locations for all the plumbing fixtures in your new house, including sinks, lavatories, tubs, showers, toilets, laundry trays and water heaters. However, if you want to know more about the complete plumbing system, these 24x36-inch detail sheets will prove very useful. Prepared to meet requirements of the National Plumbing Code, these six fact-filled sheets give general information on pipe schedules, fittings, sump-pump details, water-softener hookups, septic system details and much more. Color-coded sheets include a glossary of terms.

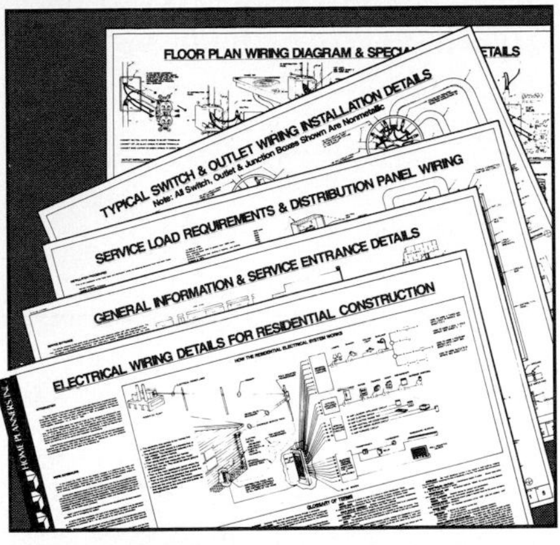

ELECTRICAL

The locations for every electrical switch, plug and outlet are shown in your Blueprint Package. However, these Electrical Details go further to take the mystery out of household electrical systems. Prepared to meet requirements of the National Electrical Code, these comprehensive 24x36-inch drawings come packed with helpful information, including wire sizing, switch-installation schematics, cable-routing details, appliance wattage, door-bell hookups, typical service panel circuitry and much more. Six sheets are bound together and color-coded for easy reference. A glossary of terms is also included.

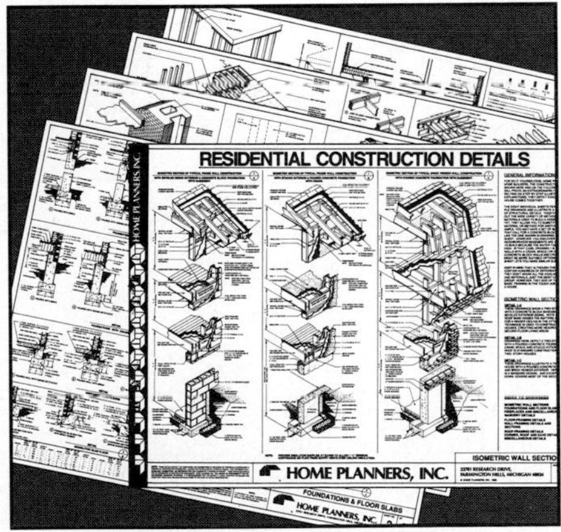

CONSTRUCTION

The Blueprint Package contains everything an experienced builder needs to construct a particular house. However, it doesn't show all the ways that houses can be built, nor does it explain alternate construction methods. To help you understand how your house will be built–and offer additional techniques–this set of drawings depicts the materials and methods used to build foundations, fireplaces, walls, floors and roofs. Where appropriate, the drawings show acceptable alternatives. These six sheets will answer questions for the advanced do-it-yourselfer or home planner.

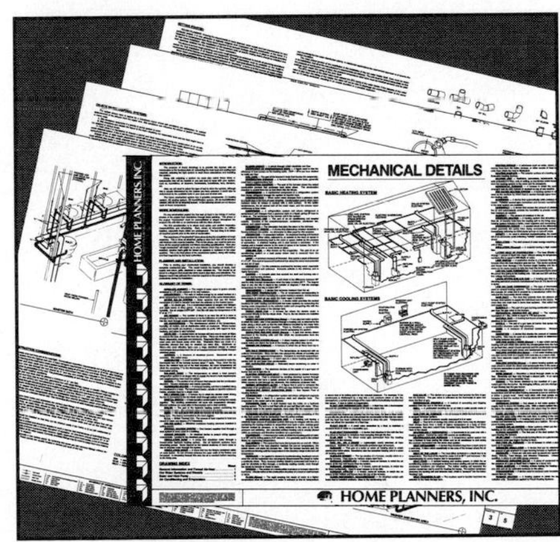

MECHANICAL

This package contains fundamental principles and useful data that will help you make informed decisions and communicate with subcontractors about heating and cooling systems. The 24 x 36-inch drawings contain instructions and samples that allow you to make simple load calculations and preliminary sizing and costing analysis. Covered are today's most commonly used systems from heat pumps to solar fuel systems. The package is packed full of illustrations and diagrams to help you visualize components and how they relate to one another.

Plan-A-Home®

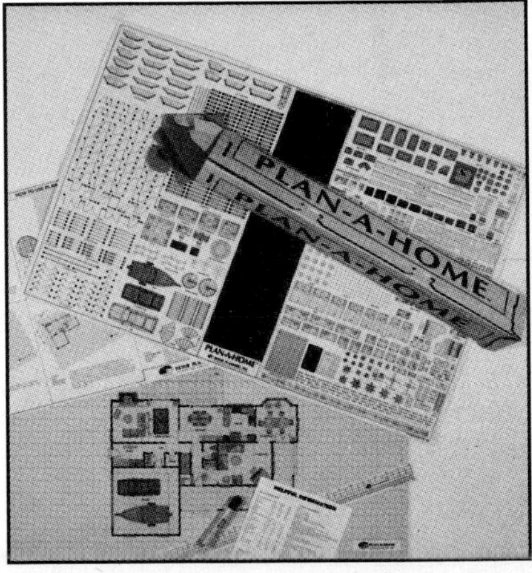

Plan-A-Home® is an easy-to-use tool that helps you design a new home, arrange furniture in a new or existing home, or plan a remodeling project. Each package contains:

- More than *700 peel-off planning symbols* on a self-stick vinyl sheet, including walls, windows, doors, all types of furniture, kitchen components, bath fixtures and many more. All are made of durable, peel-and-stick vinyl you can use over and over.
- A reusable, transparent, *1/4-inch scale planning grid* made of tough mylar that matches the scale of actual working drawings (1/4 -inch equals 1 foot). This grid provides the basis for house layouts of up to 140x92 feet.
- *Tracing paper* and a protective sheet for copying or transferring your completed plan.
- A *felt-tip pen,* with water-soluble ink that wipes away quickly.

With Plan-A-Home®, you can make basic planning decisions for a new house or make modifications to an existing house. Use with your Blueprint Package to test modifications to rooms or to plan furniture arrangements before you build. Plan-A-Home® lets you lay out areas as large as a 7,500 square foot, six-bedroom, seven-bath house.

D The Deck Blueprint Package

Many of the homes in this book can be enhanced with a professionally designed Deck Plan. Those home plans highlighted with a D have a matching or corresponding deck plan available which includes a Deck Plan Frontal Sheet, Deck Framing and Floor Plans, Deck Elevations and a Deck Materials List. A Standard Deck Details Package, also available, provides all the how-to information necessary for building *any* deck. Our Complete Deck Building Package contains 1 set of Custom Deck Plans of your choice, plus 1 set of Standard Deck Building Details all for one low price. Our plans and details are carefully prepared in an easy-to-understand format that will guide you through every stage of your deck-building project. See these pages for 25 different Deck layouts to match your favorite house.

SPLIT–LEVEL SUN DECK
Deck Plan D100

BI–LEVEL DECK WITH COVERED DINING
Deck Plan D101

FRESH–AIR CORNER DECK
Deck Plan D102

BACK–YARD EXTENDER DECK
Deck Plan D103

WRAP–AROUND FAMILY DECK
Deck Plan D104

DRAMATIC DECK WITH BARBECUE
Deck Plan D105

SPLIT–PLAN COUNTRY DECK
Deck Plan D106

DECK FOR DINING AND VIEWS
Deck Plan D107

BOLD, ANGLED CORNER DECK
Deck Plan D108

SPECTACULAR "RESORT–STYLE" DECK
Deck Plan D109

TREND–SETTER DECK
Deck Plan D110

TURN–OF–THE–CENTURY DECK
Deck Plan D111

WEEKEND ENTERTAINER DECK
Deck Plan D112

STRIKING "DELTA" DECK
Deck Plan D113

CENTER–VIEW DECK
Deck Plan D114

KITCHEN–EXTENDER DECK
Deck Plan D115

BI–LEVEL RETREAT DECK
Deck Plan D116

SPLIT–LEVEL ACTIVITY DECK
Deck Plan D117

OUTDOOR LIFESTYLE DECK
Deck Plan D118

TRI–LEVEL DECK WITH GRILL
Deck Plan D119

CONTEMPORARY LEISURE DECK
Deck Plan D120

ANGULAR WINGED DECK
Deck Plan D121

DECK FOR A SPLIT–LEVEL HOME
Deck Plan D122

GRACIOUS GARDEN DECK
Deck Plan D123

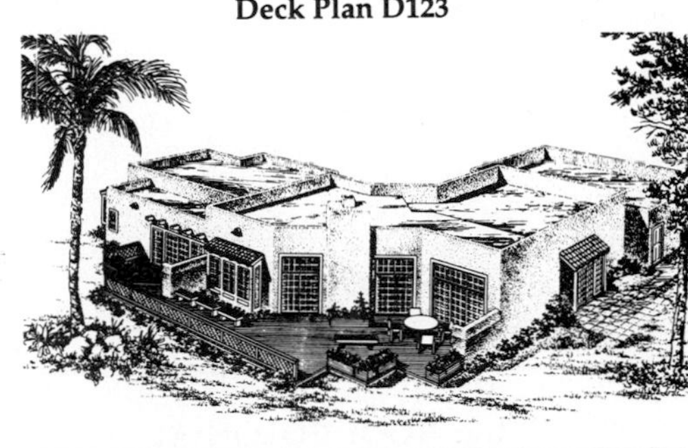

TERRACED DECK FOR ENTERTAINING
Deck Plan D124

For Deck Plan prices and ordering information, see page 248.

 Or call **Toll Free, 1-800-521-6797**.

The Landscape Blueprint Package

For the homes marked with an L in this book, Home Planners has created a front-yard landscape plan that matches or is complementary in design to the house plan. These comprehensive blueprint packages include a Frontal Sheet, Plan View, Regionalized Plant & Materials List, a sheet on Planting and Maintaining Your Landscape, Zone Maps and Plant Size and Description Guide. These plans will help you achieve professional results, adding value and enjoyment to your property for years to come. Each set of blueprints is a full 18" x 24" in size with clear, complete instructions and easy-to-read type. See the following pages for 40-different front-yard Landscape Plans to match your favorite house.

Regional Order Map

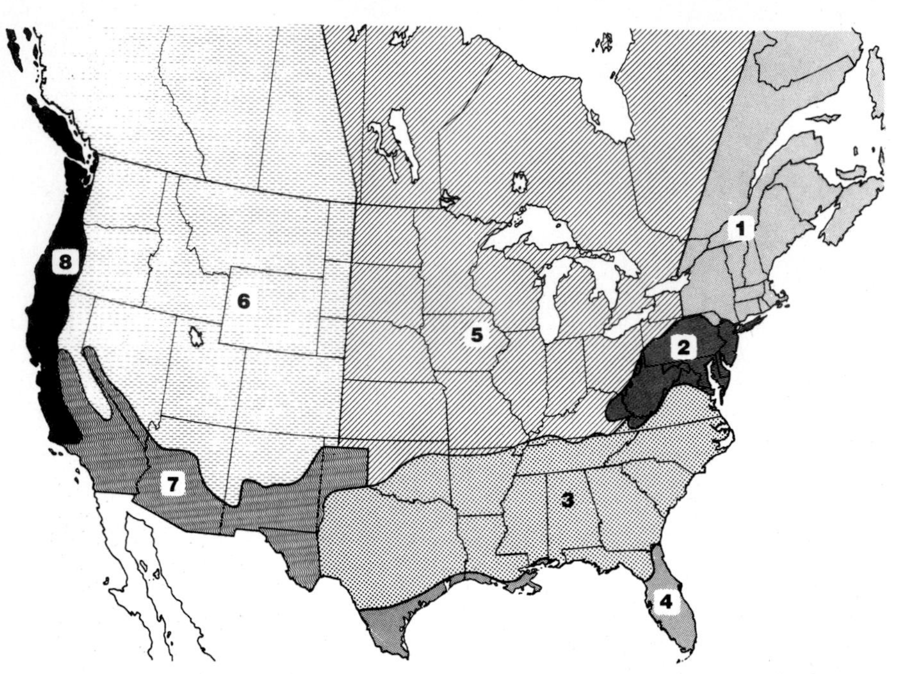

Most of the Landscape Plans shown on these pages are available with a Plant & Materials List adapted by horticultural experts to 8 different regions of the country. Please specify Geographic Region when ordering your plan. See pages 248-250 for prices, ordering information and regional availability.

Region	1	Northeast
Region	2	Mid-Atlantic
Region	3	Deep South
Region	4	Florida & Gulf Coast
Region	5	Midwest
Region	6	Rocky Mountains
Region	7	Southern California & Desert Southwest
Region	8	Northern California & Pacific Northwest

CAPE COD TRADITIONAL
Landscape Plan L200

WILLIAMSBURG CAPE
Landscape Plan L201

CAPE COD COTTAGE
Landscape Plan L202

GAMBREL–ROOF COLONIAL
Landscape Plan L203

CENTER–HALL COLONIAL
Landscape Plan L204

CLASSIC NEW ENGLAND COLONIAL
Landscape Plan L205

SOUTHERN COLONIAL
Landscape Plan L206

COUNTRY–STYLE FARMHOUSE
Landscape Plan L207

PENNSYLVANIA STONE FARMHOUSE
Landscape Plan L208

RAISED–PORCH FARMHOUSE
Landscape Plan L209

NEW ENGLAND BARN–STYLE HOUSE
Landscape Plan L210

NEW ENGLAND COUNTRY HOUSE
Landscape Plan L211

TRADITIONAL COUNTRY ESTATE
Landscape Plan L212

FRENCH PROVINCIAL ESTATE
Landscape Plan L213

GEORGIAN MANOR
Landscape Plan L214

GRAND–PORTICO GEORGIAN
Landscape Plan L215

BRICK FEDERAL
Landscape Plan L216

COUNTRY FRENCH RAMBLER
Landscape Plan L217

FRENCH MANOR HOUSE
Landscape Plan L218

ELIZABETHAN TUDOR
Landscape Plan L219

TUDOR ONE-STORY
Landscape Plan L220

ENGLISH-STYLE COTTAGE
Landscape Plan L221

MEDIEVAL GARRISON
Landscape Plan L222

QUEEN ANNE VICTORIAN
Landscape Plan L223

GOTHIC VICTORIAN
Landscape Plan L224

BASIC RANCH
Landscape Plan L225

L-SHAPED RANCH
Landscape Plan L226

SPRAWLING RANCH
Landscape Plan L227

TRADITIONAL SPLIT-LEVEL
Landscape Plan L228

SHED-ROOF CONTEMPORARY
Landscape Plan L229

WOOD–SIDED CONTEMPORARY
Landscape Plan L230

HILLSIDE CONTEMPORARY
Landscape Plan L231

FLORIDA RAMBLER
Landscape Plan L232

CALIFORNIA STUCCO
Landscape Plan L233

LOW–GABLE CONTEMPORARY
Landscape Plan L234

NORTHERN BRICK CHATEAU
Landscape Plan L235

MISSION–TILE RANCH
Landscape Plan L236

ADOBE–BLOCK HACIENDA
Landscape Plan L237

COURTYARD PATIO HOME
Landscape Plan L238

CENTER–COURT CONTEMPORARY
Landscape Plan L239

For Landscape Plan prices and ordering information, see page 248.

Or call **Toll Free,**
1-800-521-6797.

Price Schedule & Plans Index

House Blueprint Price Schedule

(Prices guaranteed through December 31, 1993)

	1-set Study Package	4-set Building Package	8-set Building Package	1-set Reproducible Sepias
Schedule A	$210	$270	$330	$420
Schedule B	$240	$300	$360	$480
Schedule C	$270	$330	$390	$540
Schedule D	$300	$360	$420	$600
Schedule E	$390	$450	$510	$660

Additional Identical Blueprints in same order................$50 per set
Reverse Blueprints (mirror image)...................................$50 per set
Specification Outlines ....$7 each
Materials Lists:
Schedule A-D $40
Schedule E $50

Deck Plans Price Schedule

CUSTOM DECK PLANS

Price Group	Q	R	S
1 Set Custom Plans	$15	$20	$25

Additional identical sets ....$5.00 each
Reverse sets (mirror image) ....$5.00 each

STANDARD DECK DETAILS

1 Set Generic Construction Details ....$14.95 each

COMPLETE DECK BUILDING PACKAGE

Price Group	Q	R	S
1 Set Custom Plans 1 Set Standard Deck Details	$25	$30	$35

Landscape Plans Price Schedule

Price Group	X	Y	Z
1 set	$35	$45	$55
3 sets	$50	$60	$70
6 sets	$65	$75	$85

Additional Identical Sets ....$10 each
Reverse Sets (Mirror Image) ....$10 each

These pages contain all the information you need to price your blueprints. In general the larger and more complicated the house, the more it costs to design and thus the higher the price we must charge for the blueprints. Remember, however, that these prices are far less than you would normally pay for the services of a licensed architect or professional designer. Custom home designs and related architectural services often cost thousands of dollars, ranging from 5% to 15% of the cost of construction. By ordering our blueprints you are potentially saving enough money to afford a larger house, or to add those "extra" amenities such as a patio, deck, swimming pool or even an upgraded kitchen or luxurious master suite.

Index

To use the Index below, refer to the design number listed in numerical order (a helpful page reference is also given). Note the price index letter and refer to the House Blueprint Price Schedule above for the cost of one, four or eight sets of blueprints or the cost of a reproducible sepia. Additional prices are shown for identical and reverse blueprint sets, as well as a very useful Materials List. Also note in the Index below those plans that have matching or complementary Deck Plans or Landscape Plans. Refer to the schedules above for prices of these plans. Some of our plans can be customized through Home Planners' Home Customizer® Service. These plans are indicated below with this symbol: 🏠. See page 251 for more information.

To Order: Fill in and send the order form on page 253—or call toll free 1-800-521-6797.

DESIGN	PRICE	PAGE	CUSTOMIZABLE	DECK	DECK PRICE	LANDSCAPE	LANDSCAPE PRICE	REGIONS
V41024	A	54						
V41034	A	55						
V41065	A	69						
V41254	B	65						
V41300	A	54						
V41301	A	53						
V41342	B	68						
V41354	A	86		D105	R	L200	X	1-3,5,6,8
V41372	A	78						
V41394	A	79		D105	R	L202	X	1-3,5,6,8
V41404	A	229						
V41406	A	192						
V41409	A	149						
V41410	A	218						
V41415	A	202						
V41416	A	202						
V41419	A	138						
V41422	A	214						
V41424	A	217						
V41425	A	150						
V41427	A	164						
V41428	A	228						
V41431	B	222						
V41432	B	196						
V41433	A	224						
V41434	A	181						
V41435	A	149						
V41437	A	175						
V41438	A	44						
V41441	A	173						
V41443	C	223						
V41444	A	137						
V41445	A	171						
V41448	A	203						
V41450	A	156						
V41451	A	205						
V41453	A	225						
V41457	A	177						
V41458	A	148						
V41459	A	216						

DESIGN	PRICE	PAGE	CUSTOMIZABLE	DECK	DECK PRICE	LANDSCAPE	LANDSCAPE PRICE	REGIONS
V41460	B	230						
V41461	B	144						
V41462	A	147						
V41464	A	157						
V41465	A	174						
V41466	A	179						
V41468	A	178						
V41470	A	197						
V41471	A	139						
V41472	A	215						
V41473	A	211						
V41474	B	212						
V41475	B	213						
V41476	B	195						
V41477	A	50						
V41478	A	135						
V41479	A	133						
V41480	A	231						
V41481	A	134						
V41482	A	210						
V41483	A	163						
V41484	A	163						
V41486	A	146						
V41488	A	147						
V41489	A	162						
V41490	A	200						
V41491	A	200						
V41492	A	162						
V41494	A	201						
V41495	A	146						
V41496	A	164						
V41497	A	134						
V41498	B	180						
V41499	B	204						
V41739	C	185						
V41802	A	55						
V41913	A	86						
V41945	B	64						
V41946	B	64						
V41974	C	127						
V41976	C	126						
V42106	B	65						
V42162	A	78		D103	R	L202	X	1-3,5,6,8
V42167	A	152						
V42168	A	152						
V42169	D	184						
V42205	B	130						
V42247	C	42						
V42379	B	97		D120	R	L212	Z	1-8
V42403	B	170						
V42405	A	142						
V42410	A	138						
V42412	A	208						
V42414	A	174						
V42416	A	44						
V42418	A	221						
V42419	A	154						
V42420	A	219						
V42421	A	148						
V42422	B	159						
V42423	A	147						
V42424	A	218						
V42425	A	146						
V42426	A	50						
V42427	A	216						
V42428	A	45						
V42429	B	206						
V42430	A	209						
V42431	A	193						
V42432	A	143						
V42434	A	43						
V42435	A	173						
V42437	A	158						
V42438	A	167						
V42439	A	220						
V42455	A	172						
V42456	B	207						
V42457	A	145						
V42458	A	227						
V42459	A	194						
V42461	A	227						
V42462	A	45						
V42463	A	169						
V42464	A	136						
V42465	B	166						
V42467	A	198						
V42468	B	227						
V42469	A	199						
V42470	B	176						
V42472	A	155						
V42476	C	182						
V42478	A	36						
V42480	A	37						
V42481	A	47						
V42482	A	168						
V42483	B	35						
V42484	A	39						
V42485	B	165						
V42486	A	34						
V42487	B	46						
V42488	A	33	■	D102	Q			
V42489	A	38						
V42490	A	160	■					
V42491	A	161	■					
V42493	C	92						
V42504	C	131						
V42505	A	59	■	D113	R	L226	X	1-8
V42510	A	79		D105	R	L200	X	1-3,5,6,8
V42511	B	112		D108	R	L229	Y	1-8
V42546	C	190						
V42548	C	191						
V42549	C	118						
V42551	B	186						
V42565	B	58		D101	R	L225	X	1-3,5,6,8
V42566	C	125						
V42579	D	129						
V42583	C	128						
V42657	B	74				L200	X	1-3,5,6,8
V42658	A	74						
V42679	C	121						
V42682	A	76	■	D115	Q	L200	X	1-3,5,6,8
V42701	C	93						
V42702	B	71						
V42703	A	70		D113	R			
V42707	A	51	■	D117	S	L226	X	1-8
V42711	B	91	■	D105	R	L229	Y	1-8
V42716	C	109				L229	Y	1-8
V42725	B	187						
V42729	b	96				L234	Y	1-8
V42753	B	70		D112	R			
V42761	B	119		D105	R	L229	Y	1-8
V42763	C	132						
V42770	B	190						
V42771	C	95						
V42772	C	94						
V42780	C	94						
V42792	B	68						
V42802	B	56	■	D118	R	L220	Y	1-3,5,6,8
V42803	B	56	■	D118	R	L225	X	1-3,5,6,8
V42804	B	56	■	D118	R	L232	Y	4,7
V42805	B	57		D113	R	L220	Y	1-3,5,6,8
V42806	B	57		D113	R	L220	Y	1-3,5,6,8

DESIGN	PRICE	PAGE	CUSTOMIZABLE	DECK	DECK PRICE	LANDSCAPE	LANDSCAPE PRICE	REGIONS
V42807	B	57		D113	R	L220	Y	1-3,5,6,8
V42821	A	98				L229	Y	1-8
V42822	A	40				L229	Y	1-8
V42823	B	90		D112	R	L229	Y	1-8
V42824	B	41						
V42825	B	52						
V42826	B	89	⌂	D116	R			
V42827	C	111				L229	Y	1-8
V42841	B	188		D108	R			
V42842	B	110		D114	R			
V42843	C	189				L228	Y	1-8
V42844	C	123						
V42846	C	124						
V42847	C	122		D112	R	L220	Y	1-3,5,6,8
V42852	A	75		D105	R	L202	X	1-3,5,6,8
V42856	C	116						
V42868	B	115						
V42878	B	49	⌂	D112	R	L200	X	1-3,5,6,8
V42883	C	73						
V42887	A	153						
V42895	D	120						
V42896	C	117						
V42923	B	88						
V42937	C	114				L229	Y	1-8
V42947	B	48	⌂					
V43184	A	140						
V43185	A	141						
V43221	A	53						
V43302	A	80	⌂					
V43313	B	82						
V43314	B	60						
V43315	D	61						
V43316	A	83						
V43331	A	81						
V43373	A	66		D110	R	L202	X	1-3,5,6,8
V43374	A	66		D115	Q	L202	X	1-3,5,6,8
V43375	A	66		D115	Q	L202	X	1-3,5,6,8
V43416	A	62	⌂					
V43417	A	85	⌂					
V43418	A	84	⌂					
V43419	B	63	⌂					
V43460	A	67						
V43501	B	87						
V44010	C	24						
V44012	A	25						
V44015	A	27						
V44027	A	26						
V44061	A	31		D115	Q			
V44113	B	15						
V44114	A	21						
V44115	B	107						
V44124	B	20						
V44125	A	13						
V44129	A	17						
V44132	B	19						
V44134	B	14						
V44147	B	105		D111	S			
V44153	A	30		D115	Q	L202	X	1-3,5,6,8
V44187	A	18						
V44207	B	106				L230	Z	1-8
V44210	A	102						
V44249	B	100						
V44254	B	101						
V44293	B	104		D102	R			
V44299	C	29						
V44302	C	28						
V44316	B	16						
V44317	B	103		D117	S			
V44319	A	32						
V44332	B	108						
V44539	C	22		D105	R			

Toll Free 1-800-521-6797

Normal Office Hours:
8:00 a.m. to 8:00 p.m.
Eastern Time
Monday through Friday
Our staff will gladly answer any questions during normal office hours. Our answering service can place orders after hours or on weekends.

If we receive your order by 5:00 p.m. Eastern Time, Monday through Friday, we'll process it the same day and ship it the following business day.

When ordering by phone, please have your charge card ready. We'll also ask you for the Order Form Key Number at the bottom of the coupon on page 253. Please use our Toll-Free number for blueprint and book orders only. For Customization orders call 1-800-322-6797, ext. 134.

By FAX: Copy the Order Form on page 253 and send it on our International FAX line: 1-602-297-6219.

For Customization: 1-800-322-6797, ext. 134

Canadian Customers Order Toll-Free 1-800-848-2550

For faster, more economical service, Canadian customers may now call in orders on our Toll-Free line. Or, complete the order form on page 253, and mail with your check indicating U.S. funds to:

Home Planners, Inc.
3275 W. Ina Road, Suite 110
Tucson, AZ 85741

By FAX: Copy the Order Form on page 253 and send it on our International FAX line: 1-602-297-6219.

The Home Customizer®

Many of the plans in this book are customizable through our Home Customizer® service. Look for this symbol on the pages of home designs. It indicates that the plan on that page is part of The Home Customizer® service.

Some changes to customizable plans that can be made include:

- exterior elevation changes
- kitchen and bath modifications
- roof, wall and foundation changes
- room additions
- and much more!

If the plan you have chosen to build is one of our customizable homes, you can easily order the Home Customizer® kit to start on the path to making your alterations. The kit, priced at only $19.95, may be ordered at the same time you order your blueprint package by calling on our toll-free number or using the order blank on page 253. Or you can wait until you receive your blueprints, spend some time studying them and then order the kit by phone, FAX or mail. If you then decide to proceed with the customizing service, the $19.95 price of the kit will be refunded to you after your customization order is received. The Home Customizer® kit includes:

- instruction book with examples
- architectural scale
- clear acetate work film
- erasable red marker
- removable correction tape
- ¼" scale furniture cutouts
- 1 set of Customizable Drawings with floor plans and elevations

The service is easy, fast and *affordable*. Because we know and work with our plans and have them available on state-of-the-art computer systems, we can make the changes efficiently at prices much lower than those charged by normal architectural or drafting services. In addition, you'll be getting custom changes directly from Home Planners—the company whose dedication to excellence and long-standing professional experience are well recognized in the industry.

Call now to learn more about how simple it can be to have the *custom home* you've always wanted.

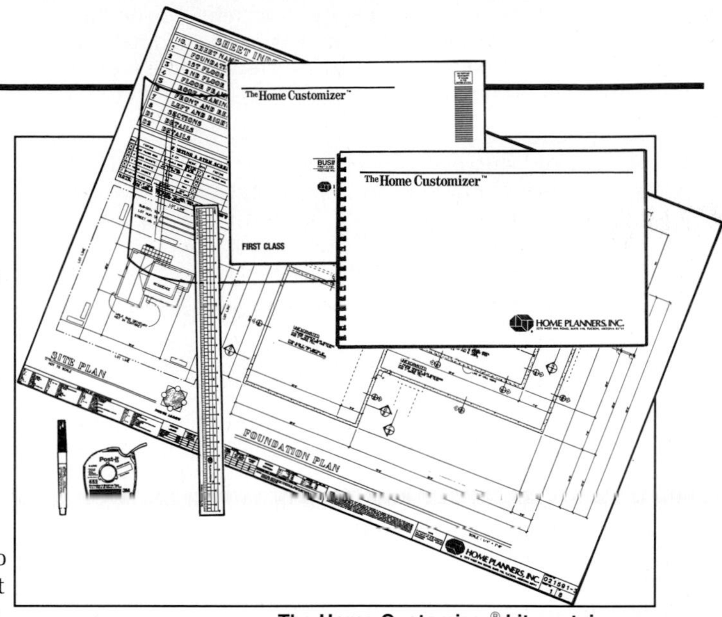

The Home Customizer® kit contains everything you'll need to make your home a one of a kind.

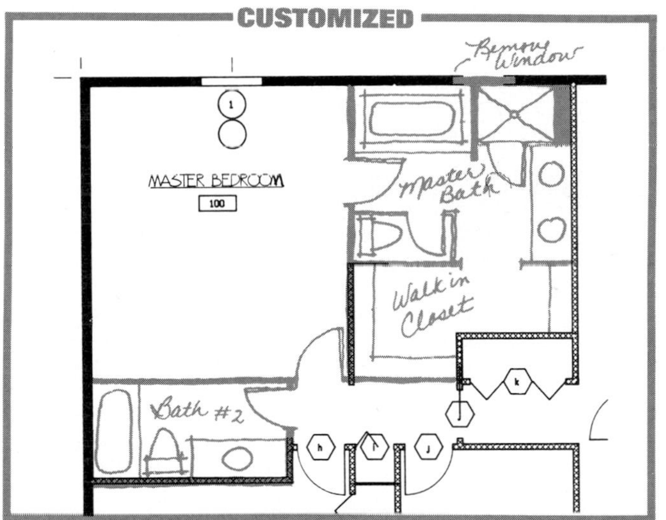

Making interior changes to the floor plan is simple and fun using the tools provided in The Home Customizer® kit!

Look for this symbol next to Home Planners' designs that are customizable.

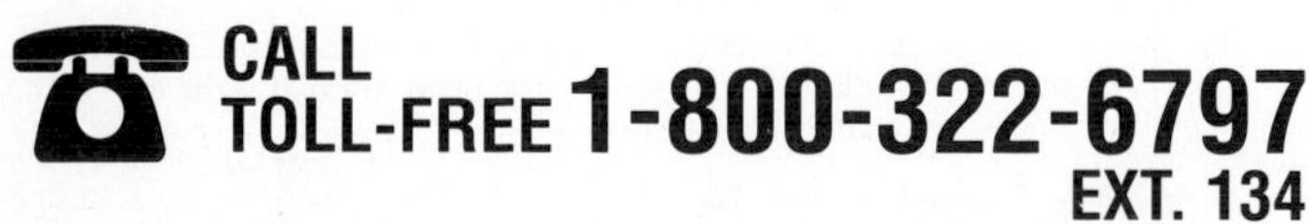

CALL
TOLL-FREE 1-800-322-6797
EXT. 134

Custom Alterations? For information about how easily this plan can be altered — at rates surprisingly below standard architectural fees — call our Home Customizer Specialist at **1-800-322-6797.**

Before You Order . . .

Before completing the coupon at right or calling us on our Toll-Free Blueprint Hotline, you may be interested to learn more about our service and products. Here's some information you will find helpful.

Quick Turnaround
We process and ship every blueprint order from our office within 48 hours. On most orders, we do even better. Normally, if we receive your order by 5 p.m. Eastern Time, we'll process it the same day and ship it the following day. Because of this quick turnaround, we won't send a formal notice acknowledging receipt of your order.

Our Exchange Policy
Since blueprints are printed in response to your order, we cannot honor requests for refunds. However, we will exchange your entire first order for an equal number of blueprints at a price of $40 for the first set and $10 for each additional set; $60 total exchange fee for 4 sets; $90 total exchange fee for 8 sets... *plus* the difference in cost if exchanging for a design in a higher price bracket or *less* the difference in cost if exchanging for a design in a lower price bracket. (Sepias are not exchangeable.) All sets from the first order must be returned before the exchange can take place. Please add $8 for postage and handling via ground service; $20 via 2nd Day Air.

About Reverse Blueprints
If you want to build in reverse of the plan as shown, we will include an extra set of reversed blueprints (mirror image) for an additional fee of $50. Although lettering and dimensions appear backward, reverses will be a useful visual aid if you decide to flop the plan. Right-reading reverses of Customizable Plans are available through our Customization Service. Call for more details.

Modifying or Customizing Our Plans
With such a great selection of homes, you are bound to find the one that suits you. However, if you need to make alterations to a design that is customizable, you need only order our Customizer® kit or call our Customization representative at 1-800-322-6797, ext. 134, to get you started (see additional information on next page). It is possible to customize many of our plans that are not part of our Home Customizer® Service.

If you decide to revise plans significantly that are not customizable through our service, we strongly suggest that you order reproducible sepias and consult a licensed architect or professional designer to help you redraw the plans.

Architectural and Engineering Seals
Some cities and states are now requiring that a licensed architect or engineer review and "seal" your blueprints prior to construction. This is often due to local or regional concerns over energy consumption, safety codes, seismic ratings, etc. For this reason, you may find it necessary to consult with a local professional to have your plans reviewed. This can normally be accomplished with minimum delays, for a nominal fee. In some cases, Home Planners can seal your plans through our Customization Service. Call for more details.

Compliance with Local Codes and Regulations
At the time of creation, our plans are drawn to specifications published by Building Officials Code Administrators (BOCA), the Southern Standard Building Code, or the Uniform Building Code and are designed to meet or exceed national building standards. Some states, counties and municipalities have their own codes, zoning requirements and building regulations. Before starting construction, consult with local building authorities and make sure you comply with local ordinances and codes, including obtaining any necessary permits or inspections as building progresses. In some cases, minor modifications to your plans by your builder, local architect or designer may be required to meet local conditions and requirements. Home Planners may be able to make these changes to Customizable Plans providing you supply all pertinent information from your local building authorities.

Foundation and Exterior Wall Changes
Most of our plans are drawn with either a full or partial basement foundation. Depending upon your specific climate or regional building practices, you may wish to convert this basement to a slab or crawlspace. Most professional contractors and builders can easily adapt your plans to alternate foundation types. Likewise, most can easily convert 2x4 wall construction to 2x6, or vice versa. If you need more guidance on these conversions, our handy Construction Detail Sheets, shown on page 241, describe how such conversions can be made. For Customizable Plans, Home Planners can easily provide the necessary changes for you.

How Many Blueprints Do You Need?
A single set of blueprints is sufficient to study a home in greater detail. However, if you are planning to obtain cost estimates from a contractor or subcontractors—or if you are planning to build immediately—you will need more sets. Because additional sets are cheaper when ordered in quantity with the original order, make sure you order enough blueprints to satisfy all requirements. The following checklist will help you determine how many you need:

_____Owner

_____Builder (generally requires at least three sets; one as a legal document, one to use during inspections, and at least one to give to subcontractors)

_____Local Building Department (often requires two sets)

_____Mortgage Lender (usually one set for a conventional loan; three sets for FHA or VA loans)

_____TOTAL NUMBER OF SETS

Toll Free 1-800-521-6797

Normal Office Hours:
8:00 a.m. to 8:00 p.m. Eastern Time
Monday through Friday
Our staff will gladly answer any questions during normal office hours. Our answering service can place orders after hours or on weekends.

If we receive your order by 5:00 p.m. Eastern, Time, Monday through Friday, we'll process it the same day and ship it the following business day. When ordering by phone, please have your charge card ready. We'll also ask you for the Order Form Key Number at the bottom of the coupon. Please use our Toll-Free number for blueprint and book orders only.

For Customization orders call 1-800-322-6797, ext. 134.

By FAX: Copy the Order Form on the next page and send it on our International FAX line: 1-602-297-6219.

Canadian Customers
Order Toll-Free 1-800-848-2550
For faster, more economical service, Canadian customers may now call in orders on our Toll-Free line. Or, complete the order form at right, and mail with your check indicating U.S. funds to:

Home Planners, Inc.
3275 W. Ina Road, Suite 110
Tucson, AZ 85741

By FAX: Copy the Order Form on the next page and send it on our International FAX line: 1-602-297-6219.

ORDER FORM

HOME PLANNERS, INC., 3275 WEST INA ROAD
SUITE 110, TUCSON, ARIZONA 85741

THE BASIC BLUEPRINT PACKAGE
Rush me the following (please refer to the Plans Index and Price Schedule in this section):

- ______ Set(s) of blueprints for plan number(s) ____________. $________
- ______ Set(s) of sepias for plan number(s) ____________. $________
- ______ Additional identical blueprints in same order @ $50.00 per set. $________
- ______ Reverse blueprints @ $50.00 per set. $________
- ______ Home Customizer® Kit(s) for Plan(s)__________ @ $19.95 per kit. $________

IMPORTANT EXTRAS
Rush me the following:

- ______ Materials List @ $40 Schedule A-D; $50 Schedule E $________
- ______ Specification Outlines @ $7.00 each. $________
- ______ Detail Sets @ $14.95 each; any two for $22.95; any three for $29.95; all four for $39.95 (save $19.85). $________
  ❑ Plumbing ❑ Electrical ❑ Construction ❑ Mechanical
  (These helpful details provide general construction advice and are not specific to any single plan.)
- ______ Plan-A-Home® @ $29.95 each. $________

DECK BLUEPRINTS

- ______ Set(s) of Deck Plan ____________. $________
- ______ Additional identical blueprints in same order @ $5.00 per set. $________
- ______ Reverse blueprints @ $5.00 per set. $________
- ______ Set of Standard Deck Details @ $14.95 per set. $________
- ______ Set of Complete Building Package (Best Buy!) Includes Custom Deck Plan ____________ (See Index and Price Schedule) Plus Standard Deck Details $________

LANDSCAPE BLUEPRINTS

- ______ Set(s) of Landscape Plan ____________. $________
- ______ Additional identical blueprints in same order @ $10.00 per set. $________
- ______ Reverse blueprints @ $10.00 per set. $________

Please indicate the appropriate region of the country for Plant & Material List. (See Map on page 244): Region __________

SUB-TOTAL $________
SALES TAX (Arizona residents add 5% sales tax; Michigan residents add 4% sales tax.) $________

POSTAGE AND HANDLING	1-3 sets	4 or more sets	
COMMERCIAL SERVICE (Requires street address - No P.O. Boxes)			
•Ground Service Allow 4-6 days delivery	❑ $6.00	❑ $8.00	$________
•2nd Day Air Service Allow 2-3 days delivery	❑ $12.00	❑ $20.00	$________
•Next Day Air Service Allow 1 day delivery	❑ $22.00	❑ $30.00	$________
POST OFFICE DELIVERY If no street address available. Allow 4-6 days delivery	❑ $8.00	❑ $12.00	$________
OVERSEAS AIR MAIL DELIVERY	❑ $30.00	❑ $50.00	$________
Note: All delivery times are from date Blueprint Package is shipped.	❑ Send COD		

TOTAL (Sub-total, tax, and postage) $________

YOUR ADDRESS (please print)
Name ________________________________
Street ________________________________
City ____________________ State ____________ Zip __________
Daytime telephone number (______) ____________________

FOR CREDIT CARD ORDERS ONLY
Please fill in the information below:
Credit card number ________________________________
Exp. Date: Month/Year ________________________
Check one ❑ Visa ❑ MasterCard ❑ Discover Card

Signature ________________________________

Please check appropriate box:
❑ Licensed Builder-Contractor
❑ Home Owner

Order Form Key
V4BP

ORDER TOLL FREE
1-800-521-6797

ORDER FORM

HOME PLANNERS, INC., 3275 WEST INA ROAD
SUITE 110, TUCSON, ARIZONA 85741

E BASIC BLUEPRINT PACKAGE
sh me the following (please refer to the Plans Index and
ce Schedule in this section):
Set(s) of blueprints for plan number(s) ____________. $________
Set(s) of sepias for plan number(s) ____________. $________
Additional identical blueprints in same order @ $50.00 per set. $________
Reverse blueprints @ $50.00 per set. $________
Home Customizer® Kit(s) for Plan(s)__________ @ $19.95 per kit. $________
PORTANT EXTRAS
sh me the following:
Materials List @ $40 Schedule A-D; $50 Schedule E $________
Specification Outlines @ $7.00 each. $________
Detail Sets @ $14.95 each; any two for $22.95; any three for $29.95; all four for $39.95 (save $19.85). $________
❑ Plumbing ❑ Electrical ❑ Construction ❑ Mechanical
(These helpful details provide general construction advice and are not specific to any single plan.)
Plan-A-Home® @ $29.95 each. $________
CK BLUEPRINTS
Set(s) of Deck Plan ____________. $________
Additional identical blueprints in same order @ $5.00 per set. $________
Reverse blueprints @ $5.00 per set. $________
Set of Standard Deck Details @ $14.95 per set. $________
Set of Complete Building Package (Best Buy!) Includes Custom Deck Plan ____________ (See Index and Price Schedule) Plus Standard Deck Details $________
NDSCAPE BLUEPRINTS
Set(s) of Landscape Plan ____________. $________
Additional identical blueprints in same order @ $10.00 per set. $________
Reverse blueprints @ $10.00 per set. $________
ase indicate the appropriate region of the country for
nt & Material List. (See Map on page 244): Region __________
B-TOTAL $________
LES TAX (Arizona residents add 5% sales tax; Michigan
idents add 4% sales tax.) $________

)STAGE AND ANDLING | 1-3 sets | 4 or more sets
)MMERCIAL SERVICE (Requires eet address - No P.O. Boxes)
:round Service llow 4-6 days delivery | ❑ $6.00 | ❑ $8.00 | $________
nd Day Air Service llow 2-3 days delivery | ❑ $12.00 | ❑ $20.00 | $________
Jext Day Air Service llow 1 day delivery | ❑ $22.00 | ❑ $30.00 | $________
)ST OFFICE DELIVERY 10 street address available. low 4-6 days delivery | ❑ $8.00 | ❑ $12.00 | $________
VERSEAS AIR MAIL ELIVERY | ❑ $30.00 | ❑ $50.00 | $________
)te: All delivery times are from te Blueprint Package is shipped. | ❑ Send COD

)TAL (Sub-total, tax, and postage) $________
)UR ADDRESS (please print)
ame ________________________________
reet ________________________________
ty ____________________ State ____________ Zip __________
iytime telephone number (______) ____________________
)R CREDIT CARD ORDERS ONLY
ease fill in the information below:
:edit card number ________________________________
cp. Date: Month/Year ________________________
neck one ❑ Visa ❑ MasterCard ❑ Discover Card
gnature ________________________________
ease check appropriate box:
❑ Licensed Builder-Contractor
❑ Home Owner
Order Form Key
V4BP
ORDER TOLL FREE
1-800-521-6797

Additional Plans Books

THE DESIGN CATEGORY SERIES

1.

ONE-STORY HOMES
A collection of 470 homes to suit a range of budgets in one-story living. All popular styles, including Cape Cod, Southwestern, Tudor and French. **384 pages. $8.95 ($10.95 Canada)**

2.

TWO-STORY HOMES
478 plans for all budgets in a wealth of styles: Tudors, Saltboxes, Farmhouses, Victorians, Georgians, Contemporaries and more. **416 pages. $8.95 ($10.95 Canada)**

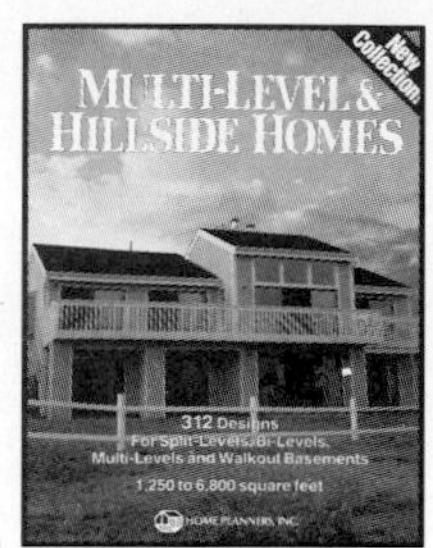

3.

MULTI-LEVEL AND HILLSIDE HOMES 312 distinctive styles for both flat and sloping sites. Includes exposed lower levels, open staircases, balconies, decks and terraces. **320 pages. $6.95 ($8.95 Canada)**

4.

VACATION AND SECOND HOMES 258 ideal plans for a favorite vacation spot or perfect retirement or starter home. Includes cottages, chalets, and 1-, 1½-, 2-, and multi-levels. **256 pages. $5.95 ($7.50 Canada)**

THE EXTERIOR STYLE SERIES

9.

THE ESSENTIAL GUIDE TO TRADITIONAL HOMES
Over 400 traditional homes in one special volume. American and European styles from Farmhouses to Norman French. "Readers' Choice" highlights best sellers in four-color photographs and renderings. **304 pages. $9.95 U.S. ($11.95 Canada)**

10.

THE ESSENTIAL GUIDE TO CONTEMPORARY HOMES More than 340 contemporary designs from Northwest Contemporary to Post-Modern Victorian. Four-color section of best sellers; two-color illustrations and line drawings throughout the remainder. **304 pages. $9.95 U.S. ($11.95 Canada)**

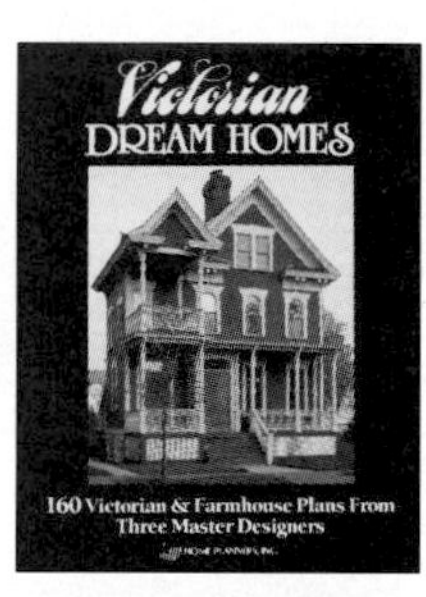

11.

VICTORIAN DREAM HOMES 160 Victorian and Farmhouse designs by three master designers. Victorian style from Second Empire homes through the Queen Anne and Folk Victorian era. Beautifully drawn renderings accompany the modern floor plans. **192 pages. $12.95 ($15.95 Canada)**

12.

WESTERN HOME PLANS
Over 215 home plans from Spanish Mission and Montere to Northwest Chateau and Sa Francisco Victorian. Historica notes trace the background and geographical incidence o each style. **208 pages. $8.95 ($10.95 Canada)**

OUR BEST PLAN PORTFOLIOS

NEW ENCYCLOPEDIA OF HOME DESIGNS
Our best collection of plans is now bigger and better than ever! Over 500 plans organized by architectural category including all types and styles and 269 brand-new plans. The most comprehensive plan book ever.

15. **352 pages. $9.95 ($11.95 Canada)**

AFFORDABLE HOME PLANS For the prospective home builder with a modest or medium budget. Features 430 one-, 1½-, two-story and multi-level homes in a wealth of styles. Included are cost saving ideas for the budget-conscious.

16. **320 pages. $8.95 ($10.95 Canada)**

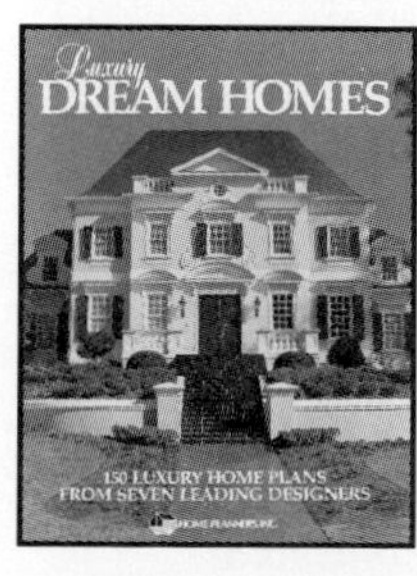

LUXURY DREAM HOMES At last, the home you've waited fo A collection of 150 of t best luxury home plar from seven of the mos highly regarded desig ers and architects in th United States. A drear come true for anyone interested in designing building or remodelin luxury home.

17. **192 pages. $14.95 ($17.95 Canada)**

HOME IMPROVEMENT AND LANDSCAPE BOOKS

5.

THE HOME REMODELER A revolutionary book of 31 remodeling plans backed by complete construction-ready blueprints and materials lists. Sections on kitchens, baths, master bedrooms and much more. Ideas galore; helpful advice and valuable suggestions. **112 pages. $7.95 U.S. ($9.95 Canada)**

6.

DECK PLANNER 25 practical plans and details for decks the do-it-yourselfer can actually build. How-to data and project starters for a variety of decks. Construction details available separately. **112 pages. $7.95 ($9.95 Canada)**

7.

THE HOME LANDSCAPER 55 fabulous front and backyard plans that even the do-it-youselfer can master. Complete construction blueprints and regionalized plant lists available for each design. **208 pages. $12.95 ($15.95 Canada)**

8.

BACKYARD LANDSCAPER Sequel to the popular *Home Landscaper*, contains 40 professionally designed plans for backyards to do yourself or contract out. Complete construction blueprints and regionalized plant lists available. **160 pages. $12.95 ($15.95 Canada)**

INTRODUCING THE NEW BLUE RIBBON DESIGNER SERIES

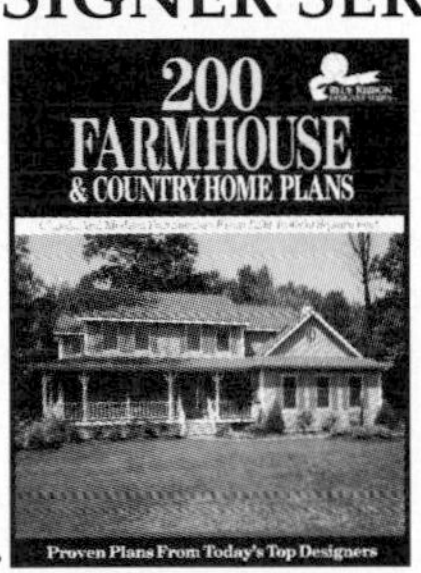

13.

200 FARMHOUSES & COUNTRY HOME PLANS Styles and sizes to match every taste and budget. Grouped by type, the homes represent a variety from Classic Farmhouses to Country Capes & Cottages. Introductions and expertly drawn floor plans and renderings enhance the sections. **224 pages. $6.95 ($8.95 Canada)**

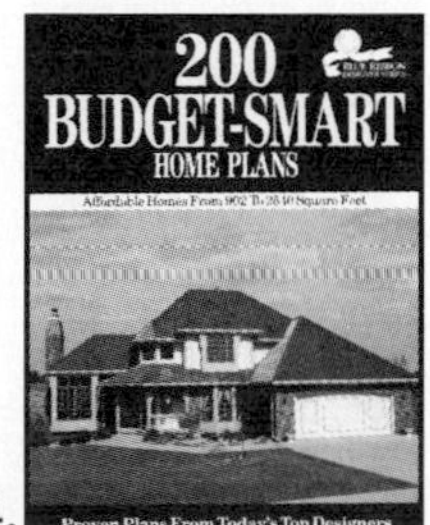

14.

200 BUDGET-SMART HOME PLANS The definitive source for the home builder with a limited budget, this volume shows that you can have your home and enjoy it, too! Amenity-laden homes, in many sizes and styles, can all be built from our plans. **224 pages. $6.95 ($8.95 Canada)**

Please fill out the coupon below. We will process your order and ship it from our office within 48 hours. Send coupon and check for the total to:

HOME PLANNERS, INC.
3275 West Ina Road, Suite 110, Dept. BK
Tucson, Arizona 85741

THE DESIGN CATEGORY SERIES—A great series of books edited by design type. Complete collection features 1376 pages and 1273 home plans.

1. _____One-Story Homes @ $8.95 ($10.95 Canada) $ _______
2. _____Two-Story Homes @ $8.95 ($10.95 Canada) $ _______
3. _____Multi-Level & Hillside Homes @ $6.95 ($8.95 Canada) $ _______
4. _____Vacation & Second Homes @ $5.95 ($7.50 Canada) $ _______

HOME IMPROVEMENT AND LANDSCAPE BOOKS

5. _____The Home Remodeler @ $7.95 ($11.95 Canada) $ _______
6. _____Deck Planner @ $7.95 ($9.95 Canada) $ _______
7. _____The Home Landscaper @ $12.95 ($15.95 Canada) $ _______
8. _____The Backyard Landscaper @ $12.95 ($15.95 Canada) $ _______

THE EXTERIOR STYLE SERIES

9. _____Traditional Homes @ $9.95 ($11.95 Canada) $ _______
10. _____Contemporary Homes @ $9.95 ($11.95 Canada) $ _______
11. _____Victorian Dream Homes @ $12.95 ($15.95 Canada) $ _______
12. _____Western Home Plans @ $8.95 ($10.95 Canada) $ _______

THE BLUE RIBBON DESIGNER SERIES

13. _____200 Farmhouse & Country Home Plans @ $6.95 ($8.95 Canada) $ _______
14. _____200 Budget-Smart Home Plans @ $6.95 ($8.95 Canada) $ _______

OUR BEST PLAN PORTFOLIOS

15. _____New Encyclopedia of Home Designs @ $9.95 ($11.95 Canada) $ _______
16. _____Affordable Home Plans @ $8.95 ($10.95 Canada) $ _______
17. _____Luxury Dream Homes @ $14.95 ($17.95 Canada) $ _______

Sub-Total $ _______
Arizona residents add 5% sales tax; Michigan residents add 4% sales tax $ _______
ADD Postage and Handling $ 3.00
TOTAL (Please enclose check) $ _______

Name (please print) _______________
Address _______________
City _______________ State _______ Zip _______

CANADIAN CUSTOMERS: Order books Toll-Free 1-800-848-2550. Or, complete the order form above, and mail with your check indicating U.S. funds to: Home Planners, Inc. 3275 W. Ina Road, Suite 110, Tucson, AZ 85741.

TO ORDER BOOKS BY PHONE CALL TOLL FREE 1-800-322-6797

V4BK

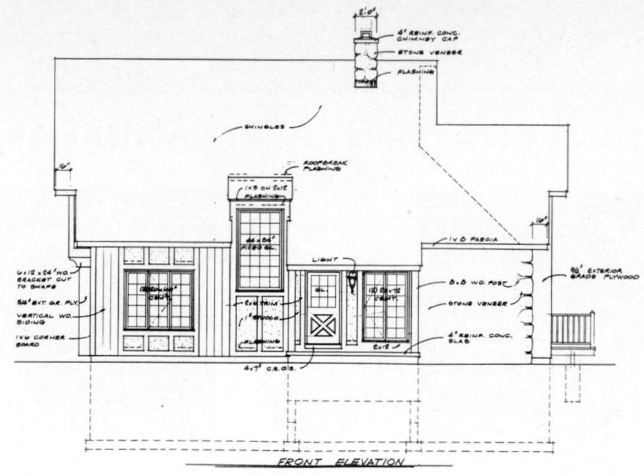

OVER 2½ MILLION BLUEPRINTS SOLD

"We instructed our builder to follow the plans including all of the many details which make this house so elegant... Our home is a fine example of the results one can achieve by purchasing and following the plans which you offer... Everyone who has seen it has assured us that it belongs in 'a picture book.' I truly mean it when I say that my home 'is a DREAM HOUSE.'"

S.P.
Anderson, SC

"We have had a steady stream of visitors, many of whom tell us this is the most beautiful home they've seen. Everyone is amazed at the layout and remark on how unique it is. Our real estate attorney, who is a Chicago dweller and who deals with highly valued properties, told me this is the only suburban home he has seen that he would want to live in."

W. & P.S.
Flossmoor, IL

"Home Planners' blueprints saved us a great deal of money. I acted as the general contractor and we did a lot of the work ourselves. We probably built it for half the cost! We are thinking about more plans for another home. I purchased a competitor's book but my husband only wants your plans!"

K.M.
Grovetown, GA

"We are very happy with the product of our efforts. The neighbors and passersby appreciate what we have created. We have had many people stop by to discuss our house and kindly praise it as being the nicest house in our area of new construction. We have even had one person stop and make us an unsolicited offer to buy the house for much more than we have invested in it."

K. & L.S.
Bolingbrook, IL

"The traffic going past our house is unbelievable. On several occasions, we have heard that it is the 'prettiest house in Batavia.' Also, when meeting someone new and mentioning what street we live on, quite often we're told, 'Oh, you're the one in the yellow house with the wrap-around porch! I love it!'"

A.W.
Batavia, NY

"I have been involved in the building trades my entire life... Since building our home we have built two other homes for other families. Their plans from local professional architects were not nearly as good as yours. For that reason we are ordering additional plan books from you."

T.F.
Kingston, WA

"The blueprints we received from Home Planners were of excellent quality and provided us with exactly what we needed to get our successful home-building project underway. We appreciate Home Planners' invaluable role in our home-building effort."

T.A.
Concord, TN